GORGIAS DISSERTATIONS 6

NEAR EASTERN STUDIES

Volume 4

Central Sanctuary and Centralization of Worship in Ancient Israel

Central Sanctuary and Centralization of Worship in Ancient Israel

From the Settlement to the Building of Solomon's Temple

PEKKA PITKÄNEN

GORGIAS PRESS
2004

ISBN 1-59333-157-6

GORGIAS PRESS
46 Orris Ave., Piscataway, NJ 08854 USA
www.gorgiaspress.com

ACKNOWLEDGEMENTS

There are various people whom I would like to thank in particular for making this dissertation and its publication possible. First of all, I want to express my heartfelt thanks to Professor Gordon Wenham, the supervisor of the thesis. He selected me to do studies with him, helped me to select a topic, and carefully guided the work. I would also like to thank Mrs Lynne Wenham and the rest of the family for their kindness. I want to thank Professor Alan Millard, the second supervisor of the thesis, for his help especially with archaeological and ancient Near Eastern material. My thanks are also due to Amihai Mazar for his help with the archaeology of the cult in the early Iron Age and Adam Zertal for his help with Mt Ebal.

I want to express my love and appreciation to my wife Sowon. She has lovingly and sacrificially supported me through this time of study. Her love and support carried me through the project. I would also like to express my heartfelt thanks to my father-in-law Yeonbok Lee, whose financial support was instrumental. My thanks are also due for my wife's family.

I want to expres my gratitude to my parents Matti and Ritva Pitkänen, my brother Saku, my sister Pirkko-Leena and her family, my sister Inka, my grandmothers Aune and Vappu, my aunts Mirja and Anneli, and my other relatives for their love and support.

It is a pleasure to thank the people in the Holy Apostles Church in Cheltenham for their support during the time I was working on the thesis, including Rev Ray and Mrs Molly Copping, the family of Peter, Chris, Ruth and Caroline Coxhead, Mr and Mrs Martin and Mary Leonard, and Mr and Mrs David and Mary Lynch. The support of the Vine Management Committee, Charlton Kings, Cheltenham, was also helpful.

Lastly, I wish to thank Dr George Kiraz for accepting this dissertation for publication and for his help in preparing the manuscript. In the final process, my thanks are also due to Dr Lieve Teugels for her work in copy editing.

מי כמוך באלהים יהוה
אדיר בשמים וגדל בחסד
ישב באדם

CONTENTS

ILLUSTRATIONS

PREFACE

This book examines the history and theology of the centralization of worship. It is based on my doctoral dissertation entitled *Central Sanctuary and the Centralization of Worship in Ancient Israel from The Settlement to the Building of Solomon's Temple: A Historical and Theological Study of the Biblical Evidence in Its Archaeological and Ancient Near Eastern Context*, with some additions and modifications.

In the Introduction, the problem of the centralization of worship is stated, making due reference to de Wette and Wellhausen from whom the current scholarly consensus originates. Also, the methodology of the investigation is outlined. Due regard is given to problems involved with historical research and archaeological investigation, including as they relate to the early history of Israel. In relation to these, an appendix which examines methodological problems of historical reconstruction has been added to the end of the book.

Chapter two examines the theology of the central sanctuary and local sanctuaries, especially from the standpoint of divine presence. In the first section, ancient Near Eastern concepts of divine presence are examined in order to provide a background based on which Israelite conceptions of divine presence can be understood better. Especially, the possibility of a simultaneous presence of a deity in both heaven and earth is emphasized. In this the role of cult places, and temples and associated cult objects in particular as the dwelling place of a god amongst ancient Near Eastern peoples is highlighted. Then, in the second section, it is first pointed out that in Israelite conception, Yahweh's presence in the midst of Israel takes place in the temple or tent of meeting through the medium of the ark, where the ark, the temple and the tent of meeting are the Israelite equivalents of an ancient Near Eastern temple and cult object. After this, it is argued that Yahweh can be present at a local altar in the context of worship, descending down from heaven to meet the worshipper. In this, an important distinction between the ark, the tent of meeting and temple versus local altars is that Yahweh's presence in the former is continuous, and intermittent at the latter.

Chapter three carries out an exegesis of the centralizing altar laws of the Pentateuch, together with an examination of their narrative and conceptual relationship to the noncentralizing altar laws of the Pentateuch. Utilising the results of Chapter two, after a brief look at the narrative setting of the Pentateuchal altar laws in Section one in order to establish that the setting of the laws in the narrative may be planned, it is argued in Section two that the Priestly material emphasizes the role of the central sanctuary as the dwelling-place of Yahweh and as a place where Israel ideally should meet together to worship Yahweh. However, the Priestly material allows local altars for worship in addition to the central sanctuary consisting of the ark and the tent of meeting. In section three, it is argued that Deuteronomy advocates centralization under ideal conditions of peace and complete settlement, but otherwise allows local altars.

Chapter four examines the history of the centralization of worship from the settlement to the building of Solomon's temple, interpreting this history by utilising theological insights gleaned from chapters one and two. The first section of the chapter examines the Shiloh statements of Jeremiah, arguing that these may be based on a reliable historical tradition, also keeping in mind the results of the latest archaeological excavations at Shiloh. Section two examines the vicissitudes of the central sanctuary between the capture of the ark from Shiloh by the Philistines at the battle of Aphek and the building of Solomon's temple. It is argued especially based on Psalm 78 that the capture of the ark signalled Yahweh's rejection of Shiloh. Consequently, Yahweh elected Jerusalem and a temple was built there by Solomon, becoming the new central sanctuary. However, no central sanctuary existed between the capture of the ark from Shiloh and the building of the temple, and consequently, there was no centralization requirement during this period. In Section three, going back in time, it is argued that according to the biblical material, there was no centralization requirement during the earliest days of the settlement. This is also attested by the existence of the tradition according to which Yahweh commanded to build an altar on Mt Ebal after Israel had entered the land. A related excursus (Section four) on Mount Ebal examines the Iron Age I remains of a structure which have been interpreted as an altar by the excavator, concluding that one cannot be certain about the nature of the structure. In Section five, it is argued that, according to the biblical material, in the last days of Joshua, Shiloh became the place where Yahweh's name dwelt and centralization was implemented. In section five, it is also argued that the book of Joshua may originate from as early as before the disaster at Aphek and the rejection of Shiloh, even though some parts of the book such as city lists are likely to derive from the period of the monarchy. In this, especially, the literary composition and rhetorical concerns of the book of Joshua point to a different provenance of Joshua from that of Judges-Kings. In section six, it is argued that centralization of worship was not possible during the Judges period because of the disturbed situation. Consequently, it was possible to worship Yahweh at local altars, as the stories of Manoah and Gideon attest.

It is concluded that according to the biblical material, the history and theology of the centralization of worship are compatible with each other from the settlement to the building of Solomon's temple, and this holds regardless of the date and provenance of the relevant biblical material. Consequently, a sixth century date for the book of Deuteronomy is no longer a necessity based on the history and theology of the centralization of worship. In addition, the history of the central sanctuary and the literary form and rhetorical concerns of the book of Joshua suggest that it and the sources it uses, such as Deuteronomy, may originate from as early as before the disaster of Aphek and the rejection of Shiloh.

ABBREVIATIONS

AASF	Annales Academiae Scientiarum Fennicae.
AB	The Anchor Bible
ABD	*The Anchor Bible Dictionary*
AfO	*Archiv für Orientforschung*
AHw	W. von Soden, *Akkadisches Handwörterbuch*. Wiesbaden, 1965-1981
ANE	Ancient Near East(ern)
ANEP	J.B. Pritchard, ed., *The Ancient Near East in Pictures*, 2nd ed. with supplement. Princeton, New Jersey: Princeton University Press, 1969
ANET	J.B. Pritchard, ed., *Ancient Near Eastern Texts Relating to the Old Testament*, 3rd ed. with supplement, Princeton, New Jersey: Princeton University Press 1969
AnOr	*Analecta Orientalia*
AO	*Archiv Orientalni*
ATD	Das Alte Testament Deutsch
AThANT	Abhandlungen zur Theologie des Alten und Neuen Testaments
BA	*The Biblical Archaeologist*
BAR	*Biblical Archaeology Review*
BASOR	*Bulletin of the American Schools of Oriental Research*

BBB	Bonner Biblische Beiträge
BECKMAN	G. Beckman, *Hittite Diplomatic Texts*. SBL Writings from the Ancient World 7. Atlanta: Scholars Press 1996, ed. by Harry A. Hoffner, Jr.
BHS	*Biblia Hebraica Stuttgartensia*
BKAT	Biblischer Kommentar, Altes Testament
BM	*Baghdader Mitteilungen*
BWANT	Beiträge zur Wissenschaft vom Alten und Neuen Testament
BZ	*Biblische Zeitschrift*
BZAW	*Beihefte zur Zeitschrift für die Alttestamentliche Wissenschaft*
CAD	*Chicago Assyrian Dictionary*
CBOTS	Coniectanea Biblica Old Testament Series
CBQ	*Catholic Biblical Quarterly*
CH	Code of Hammurabi
COS	W.W. Hallo and K.L. Younger, ed., *The Context of Scripture*. Leiden: E.J. Brill, 1997f.
EAEHL	M. Avi-Yonah and E. Stern, ed., *The Encyclopedia of Archaeological Excavations in the Holy Land*, English edition. London: Oxford University Press, 1975-1978
EBC	The Expositor's Bible Commentary
EJ	*Encyclopedia Judaica*
EJT	*Evangelical Journal of Theology*
EQ	*Evangelical Quarterly*
EVEN-SHOSHAN	A. Even-Shoshan, *A New Concordance of the Bible*, 2nd ed. Jerusalem, 1993
ExpTim	*The Expository Times*

FOSTER	B.R. Foster, *Before the Muses: An Anthology of Akkadian Literature.* Bethesda, Maryland: CDL Press, 1993
FS	Festschrift
GAG	W. von Soden, *Grundriss der Akkadischen Grammatik*, 3. auflage. AnOr 33, Rome: Editrice Pontificio Instituto Biblico, 1995
GESENIUS	W. Gesenius, E. Kautzsch and E.E. Cowley, *Gesenius' Hebrew Grammar.* 2nd ed., Oxford, 1910
GHAT	Göttinger Handkommentar zum Alten Testament
HAL	L. Koehler and W. Baumgartner, *Hebräisches und Aramäisches Lexikon zum Alten Testament.* Leiden
HANNIG	R. Hannig, *Die Sprache der Pharaonen: Grosses Handwörterbuch Ägyptisch-Deutsch (2800-950 v.Chr.).* Mainz: von Zabern, 1995
HAR	*Hebrew Annual Review*
HAT	Handbuch zum Alten Testament
HERMENEIA	Hermeneia - A Critical and Historical Commentary of the Bible
HUCA	*Hebrew Union College Annual*
IA	Iron Age
IB	Interpreter's Bible
ICC	International Critical Commentary
IDB	Interpreter's Dictionary of the Bible
IEJ	*Israel Exploration Journal*
IM	*Istanbuler Mitteilungen*
INTERPRETATION	Interpretation: A Bible Commentary for Teaching and Preaching

JBL	*Journal of Biblical Literature*
JBQ	*Jewish Biblical Quarterly*
JCS	*Journal of Cuneiform Studies*
JETS	*Journal of the Evangelical Theological Society*
JJS	*Journal of Jewish Studies*
JNES	*Journal of Near Eastern Studies*
JNSL	*Journal of Northwest Semitic Languages*
JOÜON	P. Joüon, S.J., *A Grammar of Biblical Hebrew.* Translated and Revised by T. Muraoka, 2 vols, Rome, 1996
JSOT	*Journal for the Study of the Old Testament*
JSOTSS	Journal for the Study of the Old Testament, Supplement Series
JSS	*Journal of Semitic Studies*
KAI	H. Donner and W. Röllig, ed., *Kanaanäische und Aramäische Inschriften*, 3 vols. Wiesbaden: Otto Harrassowitz, 1964
KAT	Kommentar zum Alten Testament
KHAT	Kurzer Handcommentar zum Alten Testament
KHW	J. Friedrich, *Kurzgefaßtes Hethitisches Wörterbuch.* Heidelberg: Carl Winter Universitätsverlag 1990. Unveränderter Nachdruck der Ausgabe, 1952-1966
KNUDTZON	J.A. Knudtzon, *Die El-Amarna Tafeln, mit Einleitung und Erläuterungen.* Reprint of the 1915 edition, Aalen: Otto Zeller Verlagsbuchhandlung, 1964
KS	Kleine Schriften

KTU	M. Dietrich, O. Loretz and J. Sanmartin, *The Cuneiform Alphabetic Texts from Ugarit, Ras Ibn Hani and Other Places.* Second, enlarged edition, Münster: Ugarit Verlag, 1995
KZ	*Kirchliche Zeitschrift*
LABAT	R. Labat and F. Malbran-Labat, *Manuel d'Épigraphie Akkadienne*, 6th edition. Paris: Paul Geuthner, 1994
LÄ	W. Helck and E. Otto, ed., *Lexikon der Ägyptologie*, Wiesbaden: Otto Harrassowitz, 1972f.
LBA	Late Bronze Age
LIDDELL-SCOTT	H.G. Liddell and R. Scott, *A Greek English Lexikon.* 9th ed. with Revised Supplement, Oxford: Clarendon Press, 1996
LISOWSKY	G. Lisowsky, *Konkordanz Zum Hebräischen Alten Testament.* Stuttgart: Deutsche Bibelgesellschaft, 1958, 1993
LUST	J. Lust, E. Eynikel, K. Hauspie, *A Greek-English Lexicon of the Septuagint.* 2 vols, Stuttgart: Deutsche Bibelgesellschaft, 1992, 1996
LXX	Septuagint
MB	Middle Bronze (Age)
MDOG	*Mitteilungen der Deutschen Orientgesellschaft*
NAC	New American Commentary
NASB	New American Standard Bible
NBD	J.D. Douglas, organizing ed., *New Bible Dictionary.* London: Inter-Varsity Press, 1962-1965
NCBC	New Century Biblical Commentary

NEAEHL	E. Stern, ed. *The New Encyclopedia of Archaeological Excavations in the Holy Land.* Jerusalem: The Israel Exploration Society & Carta (and Simon Schuster: New York etc.), 1993
NIB	The New Interpreter's Bible
NIBC	New International Biblical Commentary
NICOT	New International Commentary on the Old Testament
NIDOTTE	W. VanGemeren, gen. ed., *New International Dictionary of Old Testament Theology and Exegesis.* Carlisle, U.K.: Paternoster Press, 1997
NIV	New International Version
OLZ	*Orientalische Literaturzeitung*
OT	Old Testament
OTG	Old Testament Guides
OTL	Old Testament Library
PEFQS	*Palestine Exploration Fund Quarterly Statement*
PEQ	*Palestine Exploration Quarterly*
PJB	*Palästinajahrbuch*
PORTEN-YARDENI	B. Porten and A. Yardeni, *Textbook of Aramaic Documents from Ancient Egypt: Newly Copied, Edited and Translated into Hebrew and English.* Winona Lake, Indiana: Eisenbrauns and the Hebrew University, 1986
RAHLFS	A. Rahlfs, ed., *Septuaginta.* Stuttgart: Deutsche Bibelgesellschaft, 1935
RA	*Revue d'Assyriologie et d'Archéologie Orientale*
RB	*Revue Biblique*

RLA	E. Ebeling et al., ed., *Reallexikon der Assyriologie*. Berlin, 1932f.
SAA	State Archives of Assyria
SBL	Society of Biblical Literature
SOTSMS	Society for Old Testament Study Monograph Series
SPCK	Society for Promoting Christian Knowledge
StBoT	Studien zu den Bogazköy-Texten
STURTEVANT- BECHTEL	E.H. Sturtevant and G. Bechtel, *A Hittite Chrestomathy*. Philadelphia: University of Pennsylvania, 1935
TA	*Tel Aviv*
TB	*Tyndale Bulletin*
TDOT	G.J. Botterweck, H. Ringgren, ed., J.T. Willis, G.W. Bromiley, D.E. Green transl., *Theological Dictionary of the Old Testament.* Grand Rapids, Mi: Eerdmans, 1977f.
TOTC	Tyndale Old Testament Commentaries
TToday	*Theology Today*
TZ	*Theologische Zeitschrift*
UT	C.H. Gordon, *Ugaritic Textbook*. AnOr 38, Rome: Editrice Pontificio Istituto Biblico, 1998. A Revised Reprint of the 1965-1967 edition
VT	*Vetus Testamentum*
VTSup	Vetus Testamentum Supplements
WBC	Word Biblical Commentary
WThJ	*Westminster Theological Journal*
ZA	*Zeitschrift für Assyriologie*

1. INTRODUCTION

Ever since the rise of biblical criticism in the nineteenth century, Pentateuchal criticism has stood at the heart of Old Testament studies. After a century of formative development since its first recorded beginnings in the 1750's with the French physician Jean Astruc and his study of the sources of Genesis 1-2, Julius Wellhausen brilliantly formulated and presented the documentary hypothesis in his *Prolegomena zur Geschichte Israels*[1] in a way that made it the established basis of Old Testament scholarship.[2] Wellhausen's genius lay in dating P as the latest source and interpreting the rest of the Old Testament material and reconstructing the history of Israel so that it would fit with the JEDP order of the Pentateuchal sources.[3]

---

[1] Wellhausen 1905/1878.

[2] For a survey of the developments of the documentary hypothesis since its beginnings, see Archer 1994, pp. 89-98. See also Clements 1976, pp. 7-12. Cf. the social science approach of Kuhn 1960 to the history and development of natural sciences, which in many ways perfectly applies to Old Testament studies as well. According to Kuhn 1962, p. 10, "'normal science' means research firmly based upon one or more past scientific achievements, achievements that some particular scientific community acknowledges for a time as supplying the foundation for its further practice." Moreover, "When, in the development of a natural science, an individual or group produces a synthesis able to attract most of the next generation's practicioners, the older schools gradually disappear." (ibid., p. 18). Furthermore, "The new paradigm (=normal science which has become widely accepted, plus is able to create further problems for the community to resolve through research) implies a new and more rigid definition of the field. Those unwilling or unable to accommodate their work to it must proceed in isolation or attach themselves to some other group." (ibid., p. 19)

[3] See Wellhausen 1905/1878.

Since Wellhausen, a number of developments have taken place in regard to the documentary hypothesis. Until the 1960's, the development of the traditio-historical method by Gunkel, Gressmann, Alt, Noth and von Rad together with archaeological work, most notably by the Albright school, presented new challenges for the JEDP hypothesis, but these had been resolved by fitting the data into the basic framework of the hypothesis and making necessary modifications as regards the details of the hypothesis.[4] However, since the 1970's, the basic Wellhausenian consensus about the extent and dating of sources has been challenged in most of its aspects. As Wenham describes,

> Since the 1970's the comfortable consensus has begun to break up. There have been challenges to the principles of source analysis; there is uncertainty about the dating of the sources themselves and doubt about the validity of the alleged archaeological parallels. In the 1980's the debate intensified, and as we approach the end of the millennium there is no sign of it being resolved. On the one hand there are those who argue that the J source, traditionally regarded as the earliest major source, is both post-deuteronomic and post-exilic. On the other there are those who deny the existence of J and E altogether, proposing instead a pervasive Deuteronomic layer through Genesis to Deuteronomy, whereas Noth had denied that any deuteronomic hand could be discerned in Genesis-Numbers. By and large, those who adopt these approaches are also quite skeptical about the value of archaeological parallels to the Bible and tend to maintain that the Pentateuch is fictional. Going in a totally different direction, other scholars have argued that the Priestly source, traditionally supposed to be the

---

[4] See Wenham 1999a, pp. 116-118 for details. Cf Kuhn 1962, p. 33 according to whom normal science consists of "determination of significant fact, matching of facts with theory, and articulation of theory". Moreover, "Discovery commences with the awareness of anomaly, i.e., with the recognition that nature has somehow violated the paradigm-induced expectations that govern normal science. It then continues with a more or less extended exploration of the area of anomaly. And it closes only when the paradigm theory has been adjusted so that the anomalous has become the expected." (ibid., pp. 52-53).

latest source, may come from the early monarchy period with elements from the judges period. Others have suggested that both the J source and Deuteronomy may be earlier than conventional criticism suggests. No longer is it just different versions of the documentary hypothesis that find their advocates, but as at the beginning of the nineteenth century, both fragmentary and supplementary hypotheses enjoy support. Others prefer to give up trying to establish how the text originated and concentrate instead on its final form and meaning.[5]

Wenham concludes,

Among those writing most prolifically about the Pentateuch today there is thus no consensus. "Every man does what is right in his own eyes". Doubtless there is still a strong and silent majority of those who grew up with the traditional documentary hypothesis and feel no inclination to jettison it, and given the lack of an agreed alternative hypothesis there is a certain justification in a wait-and-see policy. The academic

---

[5] Wenham 1999a, pp. 118-119. For a review of the various scholarly opinions, see ibid., pp. 119-144. Cf. Kuhn 1962, pp. 82-83: "When an anomaly comes to seem more than just another puzzle of normal science, the transition to crisis and extraordinary science has begun. The anomaly itself now comes to be more generally recognized as such by the profession. More and more attention is devoted to it by more and more of the field's most eminent men. If it still continues to resist, as it usually does not, many of them may come to view its resolution as *the* subject matter of their discipline. For them the field will no longer look the same as it did earlier. Part of its different appearance results simply from the new fixation point of scientific scrutiny. An even more important source of change is the divergent nature of the numerous partial solutions that concerted attention to the problem has made available. The early attacks upon the resistant problem will have followed the paradigm rules quite closely. But with continuing resistance, more and more of the attacks upon it will have involved some minor or not so minor articulation of the paradigm, no two of them quite alike, each partially successful, but none sufficiently so to be accepted as paradigm by the group. Through this proliferation of divergent articulations, the rules of normal science become increasingly blurred. Though there still is a paradigm, few practicioners prove to be entirely agreed about what it is. Even formerly standard solutions of solved problems are called in question."

community is looking for a fresh and convincing paradigm for the study of the Pentateuch, but so far none of the new proposals seems to have captured the scholarly imagination.[6]

All in all, however, there remains one major bulwark for the Documentary Hypothesis. This is the dating of the book of Deuteronomy to the seventh century, first suggested by W.M.L. de Wette in his doctoral thesis in 1805.[7] According to de Wette, the book of Deuteronomy was written to increase the authority of the temple of Jerusalem and the Levites by regulating all sacrifices to "the place Yahweh will choose from all your tribes" and by emphasizing the role of the Levites.[8] In de Wette's view, one cannot date Deuteronomy earlier because of the ancient practice of the Hebrews to sacrifice in multiple places, as the altar law of Ex 20:21ff. and the practice of Samuel, Saul, David and Solomon attest.[9] This old practice was repudiated during the time of Josiah, and the book of Deuteronomy, composed by the priest Hilkiah and found in the temple, served this purpose.[10] Thus, de Wette dated the book of Deuteronomy based on the history of centralization, anchoring the provenance and date of the book to the temple of Jerusalem and the reform of Josiah.

Even though many twentieth-century scholars have detached the book of Deuteronomy from the reform of Josiah and may concede that a number of Deuteronomic laws may antedate the book itself, they nevertheless essentially see the book of Deuteronomy as a seventh-century product, perhaps having the

---

[6] Wenham 1999a, p. 119. Cf. Kuhn 1962, p. 77: "Though they (scientists) may begin to lose faith and then to consider alternatives, they do not renounce the paradigm that has led them to crisis". "Once it has achieved the status of paradigm, a scientific theory is declared invalid only if an alternate candidate is available to take its place." (ibid.). "The decision to reject one paradigm is always simultaneously the decision to accept another, and the judgment leading to that decision involves the comparison of both paradigms with nature *and* with each other." (ibid.).

[7] De Wette 1830/1805.

[8] De Wette 1830/1805, pp. 163-166.

[9] Ibid., p. 164n5.

[10] Ibid.

roots of its ideology in the time of king Hezekiah in the previous century.[11]

In conjunction with seeing the "place Yahweh will choose" as a veiled reference to Jerusalem, the history of centralization of sacrifices remains the main reason for dating the book of Deuteronomy to the seventh century BC. The critical consensus view of the history of centralization of sacrifices was developed by Wellhausen in the first chapter of his *Prolegomena* as a starting-point on which he built the rest of his presentation, and has been accepted as essentially unchanged by most scholars up till the present day. According to Wellhausen, there is no trace of an exclusive sanctuary for the earliest period of the Israelite history.[12] Even the latest redaction of the historical books does not criticise the multiplicity of altars and high places which existed before the building of the temple in Jerusalem. Samuel is permitted to preside over a sacrificial feast at the Bamah of his native town and Solomon is permitted to institute a similar one at the great Bamah of Gibeon at the beginning of his reign without being blamed.[13] On the other hand, according to Wellhausen, a new period in the history of worship starts with the building of the temple of Solomon.[14] After the building of the temple, no king is left uncensored for having tolerated high places. However, the view of the books of Kings, which sees the temple of Solomon as a work undertaken exclusively in the interests of pure worship and as having nothing to do with politics, is unhistorical. It idealistically projects to the past the significance which the temple had acquired in Judah shortly before the exile. In reality, the temple did not acquire the importance which it later had because of a monopoly conferred on it by Solomon, but by its own weight and as a result of political centralization which gave impetus for centralization of worship.[15] Unlike Josiah, Solomon and his successors did not abolish all other sanctuaries in order to favour his own. Especially, Elijah built an altar for Yahweh at Carmel (1 Ki 18:30-32) and

---

[11] See McConville 1993a, pp. 15-44 for a survey of the scholarship of Deuteronomy since de Wette.

[12] Wellhausen 1905/1878, p. 17.

[13] Ibid., p. 19.

[14] Ibid., p. 20.

[15] Ibid., pp. 20-21.

complained that the Israelites had destroyed the altars of Yahweh
(1 Ki 19:14).[16] Thus, if people, judges, kings, priests and prophets,
and even men like Samuel and Elisha sacrificed without hesitation
whenever an occasion arose, it is clear that during the whole of that
period nobody had even the faintest suspicion that such conduct
could be illegitimate.[17]

According to Wellhausen, the early sources J and E attest the
first stage in Israel's history, where sacrifice in multiple places is not
regarded merely as permissible, but as a matter of course.[18] Thus J
and E are to be dated as the earliest sources of the Pentateuch. In
this respect, according to Wellhausen, it is true that the liberty of
sacrifice seems to be somewhat restricted by the clause "in every
place where I cause my name to be honoured". However, this
means simply that instead of arbitrariness, the places of worship
were considered as having been selected by the Deity himself for
his service.[19]

In Wellhausen's view, the third oldest source in the
Pentateuch is Deuteronomy.[20] Moreover, the Jehovistic book of
the Covenant lies at the foundation of Deuteronomy.[21] However,
the two differ materially in one point: Deuteronomy 12 speaks for
the local unity of worship. Moreover, the law of Dt 12 has a
"polemical and reformatory nature".[22] Thus, for Wellhausen,
historical criticism has correctly assigned Deuteronomy to the
period of the attacks made on the *bamoth* by the reforming party at
Jerusalem.[23] As the Book of the Covenant and the whole Jehovistic
writing in general reflects the first pre-prophetic period in the

---

[16] Ibid., p. 21.

[17] Ibid., p. 22.

[18] Ibid., p. 29.

[19] Ibid.

[20] Ibid., pp. 32-34.

[21] "Die jehovistische Bundesbuch liegt zwar dem Deuteronomium zu grunde"; Wellhausen 1905/1878, p. 32.

[22] "Das Gesetz wird nicht müde, die Forderung der lokalen Einheit des Gottesdienstes immer und immer zu wiederholen. Es tritt damit dem, 'was wir gegenwärtig zu tun gewohnt sind', bewußt entgegen und bekämpft die bestehende Sitte, es hat durch und durch polemischen, reformatorischen Character"; Wellhausen 1905/1878, pp. 32-33.

[23] Ibid.

history of the cult, so Deuteronomy is the legal expression of the second period of struggle and transition.[24] According to Wellhausen, the historical order is all the more certain because there are compelling reasons to see a literary dependence of Deuteronomy on the Jehovistic laws and narratives.[25]

Finally, the Priestly Code is the youngest of the Pentateuchal sources, dating to the third, postexilic period of the history of the cult.[26] According to Wellhausen, there had previously been an idea that the Priestly Code is indifferent to the question of one sanctuary.[27] However, Wellhausen argues that the assumption that worship is restricted to one single centre runs through the entire Priestly Document.[28] The tent of meeting expresses the legal unity of the worship as a historical fact which has held good in Israel ever since the Exodus. Its idea is "one God, one sanctuary".[29] The tent of meeting with its encampment of the twelve tribes around it does not tolerate other sanctuaries beside itself. The encampment has no military, but has purely religious significance and derives its whole meaning from its sacred centre. There is no other place besides the tent of meeting at which God dwells and allows himself to be seen. Also, there is no place except the tent of meeting where man can draw near to Yahweh and seek his face with offerings and gifts. This view of worship pervades the whole of the middle part of the Pentateuch.[30] Thus, the unity of the cult is commanded in Deuteronomy, but is presupposed in the Priestly Code.[31] In Deuteronomy, it is a new invention, in the Priestly Code it is an already established fact. For this reason, the Priestly code is later than Deuteronomy.[32] In this respect, the tent of meeting is the copy, not the prototype of the temple at Jerusalem.[33] According to

---

[24] Ibid., p. 33

[25] Ibid.

[26] Ibid., pp. 34-38.

[27] Ibid., p. 34.

[28] Ibid.

[29] "ein Gott, ein Heiligtum"; Wellhausen 1905/1878, p. 34.

[30] Wellhausen 1905/1878, p. 35.

[31] Ibid. "Im Deuteronomium wird die Einheit des Kultus gefordert, im Priesterkodex wird sie vorausgesetzt".

[32] Ibid., pp. 35-36.

[33] Ibid., p. 36.

Wellhausen, the main point is that the tabernacle of the Priestly Code in its essential meaning is not a mere provisional shelter for the ark on the march, but the sole legitimate sanctuary for the community of the twelve tribes prior to the days of Solomon, and so in fact a projection of the later temple.[34]

Wellhausen considered the Holiness Code, Lev 17-26, as separate from the Priestly Code. According to Wellhausen, H was earlier than P.[35] However, P incorporated H into itself and in that process made a final redaction of H.[36] Whereas P assumes centralization, H still speaks for it, as a number of passages, including Lev 17, attest.[37]

Thus, Wellhausen tied together the history of centralization of worship and the dating of the Pentateuchal sources. In the early period which the sources J and E attest, worship was not centralized. In the middle period, attested by Deuteronomy, centralization was introduced. Finally, in the late period, attested by P, centralization was assumed.

After dating the Pentateuchal sources J,E, D and P based on the history of centralization, Wellhausen proceeded to reconstruct the history of other aspects of the Israelite cult based on the framework provided by the history of centralization.[38] Moreover, Wellhausen dated the material in other Old Testament books so that any material exhibiting Deuteronomistic style was composed at the same time or later than D, and any material exhibiting Priestly style was contemporaneous with or later than P.[39] Thus, for instance, if there was a Priestly passage, verse, or even word in any

---

[34] Ibid., p. 37. "Die Hauptsache bleibt indessen, daß die Stiftshütte des Priesterkodex ihrer Bedeutung nach nicht ein einfaches provisorisches Obdach der Lade auf dem Marsche ist, sondern das einzige legitime Heiligtum der Gemeinde der zwölf Stämme vor Salomo und darum also eine Projektion des späteren Tempels".

[35] Ibid., p. 378, "Jehovist Deuteronomium Ezechiel sind eine historische Reihenfolge; Ezechiel Heiligkeitsgesetz Priesterkodex müssen gleichfalls als historische Stufen begriffen werden".

[36] Ibid., p. 378.

[37] Ibid., p. 376. "Auf die örtliche Einheit des Opferdienstes wird auch in Lev 17ss. starkes Gewicht gelegt. Sie wird noch gefordert, nicht vorausgesetzt (17,8s. 19,30. 26,2)".

[38] Wellhausen 1905/1878, pp. 53-162.

[39] Except for Ezekiel and H, for which see above, p. 8.

book which otherwise could be seen to have been written earlier than P, the Priestly passage was to be considered a late, postexilic addition. Thus, Wellhausen created a logical and comprehensive view of the history of Israel and the composition of the books of the Old Testament, at the heart of which lies his interpretation of the history of centralization.

Yet, there are weaknesses in Wellhausen's view of the history of centralization. To start with, according to Wellhausen, since the books of Kings criticize ruling kings for the lack of centralization after the building of the temple, the author of the books of Kings thought that centralization should have been enforced before the time of Josiah. Yet, Wellhausen also claims that since the books of Kings do not criticize Elijah, centralization was not in actuality considered illegitimate before the time of Josiah. In other words, for Wellhausen, the books of Kings idealize the past with regard to past kings, but not with regard to Elijah. However, this logic is difficult to accept, since it assumes two mutually contradictory views held by the author of the books of Kings. The only way to resolve the contradiction is to say that the Elijah narrative was grafted into the books of Kings without any thought by the editor.[40] However, this view is difficult to maintain. The books of Kings carefully criticize past kings. And, the Elijah narratives clearly have been related thoughtfully, if not carefully, to the actions of Ahab and his son Ahaziah,[41] and thus to the books of Kings as a whole. This then suggests that the final editor had a deliberate reason to include the Elijah narrative of 1 Ki 18 without considering it contradictory with his view of centralization. Similarly, even if the author/final editor of the books of Samuel

---

[40] In fact, Wellhausen's view of centralization in this respect relies on the same method which he uses for Pentateuchal source criticism in general. Wellhausen delimits the JEDP sources according to their literary style and thought world into internally consistent sources which attest differing views of centralization and different stages of religious development. On the other hand, these sources were put together by the final redactor(s) to form the finished version of the Pentateuch without any concern that these differing views might be contradictory. Cf. Whybray 1987, pp. 120-126 for a criticism of this approach.

[41] 1 Ki 17-2 Ki 2. Similarly the Elisha narratives (2 Ki 2ff.)

knew Deuteronomy, he may have had a logically consistent reason for not criticizing Samuel for sacrificing at *bamoth*.

If one nevertheless asserts that the Elijah narrative of 1 Ki 18 was set in the books of Kings without thought, one ends up with the following circular argument: (A) The concept of centralization was created only during the time of Josiah. Therefore, any material in the books of Kings (and similarly, in any other book) which attests the concerns of centralization must be contemporaneous with or later than the time of Josiah, and any material which does not attest centralization must be earlier than the time of Josiah. (B) All material which attests the concerns of centralization is contemporaneous with or later than the time of Josiah, and all material which does not attest the concerns of centralization is earlier than the time of Josiah. Therefore, the concept of centralization was created only during the time of Josiah.

Another weakness in the Wellhausenian approach, as has been convincingly demonstrated by McConville, is that the "place which Yahweh will choose" does not necessarily refer to Jerusalem. Deuteronomy itself never directly speaks of Jerusalem,[42] and, according to McConville, throughout Deuteronomy the 'chosen place' "most naturally refers to a single place, but its requirement may be met in a number of places in succession".[43] According to McConville, in Deuteronomy's thought, "the choice of a place is not the end of a story, for Yahweh will not be bound to one place for ever".[44] Also, even if most of the Old Testament literature outside Deuteronomy speaks in favour of Jerusalem as the chosen place, there are clear indications that the Old Testament interprets "the place which Yahweh will choose" as referring to more than one location.[45] The clearest indication of a non-Jerusalemite application comes from Jer 7:12, which explicitly applies the place to Shiloh.[46] Also, according to McConville, Ps 78:60 states that

---

[42] McConville and Millar 1994, p. 110.

[43] Ibid., p. 120.

[44] Ibid., p. 122.

[45] Ibid., pp. 90-96.

[46] Ibid., p. 92. According to Wellhausen (1905/1878, p. 19), Jer 7:12 does not reflect the concerns of the premonarchic time, but of a later time. This however does not remove that fact that two places, Shiloh and Jerusalem are referred to as "the place where Yahweh let his name dwell".

Shiloh was the place where Yahweh first made his dwelling, and it is noteworthy that the verb שׁכן, which is used in Dt 12:5, is used in Ps 78:60.[47] Moreover, it has been universally acknowledged that Shiloh was a prominent sanctuary in the premonarchical period according to the books of Joshua, Judges and Samuel.[48] Finally, it has been suggested that Shechem, Bethel or Gilgal might have been central sanctuaries during the early premonarchical period, even though it must be admitted that the evidence for such a significance for any of these locations is scanty.[49]

Scholars have also questioned whether Deuteronomy's centralization requirement is absolute. Even though Welch's claim that Dt 12:14 could mean "in any of your tribes" is countered by the impossibility of such an interpretation in Dt 12:5,[50] there are other, pressing indications that Deuteronomy at least in one way or another allows for lesser altars. This is because, whereas Ex 20:22-26 and Lev 17 are the only altar laws in JE and P, respectively, there are two more altar laws in Deuteronomy besides the altar law of Dt 12. The first is Dt 16:21-22 which forbids the setting up of an Asherah beside the altar of Yahweh. This law seems to allow multiple altars,[51] which is at least at first sight blatantly in contradiction to the centralization law of Dt 12. As McConville points out, if one argues that Dt 16:21 is pre-deuteronomic, one still has to answer the question of why the final editor who wished to suppress other altars than the central altar in Jerusalem should want to include such a detail.[52]

The second "additional" altar law in Deuteronomy is Dt 27, which prescribes the building of an altar at Mt Ebal in the vicinity of Shechem right after the crossing of the river Jordan during the conquest. The altar of Dt 27 is to be made of unhewn stones, and this injunction clearly seems to refer back to the Ex 20:22-26 altar law.[53] Furthermore, there is a record in Josh 8:30-35 of the

---

[47] McConville and Millar 1994, p. 93.

[48] For a comprehensive recent discussion, including a full treatment of the history of research concerning Shiloh, see Schley 1989.

[49] See Wenham 1971a, pp. 105-109; Wenham 1993, pp. 96-99.

[50] See McConville 1984, p. 28.

[51] Cf. McConville 1984, p. 28.

[52] McConville 1984, p. 28.

[53] So also McConville 1984, p. 29.

fulfilment of this command.[54] As McConville points out, it is not
likely that the altar in Mt Ebal would have served as a sanctuary
intended by the altar law of Deut 12. According to McConville,
"This is because of the rough and primitive nature of the altar (v. 6)
and partly because an identification of the two places is nowhere
made."[55] To solve the problem of incompatibility, as with Dt 16:21,
Dt 27:5-7 has been argued to be earlier material than
Deuteronomy.[56] However, as McConville points out, once again
one has to ask the question of why the material was included in the
final form of the book.[57] As McConville notes, "This material
would probably have been too embarrassing for an author or
compiler who wanted to concentrate worship in Jerusalem to leave
in its present form".[58] Thus, according to McConville, "It is not
possible to show, therefore, that Deuteronomy requires that
worship be carried on in one place only. Its altar-law can be said to
require no more than a pre-eminent sanctuary, tacitly allowing
other, lesser altars. And this has the corollary that the law could
have arisen in an earlier period than Josiah, and have been applied
to Shiloh or Bethel, or any other sanctuary which, for any period,
was pre-eminent in Israel."[59] In this regard, it is noteworthy that
Wellhausen nowhere in his *Prolegomena* even mentions either Dt
16:21 or Dt 27.[60]

Thus, there are clear reasons to question Wellhausen and de
Wette's interpretation of the history of sacrifices. However, if one
looks at previous approaches which have more or less challenged
the Wellhausenian consensus,[61] they are few and far between and

---

[54] See below, Chapter 4.3 for a detailed exegesis of Dt 27 and Josh
8:30-35.

[55] McConville 1984, p. 29, also referring to Wenham 1971a, pp. 114ff.

[56] McConville 1984, pp. 28, 29.

[57] Ibid., p. 29.

[58] Ibid.

[59] Ibid.

[60] See Wellhausen 1905/1878.

[61] Besides McConville 1984 and McConville and Millar 1994, see
Manley 1957, pp. 122-136, Wenham 1971a and Niehaus 1992. See also
Schley 1989, pp. 11-99 which conveniently includes description of 19th
century attempts to solve the problem of why centralization was not
effected in practice in the premonarchical period.

mostly limited in scope. Also, there are a number of questions which they have not been able to answer satisfactorily. First of all, if one thinks that Shiloh may have been the chosen place,[62] or at least a central sanctuary, what are the factors on which such a claim can be based? Also, exactly how and when was Shiloh the chosen place or the central sanctuary? Further, whereas McConville asserts that Deuteronomy allows lesser altars alongside the central sanctuary based on Dt 16:21 and Dt 27, Josh 22:9-34 does not seem to allow any other sacrificial altar than the altar at the central sanctuary. Thus, what is the relationship between the central sanctuary and local altars? In this regard, as Joshua 22:9-34 seems to exhibit both Priestly and Deuteronomic features, is the view of centralization in Josh 22:9-34 Priestly or Deuteronomic? And, what is the view of the Priestly material in regard to centralization, as expounded most notably by Lev 17? Moreover, what is the relationship of the centralization requirements of the Priestly material with the centralization requirements of Deuteronomy? Also, as the tent of meeting features prominently in the Priestly material, including in Lev 17, and is also associated with Shiloh, even though not exclusively (e.g. 1 Chr 21:29; 2 Chr 1:3), what is the role of the tent of meeting in regard to centralization? Moreover, what is the meaning of the fact that the tent of meeting is replaced by Solomon's temple and that the focus changes from Shiloh to Jerusalem after the premonarchic period?

The purpose of this study is to attempt to answer these questions. For that end, I will make a detailed investigation of the material that these questions point to. First, I will make a detailed exegesis of the Pentateuchal altar laws of Ex 20:22-26; Lev 17; Dt 12 and Dt 16:21-22 in order to see how they understand the central sanctuary and centralization. I will also make a detailed investigation of Dt 27:1-8, and of Josh 8:30-35 which records the fulfilment of Dt 27:1-8. Similarly, I will investigate those passages in the Old Testament which seem to speak about Shiloh as the chosen place or as an important sanctuary in the period before the monarchy. The most important of these are Josh 22:9-34; Judges 17-21 and 1 Sam 1-4. On the other hand, Ps 78:56-72 and Jer 7:12-

---

[62] Specifically, I will use the term 'chosen place' in this study to mean a place concerning which it is thought that Yahweh has chosen it to let his name dwell there as expressed in Dt 12 and elsewhere in Deuteronomy.

17; 26:4-6, 9, besides speaking about Shiloh as an important place, also speak about its rejection, and are thus pertinent. Moreover, while 1 Sam 1-4 indisputably indicates that Shiloh is at least an important sanctuary and starts the chain of events where Shiloh is replaced by Jerusalem, the books of Samuel are characteristically less explicit in theological interpretation of the events contained in them. Therefore, I will subsume the treatment of 1 Sam 1-4 under the treatment of Ps 78:56-72 and Jer 7:12-17; 26:4-6, 9.[63] I will also refer to other biblical passages where appropriate, including parallels in the books of Chronicles to the books of Samuel and 1 Kings 1-8.

Based on the above research questions and their corresponding biblical passages, the discussion focuses naturally on the period after the settlement and before the building of the temple. As the scope of the study is limited for practical reasons, I will restrict the discussion to the period between the settlement and the building of the temple. However, as Jer 7:12-17; 26:4-6, 9, and most likely Ps 78, besides speaking about Shiloh, also directly refer to the period after the building of the first temple, I will consider the implications of these references where relevant. Naturally, the fact that the critical consensus dates the books of Deuteronomy and Joshua-2 Kings to the seventh-sixth centuries and the Priestly material to the postexilic period makes it necessary to think of at least some aspects of the conditions of these later periods as well. Nevertheless, most aspects of the problem of history of centralization which relate to the period after the building of the first temple must remain outside the scope of this study. Yet, I suspect that the period before the building of Solomon's temple is the more complex part of the problem and may give at least some indications as to how the problems of the later period could be

---

[63] Cf. Hertzberg 1964, p. 20, "The theological basis of the books of Samuel is not so obvious as that of the other historical books; it is there unobtrusively, and is more often to be read between the lines than in explicit statements." On the other hand, as Hertzberg (ibid.) puts it, the theological message of the books of Samuel is always expressed sufficiently recognizably and is told in a "masterful way" for the most part. Thus, even though I will subsume the interpretation of the events in 1 Sam 1-4 under the discussion of Ps 78:56-72 and Jer 7:12-17; 26:4-6, 9, I by no means intend to ignore what 1 Sam 1-4 say in their own right.

solved. Above all, the problem is less complex for the later period because there is no uncertainty about the chosen place. The books of Kings explicitly indicate that Jerusalem is the chosen place after the building of the temple (1 Ki 8), no other books deny this even if many of them might not mention the matter directly, and the Zion theology of the Psalms clearly emphasizes Jerusalem. Moreover, the period before the building of Solomon's temple may be suggestive for the period after the building of the temple if Shiloh was at least theoretically thought to be the chosen place or its equivalent during the time portrayed by the book of Judges. In particular, the problems posed by Gideon's and Manoah's altars are in that case similar to those produced by Elijah's actions.[64] Yet, another study may be needed for the first temple period and for the exilic and postexilic periods.

In relation to biblical material, the last 100 years have brought forward an immense amount of archaeological material both from Israel and its surrounding cultures. Archaeological material from Israel's surrounding cultures also includes written material, most notably from Egypt, Mesopotamia, ancient Anatolia, and Ugarit, which is earlier than or contemporary with premonarchic and monarchic Israel and which can be profitably used to shed light on the customs of Israel. I will include archaeological material from Israel which might be relevant to the problem at hand, such as that from Shiloh and Mount Ebal, and certain material related to cultic matters.[65] As regards material outside Israel, I have especially included material which relates to ancient Near Eastern

---

[64] Thus, I will attempt to shortly sketch how the Elijah narrative could be viewed when looking at Gideon's altars. Note also that an overall similarity between the Gideon and Elijah narratives has been recognized; see Gregory 1990, pp. 143-144, and cf. O'Connell 1996, p. 152n189.

[65] In fact, overall, it has to be said that the number of cult places which have been attested archaeologically is small during the period from the settlement to the building of Solomon's temple. Gilmour considers only the "Bull Site", Mt Ebal and Ai from the central hill country as sites which can be interpreted cultically in the Early Iron Age. (Gilmour 1995; see also his summary map on p. 428 listing all sites with cultic finds in Early Iron Age Palestine). As far as the Late Bronze Age is concerned, the data are not very plentiful either (see Ottosson 1980 who treats the most important temples and cult places in Palestine from the Early Bronze Age until the end of the Iron Age).

conceptions of divine presence and absence, as the presence of gods is firmly related to cultic matters both in Israel and the ancient Near East. Especially, as the "coming" of Yahweh in Ex 20:24 seems to be connected with divine presence, and at least at first sight seems to contrast with the Priestly conception that the tent of meeting is the dwelling-place of Yahweh (Ex 25:8), clarifying at least some aspects of the Israelite view of divine presence might be helpful in understanding the mutual relationship between the central sanctuary and local altars, and looking at the matter in comparison and contrast to ancient Near Eastern beliefs of divine presence might help in clarifying the resulting picture further. In this context, and especially drawing on ancient near Eastern concepts, I will also briefly attempt to treat the seemingly complex problem of divine presence in Deuteronomy as it relates to the central sanctuary.[66]

I have chosen a certain number of methodological presuppositions for the study. As is natural for the task ahead, I will not assume a date for Deuteronomy.[67] Also, I will not assume Pentateuchal source division.[68] However, I will interact with critical

---

[66] For a review of the problem, including history of scholarship, see McConville and Millar 1994, pp. 110-116. See also Weinfeld 1972, pp. 191-209.

[67] Cf. for this and the following assumptions the comments in Kuhn 1962, p. 84: "The transition from a paradigm in crisis to a new one from which a new tradition of normal science can emerge is far from a cumulative process, one achieved by an articulation or extension of the old paradigm. Rather, it is a reconstruction of the field from new fundamentals, a reconstruction that changes some of the field's most elementary theoretical generalizations as well as many of its paradigm methods and applications". Also, "So long as the tools a paradigm supplies continue to prove capable of solving the problems it defines, science moves fastest and penetrates most deeply through confident employment of those tools. The reason is clear. As in manufacture so in science - retooling is an extravagance to be reserved for the occasion that demands it. The significance of crises is the indication; they provide that an occasion for retooling has arrived." (ibid., p. 76).

[68] The main reasons for this are as follows, as elaborated especially by Whybray:

1. "Many different explanations could be given of the process by which the Pentateuch attained its present form. The Documentary

consensus views where necessary in the argumentation. On the other hand, I recognize that there are various literary styles in the Pentateuch, which can be divided into Priestly, Deuteronomic and Narrative styles, however elusive the exact delimitation of material according to these might be. Overall, what I will call Priestly material roughly corresponds to P together with H, Deuteronomic

---

Hypothesis in its classical form is a particular and elaborate example of one main type of literary theory, which has predominated for many years" (Whybray 1987, p. 129; cf. our quotations of Kuhn 1962 above).

2. The documentary hypothesis cannot account for all data of the Pentateuch. Especially, in this respect, "It was universally admitted that the distinction between the earliest documents, J and E, was frequently blurred." (Whybray 1987, p. 129) Cf. also e.g. Num 32 where a satisfactory source division between JE and P has not been successful (see Gray 1903, p. 426).

3. The documentary hypothesis is dependent on an evolutionary view of the history of Israel, but "it is now recognized that the religious phenomenon of Yahwism and Judaism was far more complicated, and its history less unilinear, than Wellhausen supposed it to have been". (Whybray 1987, p. 43).

4. "The authors of the documents are credited with a consistency in the avoidance of repetitions and contradictions which is unparalleled in ancient literature (and even in modern fiction), and which ignores the possibility of the deliberate use of such features for aesthetic and literary purposes." (Whybray 1987, p. 130) At the same time, the redactors who put the documents together are supposed to have left even major inconsistencies intact (ibid., pp. 120-122).

5. "The breaking up of narratives into separate documents by a 'scissors and paste' method not only lacks true analogies in the ancient literary world, but also often destroys the literary and aesthetic qualities of these narratives, which are themselves important data which ought not to be ignored." (Whybray 1987, p. 130)

6. "Too much reliance was placed, in view of our relative ignorance of the history of the Hebrew language, on differences of language and style. Other explanations of variations of language and style are available, e.g. differences of subject-matter requiring special or distinctive vocabulary, alternations of vocabulary introduced for literary reasons, and unconscious variation of vocabulary." (Whybray 1987, p. 130)

Whybray himself, after arguing against the methodology and results of source (and also traditio-historical) criticism (for details, see Whybray 1987, pp. 17-219), dispenses with source division altogether and takes the Pentateuch as a literary unity (see ibid., pp. 221-242).

material roughly corresponds to any material exhibiting the style of the book of Deuteronomy, and Narrative material roughly corresponds to JE. As might be expected, I will not assume the dating of the Pentateuchal sources, and I will not assume the dating of material exhibiting any of the Priestly, Deuteronomic or narrative styles. Also, for these reasons I will not assume the dating of any relevant Old Testament books if this dating is based on the critical consensus date of the Pentateuch. On the other hand, for these reasons I will pay special attention to the issues of dating of the biblical passages I focus on and any other relevant material. In the dating of the passages, I will try to take note of the implied rhetorical goals of the passages and other relevant material in question.[69] As a consequence of not assuming dates for biblical books exhibiting the various Pentateuchal styles, and also due to the recent challenges against the unity of the so-called Deuteronomistic History, I will not assume *a priori* that Joshua-2 Kings together with the book of Deuteronomy is necessarily a unified literary whole and the work of one author.[70]

Moreover, I will proceed with the recognition that the interpretation of archaeological material includes a number of problems. First of all, the archaeological record is only a sample of the physical material which existed in the past and is thus subject to the accidents of survival. Also, the identification of archaeological sites is often unclear or disputed. Moreover, as pertains religious matters, it is not always clear whether certain archaeological remains should be interpreted from a cultic standpoint.[71] Further, in this, if a particular site or artefact can be interpreted as cultic, it is not always clear whether the site or artefact was used by Israelites or by Canaanites. Even if a cultic site or artefact was used by Israelites, there still remains the problem of whether the usage is to

---

[69] For a comprehensive treatment of rhetorical criticism and its application to the book of Judges, see O'Connell 1996.

[70] See Noth 1991/1943 for the theory of the Deuteronomistic History. See McConville 1997 for a recent survey of scholarship of Joshua-2 Kings especially after Noth. See also especially Westermann 1994, who argues that the books of Joshua-2 Kings are separate works rather than a connected, unified whole.

[71] Cf. e.g. Mazar 1990a and Ahlström 1993, *passim* for accompanying issues and problems of interpretation.

be considered to have been legitimate according to orthodox/canonical Yahwism or whether it is to be considered syncretistic. One's interpretation of these matters hinges on one's view of the written materials of the Old Testament, including their dating. Thus, whether one thinks that a cultic site or artefact which does not fit with orthodox/canonical Yahwism could actually have been conceived as illegitimate by the people who produced it or used it, or that the view of illegitimacy is a creation of later religion which the Old Testament documents attest, depends on how one dates the material of the Old Testament.[72]

On the other hand, specifically, I will not try to solve archaeological problems relating to the early history of Israel. Certainly, the early history of Israel has in many ways been a subject of heated debate in the past, and continues to be a problem in the present as well. This is above all because there is no direct archaeological proof of a conquest[73] either in the 13th or the 15th century BC. On the other hand, there are good reasons to think that an extensive settlement process took place in the Israelite hill country from the beginning of Iron Age I, whichever way one interprets the causes and implications of that settlement.[74] However, the current scholarly consensus has largely rejected the historically important conquest, peaceful infiltration and peasants' revolt models, favouring models which explain the settlement in terms of indigenous origins.[75]

There are also problems with the correlation of archaeological and biblical data for later periods. Sure, scholars have traditionally been fairly positive about this correlation, and consequently about the usability of the biblical material for historical reconstruction from the period of Judges on. Recently, however, there have been strong challenges even about whether the biblical material can be

---

[72] For this problem, see already Wellhausen 1905/1878, esp. pp. 17-20 from a literary standpoint, and most notably Ahlström 1993 from an archaeological standpoint.

[73] And even less so for the Exodus, but see Hoffmeier 1997.

[74] See especially Finkelstein 1988, and cf. e.g. Coote and Whitelam 1987, Thompson 1992, Dever 2001, Mazar 1990a.

[75] See e.g. Dever 2001, p. 41 and passim. For a history of scholarship on the early history of Israel, see Thompson 1992, pp. 1-170; Hoffmeier 1997, pp. 3-51.

used at all for reconstructing the history of Israel before the exile. According to such scholars as T.L. Thompson, N.P. Lemche and P.R. Davies, the biblical Israel is a scholarly construction from the Persian and Hellenistic periods and the biblical texts cannot be used for historical reconstruction of real Israel before the exile.[76] Keeping these considerations in mind, how are we to justify a study which will examine textual evidence about the early history of Israel?

First of all, it has to be noted that one can study the picture that texts give without any regard to their historicity, and this will be a main starting point for the present work. I will concentrate on the picture that the Old Testament documents themselves build about the early history of Israel. Only after that I will ask the question of whether and how much this picture may correspond to historical reality.

However, I must also add that I do not share the scepticism of Lemche, Davies and Thompson about the value of using biblical documents for reconstructing the history of Israel before the exile. There are a number of reasons for this. First of all, according to these scholars, the biblical documents cannot be used for historical reconstruction unless data contained in them can be verified from contemporary extrabiblical documents.[77] It is true that, say, if one were to imagine a court case where there is only one witness, it might be that the court would not accept the testimony of the witness. However, this would not yet mean that the witness cannot be trustworthy, unless he or she can be falsified. As one cannot travel to the past to verify the testimony, it would be beyond the court's reach to verify the testimony about the past in such a case. The analogy with biblical studies should be clear. Moreover, in fact, there is much positive archaeological evidence from before the exile which corroborates a lot of what the corresponding biblical texts portray.[78]

---

[76] See esp. Lemche 1998; Thompson 1992; Thompson 2000; Davies 1992; and cf. Finkelstein and Silberman 2001 who have similar tendencies but are less radical than Thompson, Davies and Lemche.

[77] See e.g. Lemche 1998, pp. 29-30.

[78] See esp. Dever 2001 for many details. See also Mazar 1997 which gives comprehensive reasons against the lowering of IA chronology recently proposed by Finkelstein which, if accepted, would result in

Secondly, the abovementioned scholars state that since the biblical texts are late, they are deemed to be unreliable.[79] Yet, they make this assertion of lateness by relying on the results of biblical criticism which is largely based on a literary examination of the biblical documents.[80] However, how about if one were to be able to give literary critical reasons for an earlier dating of the documents? In fact, the discussion which follows in this book pays extensive attention to dating based on a literary examination of the selected texts precisely for this reason. Moreover, even if a late dating for the composition of biblical books is granted, I disagree with Lemche that if the historical material in question has been utilised later, it cannot be taken as trustworthy even if it originates from the time of the events which it portrays.[81] There are well known cases where literary material has been transmitted reliably through centuries in the ancient Near East.[82] However, I agree with the minimalists, and for that matter with most scholars, in that one has to examine literary material carefully before accepting its historical testimony.

Thirdly, it has to be said that even if a historical reconstruction is logically consistent and explains the available historical record, it does not yet necessarily follow that such a reconstruction is a good approximation of historical reality. This is because based on theoretical considerations, one always needs to think of the possibility of the existence of multiple substantially differing reconstructions which are logically consistent and explain the available historical record.[83] Consequently, the claims of these scholars about the validity of their own historical reconstructions should be taken with caution.

As regards the book of Joshua in particular, even if there is no clear evidence of a conquest and even if it were certain that a conquest never took place, it would not yet automatically follow

---

considerably making the reliability of the biblical accounts about the period of the United Monarchy in particular suspect; cf. Dever 2001, pp. 43-44.

[79] See e.g. Lemche 1998, pp. 25-30.

[80] See ibid.; Thompson 1992, pp. 88-112.

[81] See Lemche 1998, pp. 25-30.

[82] See below, Chapter 4.1.

[83] For this, see below, Appendix.

that the whole of the book of Joshua should thereby be discarded as nonhistorical. A careful examination of the book might nevertheless reveal some historical information. In this respect, one should add that the book of Joshua is often read as portraying a quick and comprehensive conquest and settlement, but is such a reading justified upon closer examination? Keeping these comments in mind, it seems better to take the textual evidence as one witness, whether more or less reliable, and archaeological evidence as another, and use both to try to build a plausible picture about the early history of Israel. Naturally, if such a method is adopted, results in this difficult area cannot be but tentative.[84] Moreover, as this book focuses on the history and theology of centralization and the central sanctuary, it is by no means its intention to try to solve all problems which relate to the correlation of biblical and archaeological material, including the conquest narratives of Joshua.

A further comment should be made about how one should read Old Testament literary material. Even if late twentieth and early twenty-first century Western culture often discredits the possibility of divine intervention in human affairs, this was not the case in the ancient Near East. On the contrary, in the ancient Near East, divine intervention in human affairs was considered a self-evident aspect of life, with (at least practically) all known ancient Near Eastern literary works more or less reflecting this fact. Moreover, if one wished to discredit historical sources because they attest the viewpoint of their writer, perhaps even in a propagandistic way, it would be difficult to study history at all. Especially, as is well known, a lot of ancient Near Eastern historiography has been written from the viewpoint of the writer and his society, and often includes propagandistic features.[85] Yet, regardless of these propagandistic features and the belief in divine intervention in the documents, ancient Near Eastern historians carefully consider whether any historical reconstruction can be made from these sources. Thus, nothing less should be allowed for the Old Testament as it is a collection of ancient Near Eastern

---

[84] Of course, such caution should be exercised with other texts and periods as well, even if to a lesser extent.

[85] See e.g. Younger 1990.

documents.[86] In this respect, as it is well known that narrative and theology are generally inseparable in ancient Near Eastern historiography,[87] I will assume that the same applies to the Old Testament as well, unless there are compelling reasons to think otherwise.[88]

Then, as far as the particulars of the comparative evidence of the ancient Near Eastern material outside the Old Testament are concerned, even though the study of the ancient Near East is divided into various branches, such as Egyptology, Sumerology, Assyriology, Hittitology and Ugaritic studies, and each is a complex field on its own, with a few exceptions I have tried to treat relevant Ancient Near Eastern material from a broad standpoint across the field as a whole. I have also tried to include only conclusions and interpretations which generally are thought to be firmly established.[89]

The primary issue to which this study hopes to contribute is the history of centralization of sacrifices in the period between the settlement and the building of Solomon's temple. A related issue is the role of the central sanctuary and local altars and their mutual relationship, and this study will focus on it where appropriate in order to solve the problems relating to the history of centralization. Moreover, as is clear from the previous discussion and elsewhere, the history of centralization is connected with a number of other complex issues. These include Pentateuchal source division and the dating of the Pentateuchal sources, the question of the

---

[86] Cf. Younger 1999, pp. 205-206, according to whom ignoring the biblical evidence outright "would be like ignoring the Annals of Sargon in a reconstruction of the fall of Samaria because of a perceived bias in his writings".

[87] See e.g. Younger 1990 for many examples.

[88] Cf. Younger 1990. Cf. also Van Seters 1983 for another stimulating treatment of ancient Near Eastern and Israelite historiography, regardless of whether one finds a number of its methods and conclusions acceptable.

[89] Naturally, there is variation in the ancient Near Eastern cultures, both regionally and at various time periods. Yet, there is an overall similarity as well, and it is above all the common factors that I will attempt to draw from. Also, due to a broad approach, I will generally not discuss the relevant ancient Near Eastern sources in their original languages.

Deuteronomistic History, the dating of the books of Joshua-2 Kings, including the date of Joshua and its relationship to the Pentateuch and to Judges-2 Kings,[90] the dating of a number of other Old Testament books, the interpretation of archaeological material from Israel, the question of the literary unity of the Pentateuch and other Old Testament books, the history of priesthood,[91] profane slaughter,[92] centralization of other Israelite institutions such as the Passover,[93] and divine presence in Deuteronomy.[94] I will introduce these issues and address them when they arise naturally from the investigation of the passages which relate to centralization of sacrifices in the period between the settlement and the building of Solomon's temple.

A word must be said about the order of presentation. I have chosen to treat Chapter 1, *Centralization and the Period from the Settlement to the Building of Solomon's Temple* in a topical rather than chronological order, as this is more helpful for the development of the argument.

---

[90] See Auld 1980 for a review of issues relating to the problem of whether the book of Joshua is a part of a Hexateuch or a Deuteronomistic History, including history of modern scholarship.

[91] See Cody 1969 for issues involved in the history of Israelite priesthood, and also Schley 1989 as the problem relates to Shiloh and the premonarchical period.

[92] For the classic statement of profane slaughter, see Wellhausen 1905/1878, pp. 53-79. For a recent treatment, including history of scholarship, see McConville 1984, pp. 39-55.

[93] For the classic statement of feasts, including Passover, see Wellhausen 1905/1878, pp. 80-114. For a recent treatment, including history of scholarship, see McConville 1984, pp. 99-123. See also Levinson 1997, pp. 53-97 as regards Passover in Deuteronomy.

[94] See von Rad 1953/1948, pp. 37-44; Weinfeld 1972, pp. 191-209; Wilson 1995 for the issues involved with divine presence in Deuteronomy.

2. DIVINE PRESENCE AND CENTRALIZATION

2.1. Divine Presence in the Ancient Near East

As the Israelites shared a common cultural heritage with the other people of the ancient Near East, let us start by clarifying general ancient Near Eastern conceptions of divine presence. These will help us understand better the Israelites conceptions about the ark, the tent of meeting and the temple, and sanctuaries outside the context of the ark, the tent of meeting and the temple,[95] to be discussed in the subsequent sections of Chapter 2. Overall, our principal aim is to use the results of Chapter 2 to illuminate the Pentateuchal requirements of centralization which will be discussed in Chapter 1 and the history of the central sanctuary and centralization which will be discussed in Chapter 1.

In the ancient Near East, gods were thought to be present both in heaven[96] and on earth. First of all, it is clear that a god could be present in heaven. For instance, the Mesopotamian sun god Shamash was present in the sun,[97] Ishtar was seen as the goddess of the morning and evening stars,[98] and the ancient Near Eastern mythologies speak of various actions of gods in the heavenly realm.[99]

On the other hand, gods could be present on earth. The most important and conspicuous place where a god could be present on earth was a temple which was considered an earthly house of a god.

---

[95] Cf. also above, Introduction, p. 15.

[96] I use this term to include the underworld and other cosmic localities.

[97] Jacobsen 1987, p. 17. This would naturally also be true for the Egyptian sun god Re (cf. *ANET*, p. 8, where Re says: "Behold ye, I am here in the sky in my [proper] place"), and for the Hittite sun god (^{d}UTU, usually taken as 'Istanus'; see Gurney 1977, pp. 8, 10, 11, 14; *KHW*, p. 300).

[98] Jacobsen 1987, pp. 17-18.

[99] See e.g. Dalley 1989 for Mesopotamia.

As Hutter points out, "Die Sumerer nannten den Tempel É, womit auch ein Wohnhaus bezeichnet werden könnte."[100] Also, the use of the word *bīt ilim* for a temple in Akkadian[101], *pr* in Egyptian,[102] É.DINGIR in Hittite[103], and *byt/bt* in Ugaritic[104] reflects this fact.[105]

The presence of a god in a temple occurred through a cult object, which could either be an anthropomorphic[106] or a theriomorphic[107] statue representing the god, a divine symbol[108] or a cult stela.[109] The cult object was made and dedicated to provide a locus for the god's presence.[110] In this respect, both Mesopotamians and Egyptians thought essentially in the same way about divine images,[111] even though one might perhaps say that in Mesopotamia, an image which was properly consecrated was in general rather equated with the god in question,[112] whereas in

---

[100] Hutter 1996, p. 80.

[101] See Hutter 1996, p. 80; *AHw*, p. 133.

[102] See HANNIG, p. 278.

[103] See *KHW*, p. 270.

[104] See *UT*, p. 371.

[105] Cf. also e.g. Wiggermann 1996, esp. p. 1861, Te Velde 1996, p. 1732, and McMahon 1996, p. 1992.

[106] So especially in Mesopotamia; see e.g. Oppenheim 1964, pp. 184-185.

[107] So often in Egypt; see e.g. Hornung 1996.

[108] For Egypt, see Hornung 1996; for Mesopotamia, see Green 1996.

[109] For a study of aniconic cult objects in the ancient Near East, including cult stelae, see Mettinger 1995. See also Hutter 1993.

[110] See e.g. Jacobsen 1987; Lorton 1999. See also Jacobsen 1987, pp. 23-28; Walker and Dick 1999 and Lorton 1999, pp. 147-179 for the "opening of mouth" or "washing of the mouth" rituals in Mesopotamia and Egypt which would disassociate the cult object from human sphere and prepare it for sacred use.

[111] See Lorton 1999, p. 181n75. Cf. McMahon 1996, p. 1990 for (similar) related concepts in the Hittite realm. Cf. also the discussion of god images in Ugarit in De Tarragon 1980, pp. 98-112 which implies that the related concepts were not radically different in Ugarit either. Cf. also Jdg 17:3-5; 18:24.

[112] See Jacobsen 1987, pp. 16-17; cf. Thureau-Dangin 1975 where cult statues are spoken of as gods.

Egypt, gods and images were rather seen as separate.[113] The presence of the god in an image was seen as continuous in normal circumstances, even though an aspect of daily rejuvenation of the godly power in the image was also included in Egypt in the late period.[114]

Moreover, it is clear that a god's presence in heaven and earth could be simultaneous. This is demonstrated by the fact that for instance, the sun god Shamash still remained in the sky even if he was present in his sanctuary.[115] Furthermore, a god could be simultaneously present in more than one locality on earth, as there could at one time exist more than one temple dedicated to a particular god.[116] The ancient Mesopotamian concept of the simultaneous presence of gods in heaven and on earth has been described by Jacobsen,

> In saying that the cult statue is the form of the god filling with its specific divine content we do not wish to suggest the image of a vessel filled with different content, or even of a body with a god incarnate in it. We must think, rather, in terms of a purely mystic unity, the statue mystically becoming what it represents, the god, without, however, in any way limiting the god, who remains transcendent.[117]

We should also point out that in Mesopotamia, a temple was conceived of as a place of cosmic significance,[118] and such

---

[113] See Morenz 1960, p. 151; Assmann 1984, pp. 53-57; Lorton 1999, esp. pp. 179-201.

[114] See Lorton 1999, pp. 179-201; cf. Assmann 1984, pp. 50-58. Note also that during the time of Akhenaten, when the sun god was elevated (at least practically) as the sole god and images were banned, the sun god's presence was manifested in the temple through sunlight, and thus the sun god was not present in the temple (or in the world) during the night, but the sun god's presence in the temple (and in the world) was repeatedly renewed every morning (see Hornung 1999, pp. 72-73, 95-96).

[115] See Jacobsen 1987, pp. 17-18; for Egypt, see Lorton 1999.

[116] Jacobsen 1987, p. 17; Lorton 1999, p. 134n14; cf. George 1993 for Mesopotamian temple lists, among many examples for instance the Khorsabad temple list on pp. 41-42 which names temples for Ishtar in various localities.

[117] Jacobsen 1987, p. 22.

[118] George 1993, p. 59; Hutter 1996, pp. 82-83; cf. Hurowitz 1992, pp. 335-337.

ceremonial names of temples as É.TEMEN.AN.KI[119] (House, a Foundation of Heaven and Earth), É.DUR.AN.KI[120] (House, a bond of Heaven and Earth) and their variations[121] suggest that temples were also seen as places where heaven and earth met.

The relationship between a temple, god and image is illustrated well by ancient Near Eastern temple building accounts. According to Hurowitz, the major highlight of a temple building project is the moment during dedication ceremonies when the god enters into the temple:

> All of the sources relating to the dedication of a temple say either that the king brought the god into the temple and seated him in his place of happiness, or that the god entered the temple. Some sources even state that the king held the (statue of the) god by the hand and led him in a procession to the temple (see the inscriptions of Esarhaddon, Assurbanipal and Nabonidus). In addition to this, the annals of Tiglath-pileser I tell us that the dedication ceremony is called *tērubat bītim*, 'the entry into the house' (E. Wallis Budge and L.W. King [eds.], *Annals of the Kings of Assyria* 87 VI 90-93).[122]

As Hurowitz describes, and which further illustrates the role of temples and images, the major difference between temple and palace dedication ceremonies is that,

> This crucial element of the god entering and sitting in his temple is entirely absent from the inscriptions relating to the building and dedication of palaces. Instead, all the accounts of palace dedications, with no exception, state that the king 'invited' or 'called' (*qarû*) the gods of the city and the land into the new palace. This invitation was so that the gods might join the party and celebrate along with people, the princes and the king. The gods were invited to participate in the celebrations, but not to stay! Sargon's account of the dedication of Dur-Sharrukin even says that the gods

---

[119] George 1993, p. 149.

[120] Ibid., p. 80.

[121] See ibid., *passim.*

[122] Hurowitz 1992, p. 272.

returned to their cities following the dedication of the palace.[123]

Hurowitz sums up,

> The difference in the nature of the dedication ceremonies and the role of the gods in them derives, naturally, from the different functions of the buildings. In a temple dedication ceremony, the god takes up residence in his own new house, while in a palace dedication ceremony the god is only an honored guest in the house of the king.[124]

The favour of the gods was important for the prosperity of the people concerned, and the favourable disposition of a god was connected with his presence. This can clearly be seen from the fact that the worst that could happen to a city or land was that its god or gods would become angry. Such an anger would in general be a portent of a catastrophe, such as an enemy invasion and the destruction of the city or land. In this respect, a catastrophe would often be interpreted as a result of the displeasure of the gods. In fact, this displeasure was especially manifested by a deity leaving his/her sanctuary, described by a number of ancient Near Eastern documents.[125] Even if no particular reason for irritation is given, and even if divine abandonment was almost rather the result than the cause of the catastrophe,[126] as is the case with two Sumerian laments, the Lamentation over the Destruction of Ur[127] and the Lamentation over the Destruction of Sumer and Ur[128], these laments nevertheless clearly express the dismay of their composers that the gods have abandoned their temples, and the desire that the gods would return to their previous dwelling places. The Lamentation over the Destruction of Ur starts as follows,

---

[123] Ibid., p. 272.

[124] Ibid., pp. 272-273.

[125] For a summary treatment of these, see Block 1988, pp. 125-161 and Niehaus 1995, pp. 136-140.

[126] So Block 1988, p. 132; cf. however Cooper 1983, p. 21, "a city can be destroyed only when its god has left".

[127] See Kramer 1940; Translation also in *ANET*, pp. 455-463.

[128] See Michalowski 1989; Translation also in *ANET*, pp. 611-619, and *COS* 1, pp. 535-539.

expressing the fact of divine abandonment in the land as a whole (lines 1-6):[129]

> He has abandoned hi[s] stable, his sheepfold (*has been delivered*) to the wind;
>
> The wi[ld o]x has abandoned his stable, his sheepfold (*has been delivered*) to the wind.
>
> The lord of all the lands has abandoned (his stable), his sheepfold (*has been delivered*) to the wind;
>
> Enlil has abandoned...Nippur, his sheepfold (*has been delivered*) to the wind.
>
> His wife Ninlil has abandoned (her stable), her sheepfold (*has been delivered*) to the wind;[130]

Lines 237-240 express the connection with temple abandonment and plunder (at Ur):

> Its lady like a flying bird departed from her city;
>
> Ningal like a flying bird departed from her city;
>
> On all its possessions which had been accumulated in the land, a defiling hand was placed;
>
> In all its *storehouses* which abounded in the land, fires were kindled.[131]

Lines 373-384 express the desire by the people for return:

> O my queen, verily thou art one who has departed from the house; thou art one who has departed from the city.
>
> How long, pray, wilt thou stand aside in the city like an enemy?
>
> O Mother Ningal, (how long) wilt thou hurl challenges in the city like an enemy?
>
> Although thou art a queen beloved of her city, thy city...thou hast abandoned;
>
> [Although] thou art [a queen beloved of her people], thy people...thou hast abandoned.
>
> O Mother Ningal, like an ox to your stable, like a sheep to thy fold!
>
> Like an ox to thy stable of former days, like a sheep to your fold!

---

[129] Note also that, as is often the case, the text has been reconstructed from several tablets and fragments (see Kramer 1940, pp. 14-15; *ANET*, p. 455).

[130] Kramer 1940, pp. 16-17; *ANET* (translated by Kramer), p. 455; followed by 30 more lines of similar description.

[131] Kramer 1940, pp. 42-43; *ANET*, p. 461. Cf. Block 1988, p. 132.

> Like a young child to thy chamber, O maid, to thy
> house!
> May Anu, the king of the gods, utter thy *"'tis enough"*;
> May Enlil, the king of all the lands, decree thy
> (favorable) fate.
> May *he* return thy city to its place for thee; exercise its
> queenship!
> May *he* return thy city to its place for thee; exercise its
> queenship![132]

Another Sumerian lament, the 'Curse of Agade'[133] expresses (among other things) how Inanna leaves her temple in Agade and turns against the city. The curse starts with a positive description of life when Inanna is favourable to the city (lines 4-24):

> And then, to Sargon, king of Agade,
> Enlil, from south to north,
> Had given sovereignty and kingship -
> At that time, holy Inanna built
> The sanctuary Agade as her grand woman's domain,
> Set up her throne in Ulmaš.
> Like a youngster building a house for the first time,
> Like a girl establishing a woman's domain,
> So that the warehouses would be provisioned,
> That dwellings would be founded in that city,
> That its people would eat splendid food,
> That its people would drink splendid beverages,
> That those bathed (for holidays) would rejoice in the
> courtyards,
> That the people would throng the places of celebration,
> That acquaintances would dine together,
> That foreigners would cruise about like unusual birds in
> the sky,
> That even Marhaši would be reentered on the (tribute)
> rolls,
> That monkeys, mighty elephants, *water buffalo*, exotic
> animals,
> Would jostle each other in the public squares -
> Throughbred dogs, lions, mountain ibexes, alu-sheep
> with long wool -

---

[132] Kramer 1940, pp. 62-65; *ANET*, p. 462; cf. Kramer 1963, p. 144.
[133] See Cooper 1983; an older translation also in *ANET*, pp. 646-651.

(So that all this might happen), Holy Inanna did not
     sleep.[134]

After a further description of prosperity in lines 25-53,
suddenly the tone changes (lines 54-62):

How/thus in Agade's city-gate...!
Holy Inanna knew not how to accept those offerings
     there;
Like an aristocrat, talking about founding a house, she
     could not get enough of those luxuries,
But the word from Ekur[135] was as silence.
Agade was reduced to trembling before her, and
She grew anxious in Ulmaš.
She withdrew her dwelling from the city,
Like a young woman abandoning her woman's domain,
Holy Inanna abandoned the sanctuary Agade.[136]

Troubles were then seen to ensue. According to lines 83-85,

That the kingdom of Agade would no longer occupy a
     good, lasting residence,
That its future was altogether unfavorable,
That its temples would be shaken and their stores
     scattered.[137]

Whereas the above examples do not give clear reasons for
divine temple abandonment,[138] the latter part of the Curse of
Agade clearly indicates that a violation of a god's sanctuary can
provoke a god's wrath. After Inanna has left the city and troubles

---

[134] Cooper 1983, pp. 50-51.

[135] Ekur was the temple of Enlil in Nippur (cf. George 1993, p. 116 no. 677), and the reference is thus to the word of Enlil (see Cooper 1983, p. 240).

[136] Cooper 1983, pp. 52-53; cf also Block 1988, p. 133. In fact, Cooper (1983, pp. 236, 239-240) suggests that the reason why Inanna could not accept the gifts and left was that there was not a proper temple for her in Agade, and Enlil did not allow the building of one. However this may be, Cooper himself (ibid., pp. 21-22) explicitly emphasizes the motive of divine abandonment in the composition, pointing out especially lines 60-62,

uruki-ta dúr-ra-ni ba-ra-gub
ki-sikil ama₅-na šub-bu-gim
kù ᵈinanna-ke₄ èš a-ga-dèᵏⁱ mu-un-šub.

[137] Cooper 1983, pp. 54-55.

[138] Except a decree of Enlil for which no reason is given (see Block 1988, p. 133; Cooper 1983, pp. 29-30, 240, and n. 135 above).

have ensued, Naram-Sin, the ruler of Agade accepts the situation
for seven years (lines 87-92). However, after this he goes and
ransacks Ekur, the temple of Enlil at Nippur (lines 97-144). Enlil
then avenges the deed, and as a final result (following a calamity to
the land of Sumer as a whole) Agade is completely destroyed (lines
145-281).

On the other hand, there are also examples where a violation
is seen as a direct cause of divine temple abandonment. In the
Middle Assyrian "Tukulti-Ninurta Epic" (13th century BC), the
Assyrian victory over Kashtiliash IV, the king of Kassite Babylon is
interpreted as a result of his gods' abandoning him due to his
covenant breaking. According to the material,

> [The gods became angry at] the king of the Kassites'
>   betrayal of the emblem [of Shamash]
> Against the transgressor of an oath (*e-tiq ma-mi-ti*),
>   Kashtiliash, the gods of heaven and netherworld [
>   ].
> They were [angry] at the king, the land and the people [
>   ],
> They [were furious and with] the willful one, their
>   shepherd.
> His lordship, the lord of the world, became disturbed,
>   so he [forsook] Nippur,
> He would not approach [ ] (his) seat at Dur-Kurigalzu.
> Marduk abandoned his sublime sanctuary, the city
>   [Babylon],
> He cursed his favorite city Kar-[   ].
> Sin left Ur, [his] holy place [   ],
> Sh[amash became angry] with Sippar and Larsa,
> Ea [ ] Eridu, the house of wisdom [   ],
> Ishtaran became furious w[ith Der   ],
> Annunnitu would not approach Agade [   ],
> The lady of Uruk cast [off her   ]:
> (All) the gods were enraged [   ][139]

Also, the sin of the people could be the cause of divine temple
abandonment. The bilingual (Sumerian/Akkadian) text K 4874
from around the time of Nebuchadnezzar I (12th century BC)
clearly demonstrates this:

---

[139] FOSTER, vol 1, p. 212, lines 32'-46'; Akkadian in Lambert 1957-58,
pp. 42, 44; cf. Niehaus 1995, pp. 137-138.

> At that time, in the reign of a previous king, conditions changed.
> Good departed and evil was regular (*da-mi-iq-ti is-si-ma le-mu-ut-tu sad-rat*).
> The lord became angry and got furious,
> He gave the command and the gods of the land abandoned it [...] its people were incited to commit crime.
> The guardians of peace became furious, and went up to the dome of heaven, The spirit of justice stood aside.
> ..., who guards living beings, prostrated the peoples, they all became like those who have no god,
> Evil demons filled the land, the namtar-demon .[...]..., they penetrated the cult centres.
> The land diminished, its fortunes changed.
> The wicked Elamite, who did not hold (the land's) treasures in esteem, [...] his battle, his attack was swift,
> He devastated the habitations and made them into a ruin, he carried off the gods, he ruined the shrines.[140]

Mesopotamian divine temple abandonment often involved the departure of the image from the temple in question.[141] As Block describes it, even if the event was on the human level to be seen simply as a spoliation of the image, on the cosmic level, the party which had lost the image interpreted the event as the god himself having arranged it.[142] If the image was received back, it was interpreted as a sign that the god returned of his own volition.[143] On the other hand, at least for the Neo-Assyrians, the spoliation of the enemy's images "was meant to portray the abandonment of the

---

[140] Lambert 1967, p. 130, lines 15-24. Akkadian in ibid., pp. 128-129; copies of tablets in ibid., pp. 134-138; for dating, see ibid., pp. 126-127. Cf. also Block 1988, p. 136.

[141] See Block 1988, pp. 134-135; Niehaus 1995, pp. 139-140.

[142] Block 1988, pp. 134-135, discussing the prophetic speech of Marduk, from the time of Nebuchadnezzar I of Babylon in the 12th century BC. Cf. Oppenheim 1964, p. 184: "The god moved with the image when the latter was carried off - expressing thus his anger against his city or the entire country."

[143] Block 1988, p. 135.

enemy by his own gods in submission to the superior might of Assyria's god, Ashur".[144]

Thus, it is clear that it was important for the ancient Near Eastern people to secure divine favour and presence. In this, the cult of the god was instrumental.[145] The principal locality where the cult took place especially in Egypt and Mesopotamia was the temple where, as discussed above, the god was considered to be present.[146] And, as Postgate spells out for early Mesopotamia, and which no doubt applies to the ancient Near East as a whole, "To please the god and ensure his or her continued presence, ... the building had to be splendid."[147]

Finally, divine presence was important in the ancient Near East for war and for oaths and treaties. There is evidence from Egypt that statues of deities accompanied the king when he led his army into foreign lands.[148] Neo-Assyrian sources indicate that

---

[144] Cogan 1974, p. 40 (see also ibid., pp. 9-41); cf. Niehaus 1995, pp. 139-140. Cf. Parpola 1987, p. 10 Fig. 4, and ibid., p. 137 Fig. 32 which depict the carrying off of gods from a defeated city by Tiglath-Pileser III (745-727 BC). Cf. also 2 Sam 5:21, pointed out by Niehaus 1995, p. 140.

[145] According to Wiggerman 1996, in Mesopotamia, neglecting the cult was high treason against the gods. Cf. Oppenheim 1964, p. 184, "Fundamentally, the deity was considered present in its image if it showed certain specific features and paraphernalia and was cared for in the appropriate manner, both established and sanctified by the tradition of the sanctuary." According to te Welde 1996, p. 1731, as regards Egypt, "If the gods were not worshiped, they would leave Egypt, and cosmic disasters would occur. The state would fall apart and be destroyed by enemies and rebels. Individuals would become the victims of illness and premature death. (Such catastrophes are narrated in the restoration stela of Tutankhamun and in the Ptolemaic period Papyrus Jumilhac.)" Cf. McMahon 1996, p. 1993 for the Hittite realm: "Nothing angered the gods more than neglect of the required cult."

[146] Thus as regards official religion, which most surviving documents in Mesopotamia and Anatolia represent (see Wiggermann 1996, p. 1859; McMahon 1996, p. 1981). For a rare study of family religion in Babylonia and Syria, see van der Toorn 1996. As regards Egypt, most religious texts are concerned with official religion or with funerary cults (see James 1979, p. 132).

[147] Postgate 1992, p. 264.

[148] Lorton 1999, p. 145n35, noting also that these were "presumably not" cult statues from temples.

divine emblems were customarily carried to battle.[149] They acted as substitutes for god-images, seemingly for the reason that god images could have been damaged during a campaign.[150] There exist pictures which depict the king worshipping before these emblems.[151]

Another context where divine presence was important was oaths and covenants. We know that in the Old Babylonian time an oath had to be made in the presence of a god.[152] Thus, it would be customary to go to a temple to swear oaths in the case of a legal dispute. However, besides going to a temple to take an oath in a legal dispute, it was also customary to bring divine symbols to the locality of the witness, and the witness was then to swear in the presence of the these symbols and thus in the presence of the gods represented by the symbols.[153] Postgate gives the following examples from Old Babylonian times: (a) "The divine hand of Dingir-mah, the divine Dog of Gula, the divine Spear-symbol of Ištar, these gods they placed inside the orchard, and Sabum swore to Matiya and Belu as follows ..."; (b) "Iddin-Enlil appealed to the judge of Larsa, and the mayor of the village of Kutalla and the village elders were present and (for) Iddin-Enlil the axe of Lugal-kidunna was taken up and it went round the orchard and he made a solemn declaration and took (the orchard)."; (c) "(The elders) committed Apsu-ilišu to the Emblem of Šamaš, (to swear) by [or:

---

[149] See Mayer 1983, pp. 68-69, line 14 on Sargon's campaign against Urartu: a-na ^{kur}Zi-kir-te ù ^{kur}An-di-a ša ^{d}URÌ.GAL^{d}IM u-ri-gal-li a-li-kut maḫ-ri-ia ú-šat-ri-ṣa ni-ir-šu-un. See also Younger 1990, p. 93 for the time of Ashur-Dan II (9th century BC), and Budge 1914, plates XVI.2 and XVII.2 for pictures.

[150] Pongratz-Leisten, Deller and Bleibtreu 1992, pp. 291-292; One might also think of the possibility of a loss of the image; according to Block (1997, p. 8), "Since the statue of a god was perceived to be indwelt by the spirit of the divinity, no experience could be more devastating psychologically than to lose the image".

[151] See Cogan 1974, p. 62 Fig. 1 (the same in Mettinger 1995, p. 42, Fig. 2.1); ANEP no. 625.

[152] See CH, e.g. §§ 9, 23.

[153] Postgate 1992, pp. 280-281; see also Spaey 1993; Mettinger 1995, p. 41.

in] the reed *kilkilu* in the gate(?) of Nungal inside the ring of flour, and he 'pulled out' the symbol of Šamaš...".[154]

Divine presence was also important when making treaties. The text of Esarhaddon's Succession Treaty states the divine witnesses as follows: (treaty) "(which he) confirmed, made and concluded in the presence (*ina IGI*) of Jupiter, Venus, Saturn, Mercury, Mars and Sirius; in the presence of Assur, Anu, Ill[il], Ea, Sin, Šamaš, Adad, Marduk, Nabu, Nusku, Uraš, Nergal, Mullissu, Šerua, Belet-ili, Ištar of Nineveh, Ištar of Arbela, the gods dwelling in heaven and earth, the gods of Assyria, the gods of Sumer and [Akka]d, all the gods of the lands".[155] Also, we know from ancient Near Eastern sources that treaties were typically deposited in the presence of gods, and this naturally implies a sanctuary/sanctuaries of these gods as a place of deposit. For instance, the Hittite treaty between Hattušili III of Hatti and Ulmi-Teshup of Tarhuntassa states: "The treaty tablet has already been made, and it shall be placed in Arinna in the presence of the Sun-goddess of Arinna."[156] Or, Hattušili states that "Which enemy countries I conquered one after the other, while still young, these I will describe separately on a tablet and will lay it down before the goddess (*PANI* DINGIR-*LIM*)".[157] Or, the Letter from Ramses II of Egypt to Kupanta-Kurunta states: "The written version of the oath which [I made] for the Great King, the king of Hatti, my brother, has been set at the feet of [the Storm-god] and before the Great Gods. They are witnesses [to the words of the oath]. And the written version of the oath which the Great King, [the King of Hatti, my brother], made for me [has been set] at the feet of the Sun-god (*ina šu-pa-al GÌR.MEŠ ša ᵈUTU*) of [Heliopolis] and before the Great Gods (*a-na pa-ni DINGIR.MEŠ GAL.MEŠ*). They are witnesses to the words [of the oath]."[158]

---

[154] Postgate 1992, p. 281.

[155] Parpola and Watanabe 1988, p. 29.

[156] BECKMAN, p. 105 (§5). Hittite text in van den Hout 1995, p. 34, lines 38'-39'.

[157] Apology of Hattušili 1.73-74, in *COS* 1, p. 200 (transl. & ed. by T.P.J. van den Hout). Hittite text in STURTEVANT-BECHTEL 1935, pp. 49-51.

[158] BECKMAN, p. 125 (§§ 6-7). Treaty in Akkadian; text in Edel 1994, vol 1, p. 76, lines 14'-19' (see also ibid., plate XVIII for the cuneiform).

Thus, we may summarize that in the ancient Near East, divine presence was an important aspect of religious life. Divine presence was important at least as a guarantee of safety and prosperity, in war and in the case of oaths and treaties. A god could be present on earth above all through its image (or symbol), and a temple was an earthly house of a god where the god resided through its image (or symbol).

2.2.   Divine Presence in Israel

2.2.1.   The Role of the Ark, the Tent of Meeting and the Temple

Having clarified general ancient Near Eastern conceptions of divine presence, let us next look at Israelite concepts, starting by an examination of the role of the ark, the tent of meeting and the temple. Our main aim is to clarify that the ark of the covenant was the Israelite functional equivalent of an ancient Near Eastern god image,[159] and that the temple of Solomon and the tent of meeting were the equivalent of an ancient Near Eastern temple as a house of god.[160] Also, we will look at the implications of this functional equivalence between Israel and the ancient Near East, especially as it relates to Yahweh's presence on earth in a sanctuary according to Deuteronomy. On the other hand, we will also pay attention to how the Israelite conceptions differed from those of the ancient Near East, especially as regards the ark.

That the ark, the tent of meeting and the temple were functionally equivalent to ancient Near Eastern god images and temples can be seen in a number of ways. First of all, as Hurowitz has pointed out, if one compares the biblical accounts of the building and dedication of the tent of meeting in the Priestly material (Ex 25-31, 35-40; Lev 8-10; Num 7) and Solomon's temple

---

[159] Cf. Miller and Roberts 1977, p. 9 and *passim* on this role of the ark.

[160] Cf. Haran 1978, according to whom the tent of meeting was a "portable temple". Note also that this concept holds irrespective of whether one considers that the tent of meeting tradition is historical or not.

(1 Ki 5:15 - 9:25; parallel in 1 Chr 17 - 2 Chr 8), they follow the following ancient Near Eastern literary pattern:[161]

> (1) the circumstances of the project and the decision to build
>
> (2) preparation, such as drafting workmen, gathering materials
>
> (3) description of the building
>
> (4) the dedication rites and festivities
>
> (5) blessing and/or prayer of the king, etc.
>
> (6) blessing and curses of future generations
>
> [+] other occasional elements[162]

If we now think of the biblical accounts of the building of the tabernacle and the building of the temple in the Old Testament, in both cases Yahweh's *kabod* takes residence in the new building after the ark has been brought into the tabernacle or the temple (see Ex 40:21, 34-35 for the Tabernacle; 1 Ki 8:6-10 [cf. 2 Chr 5] for the temple).[163] Thus, the bringing in of the ark to the temple/tent of meeting corresponds to an Assyrian *tērubat bītim*, the entry of the god to the house.[164] On the other hand, when the ark is captured from the Israelites at the battle of Aphek (1 Sam 4), Phinehas' wife, at her last, utters: גלה כבוד מישראל (1 Sam 4:21, 22), signalling that

---

[161] Hurowitz 1992, p. 64. In fact, according to Hurowitz (1992, see esp. pp. 312-313), the literary pattern is specifically Mesopotamian. However, Millard points out that the concepts and the sequence of events are so general to the ancient Near East that they and their written description need not be considered to be specifically Mesopotamian, but as general ancient Near Eastern (A.R. Millard, personal communication, May 2000).

[162] According to Hurowitz (1992, p. 22), this ancient literary pattern also underlies "the story of rebuilding the (Second) Temple in Ezra 1-6, Nehemiah's account of repairing the Walls of Jerusalem, and perhaps even Josephus' account of the Herodian rebuilding and aggrandizement of the Temple".

[163] So expressly Hurowitz 1992, pp. 267-268.

[164] See Hurowitz 1992, pp. 260-277 and cf. above, p. 28. Note that there is no reference to Yahweh's *kabod* filling the tent for the ark in 2 Sam 6, even though the celebrations in 2 Sam 6 resemble those of temple dedication ceremonies (see Hurowitz 1992, pp. 269-270 for the similarity of the literary pattern of 2 Sam 6 and 1 Ki 8). See also Miller and Roberts 1977, pp. 79-81 for a text describing the entrance of Marduk to Babylon.

Yahweh has left the land.[165] Similarly, there is a description of the departure of God's *kabod* in Ezekiel 8-11 from the temple before its destruction by the Babylonians.[166] Even though the ark is not mentioned directly in the Ezekiel passage, the connection of the ark with Yahweh's presence is confirmed by the fact that the ark was lost at the time of the destruction of the first temple,[167] and, according to the rabbis the ark and the *shekinah*, or God's presence were among a list of five things missing from the second temple.[168] The fact that the *shekinah* was missing is perfectly logical, as the symbol of *shekinah*, the ark, was missing.

Furthermore, the role of the ark in battle is similar to that of ancient Near Eastern divine symbols.[169] According to Numbers 10:33-36,[170] when the ark set out, Moses said,

קומה יהוה ויפצו איביך וינסו משנאיך מפניך:

Arise Lord, let your enemies be scattered, and let those who hate you flee before you.

Moreover, when the ark came to rest, he said:

שובה יהוה רבבות אלפי ישראל:

Return, Yahweh, to the myriads of Israel.[171]

Similarly, in Joshua 1-8, the ark is carried in front of the people (e.g. Josh 3:6; 6:8-9). In Numbers 14:41-45,[172] the ark, and thus the presence of Yahweh does not move with the people, resulting in defeat (cf. Dt 1:42), and in 1 Sam 4:7, when the ark comes to the Israelite camp, the Philistines are described as being afraid that God has come to the camp.[173]

---

[165] Cf. Mettinger 1982, p. 121; Miller and Roberts 1977, pp. 64, 66.

[166] See Block 1988, pp. 150-159; Block 1997; and Block 1997a, pp. 276-360. See also Mettinger 1982, pp. 97-103.

[167] According to the apocryphal 2 Macc 2:4-5, the prophet Jeremiah took the ark and hid it in a cave.

[168] As pointed out by Hurowitz 1992, p. 146n1 and Clements 1965, p. 126n2; see these for a full list of things missing according to the rabbis.

[169] Cf. above, p. 35.

[170] Generally attributed to JE; see Wenham 1981, p. 19.

[171] Cf. also below, p. 42n177.

[172] Generally attributed to JE; see Wenham 1981, p. 19.

[173] Cf. Miller and Roberts 1977, pp. 32-36 for 1 Sam 4:1-12. Note also that in 2 Sam 11:11 the ark accompanies the Israelites on their campaign to Rabbah.

Also, the placing of the ark in the house of Abinadab in Kiriath Jearim (1 Sam 7:1) has its parallel in the ancient Near East. According to Hurowitz, "The use of temporary housing, institution of cultic dues and performance of mourning rites for gods who were for some reason or other displaced from their own sanctuaries are practices known also from several Mesopotamian texts".[174]

Thus, the ark and the tent of meeting/temple are functionally similar to ancient Near Eastern temples and god images. Yet, there are differences between the ark and ANE god images which make the ark a unique cult object. A very important distinction between the ark and ancient Near Eastern god-images is that whereas most of the ANE god-images were anthropomorphic (or perhaps theriomorphic) representations of the corresponding deity, this is not the case for the ark.[175] The ark is in no way a representation of Yahweh or what he might look like. This is perfectly in agreement with the prohibition of images as expressed by the ten commandments of the Sinai covenant (Ex 20:4-5) and repeated in the ten commandments of the Moab covenant in Deuteronomy

---

[174] Hurowitz 1992, p. 329, including pp. 328-329 for examples from ANE. There is however no evidence for specific cultic mourning for the ark at Kiriath Jearim. Also, the impression one gets from the books of Samuel is that the ark is not to be seen as functional in the same sense as in Shiloh or in Jerusalem during its stay at Kiriath Jearim even if one thinks that Yahweh's presence might nevertheless be connected continuously with the ark. The ark is lodged in a private house (similarly 2 Sam 6:10-11 where the ark is lodged in the house of Obed-Edom), and according to 1 Sam 7:1, Abinadab is rather a caretaker of the ark (the word שמר is used; cf. the fate of his son when he touches the ark in 2 Sam 6 [cf. Haran 1978, p. 80]), and rather than coming to Kiriath Jearim, the people would rather gather at Mizpah (1 Sam 7:5-14) and elsewhere, including for cultic activities. As Eissfeldt (1962-1979a/1973, pp. 5-6) suggests, the houses of Abinadab and Obed-Edom should rather be taken as temporary lodgings for the ark arising from necessity (Notunterkünfte).

[175] One should also note that there is no record of a ritual for the initiation of the ark such as the "opening of mouth" rituals of the ancient Near East (cf. above, p. 26n110).

(Dt 5:8-9; cf. Dt 4:12-19). In Israelite thinking, Yahweh is above all
a transcendent god and is not to be represented by images.[176]

In this regard, whereas in the ancient Near East, gods take
their residence *in* the god image, Yahweh is not present *in* the ark,
but *at* the ark. Yet, it is not clear how Yahweh is present at the
ark.[177] The expression ישׁב הכרבים (see 1 Sam 4:4; 2 Sam 6:2; 2 Ki

---

[176] On the other hand, there are passages in the Old Testament in
which Yahweh reveals himself anthropomorphically; e.g. Gen 18 (ascribed
to J; see Wenham 1994, p. 44); Ex 24:9-11 (ascribed to J or E; see Childs
1974, p. 500); Ex 33:18-23 (ascribed to J or E or both; see Childs 1974,
pp. 584-585), and in Ezekiel (e.g. Ez 1:26-28). Should one wish to think
that Yahweh should in general be thought of in anthropomorphic terms
in JE and P, one could then deduce that Yahweh was
anthropomorphically in the midst of the fire at Sinai, but the common
people could not see this anthropomorphic form due to the distance, fire
and the clouds in the JE account (for source criticism, see Childs 1974,
pp. 344-347) of Ex 19:14-25 (Ex 19:18: whole mountain filled with smoke
when Yahweh descends in fire, Ex 19:21-24: ordinary people [and perhaps
priests; cf. v. 22 with v. 24] cannot approach *to see* Yahweh
[פן־יהרסו אל־יהוה לראות; v. 21] but must look from distance, from
outside a marked border). Then, Dt 4:12-13 basically expresses the same
matter: the distance, the fire, the smoke, and that the people could not see
Yahweh. This *experience* of the Sinai theophany by the people of Yahweh's
תמונה hidden behind the fire and clouds then is the reason for the
prohibition of images (Dt 4:15-18; cf. also the אצבע אלהים, the 'finger of
God' in Dt 9:10). In this respect, one has to add that Yahweh's separation
from ordinary people at Sinai is compatible with his separation from
ordinary people in the Holy of Holies inside a temple/tent of meeting.
Finally, it is interesting that even though Yahweh revealed himself
anthropomorphically to Moses and the elders of Israel at Sinai, Ex 33:18-
23 (generally assigned to JE and/or separate material; see Childs 1974, p.
584) suggests that he showed only a limited side of himself to them. This
finds an analogy with especially Mesopotamian god images. Even though
a god image was equated with the corresponding god after a proper
dedication in ancient Mesopotamia, the god nevertheless transcended the
image and there was more to the god than the image.

[177] Also, Num 10:33-35 (quoted above, p. 40) could perhaps be read to
suggest that in battle or on the move, Yahweh as if arises from
dwelling/resting at the ark and fights for Israel, and then returns back to
dwell/rest at it once the ark sets down for a new campsite (cf. also Ps
132:8, 13-14; 1 Chr 28:2).

19:15; 1 Chr 13:16; Ps 80:2; Is 37:16; cf. Ps 99:1) does not indicate any specific location as the preposition is missing.[178] Thus, it is not clear that the cherubim formed a throne on which Yahweh was sitting.[179] The problem of localization and a direct concept of a cherubim throne is made more difficult by the two additional cherubim in the Holy of Holies of Solomon's temple (see 1 Ki 6:23-28; 1 Ki 8:7; 1 Chr 28:18; 2 Chr 3:10-13; 2 Chr 5:8). As Woudstra observes, "Was Yahweh henceforth to be thought as seated above, or between, or beneath, the first pair or the second? If the cherubim were thought to represent his throne, how, then, was Yahweh's exact position to be regarded?"[180] Moreover, "How could he (Solomon) have made a throne above a throne?"[181] Woudstra concludes:

> Solomon's action can only be understood if the phrase *yošev hakkerubim* is detached somewhat from the position of the cherubim on the ark. The ark-cherubim, together with the other cherubim found in the sanctuary, jointly served to stress the majesty and the heavenly character of the One who was pleased to dwell below. This idea was capable of being enhanced by the making of another pair of cherubim and by placing the ark beneath them. The cherubim which Solomon made thus strengthened the idea of the original cherubim. But that idea was not to provide a throne-like structure for Yahweh. Although the idea of the ark as throne may be retained in a general way the figure must not be pressed to the point at which the

---

[178] Cf Woudstra 1961, pp. 85-87. The Priestly description of Ex 25:22 states:

ונועדתי לך שם ודברתי אתך מעל הכפרת מבין שני הכרבים אשר על־ארון העדות

"And I will meet with you there and will speak with you from upon the cover, from between the two cherubs which are on the ark of the testimony". Cf. Num 7:89.

[179] See Mettinger 1982, pp. 21-22 and Mettinger 1995, pp. 102-103 for pictures of ANE cherubim thrones.

[180] Woudstra 1961, p. 90, noting also that it has been thought that the large cherubim may have formed a *merkaba* (with wheels) similar to that seen by Ezekiel in his vision (based on 1 Chr 28:18). Cf. Mettinger 1982, pp. 35-36, 105.

[181] Woudstra 1961, p. 90.

exact position of the cherubim on the ark is expected
to supply the features of a throne-structure.[182]

Another interesting aspect of the ark is that it is associated
with Yahweh's footstool (Ps 99:5; 132:7; 1 Chr 28:2), even though
the word הדם is also used literally (Ps 110:1), or to speak of the
earth (Isa 66:1) and of Zion (Lam 2:1).[183] Even if Ps 99:5; 132:7; 1
Chr 28:2 referred to the temple as Yahweh's footstool,[184] the ark
would nevertheless also be implied as it is the locus *par excellence* of
the presence of Yahweh.[185] Then, the depositing of law tablets in
the ark (Ex 25:21; Dt 10:1-5; 31:26) would be very much in line
with the ancient Near Eastern custom of depositing treaty tablets
in the divine presence.[186] As seen above (p. 37), the letter of
Ramses to Kupanta-Kurunta explicitly speaks about depositing a
treaty under the feet of a god: "The written version of the oath
which [I made] for the Great King, the king of Hatti, my brother,
has been set at the feet of [the Storm-god] and before the Great
Gods. They are witnesses [to the words of the oath]. And the

---

[182] Ibid., pp. 90-91.

[183] Cf. Fabry 1978, p. 331.

[184] This would then perhaps mean that Yahweh, who is
dwelling/sitting in heaven, had his "feet" in the temple (cf. Isa 66:1; Lam
2:1). On the other hand, Ez 43:7 speaks of the temple as the place of both
the future throne of Yahweh and of the sole of his feet.

[185] If the ark is meant, it is even possible that the *kapporet* would
specifically be the footstool. In relation to this, one should note the
intriguing suggestion that the word *kapporet* may be related to Egyptian *kp
n rdwj* (Görg 1977; Mettinger 1982, pp. 87-88), literally "sole of the feet".
HANNIG (p. 880) suggests the meaning "Thronsockel" ("throne
pedestal") for *kp n rdwj*, indicating however that the meaning is not
certain. This would then be another parallel to the word *kapporeth* besides
the Akkadian *kapāru*, to purify cultically (see *AHw*, pp. 442-443, D-stem;
cf. *HAL*, p. 470). Cf. also Fabry (1978, pp. 327-328) who notes that a
footstool could be a pedestal of a divine statue in Mesopotamia, and thus
the perceived image could be Yahweh standing or sitting (more or less)
invisibly above the ark, with his feet on the *kapporeth* (cf. also Frankfort
1996, p. 161 Fig. 186 of Assurnasirpal II with his feet resting on a
footstool). In any case, these considerations would, incidentally, fit with
the idea that *kapporet* is part of both purification from sin (Lev 16:14-16)
and the presence of Yahweh (Ex 25:21-22; Lev 16:13).

[186] Cf. above, p. 37 for the ANE custom.

written version of the oath which the Great King, [the King of Hatti, my brother], made for me [has been set] at the feet of the Sun-god of [Heliopolis] and before the Great Gods. They are witnesses to the words [of the oath]."[187] It has to be emphasized in this context that, especially as regards Deuteronomy, nothing in Dt 10:1-5; 31:26 is in contradiction to the ancient Near Eastern custom; rather, the texts are perfectly compatible with the custom of placing treaties in the divine presence.[188] Also, Jeremiah's statement that the ark will not feature prominently in the future (Jer 3:16-17) does not deny the ark's role as a locus of divine presence.[189] Rather, the passage indicates that divine presence will be manifested without the *existence/medium* of the ark in the future, and this is perfectly compatible with the loss of the ark during the exile.[190]

---

[187] Quoted also by de Vaux 1972/1967, p. 148.

[188] *Contra* von Rad 1953/1948, p. 40 (cf. von Rad 1965a/1931, pp. 106-107, "Deuteronomy's view of it [the ark] as a receptacle for the tables of the law is an obvious 'demythologizing' and rationalizing of the old view [of the ark as a seat of Yahweh's presence]"), and *contra* Weinfeld 1972, p. 208; cf. Wenham 1993, p. 100. Note also that the expression ארון ברית יהוה (or a slightly variant form of it; see Woudstra 1961, pp. 73-74 for a listing of all appellations of the ark) which connects the ark with a covenant with Yahweh is used of the ark in Josh 3-6 and in 1 Sam 4 where the ark acts as a functional equivalent to ancient Near Eastern god images. Similarly, 1 Ki 8:9 indicates that the ark which is just making a *tērubat bītim* in the style of ancient Near Eastern god images (recall above, p. 39) contains the law tablets of the covenant made at Sinai (cf. Dt 10:5). Note also that it is natural to consider that OT covenants parallel ANE treaties (see e.g. Thompson 1963; Walton 1989, pp. 95-107; Weinfeld 1972).

[189] *Contra* Weinfeld 1972, p. 208. In fact, the parallelism between vv. 16 and 17 associates the ark with the throne of Yahweh for the present time of the implied narrative context. Cf. Holladay 1986, p. 121, "Verse 17 is a prime datum to reinforce the thesis that the ark was understood to be a throne of Yahweh."

[190] Cf. above, p. 40 on the loss of the ark. In this respect, what is the point of calling Jerusalem the throne of Yahweh in v. 17, if Yahweh himself is seen to reside only in heaven? Rather, Jer 3:17 is a promise of the future presence of Yahweh in Jerusalem, to be seen also from the exilic standpoint of the divine abandonment of Jerusalem by Yahweh

An important point to be observed is that there existed only one ark of the covenant, the symbol of Yahweh's presence. This strongly implies that there could at one time be only one "house of Yahweh" where the ark and thus Yahweh himself would be present. This of course does not take away the possibility that Yahweh could manifest himself in a theophany as he did in Sinai to Moses during the covenant making, to Elijah at Horeb (1 Ki 19), and at other places and occasions during the history of Israel. But, as the Priestly material indicates, the tent of meeting containing the ark as the *locus specificus* is *the* place where Yahweh dwells among his people Israel (Ex 25:8),[191] and the same applies to the temple of Solomon (1 Ki 8:10-13).

---

which was manifested by the loss of the ark and the destruction of Jerusalem.

[191] That gods could be present in more than one sanctuary at the same time in the ancient Near East (see above, p. 27) provides a natural solution to the problems associated with the question of Yahweh's continual vs. intermittent presence in regard to the tent of meeting. Yahweh may be continually present inside the tent of meeting and yet manifest his presence in a special way on special occasions in another place (For history of scholarship of the problem, see Mettinger 1982, pp. 83-85; Note however also that both a continuous presence and special manifestations of *kabod* are attested in material assigned to P, and that scholars have found it difficult to separate P into separate subdocuments which would contain only one of these concepts [see Kuschke 1951, pp. 87-88]). Thus, one may agree with Mettinger (1982, p. 89) when he says, "It therefore seems probable that the *kabod* was conceived of as continuously present, and further, as being theoretically visible above the *kapporet*. But in addition to the continual Presence in the privacy of the sanctuary, the texts also describe *public* manifestations of the majesty of God which take place outside the tabernacle. Such manifestations take place in part on solemn occasions, as when the *kabod* 'settles' upon Sinai (Exod 24:15-18), or when Aaron undertakes his first sacrifice (Lev 9:5-6, 23-24); and in part in critical situations when the people hesitate to submit to God's will (Exod 16:7, 10; Num 14:10; 16:19; 17:7)." Connected with this, it is worth observing that Ex 33:7-11 describes a tent, an act which according to the Pentateuchal narrative sequence takes place before the making of the ark and the tabernacle where the ark is located, and that Numbers 11:6-30; 12:4-10 and Dt 31:14-15, regardless of whether one thinks that the tent in question on each occasion is that of Ex 33:7-11 or the Priestly tabernacle, concern special occasions (see e.g. von Rad

Moreover, there is no description of a legitimate cult with an associated priesthood in the Old Testament except in association with the ark and the temple and the tent of meeting.[192] In fact, the priesthood and cult associated with the tent of meeting and the temple are, speaking in general terms, similar to the cult which would go on in an ancient Near Eastern temple containing a divine image. In this respect, as indicated above,[193] according to the conceptions of ancient Near Eastern people, if the gods were not to be present in the temple(s)/land, or left the temple(s)/land, it would be a sign of a catastrophe. This is perfectly consistent with the Priestly material, according to which if the Israelites are holy and respect Yahweh's sanctuary, Yahweh will continually dwell among them.[194] On the other hand, as Joosten expresses it, the sins of the people "force the godhead out of his sanctuary".[195] Moreover, as Joosten points out, this happened during the time of Ezekiel, as expressed in Ezek 1-11.[196] Similarly, Yahweh abandoned Israel and left the sanctuary of Shiloh during the premonarchical period.[197] The matter involved both the sins of the priesthood (1 Sam 2:12-17, 27-36; 3:10-14) and the sins of the people (Ps 78:56-58).[198]

With this background in mind, it is a little difficult to think that Deuteronomy would deny the presence of Yahweh in the temple or the tent of meeting, especially when there is no explicit

---

1953/1948, pp. 42-43; Haran 1960; 1978, pp. 260-275; de Vaux 1972/1967, p. 143; Knohl 1997; Milgrom 1989, pp. 386-387 for the problem of two tents).

[192] Provided that the tradition which associates the tent of meeting with Shiloh is correct; for more on this, see below, Chapter 1, especially 4.2.

[193] See above, p. 29f.

[194] Cf. Joosten 1996, pp. 125-127, referring especially to Lev 26:11.

[195] Joosten 1996, pp. 127-128. The possibility of withdrawal is implied in Lev 26:11-12, part of Lev 17-26, material generally attributed to H. However, based on ancient Near Eastern parallels, it is self-evident that the same concept applies to material attributed to P as well (cf. also Ex 33:3 which is generally attributed to JE [see Childs 1974, p. 584]).

[196] Joosten 1996, p. 127. Cf above, p. 40.

[197] See above, p. 39.

[198] For more on the issues surrounding the loss of the ark at the disaster of Aphek, see Chapter 4.2 below.

denial of Yahweh's presence in a sanctuary in Deuteronomy. In this respect, to say that the lack of explicit mention of Yahweh's presence on earth is the same as denying it is essentially an *argumentum ex silentio*. However, what is more, a number of features in Deuteronomy rather suggest Yahweh's presence on earth and/or in a sanctuary. First of all, Dt 23:19 speaks about בית יהוה אלהיך, and as we have seen above, a 'house' of a god in the ancient Near East is a place where the god dwells.[199] Therefore, Dt 23:19 clearly implies that Yahweh dwells on earth. Moreover, as indicated above, the picture of the ark in Deuteronomy is compatible with Yahweh's divine presence at the ark.[200] Where the ark is, there is also Yahweh's presence. In this respect, if the Deuteronomic editor of 2 Sam 7 or 1 Ki 8[201] wanted to polemicize against Yahweh's dwelling on earth, one has to consider his polemics as very clumsy since he left intact 2 Sam 7:5-7 and 1 Ki 8:10-13 which affirm Yahweh's presence on earth.[202] Furthermore, we have to remember that especially in Egypt, heaven was the primary dwelling-place of gods,[203] and consequently, it would not be odd if Deuteronomy

---

[199] See above, Chapter 2.1, p. 25f.

[200] See above, p. 45.

[201] One should also ask whether 1 Ki 8:14-61 reflects Deuteronomic or exilic concerns and how much (cf. also Haran 1969a, pp. 260-261 who points out that D and Dtr do not necessarily share the same views; similarly Wellhausen 1905/1878, p. 278). Moreover, since prayers in the ancient Near East were typically spoken in a temple in divine presence and were part of the cult (Cf. Oppenheim 1964, p. 175: "Prayers in Mesopotamian religious practice are always linked to concomitant rituals."; Morenz 1960, p. 102 for Egypt; de Roos 1996, p. 1998 and Lebrun 1980 for the Hittite realm; cf. also the fact that many, if not most Psalms, which certainly contain prayer, must have been part of temple worship in Israel, both during the first and the second temple [cf. e.g. Craigie 1983 et al.]), it would be odd that the lack of explicit mention of cult in 1 Ki 8:14-61 should prove that, as Weinfeld (1972, p. 209) asserts, "The sanctuary is here conceived as a house of prayer and not as a cultic centre."

[202] Moreover, as Haran (1969a, p. 259) notes, the idea of transcendence of God does not quite fit with the idea of centralization of the cult in one place.

[203] According to Lorton (1999, p. 134n14), "considering only the example of the sun-god, it should be obvious that the essence of the deity

emphasized this aspect of divine presence. Further, in the ancient
Near East, a god's name was associated with its presence. A
Sumerian poem speaking of Enlil is illustrative in this respect:

> When your name rests over the mountains, the sky
>   itself trembles;
> The sky itself trembles, the earth itself shivers.
> When it rests over the mountains of Elam,
> When it rests over the horizon,
> When it rests over the "foundation of the earth",
> When it rests over the farthest reaches of the earth,
> When it rests over the surface of the earth,
> When it rests over the awe-inspiring mountains,
> When it rests over the high mountains,
> When it rests over the powerful (?) mountains,
> When it rests over the mountains and over the wide
>   sky, the sky itself [trembles].[204]

---

was first and foremost in the sun itself, while only part of it could be in
his cult statue". Cf. also the Instruction of Any (7.16) from the New
Kingdom (text in *COS* 1, pp. 111-115, translator M. Lichtheim), "God of
this earth is the sun in the sky, while his images are on earth" (cf.
Assmann 1984, p. 55; Lorton 1999, p. 192n107 for discussion). Cf. also
the Amarna religion, where the sun was the only god and his presence was
not manifested by images, but through sunlight emanating from the sun
itself (Hornung 1999, pp. 72-73, 95-96; see also ibid., p. 77 Fig. 18). Cf.
also Hornung 1983/1971, p. 191, "Every god is 'transcendent' in the
sense that his being reaches beyond that of this world and its norms", and
(ibid.), "simply because the locus of being and action of Egyptian gods is
not on earth, they must be transcendent". It also has to be noted that,
according to Hornung (ibid., p. 110), Hathor is manifested in various
forms: human (a lady), a cow, or a mixture of these (a cow head with a
human face; woman with cow's head). However, the true form of a god in
Egypt is "hidden" and "mysterious" (see ibid., p. 124).

    [204] Niehaus 1995, p. 193. For the Sumerian, see Kutscher 1975, pp.
86-89 (lines 62-72); cf. also ibid., pp. 99-100 for lines 119-125 which are
similar to lines 62-72. The text of the lament has been pieced together
from several fragments, ranging from the Old Babylonian to Seleucid
periods. However, the important lines 62-63 with
mu-zu kur-ra mu-un-ma-al-la-šè
    an ní-bi nam-dúb-[ba]
an ní-bi nam-dúb ki ní-bi nam-[sìg]
are attested in a fragment which according to Kutscher most likely comes
from Old Babylonian times (see Kutscher 1975, pp. 8-10, 86-87).

In fact, there is a passage even in the book of Deuteronomy itself which closely associates Yahweh and his name. According to Dt 28:58,

אם־לא תשמר לעשות את־כל־דברי התורה הזאת
הכתובים בספר הזה ליראה את־השם הנכבד והנורא
הזה את יהוה אלהיך:

> If you do not carefully do all the words of this law written in this book to fear this honorable and awesome name, Yahweh your God.[205]

Also, as Wilson points out, the expression *lipne YHWH* ('before the LORD') occurs twenty-five times in Deuteronomy, out of which sixteen are found within chapters 12-26, the main legal section of the book.[206] According to Wilson, there are good reasons to take the expression literally as indicating the presence of Yahweh at the sanctuary.[207] Wilson summarizes,

> An understanding of לפני יהוה in Deut. 12-26 as referring to the Presence of YHWH localized at the sanctuary is consistent with its general characteristics in these chapters, the particular contextual features evident for the occurrences in 18:7; 19:17 and 26:5, and the usage of identical expressions in connection with both humans and the Deity elsewhere in the OT.[208]

In any case, even if one does not accept Wilson's conclusions, one could easily take (or mistake!) the expression *lipne YHWH* in Dt 12-26 to refer to Yahweh's actual presence in the chosen place.[209] Then, how can one say that Deuteronomy polemicizes against Yahweh's presence on earth?[210] From this it follows that we may suspect that to deny that the expression *lipne YHWH* does not allow Yahweh's presence on earth in the central sanctuary is circular argumentation: (A) According to Deuteronomy Yahweh is not present on earth in the sanctuary. Therefore, *lipne YHWH* in Dt 12-26 and in the rest of Deuteronomy cannot refer to Yahweh's

---

[205] As pointed out by Niehaus 1985, p. 211. Cf. also 2 Sam 6:2,

ארון האלהים אשר־נקרא שם שם יהוה צבאות ישב הכרבים

[206] Wilson 1995, p. 131.

[207] See ibid., pp. 131-197 for a very detailed treatment.

[208] Ibid., p. 197.

[209] Scholarly lack of uniformity in interpretation of the expression in 12-26 also attests this; see Wilson 1995, pp. 131-132.

[210] *Contra* von Rad 1953/1948, pp. 38-39; Weinfeld 1972, p. 195.

actual presence on earth (B) *Lipne YHWH* in Deuteronomy does not refer to Yahweh's actual presence on earth. Therefore, according to Deuteronomy Yahweh is not present on earth in the sanctuary.

Finally, we may add that there are a number of instances in Deuteronomy where Yahweh's (temporary) presence on earth is clearly implied outside the context of a sanctuary.[211] The description of Yahweh's theophany in fire at Mount Sinai is interesting, as it fits very well with the idea that Yahweh is present simultaneously both in heaven and on earth. When Yahweh descended on Sinai, he was still simultaneously present in heaven as well.[212] The earthly side of this simultaneous presence is indicated by the state of affairs that Yahweh's תמונה was manifested on earth at the mountain, even though hidden behind the fire, clouds and darkness (Dt 4:12, 15, 36).[213] In this respect, Yahweh writes on the new law tablets (Dt 4:13; 9:10; 10:1-5), even with his finger (Dt 9:10),[214] and the descriptions of the interactions between Yahweh and Moses in Dt 9-10 imply closeness of Yahweh and Moses (Moses goes up to the mountain to meet Yahweh [Dt 9:9; Dt 10:1, עלה אלי ההרה]; Yahweh speaks with Moses at the mountain [Dt 9:12]; Yahweh gives Moses the tablets of stone which he has written [9:9-10]). On the other hand, Deuteronomy 4:36 could say that the words came from heaven in order to emphasize the heavenly character and thus the ultimate transcendence and majesty of Yahweh.

Thus, when one points out that the "coming" of Yahweh in the material commonly attributed to the JE sources[215] implies that Yahweh "comes" from another realm, that is, heaven, all of the Narrative (JE), Priestly and Deuteronomic material of the Pentateuch is fully compatible with Yahweh's presence and dwelling both in heaven and on earth. And, it has to be emphasized that the possibility of simultaneous presence both in heaven and on

---

[211] Cf. Fretheim 1968, p. 7n. 41, who lists Dt 1:30, 33; 2:7; 4:7, 37; 7:21; 9:3; 20:4; 23:14; 31:3, 6, 8.

[212] In line with typical ancient Near Eastern conceptions of divine presence; recall above, Chapter 2.1, p. 25f.

[213] Cf. above, p. 42n176.

[214] Cf. above, p. 42n176.

[215] Cf. further below, Chapter 2.2.2

earth (including multiple places) is fully in line with general ancient Near Eastern conceptions of divine presence.

In summary, the ark and the tent of meeting and temple are analogous to ancient Near Eastern god images and temples. Yahweh is (basically) continually present on earth at the ark which is normally kept in the tabernacle or temple, the house of Yahweh.

Having clarified some aspects of Yahweh's presence with regard to the ark and the tent of meeting and temple, let us proceed to an examination of Yahweh's presence outside that context and how this impinges on biblical views of the central sanctuary and other places of worship.

2.2.2.   Ex 20:22-26 and the Presence of Yahweh Outside the Context of the Ark, the Tent of Meeting and the Temple

As Ex 20:24 speaks about the "coming" (using the verb בוא) of Yahweh in the context of building an altar and performing sacrifices on it, one may suspect that a careful investigation of Ex 20:22-26 might help to further understand Israelite conceptions of divine presence in relation to worship. Consequently, we will especially focus on the concept and implications of the "coming" of Yahweh to an altar described in Ex 20:22-26, which at least at first sight seems to be different from the idea of continual presence of Yahweh in the context of the ark, the tent of meeting and the temple. Also, an investigation of Ex 20:22-26 will serve as a preliminary for us for the discussion of centralization in the Pentateuch in Chapter 1 below, as Ex 20:22-26 is considered as the representative of the centralization view of the J and E sources.[216] To help interpret Ex 20:22-26, let us first look at relevant critical issues surrounding these verses, especially as regards their unity.

The altar law of Ex 20:22-26 is part of Ex 20:22-23:33, the so-called Covenant Code. As far as the provenance of the Covenant Code is concerned, Childs describes the matter succinctly from the standpoint of source-critical approaches:

> At the height of the literary-critical period much attention was given in determining to what literary sources the Book of the Covenant was to be assigned. Wellhausen first assigned it to the J source in contrast

---

[216] Cf. Wellhausen 1905/1978, pp. 28-29.

to the 'ethical Decalogue' of E (*Composition*, 1st ed. 1876), but retracted his opinion in 1889 in the light of Kuenen's criticism. Others attempted to assign the book to E (Jülicher). However, from the time of Bäntsch's monograph of 1892 a growing consensus had emerged that the Book of the Covenant was an older collection of laws which was independent of the usual critical sources. Usually it was thought that the secondary framework into which it had been placed was that of E.[217]

This view has prevailed till the present day,[218] even though at present there is, as Van Seters expresses it, "a consensus among scholars that the Covenant Code did not come into existence at one time but is the result of various layers of redactional activity."[219] Thus, naturally, there has been a lot of discussion concerning the prehistory of the collection.[220]

Another major area of research has been the relationship of the laws of the Book of the Covenant to known ANE cuneiform laws.[221] However, these issues do not concern us too much here, except as they relate to the altar law. Yet we must say immediately that there are no known cuneiform legal parallels to the Pentateuchal altar laws. Thus, we are left here with issues relating to the prehistory of the altar law of Ex 20:22-26. One should however mention that the parallels to cuneiform legal corpora speak rather for an early than late provenance of the legal material in the Book of the Covenant.[222] Also, in any case, the Ex 20:22-26 altar law is associated with J and E, which are generally considered to be the earliest sources of the Pentateuch.[223]

A number of scholars have thought that Ex 20:24-26 formed an original altar law, and that verses 22 and 23 are later addition.

---

[217] Childs 1974, p. 452.

[218] Van Seters 1996, p. 319.

[219] Van Seters 1996, p. 319. Westbrook is however an example of an exception to diachronic approaches. He sees the Covenant Code as static and synchronic. See Levinson, ed. 1994 for details.

[220] See commentaries, e.g. Childs 1974 and Durham 1987.

[221] See e.g. Levinson, ed. 1994.

[222] Cf. e.g. Westbrook 1994, incl. pp. 21, 28.

[223] Even if some scholars, such as Van Seters, have challenged the priority of JE (see Van Seters 1996).

According to Childs, "the overwhelming number of critical
commentaries (Bäntsch, Noth, Te Stroete, etc.) judge vv. 22-23 to
be later redactional framework, and therefore without exegetical
significance".[224] Also, it is often thought that since the laws
following Ex 21:1 are preceded with a heading "these are the
מִשְׁפָּטִים that you are to set before them" in 21:1, and because Ex
20:22-26 is cultic legislation in contrast to the "מִשְׁפָּטִים", the
regulations of 20:22-26 are not under the "מִשְׁפָּטִים", but have been
added in separately.[225]

However, there are good reasons for seeing unity and design
in the arrangement. Even though the altar law is slightly separate
from what follows after the title מִשְׁפָּטִים in 21:1, including in its
content matter, the two entities are logically compatible.
Furthermore, as Sprinkle observes, the word "before them
(לִפְנֵיהֶם)" in 21:1 refers to Israelites (בְּנֵי־יִשְׂרָאֵל), who are
mentioned in 20:22, and thus it is natural to see 21:1 as referring
back to 20:22.[226]

As regards the setting of the altar law in relation to the
surrounding narrative, commentators agree that v. 22 serves as a
redactional link. That God is portrayed as speaking from heaven
seems at first to contradict the portrayal of J and E according to
whom God is present on the mountain.[227] For this reason, the
passage rather could be taken to have affinities with D, as it is often
considered that Deuteronomy portrays God as present only in
heaven.[228] However, as was discussed before,[229] such a dichotomy
regarding divine presence is unnecessary. In ancient Near Eastern
thinking, a god could be present both on heaven and earth, even

---

[224] Childs 1974, p. 465.

[225] Sprinkle 1994, p. 31.

[226] Sprinkle 1994, p. 31. Cf. also Van Seters 1996, p. 325.

[227] See Noth 1962, pp. 175-176; cf. Childs 1974, pp. 348-350,
according to whom it is difficult to distinguish between J and E in Ex
19:1-25; 20:18-21.

[228] Cf. above, Chapter 2.2.1. According to Childs 1974, p. 465, v. 22
may come from the Deuteronomist. According to Weinfeld 1972, pp.
206-207n4, the verse "appears to be a deuteronomic accretion". Mettinger
(1982, p. 48n37) follows Weinfeld, stating that "Exod 20:22 is a Dtr
accretion, as was pointed out by Weinfeld (1972: 206f. n.4)".

[229] See above, Chapter 2.1 and 2.2.1.

simultaneously and in many places, and there is no reason to deny that the same could apply to Yahweh's presence in Israel. Furthermore, the biblical evidence clearly indicates that Yahweh could manifest his presence outside the context of the ark, the temple or the tent of meeting.[230] Thus, one should rather think that Ex 20:22 is a solemn way of proclaiming that the God who is present at Sinai has come down from his heavenly dwelling place, and ultimately the origin of the speech is from heaven, a realm inaccessible to man. In other words, the expression that Yahweh has spoken from heaven emphasizes Yahweh's majesty by emphasizing his transcendence.[231]

Furthermore, if one compares Ex 20:22 with Ex 19:3-4, there is clear parallelism between these passages in two levels: "say this to the sons of Israel" and "you have seen".[232] If on the other hand one looks at the source analysis of Ex 19, one notices that verses 3b-4 where both these expressions occur, are assigned to a Deuteronomic redactor.[233] If this assignment is warranted, since the word "before them (לִפְנֵיהֶם)" in 21:1 refers back to the Israelites (בְּנֵי־יִשְׂרָאֵל) who are mentioned in 20:22,[234] one would have to conclude that a Deuteronomic editor did a great deal in setting the Book of the Covenant into its present narrative setting in the Pentateuch. This then would reinforce the idea often held that a Deuteronomic editor reworked and transformed the legislation of the Book of the Covenant when forming the Deuteronomic legislation.[235] However, it would also mean that the Deuteronomic editor thought carefully how to edit the material, and thus had a fully considered reason to put the Book of the

---

[230] E.g. Gen 18 (Abraham and Sodom); Ex 19-34 (covenant-making at Sinai); 1 Ki 19:11-18 (Elijah at Horeb) etc.

[231] Cf. Sprinkle 1994, pp. 30-31; and cf. above, p. 51.

[232] So Childs 1974, p. 465 as regards to the first parallel. The first expression ("say this to the Israelites") is slightly different in 19:3, but due to the parallelism "house of Jacob"/"sons of Israel" in the verse, this seems to be of no particular significance.

[233] Childs 1974, p. 345.

[234] Cf. above, p. 54.

[235] So already in the time of Wellhausen, including Wellhausen himself (see Wellhausen 1905/1878, pp. 32-33; cf. above, p. 6); see also e.g. Levinson 1997.

Covenant into its present narrative setting (or at least to retain it there), even though certain parts of its legislation, such as those concerning centralization, supposedly contradict the legislation of Deuteronomy. This would then rather suggest that the Deuteronomic editor may have had a way of looking at the material together so that there was no perceived contradiction, or at least he perceived no major contradiction.

In any case, if one looks at only vv. 24-26 as totally separated from their context, v. 24 speaks about Yahweh's "coming" to the worshipper in the context of a local altar. As Yahweh will "come", this indicates that he is not dwelling at the local altar. Then, if one looks at the matter from the standpoint of divine presence, first of all, one has to point out that an altar is generally associated with offerings and thus cult, whether private or public. On the other hand, at least the cult of an ancient Near Eastern temple, and similarly the cult at the Israelite tent of meeting/temple was intended to occur in divine presence. Furthermore, as we have seen, divine presence is associated with blessing throughout the ancient Near East and in Israel.[236] Then, divine presence and blessing are spoken of also in the context of Ex 20:24-26. Ex 20:24 indicates that Yahweh will "come" to the worshipper and bless the worshipper in every place where he "causes his name to be remembered":

בכל־המקם אשר אזכיר את־שמי אבוא אליך
וברכתיך[237]

In the context of the altar-law of Ex 20:24-26, this then would mean that Yahweh will be present at an altar described in Ex 20:22-26 if such an altar is erected at a suitable place and offerings offered on it. In other words, an altar as described in Ex 20:22-26

---

[236] Cf. also Levine 1974, p. 41n106, "the cult was the stuff of ancient religions, not because it expressed lofty notions of an abstract character, but because it worked to secure the blessings of life for the people, individually and collectively".

[237] Note also that if Yahweh's "coming" to a place is associated with his "causing to remember his name" in a place (Ex 20:24), it would be quite logical to infer that Yahweh's "dwelling" in a place should be associated with his "placing his name to dwell" in a place (Dt 12:5).

acts as a *locus* at which Yahweh's presence is manifested.[238] Then, since in the ancient Near East images acted as a locus of a god's presence, an earthen altar in Israel serves a purpose analogous to that of ancient Near Eastern god images.[239] Furthermore, this implies that god images are not necessary, but an earthen altar is enough to secure Yahweh's presence and blessing.

This also fits perfectly with Ex 20:23. According to Ex 20:23, Israelites are forbidden to make gods of silver (אלהי כסף) or gods of gold (ואלהי זהב), and if one connects verse 23 with v. 24, the thought is exactly that the Israelites are not to make either silver or golden images, but are to make an earthen altar instead.[240] In other

---

[238] Similarly Robertson 1948, p. 14. According to Levine 1993, p. 199, "In the earliest performances of cultic rites associated with outdoor altars, it was assumed that the deity was not automatically to be found at the site of worship." Moreover, according to Levine (ibid.), the deity which normally resides in the heavens descends to earth and arrives at the site in response to his worshippers. Furthermore, "also relevant in the provisions of Exodus 20, is the theme of divine arrival at the altar site" (ibid., p. 202). Levine also points out Gen 18:21-22 (Yahweh's descent to Sodom and Gomorrah); Micah 1:3 (Yahweh's descent to tread the high places of the earth); Jdg 13:20 (Manoah and the angel's ascent heavenward in the sacrificial flame of fire); 1 Ki 18:24, 38 (the fire from heaven at Carmel) and Gen 28 (the ascension and descension of angels between heaven and earth and the descent and presence of Yahweh with Jacob) as expressing the "vertical dimension" of divine presence (ibid., pp. 199-203), and Num 23 as an example where the deity arrives to Balaam in response to offerings (עלות; Levine 1974, p. 23). Finally, according to Levine (1993, p. 204), in a pertinent place, the "dramatic appearance of the deity in response to sacrificial worship" is "a phenomenon which occurs anew each time the deity is ritually invoked, or attracted", and, "This is what it meant to say that a worshipper stood *lpny YHWH* 'in the presence of YHWH'".

[239] Cf. Levine 1974, p. 78, according to whom in the Ex 24 blood ritual half of the sacrificial blood was dashed against the altar and the other half upon the assembled people, and that this bound the two "parties" of the covenant together, and the altar represented the deity. Cf. also Durham (1987, p. 343), according to whom the altar in Ex 24 is "the symbol of Yahweh's Presence".

[240] Note that the idols in v. 23 could either be made "with me" (אתי; regarding אלהי כסף) or "for yourself" (לכם; regarding אלהי זהב), whereas an altar in v. 24 is to be made "for me" (לי), speaking from Yahweh's

words, god images are neither necessary nor allowed as the locus of Yahweh's presence. This also means that whether or not v. 23 was an original part of vv. 24-26, in its present form it fits well with the thought of these verses.

This contrast between god images and altars could then help towards solving the puzzling problem of why an earthen altar is commanded.[241] The simple form of the earthen altar, and on the other hand the prohibition of working the stones if a stone altar is built instead, could help make it certain that one would not be able to make the altar into an image of Yahweh or anything resembling one. An altar as envisaged by Ex 20:22-26 would then fit perfectly with the aniconic character of Israel's faith. However, the prohibition of tools may also include injunction against adopting Canaanite altars made of finished stone.[242]

On the other hand, there may be a further reason why an earthen altar is commanded. When one thinks that the worshipper is on earth and Yahweh is in heaven, an altar where Yahweh "comes" acts as a meeting place between Yahweh and the

---

perspective. In other words, the idols show either no allegiance for Yahweh or a shared allegiance, whereas an altar shows allegiance to Yahweh only.

[241] See Sprinkle 1994, pp. 41-42 for a summary of attempted solutions.

[242] So Childs 1974, p. 466 and Durham 1987, p. 320, both referring to Conrad, *Studien zum Altargesetz: Ex 20:24-26*, Marburg Dissertation 1968, which was unavailable to me. As regards v. 26, it is entirely possible that nothing was worn under a typical loincloth of the time (cf. Dt 25:11; see also e.g. *ANEP* for the clothing of ancient Near Eastern people). Then, going up the stairs would mean lifting one's knee higher than usual, and the genitals could thus be exposed more easily. The tension caused in the loincloth would also show one's bodyline from behind, including the buttocks (Mrs S. Pitkänen, personal communication, December 1999). On the other hand, perhaps Ezekiel's altar (Ezek 43:17) could include stairs since it was for the use of priests only (Ezek 43:18-27; 46:1-15), and one may assume that they were properly clothed (cf. Ex 28:42-43; Lev 6:10; cf. Sprinkle 1994, p. 49; Durham 1987, p. 320). Of course, as Sprinkle notes, it is possible that the injunction was also against Canaanite cult practices, "since Canaanite altars known from archaeology often had steps, and Canaanite worship is believed to have included sexual elements" (Sprinkle 1994, p. 49; cf. Childs 1974, pp. 466-467). Cf. also Margueron 1975, pl. VII.2 for a stepped altar at Emar.

worshipper, and thus between heaven and earth.[243] Then, it is possible that an earthen altar is commanded in order to stress that it is an earthly meeting place between Yahweh and the worshipper who is on earth. This would then fit with the command that since Yahweh has spoken from heaven (v. 22), people are to make an altar of earth (v. 24). Thus, it may be that heaven and earth are slightly punningly contrasted in vv. 22 and 24, with the word אדמה used to describe the building material of the altar, and yet suggesting the association heaven/earth usually expressed by the word pair שמים/ארץ (Dt 4:26; 30:19; 32:1).

This then would also suggest that vv. 22 and 24 belong together. Moreover, when one remembers that in the ancient Near East, gods dwell in heaven, Yahweh's "coming" implies that he "comes" to the local altar from heaven and not from another earthly locality. Furthermore, Yahweh's "coming" specifically implies that in the context of the Exodus altar law, Yahweh is normally present in heaven and not on earth. Then, as Yahweh "comes" from heaven in v. 24 and speaks from heaven in v. 22, this suggests that verses 22 and 24 are connected with each other conceptually.

Thus, we may conclude that there are good reasons to see vv. 22-26 as a conceptual unity.[244] This specifically suggests that v. 22

---

[243] Cf. also the comments above, p. 27 on temples as meeting places between heaven and earth.

[244] Note also that one may arrange vv. 22-24 according to the following palistrophic structure, where word pairs (e.g. AA') contrast with each other. (Exceptions: words in parentheses in the beginning of v. 22 do not have a correspondence; D' has two of D to contrast it):

(A)	(אתם) ראיתם (כי מן־)
(B)	השמים
(A')	דברתי
(C1)	עמכם
(D)	לא תעשׁון
(C1')	אתי
(E)	אלהי כסף
(E)	ואלהי זהב
(D)	לא תעשׂו
(C2)	לכם
(E')	מזבח

either belongs to the original altar law, or at least that the editor who added it saw no contradiction between it and the rest of the altar law. Thus, it is entirely possible that v. 22 is not Deuteronomic redaction, but an integral part of the original altar law. Even if v. 22 were an addition by a Deuteronomic editor, this would nevertheless strongly imply that the Deuteronomic editor essentially shared the thought world of the Exodus altar law as regards divine presence.

In any case, coming back to the interpretation of v. 24, it is by no means clear in what way Yahweh "comes" to be present in the place where the altar is. Whereas Yahweh is somehow localized above the ark,[245] there is no indication that Yahweh would be on or above the local altar, at its side etc., and there is no indication of the mode of Yahweh when he "comes" to the worshipper. This suggests that Yahweh's presence at a local altar is not tied to space, but Yahweh is present freely at the location, and this is compatible with the accounts of Yahweh's theophanies outside the context of local altars, the ark, the temple and the tent of meeting.[246] This freedom of Yahweh then also gives further ground for the prohibition of images, as an image is a cult object inside which a deity takes its dwelling.[247] For this same reason, a *massebah* as a seat of Yahweh's presence would not be compatible with orthodox/canonical Israelite worship,[248] even if one might say that

---

אדמה	(B')
תעשה־	(D')
לי	(C2')

[245] Cf. the discussion above, p. 42.

[246] E.g. Gen 18; 1 Ki 19:9-18.Note also the theophanies at the doorway of the tent of meeting in the Pentateuch (e.g. Ex 33:9; Num 12:5; Dt 31:15) which occurred outside at least a direct context of the ark (cf. above, p. 46n191). Note also the pacts of David and Jonathan (1 Sam 18; 20; 23), where at least the pact of 1 Sam 23:14-18 was made לפני יהוה (1 Sam 23:18) and the context (at Horesh, in the desert of Ziph) strongly suggests that the pact did not take place in a shrine (see esp. Sheriffs 1979, pp. 59-61).

[247] See above, Chapter 2.1.

[248] That *masseboth* were used in Palestine as a seat of divine presence and/or as a representation of a god is suggested by a number of factors. The finds at Arad from IA II (see e.g. Mettinger 1995, pp. 143-149) and

Hazor from LBA (see e.g. Mazar 1990a, pp. 253-254; Ottosson 1980, pp. 39-41), where *masseboth* were found at the "holy of holies" of the cultic site concerned strongly suggest that they were used as seats of divine presence, as it was normal to place god image(s) to the holy of holies of a temple or shrine. Also, Wenham (1994, p. 224) notes that, "the eighth-century Sefire treaties speak of the stones on which the treaties are inscribed as *bty ᵓlhy* 'bethels, houses of the gods' (Sefire 2.C.2-3, 9-10)". Moreover, according to Hutter (1993, pp. 91-99), in the Hittite realm, stelae were seen as representations of a deity. For instance, according to Hutter (ibid., p. 93), KUB VII 24 Vs. 1-5 says, "Berg Malimaliya: Von altersher gab es kein Götterbild. Seine Majestät Tudhaliya (machte) die Statue eines Mannes aus Eisen von 1 1/2 Spannen, die Augen aus Gold; sie steht auf einem Löwen aus Eisen. In den Tempel des Berg(gotte)es Kukumuša bringt man sie; als Stele stellt man (ihn) in Tuhniwara auf einen Felsblock." Further, according to Hutter (ibid., p. 94), in the list of steles in KUB XXXVIII 15, the following is said, "Iruš: eine Stele (ⁿᵃ⁺ZI.KIN), Ta[hat sie gemacht. Ein Schaf, ein Gefäß mit Bier <und> Brot [gibt man] vo[n der Stadt (?)]. Der neue Gott ist eine Stele. Ta[hat sie gemacht]. ... Milkuš: eine Stele, Palla[š hat sie gemacht]." On the other hand, as far as Syria (from an earlier time than the Hittite realm) is concerned, Durand (1985, p. 83) suggests that a number of examples indicate that rather than seeing Syrian stelae as functionally similar to statues of gods, they could rather be seen as "temporary" symbols for specific ceremonies ("Ce qui est le plus curieux semble être l'affirmation que ces bétyles ne représentent pas des réalités religieuses définitives, pierres que l'on dresse et à qui un culte sera rendu désormais, mais des symboles 'épisodiques' que l'on amene pour une cérémonie précise. Il est peu vraisemblable qu'il faille tirer de nos documents, par exemple, que les trois bétyles mentionnés ci-dessus représésentaient les statues des divinités mêmes des temples le Mari. La lettre de Bannum, ci-dessus, semble prouver que l'envoi du *sikkanum* fait partie des *préliminaires* nécessaires à la fête d'Eštar. Rien ne nous dit ce que ces bétyles devenaient, une fois la fête finie et leur rôle tenu."). On the other hand, we might add that even if these Syrian standing stones had only temporary use for specific ceremonies, might one even think that the gods were nevertheless present in them temporarily for the ceremony? We must conclude that it may be impossible to know the role of these Syrian standing stones for certain. For these reasons, it may also be difficult to say exactly how Jacob perceived the *massebah* he set up (Gen 28:18-22; 35:14; cf. [esp.] Wenham 1994, pp. 217-226, 326; Hutter 1993, pp. 99-103 for analyses of the passages). Besides thinking of the *massebah* as a seat of Yahweh, Jacob may have thought of it as a temporary symbol of Yahweh, and moreover (A.R.

a *massebah* is strictly speaking not an image. Thus, the Exodus altar
law of the Covenant Code is fully compatible with the exclusion of
masseboth as a seat of Yahweh's presence.[249] However, it is
completely another matter whether all usage of standing stones
should be considered as illegitimate in Israel. One may think that a
standing stone could be erected as a sign or witness, or could even
mark a sacred area as long as it was not seen as a seat of Yahweh.[250]
For instance, the stones in Ex 24:4 symbolized the twelve tribes of
Israel, the stones in Joshua 4 were intended as signs (Josh 4:6-8, 21-
24), and Dt 27:1-8 orders stones to be set up together with the altar
of Yahweh at Mt Ebal.[251] In fact, Josh 4:6-8, 21-24 and Dt 27:1-8

Millard, personal communication, May 2000), symbolizing that he would
later build a house of Yahweh at the site. In any case, one must also stress
that the Jacob narratives portray the pre-Mosaic time, and thus even if
Jacob perceived the *massebah* as a seat of Yahweh, it does not necessarily
need to be taken to indicate that this would have been acceptable for
people after the time of Moses.

[249] This even if one thinks that verses 22-23 are later addition, even
though there are strong reasons for seeing them as part of the original
altar law, as seen above.

[250] Cf. Pagolu 1995, p. 113. Naturally, a *massebah* as a symbol of
Canaanite worship would not have been acceptable either (Dt 7:5; 12:3; cf.
Pagolu 1995, p. 114).

[251] For a general treatment of Dt 27 and Josh 8:30-35, see below,
Chapter 4.3. The standing stones at Gezer from the pre-Israelite period
(MB II) are intriguing. As Ottosson (1980, p. 94) describes, the 'Gezer
High Place' "consists of 10 tall monoliths standing in a straight line
running north-south. All of them had been erected at the same time. The
bases of the stones were surrounded by a platform built of undressed
stones with a curb of boulders. To the west of the fifth and sixth stones
was a large stone block with a rectangular hole at the top. The stones were
erected inside the 'Inner Wall', also dated to MB II." (Ottosson 1980, p.
94, with a picture in ibid., p. 95; cf. W.G. Dever, *ABD* II, pp. 998-1003;
NEAEHL, pp. 496-506, including a bibliography of the excavations;
Mettinger 1995, pp. 184-186. Note also that the stone block with a hole at
the top may be a socket for a now-missing monolith [Dever, *NEAEHL*,
p. 501; cf. Dunand 1958, vol II, p. 645, Fig. 768; vol II, Atlas, plates xxi.3,
xxii-xxiv for similar stone blocks with a hole at the top in the stelae
temple in Byblos]). Even though a cultic interpretation for the site is
deemed as the most probable, the matter is not considered as certain
(W.G. Dever, *ABD* II, p. 1000; *NEAEHL*, p. 501; Ottosson 1980, p. 94;

specifically show that even Deuteronomy accepts a memorial usage of *masseboth*,[252] as it is extremely difficult to detach either Josh 4:6-8, 21-24 or Dt 27:1-8 from a Deuteronomic context, especially as the children's questions in Josh 4:6-8, 21-24 are very similar to those in Dt 6:20ff.,[253] and as it is difficult to think why Dt 27 would have been taken in to the book of Deuteronomy or retained in it if it were seen as contradictory to the rest of the book.[254] We should also add that according to Josh 24:26, Joshua "set up a great stone under the oak which is in the sanctuary of Yahweh". This stone is not to be understood as a seat of Yahweh, since, even though the stone is spoken of in anthropomorphic terms (v. 27), the text, beside stating that the stone is a witness (עדה), states that the stone "has heard all the words of Yahweh" (שמעה את כל־אמרי יהוה), and the stone is thus seen as separate from Yahweh. Finally, the מצבה אצל־גבולה ליהוה in Isa 19:19-20 is "for a sign and for witness" (לאות ולעד).[255]

There is evidence also outside the Ex 20:22-26 altar law that it is enough to have an altar without a specific cult object as a seat of Yahweh in order to be in the presence of Yahweh in a cultic

---

Mettinger 1995, p. 186). In any case, the size and the look and feel of the stones and the installation as a whole does not discount a possibility of monumental usage (cf. W.G. Dever, *ABD* II, p. 1000; *NEAEHL*, p. 501, who speaks of "monumental architecture" even though he suggests a cultic interpretation). One also has to note that even though the structure ostensibly dates from the Middle Bronze Age, according to Dever, it may have been reused in the Late Bronze Age (*NEAEHL*, p. 501), and according to Mettinger (1995, p. 186; referring to oral communication with Ussishkin), "we should not discount the possibility that the installation was visible (and used?) as late as the Iron Age". Finally, in any case, it is generally acknowledged that standing stones can have other than cultic functions (see Hutter 1993, p. 87).

[252] Thus, Dt 16:21-22 can be understood to mean that a *massebah* as a seat of Yahweh (or, naturally, as a seat or symbol of another god) would not be acceptable by an altar (cf. also below, p. 104). Cf. also Lev 26:1.

[253] See Noth 1953, pp. 37, 39 on Josh 4:6-8, 21-24.

[254] For a detailed examination of the literary questions relating to Dt 27, see below, Chapter 4.3.

[255] Cf. Pagolu 1995, p. 111. Cf. also 2 Sam 18:18, which attests a memorial usage/meaning of a *massebah* (It is also called a monument [יד אבשלם] later in the verse).

context. In 1 Sam 21, David comes to Nob to the priest
Abimelech. According to 1 Sam 21:7, the bread of presence was
taken out from *lipne YHWH* in order to be replaced with fresh
bread. When one couples this with the description that Abimelech
who was serving at the sanctuary in question is in all likelihood to
be understood to be a descendant of Eli (1 Sam 14:3; 22:20), it
would be quite logical to infer that the tent of meeting was at Nob
at the time, having been taken there after the disaster at Aphek (1
Sam 4).[256] However, the ark was not inside the tent of meeting, but
was at Kiriath Jearim (1 Sam 7:1-2; cf. 2 Sam 6).[257] Thus, it would
be entirely plausible that the Holy of Holies should be understood
as empty at the time. Yahweh was not dwelling in the tent of

---

[256] According to Cody (1969, p. 85), "The very presence of the Nob
incident in the narrative of David's rise to kingship, along with the fact
that the narrative takes the nature of the Nob sanctuary quite for granted
and quite without need of explanation, suggests that the sanctuary is the
successor of Shiloh as the covenantal sanctuary, and that the priests
attending it are the successors of the priesthood of Shiloh." Moreover
(ibid.), "The genealogical tie of Abimelech and his house to Eli, too, is a
strong indication that Nob was the heir of the sanctuary of Shiloh." Even
though a number of scholars more or less have acknowledged that Nob
was the successor of Shiloh, and have acknowledged that the mention of
the bread of presence fits perfectly with Lev 24:5-9; Ex 25:30; 40:23; Num
4:7 (see Hertzberg 1964, pp. 179-180; McCarter 1980, pp. 349-350, Stoebe
1973, pp. 393, 395, Klein 1983, pp. 213-214), with Hertzberg (1964, p.
179) even suggesting that the associated shrine was a tent shrine, they
have been reluctant to suggest that this might also imply that the tent of
meeting was at Nob (see Hertzberg 1964, pp. 179-180; McCarter 1980,
pp. 349-350, Stoebe 1973, pp. 393-395, Klein 1983, pp. 213-214; cf. Smith
1912, p. 198), obviously based on the scholarly consensus of the late
dating of P and the idea that its tent of meeting tradition is unhistorical
(cf. above, p. 7). See further below, incl. p. 139f. for considerations of the
nature of the sanctuary at Shiloh during the premonarchical period and of
the historical plausibility of the tent of meeting tradition. Note also that
Hertzberg 1964, pp. 178-179 suggests that only the priests were at Nob,
whereas the associated shrine was somewhere else (more or less) nearby.
However, the/an ephod was at the site (1 Sam 21:10), and 1 Sam 22:10
rather hints that cultic activity occurred at Nob.

[257] For an examination of the overall reasons for the separation of the
ark and the tent of meeting after the disaster of Aphek, see below,
Chapters 4.1 and 4.2.

meeting any more, but could however "come" and be present there in the context of worship at the altar of the tent of meeting. Similarly, when David set up the tent of meeting and cultic worship at Gibeon (1 Chr 16:39-42), the ark was not in Gibeon but in Jerusalem (see v. 37). Moreover, 2 Chr 1:6 explicitly states that Solomon offered *lipne YHWH* on the bronze altar of the tent of meeting at Gibeon, even though the ark was in Jerusalem (see v. 4).

Finally, looking at Ex 20:22-26, it seems clear that the law allows altars in multiple places.[258] On the other hand, is there any limitation as to where an altar may be built? According to Lohfink, "die Altarformel des Bundesbuches grenzt die Möglichkeiten des Kultes zunächst einmal ein (was manchmal übersehen wird). Nicht überall darf Jahwekult geschehen, sondern nur an Orten mit einer bestimmten Qualität."[259] However, one also has to note that the altar law of Ex 20:22-26 does not prescribe any penalty if an altar is built in some other place than one where Yahweh "has caused his name to be remembered". Rather, the law merely states that Yahweh will come to the worshipper and bless him if the place is "right". No curse or punitive action on behalf of the deity is indicated, even if the place is not "right". In other words, based on the Exodus altar law, an altar may be built anywhere, but building one in a right place is accompanied with a promise of Yahweh's presence and blessing.

Thus, the altar law of Ex 20:22-26 implies that a cultic place outside the context of the ark, tent of meeting and temple requires only a simple altar in order to secure Yahweh's presence and blessing. No other cult objects are necessary.[260] Then, local altars as expressed by Ex 20:22-26 contrast with the ark and the tent of meeting and the temple first of all in that the local altars are not a place of Yahweh's permanent presence. They are not a house of Yahweh, or associated with a house of Yahweh, but are places where Yahweh will "come" to meet the worshipper. On the other hand, the ark is basically the seat of Yahweh's permanent presence,

---

[258] See Childs 1974, p. 447 for a reference to an interpretation of the Ex 20 altar law as referring to one place only and its refutation by Childs.

[259] Lohfink 1991, p. 168.

[260] For considerations of the presence of Yahweh at the local scene in a setting where all worship should be centralized, see below, Chapter 4.5, p. 199f.

and functionally equivalent to ancient Near Eastern god images. The fact that the local altar would be of simple nature would contrast it with the elaborately constructed altar of the tent of meeting and the temple. Also, we should note here the simple and clear fact that no Priestly injunctions or prerogatives exist in the biblical texts for local altars,[261] whereas a more or less elaborate Priestly cultus, analogous to ancient Near Eastern temple worship, is centered around the ark, the tent of meeting and the temple. Thus, the ark, the tent of meeting and temple far outshine the external form and purpose of local altars, and the "system" of the ark together with the tent of meeting or the temple is worthy of a designation *central sanctuary*.

Thus, besides the concept of divine presence in Deuteronomy, whereas according to the Wellhausenian system the altars described in J and E reflect an early and simple decentralized mode of worship from which a later complicated centralized worship developed, according to our interpretation, the simple altars described in material assigned to J and E speak about local modes of worship, distinct from the elaborate cultic system of the ark, the tent of meeting and the temple described elsewhere. Moreover, based on our considerations in Chapter 2, the local and central modes of worship can fundamentally be seen to be rather complementary than contradictory to each other.

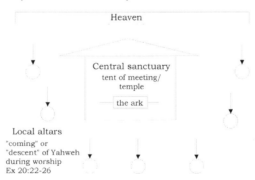

Figure 1: Divine presence at the central sanctuary and at local altars

---

[261] Also, it seems that any Israelite may sacrifice at them (cf. Haran 1978, p. 63).

On the other hand, if we look at the Pentateuchal legislation, at least at first sight it seems that some of the Pentateuchal legal material wishes to limit all sacrifices to one sanctuary only. This then brings us to an important question to which we will turn next: What is the purpose and meaning of centralization, also in light of the results we have obtained thus far regarding the role of the central sanctuary and local sanctuaries?

3. CENTRALIZATION IN THE PENTATEUCH

3.1. Centralization and the Narrative Setting of Pentateuchal Legal Material

In its present form, the legal material of the Pentateuch has been placed in a narrative setting. Therefore, let us start our investigation of centralization in the Pentateuch by examining if this narrative setting suggests any implications for our understanding of centralization in the Pentateuch. We will also keep in mind that the Wellhausenian approach has devoted little if any attention to the idea that the overall narrative placement of the Pentateuchal legal material may have involved meaningful design.[1]

If one looks at the narrative arrangement of the Pentateuch, its first legal material consists of Ex 12-13, the Passover and firstborn legislation. This legislation is generally considered to consist of a mixture of J and P material, with 12:1-20, 28, 40-51; 13:1-2 customarily assigned to P.[2] From the standpoint of our investigation, it is important to note that the P material of the Passover does not advocate centralization; rather, the Passover lamb is to be sacrificed (cf. Ex 34:25) and eaten at private homes. On the other hand, it is a well-known fact that Deuteronomy centralizes the Passover celebrations to the 'chosen place' (Dt 16), as against the JE regulations for which the feast was local as well. Wellhausen explained this by basically saying that the Priestly writer

---

[1] Cf. above, p. 9n40 and p. 16n68 (including references to Whybray 1987) on the role of redactors in putting together the Pentateuchal sources J, E, D, and P in Wellhausenian thinking.

[2] Childs 1974, p. 184.

returned the festival to its family setting in his legislation.[3] However, we may note at this point that if Passover sacrifices are done in private homes, this does not quite fit with Wellhausen's idea that P assumes centralization.[4]

The next legal material in the Pentateuch consists of the Decalogue and the Covenant Code, Ex 20:1-17; 20:22-23:33. As was mentioned above,[5] in the early days it was customary to consider that the Covenant Code belongs to J or E, but later it was agreed that the Covenant Code was an older collection of laws independent of the usual critical sources, and put in its present position by E.[6] Similarly, the Decalogue was originally assigned to E, but it too was later seen as an independent unit put into its present narrative context by E, or perhaps by the compilers of Exodus.[7] One should also add here that it is generally considered that vv. 23-25a, 31b-33 of the parenetic epilogue Ex 23:20-33 of the Covenant Code are a D addition. On a conventional interpretation of the altar law of Ex 20:22-26, neither the Decalogue nor the Covenant Code advocate centralization. On the contrary, the altar law legislates with multiple places of sacrifice in mind. Moreover, in a number of places in the Book of the Covenant there is an exhortation to come to God in a judicial context (אֶל/עַד־הָאֱלֹהִים; Ex 21:6; 22:8, 9), and these references are in general interpreted to concern local sanctuaries.[8] However, one should keep in mind that while the explanation of the phrase אֶל/עַד־הָאֱלֹהִים as a reference to local sanctuaries is the one most easily conceived, the interpretation of the phrase is nevertheless not certain.[9] Then, if there are D additions in the Covenant Code, one

---

[3] See Wellhausen 1905/1878, p. 103; cf. Childs 1974, p. 186. I will not go here into the discussion of the question of the relationship of *pesah* and *massoth* in the festival and the theories of their historical development.

[4] Cf. above, p. 7.

[5] See above, p. 52.

[6] Childs 1974, pp. 452.

[7] Durham 1987, pp. 282-283. As might be expected, it has also been considered that the ten commandments have experienced diachronic development (see ibid., p. 280).

[8] See Durham 1987, p. 321.

[9] Other suggested alternatives are that אֱלֹהִים means (i) 'judges' or 'rulers', (ii) the place of the court, (iii) gods, and (iv) *teraphim* in the context

might specifically ask why the Deuteronomic editor did not take issue with the decentralized picture of the Covenant Code.

The covenant code is followed by the blueprints of the tabernacle, Ex 25-31, all part of P.[10] The blueprints are followed by the description of making the tabernacle, Ex 35-40, which is in many places a verbatim repetition of what has already been described in Ex 25-31. All of Ex 35-40 is assigned to P as well.[11]

The two 'versions' of the tabernacle and its furnishings are sandwiched by a narrative of a covenant violation and a subsequent covenant restoration, Ex 32-34. The narrative includes embedded legal material for the restoration of the covenant, Ex 34:10-28. This legal material is commonly assigned to J, even though further JE, Priestly and Deuteronomic redaction is generally posited as well.[12] Conceptually, and without going into a consideration of the possible reasons for the literary arrangement of Ex 25-40 as a whole and the place of Ex 32-34 within it, one can safely say that Ex 34:10-28 belongs to the time before the construction of the tabernacle from the perspective of the narrative. It is in no way dependent on the tabernacle or its construction even though the instructions for the construction of the tabernacle precede it from the standpoint of strict literary sequence. And, it is important to note in this context that none of the legal material of Ex 34:10-28 advocates centralization, at least not directly.[13]

After the construction of the tabernacle, practically all legal material which is included in or embedded into the subsequent narratives until the end of the book of Numbers is Priestly. It is

---

(Sprinkle 1994, p. 56). Sprinkle himself advocates the teraphim option in the sense of 'figurines of ancestors' (ibid., pp. 57-60).

[10] See Childs 1974, p. 529 for the source assignment.

[11] See Durham 1987, p. 473 for source-critical issues regarding the chapters.

[12] Durham 1987, p. 458.

[13] Ex 34:23-24 (quoted below, p. 100) could actually be taken either in a decentralized or centralized sense, depending on one's general approach to local sanctuaries versus central sanctuary. This fits with the fact that v. 23 is generally taken to belong to J, but v. 24 often to D (see Durham 1987, p. 458 for a detailed source division of Ex 34:10-28). It is also worth noting that Van Seters (1996, pp. 330-331) takes Ex 34:23 as a reference to appearing at the central sanctuary.

also important to note that the Priestly legislation is generally seen to be at least a reasonably unified whole, except for Lev 17-26, the so-called Holiness Code. We will discuss the relationship of the Holiness Code to the rest of the Priestly material below as it relates to the altar law of Lev 17, but for the moment, suffice it to say that the Holiness Code is generally seen to have many affinities with P, and thus one is considered to be an offshoot of the other, whichever is deemed to be first by the scholar in question. Also, it is appropriate to recall here that according to Wellhausen, H was earlier than P, and whereas P assumes centralization, H still speaks for it.[14]

Finally, in narrative sequence, the Pentateuch is concluded by the book of Deuteronomy. Even if the book of Deuteronomy is often not thought to be a unified whole from a compositional standpoint,[15] it is difficult to avoid at least the impression that in its present form, the book argues for centralization of worship, especially based on the contents of Dt 12.[16]

Now, one should ask the question of what is the purpose of the arrangement of the legal material in the Pentateuch as spelled out above. Even if one takes the view that the Pentateuch is an amalgam of diverse materials put in place at diverse times, as is generally done, one question that has to be asked is: Why did the final editor who put each successive layer of legal material into place keep the earlier material even though it was at least seemingly contradictory to the later material, especially as regards centralization?[17] For instance, if the Priestly author repealed the law allowing profane slaughter, why did he on the other hand leave in place the Deuteronomic injunction which allows it? Or, similarly, why were the various at least seemingly contradictory regulations concerning the centralization of the Passover left in their respective places? Or, why was the Covenant Code put together in the Pentateuch with Deuteronomy if it was seen as contradictory to Deuteronomy, especially as regards centralization?

---

[14] See above, p. 8.

[15] See notably Wellhausen 1963/1876, pp. 187-208, and Weinfeld 1991, pp. 9-13 for the issues involved.

[16] Cf. Weinfeld 1991, p. 16.

[17] Cf. above, p. 16n68, item no. 4.

On the other hand, if we look at the total arrangement of legal material in the Pentateuch, leaving aside the question of how Dt 16:21-22 and Dt 27 might relate to the apparently centralizing concerns of the book of Deuteronomy,[18] we may observe that *all ostensibly uncentralized material has its setting in the time before the construction of the tabernacle* in the wilderness. Moreover, if one looks at this material without regard to its narrative setting, it neither knows anything of nor at least ostensibly hints at the construction of the tabernacle. Neither does it by itself contain any hint about centralization. One may then ask: If the Pentateuch is a haphazard collection of diverse materials, how is it possible that this arrangement has resulted?[19]

---

[18] See below, Chapters 3.3 and 4.3 for considerations of this matter.

[19] Note also that at least some of the material in Exodus implies that it has been set into the present narrative with a full knowledge and understanding of the following events of the establishment of the wilderness cult. For instance, in Ex 19-24, the seemingly innocent prohibition of priests approaching the mountain where Yahweh descends (Ex 19:22, 24 [generally not assigned to P; see Childs 1974, p. 345; Durham 1987, pp. 268-269]) suggests this. The narrator hints at what is to come later as regards to priesthood (cf. Sprinkle 1994, p. 22), even if he did not refer directly to the Aaronide priesthood in the verses (cf. Kaiser 1990, p. 419). Moreover, there is reason to think that the legal material of Ex 19-24 has been integrated carefully into the narrative. For instance, as Sprinkle convincingly suggests, the Decalogue and the Book of the Covenant have been crafted to the surrounding narrative of Ex 19-24 by means of a technique called resumptive repetition. According to Sprinkle (1994, p. 19), "The essence of this technique is that the narrator tells a story once, then picks up the story again somewhere in the chronological sequence and retells it, often expanding the story or telling it from a different point of view." By applying this principle, Sprinkle is able to solve practically all problems of chronology in Ex 19-24 (for details, see ibid., pp. 18-24). What is more, Sprinkle shows how the arrangement of the material in fact has served the author in helping him to communicate his message effectively (for details, see ibid., pp. 24-27). Sprinkle also suggests a number of features which link the legal material of the book of Covenant and the surrounding narrative (see ibid., pp. 29-34, and also the discussion of Ex 20:22-26 above, Chapter 2.2.2). Besides these considerations of Ex 19-24, we might add that the sandwiching of Ex 32-34 between the two versions of the tabernacle blueprints of Ex 25-31 and Ex 35-40 (cf. above, p. 71) suggests more than casual putting together of

A further intriguing question to be asked in regard to the narrative setting of the Pentateuchal legal material is why the Priestly material has been set in the wilderness in a camp arranged around the tabernacle. This question remains valid regardless of whether one believes that the legislation was actually given in the wilderness and depicts real conditions or whether one believes that it is later fiction, as the time of application of the material in the wilderness would have been very limited in comparison with its application in settled conditions in the land. The question becomes even more intriguing when one bears in mind that a number of the Priestly laws explicitly relate to the conditions in the land. To repeat: Why is a major part of the Priestly legislation, including the centralization law of Lev 17, speaking in terms of the camp and wilderness, whereas some laws, such as the Passover law (Ex 12), leprosy laws (Lev 13-14) and laws of first fruits (Lev 23:10-14 [H]) directly regulate for the conditions in the promised land? Specifically, what would the author of the centralization law and the law of profane slaughter in Lev 17 wish to communicate to people already settled in the land by specifically taking the camp as a frame of reference, since it is clear that he could have formulated the laws otherwise as some of the Priestly laws which directly refer to settled conditions indicate?

Moreover, what is the rhetorical purpose of the fact that the book of Deuteronomy portrays itself as a speech of Moses, and that the book as a whole, including its legal material, has its narrative setting on the verge of the promised land, and specifically after the JE and Priestly legislation in narrative sequence?

Finally, what is the rhetorical purpose of placing the decentralizing legislation of Exodus into a narrative setting of a covenant at Horeb with the exodus generation,[20] whereas the (at

---

the material, and it is difficult to think how this could be possible unless the person responsible for the arrangement knew both the Priestly material of Ex 25-31; 35-40 and the legal material of Ex 34. Thus, these considerations of Ex 19-40 also suggest both a careful literary arrangement of Ex 19-40, and especially the mention of priests in Ex 19:22, 24 may even suggest that the Priestly material is prior to the narrative material in Exodus (for the priority of Priestly material in Genesis, see Wenham 1999b).

[20] Except Ex 12-13 which are set in Egypt.

least seemingly) centralizing legislation of Deuteronomy has a narrative setting of a covenant at the plains of Moab with the next generation?[21] Why is the Priestly legislation not directly set as a covenant, and on the other hand spans the time interval between the covenants at Horeb and Moab?[22] Let us proceed into the interpretation of the altar laws in the Priestly material and in Deuteronomy with these considerations and questions as a starting-point.

3.2.   Lev 17:1-15 and Centralization in the Priestly Material

As Leviticus 17 is the centralizing law *par excellence* of the Priestly material, we will base our discussion of centralization in the Priestly material on a detailed examination of Lev 17. In order to interpret Lev 17, we will start by discussing relevant critical questions surrounding the chapter. We will also keep in mind our larger considerations regarding the narrative arrangement and relationship of the various legal material of the Pentateuch.[23]

As discussed above,[24] Lev 17 is part of the Priestly legislation of the Pentateuch which spans Exodus to Numbers. The Priestly material, including its legal material, is generally divided into two sources, the Priestly Torah (P) and the Holiness Code (H). As Joosten describes, "The distinct character of the collection of laws in Leviticus 17-26 was first recognized in the 19th century. In 1877 it was given the name 'Holiness Code' (*Heiligkeitsgesetz*) by Klostermann, and this fitting appellation has stuck ever since."[25] However, it has to be emphasized that, as Joosten expresses it, "H shares much of its language and ideas with P".[26]

---

[21] Note also that Dt 28:69 explicitly connects the Sinai and Moab covenants (cf. Reuter 1993, p. 229), and recall that it is generally thought that the Covenant Code and Deuteronomy are closely connected with each other (cf. above, pp. 6, 55, 70).

[22] Passover and firstborn laws in Ex 12-13 include Priestly material as well, though.

[23] Cf. above, Chapter 3.1.

[24] See above, Chapter 3.1.

[25] Joosten 1996, p. 5.

[26] Ibid., p. 13.

Whether Lev 17 actually belongs to the Holiness Code has been debated since the identification of the Holiness Code.[27] According to Hartley, "Since this speech deals solely with sacrifices, it is more in accord with the preceding legislation than with the following material, which treats primarily ethical and purity issues."[28] Moreover, "Because of its concern with sacrifices and its location, a few scholars group it with chap. 16."[29] Yet, Hartley points out that the note in Lev 16:34 that Israelites complied with Yahweh's instructions sets Lev 16 off from the following,[30] and that the desire to remove all forms of pagan practices in Lev 17 is in accord with the Holiness Code.[31] On the other hand, according to Hartley, the concern in Lev 17 about eating blood (vv. 10-14) is fitting for P.[32]

The language of Lev 17 has affinities with both H and P. Without going into full details, as it is not necessary for this investigation, the following examples given by Hartley illustrate the matter.[33] Affinities with H include the following: "The use of the divine first person (vv. 10-12, 14; cf. 26:3, 6, 17), the אִישׁ אִישׁ מִבֵּית יִשְׂרָאֵל, 'any Israelite' formula (vv. 3, 8, 10, 13), the cut-off penalty in the divine first person (v. 10; cf. vv. 4, 9, 14; 20:5) and the penalty נָשָׂא עֲוֺנוֹ, 'he is held responsible' (v. 16)".[34] On the other hand, affinities with P include the following: The usage of

---

[27] Hartley 1992, p. 250.

[28] Ibid.

[29] Ibid.

[30] Ibid.

[31] Ibid., p. 251.

[32] Ibid.

[33] As Hartley 1992, pp. 248-249 discusses, a number of expressions which have been listed as occurring in either P or H but not in the other, occur elsewhere in the Old Testament, and thus are not unique to P or H, complicating the analysis of distinctiveness between P and H. Thus, the analysis of Schwartz 1996, p. 37 in regard to Lev 3-7 is not quite as certain as it seems. One should also add that as the vocabulary of the OT is about 10,000 words whereas the vocabulary of a living language is at least 50,000 plus, we have no way of knowing what sort of oral pool was available at the time of the writing of both codes, and thus the distinctiveness is not necessarily a matter of the availability of vocabulary, but can as well be a matter of choice based on subject matter, at least in a number of cases.

[34] Hartley 1992, p. 251.

"אהל מועד, 'the Tent of Meeting' (vv. 4, 5, 6, 9), והקטיר החלב, 'and he is to smoke the fat' (v. 6), לריח ניחח ליהוה, 'a soothing aroma to Yahweh' (v. 6), and קרבן, 'offering, oblation' (v. 4)".[35]

It has been argued that if one takes Lev 17 as part of the Holiness Code it would fit with the practice of other biblical law codes which also put cultic laws at their beginning, as Ex 20:22-26 starts the Book of the Covenant, Dt 12 starts the code of Deuteronomy, Ezek 40-42 starts Ezek 40-48 and Ex 25-31 starts the Priestly material.[36] This together with the break at the end of Lev 16 is perhaps the strongest argument for assigning Lev 17 to H, even though one might also add that like Deuteronomy, H concludes with blessings and curses, and that the paraenetic elements in H of explaining and motivating the laws are unique in comparison with P.[37] Yet, this argumentation has its weaknesses. Since P is rather commenced by Ex 12 than by the Tabernacle blueprints, one cannot strictly speaking say that P starts with cultic regulations. Also, there are no blessings and curses in P. Moreover, besides noting that Ezek 40-48 contains no blessings and curses, one may even ask whether it should be considered as a law code at all.

Furthermore, scholars have not agreed about the relative dating of P and H. As Joosten describes, until recently the analysis of the relationship of the two codes was based on the following premises: "a) that the original Holiness Code has been edited by, or in the spirit of, P; and b) that the P-redaction had been preceded by the redactional activity of the author(s) of the Holiness Code. The second step was to distinguish between the older laws and the (mostly paraenetic) redactional framework added by the authors of the original work. Further complexity was introduced when two, three or even four different hands were distinguished in the redactional elements."[38] Yet, recent scholars have questioned this approach. Besides criticizing the subjective criteria of the literary analysis (which is reinforced by the fact that no two analyses

---

[35] Ibid.

[36] Hartley 1992, p. 251, referring to earlier commentators, such as Bertholet and Eissfeldt. See also Joosten 1996, p. 6.

[37] Joosten 1996, p. 6.

[38] Joosten 1996, p. 7. Cf. Wellhausen 1905/1878, pp. 52, 374-383.

coincide exactly),[39] the order of the two codes has been reversed.[40] Especially, Knohl has argued that H was composed and edited by an H school, and H "clearly" postdates the work of the P school who edited P.[41] In fact, Knohl even thinks that HS is the final editor of the Pentateuch.[42]

A major argument for Knohl in favour of such analysis is that there are passages with the characteristics of Lev 17-26 outside the confines of Lev 17-26, and that this has been somewhat of a problem for scholars to explain.[43] As Knohl points out, there is no agreement about identifying the H fragments outside Lev 17-26.[44] Also, according to Knohl, the recognition that signs of H appeared in writings spread out over the entire Priestly work led some scholars even to doubt the very existence of H as a separate unit within the Priestly source.[45] For Knohl, seeing H as later than P enables a better appropriation of the H material outside Lev 17-26.

Knohl also further challenges the conventional source division between P and H. According to Knohl, many sections outside the Holiness Code that have hitherto been attributed to P are really part of the writings of the H school.[46] Given the fact that Knohl's source criticism is on many accounts a convincing alternative to previous approaches, one must say that the question of the composition of the Priestly material of the Pentateuch, including the existence, extent and mutual relationship of P and H is far from settled.

Also, if one reads both P and H without taking Lev 17 into consideration, neither code seems to include a centralization requirement. As regards P, according to Milgrom, "P does not

---

[39] See Joosten 1996, p. 8.

[40] Joosten 1996, pp. 13-14.

[41] Knohl 1995, p. 6. Note that Knohl (ibid., p. 112) thinks that the Priestly phrases requiring centralization of the cult in Lev 17 "are not formulated in the 'pure', precise language of PT, but are PT phrases adapted in the spirit of HS".

[42] Ibid., pp. 101-103; p. 200.

[43] Ibid., p. 2.

[44] Ibid., p. 3. According to Joosten 1996, pp. 15-16, "Important passages are Ex 6:6-8; 31:13-17; Lev 11:44f; Num 10:8-10; 15:38-41."

[45] Ibid., p. 3, giving references as well.

[46] See ibid., p. 6; pp. 56-110.

claim that the Tabernacle is the only legitimate sanctuary. There is neither admonition nor ban against worshiping at other altars".[47] Milgrom adds, "P requires a central but not a single sanctuary".[48] Also, as is well known, and as referred to before, most of the injunctions concerning sacrifices in P have camp conditions in the wilderness as their literary setting, with Israel settled around the camp in close proximity. The laws do not directly relate what should happen after the camp setting is no longer valid, but the matter is left to interpretation. As regards H, the camp paradigm still holds, and furthermore, if one excludes Lev 17 from consideration, there seems to be no direct requirement for centralization in H either. In fact, except for Lev 19:20-22 and 24:1-9, the central sanctuary is hardly mentioned in Lev 18-26. In this respect, one can read Lev 18-26, including the festival regulations in Lev 23, in the same way as one can read P, that is, as demanding a central but not a single sanctuary. For instance, if one were to read Lev 23 by itself, one could interpret the material without recourse to a central sanctuary. Especially, Lev 23:4-8; 9-14 and 23:15-22 could by themselves be interpreted from a context of a local altar/sanctuary only. The offerings in Lev 23:15-21 could also be seen (at least partly) as common offerings representing more than one person as a relatively large amount of animals is involved in vv. 18-19. Finally, the mention of sanctuaries (מקדשים) in Lev 26:31 could be taken to mean either that sanctuaries are bad in themselves, or that sanctuaries which by themselves are legitimate would be destroyed as a result of the curses.

Thus, the interpretation of whether P or H (or both) requires centralization depends on whether one assigns Lev 17 to P or H

---

[47] Milgrom 1991, p. 32. Cf. Wellhausen 1905/1878, p. 34 concerning the views of his time, "Über den Priesterkodex ist die meinung verbreitet, daß es sich in diese Sache ziemlich indifferent verhalte, weder die Vielheit der Opferstätten erlaube, noch auf die einheit Gewicht lege, und daß ihm dieser Haltung wegen die Priorität vor der deuteronomium zukomme." Note also that the Passover sacrifice (Ex 12; cf. Ex 34:25) is decentralized in P, occurring at individual homes (cf. above, p. 69).

[48] Milgrom 1991, p. 34.

(or both).[49] In other words, the interpretation of the requirement of centralization in both P and H depends on one's interpretation of Lev 17 and on the question of which lawcode Lev 17 originally belonged to. As Lev 17 is a mixture of both P and H, it it is reasonable to think that one cannot deny the possibility that the writer / incorporator of Lev 17 was aware of material pertaining to both P and H. It is even possible to think that there existed a centralization requirement which first belonged to either P or H, whichever was first, and included only the form and vocabulary of this earlier code, but was edited in view for the latter code as well and incorporated in its present place when the two codes were combined.[50]

Thus, because Lev 17 is a mixture of P and H features and there is no agreement as to the relative order of P and H, or even whether they ever existed as separate entities, the problem of the internal prehistory of the Priestly material is very difficult, including the view of centralization in P and H. Thus, we may conclude that it is safest if we look at Lev 17 as it is embedded to the Priestly material in its final form in its current literary arrangement and setting.

Let us then look at what Lev 17 says about centralization. Let us start by looking at the chapter as a whole. Schwartz, who has written two detailed articles about Lev 17,[51] has argued that the chapter is a unit consisting of five paragraphs (vss. 3-7; 8-9; 10-12; 13-14; 15-16).[52] According to Schwartz, "The first four share a common formulational mold, and all five mention explicitly, or refer obliquely to, the threat of כרת. The first two paragraphs, as seen from their similar style and vocabulary, are a unit, dealing with sacrificial animals and the place of their slaughter. The last two paragraphs too are a unit; they are the sub-sections of the blood prohibition of the third."[53]

---

[49] Keeping in mind from above that scholarly consensus somewhat hesitantly assigns the passage to H, for which the strongest argument is the current literary placement of the chapter as preceding Lev 18-26.

[50] Cf. Elliger 1966, pp. 224-225 for a source-oriented approach to Lev 17 which postulates P redactors on an H "Grundschicht".

[51] Schwartz 1991; Schwartz 1996.

[52] Schwartz 1991, pp. 36-37; Schwartz 1996, p. 16.

[53] Schwartz 1996, p. 16; Cf Schwartz 1991, pp. 37-42 for details.

Also, according to Schwartz, "All the lines of the formal analysis lead to the following view of the balanced and designed structure of the chapter: the first three paragraphs contain three prohibitions, arranged in ascending order of severity. The last of these three, which is of course the most absolute and most severe, draws in its wake two positive commands which are its subsections and which expand upon and clarify it. These last two - or, to be precise, the last three, since they are a unit - are arranged in descending order of severity. The five paragraphs thus make up an inverted 'V', at the zenith of which stands the absolute prohibition of partaking of blood and its rationale. This section, vv. 10-12, is therefore the axis upon which the chapter revolves."[54]

Schwartz continues, "The merest glance at the content leads to the same conclusion: all five paragraphs deal with the legitimate and correct manner of disposing of the blood of those animals which may be eaten. The first two speak of sacrificeable animals - which, in the view of this chapter, must indeed be sacrificed - and the last two speak of animals which, though they may be eaten, may not be sacrificed. At the center, between the first two and the last two, stands the axiom upon which all four depend: that partaking of blood is prohibited."[55]

One has to note here that vv. 8-9 do not speak about blood. Yet, in the light of comparing v. 9 with v. 4, it is conceivable that bloodguiltiness would be accounted to a man who does not bring either an *olah* or *zebah* to the tent of meeting. Thus, whether one fully accepts Schwartz's analysis of the structure of the chapter as a whole, Schwartz has made a case for the literary unity of the chapter and the importance of the blood prohibition in it.

After having noted the centrality of the blood prohibition in regard to Lev 17, we must note that the question of why blood is prohibited, important as it is, is not all that relevant for the present discussion. However, one point needs attention. Suffice it to say that we agree with Rendtorff who asserts that the general value and importance of blood for expiation is the reason given in v. 11 for

---

[54] Schwartz 1991, pp. 42-43.
[55] Schwartz 1991, p. 43.

the blood prohibition.[56] Also, it is good to recall here that all biblical law codes forbid the consumption of blood.[57]

Thus, we are left with the centralizing requirements of verses 3-9 which, even though they connect with vv. 10-16 and may be subservient to them, can nevertheless be interpreted relatively independently. Turning aside from vv. 10-16, let us first look at vv. 8-9.

The interpretation of vv. 8-9 does not seem very complicated. The law states that all *olah* and *zebah* sacrifices are to be brought to the tent of meeting. The law is thus about cult centralization. There seem to be only two issues of some uncertainty. First, it is often thought that the usage of *olah* and *zebah* is a merism, i.e. the two terms cover all sacrifices.[58] This is possible, even though one cannot be absolutely certain. Secondly, one should notice that from the standpoint of its present narrative setting, the law assumes a wilderness setting with the Israelites camped around the tent of meeting, and it is not directly stated whether and how the law should be applied after the settlement when the distance to the central sanctuary would complicate its application. We will discuss this matter further below.

On the other hand, the interpretation of vv. 3-7 is difficult, and these verses thus form the *crux interpretum* of Lev 17 in regard to centralization. To start with, as Schwartz has given good reasons to consider vv. 3-7 as a literary and legal unity,[59] we will concentrate on the final form of the text. Assuming then that the passage is to be taken as a unity, one needs to recognize that since rabbinic times

---

[56] Rendtorff 1995, pp. 26-27. His article is a response to Milgrom 1971, who argues that Lev 17:11 refers only to the *shelamim* offering, and speaks about expiation against a crime given in Lev 17:4, an unauthorized killing of an animal.

[57] Cf. Brichto 1976, p. 42n32: "The blood taboo, present in so many places in the Bible ... is so old and ingrained that it cannot be used for the dating of sources." One should also note that if P is separated from H, Gen 9:1-6, which is assigned to P, nevertheless contains a blood prohibition (see e.g. Brichto 1976, pp. 19-20; c.f. Wenham 1987, pp. 167-169 concerning Gen 6-9 source analysis).

[58] See Hartley 1992, p. 273; Brichto 1976, p. 25.

[59] See Schwartz 1996, pp. 17-18.

there has been a debate regarding the substantive content of the legislation of Lev 17:3-7.[60] According to Schwartz,

> The two sides of the question are represented in Talmudic literature by R. Ismael and R. Akiba, the former claiming that the intent is to outlaw what he called "profane" slaughter, i.e., the slaughter of oxen, sheep, or goats without first presenting them as an offering to YHWH, and the latter claiming that the intent is to prohibit making sacrifices to YHWH of oxen, sheep or goats outside of the single sanctuary, in other words, that this is what scholars call a law of cult-centralization.[61]

The question of interpretation hinges on the meaning of the verb שחט in v. 3. According to Hartley,

> The word שחט, "slaughter", has both a popular meaning for ordinary slaughtering of an animal (e.g., as Gen 37:31) and a restricted cultic meaning for the ritual slaughter of an animal (1:5). The big question is whether שחט is used broadly or restrictively."[62]

It is possible to take the meaning of שחט in both ways in v.3. Even though Levine has argued that "In the ritual texts of the Torah the verb שחט never has the general sense of 'slaughtering' that it has in other, less detailed biblical texts",[63] we must note the usage of the verb in the following Priestly passages: Lev 14:5 ("leper"); Lev 14:50, 51 ("leprous" house); Num 19:3 (purification heifer). In none of these passages does the verb שחט indicate sacrifice, and neither does the killing even occur in front of the tent of meeting. On the other hand, the killing of the animal concerned in these passages is part of a ritual. The question then hinges on whether the word שחט means ritual slaughter in the Priestly material or whether the meaning comes from the fact that the context of the killing always is a ritual in the Priestly material. It may be impossible to decide for certain.

Let us next look at v. 3. The animals referred to in the verse are the same as referred to in the law of *shelamim* in Lev 3 (שור vs

[60] See Schwartz 1996, p. 18.
[61] Schwartz 1996, p. 18.
[62] Hartley 1992, p. 269.
[63] Levine 1989, p. 113.

בקר in Lev 3:1; כשב vs כשב in Lev 3:7; עז vs עז in Lev 3:12). A bird which would refer to an *olah* (Lev 1: 14-17) is not mentioned. Also, in the law of the burnt offering in Lev 1, only a male ox, lamb or goat may be offered in front of the tent of meeting, whereas neither Lev 17:3 nor Lev 3 makes a distinction between male or female. Further, the fact that vv. 5-6 of Lev 17 are about *shelamim*[64] reinforces the idea that vv. 3-4 concern animals that are fit for *shelamim*.[65] Thus, the law of Lev 17:3-7 revolves around *shelamim*.

After these observations, let us first read the rest of the law as if it refers to *shelamim* sacrifices only, and not to profane slaughter. Hartley gives the following motivation for the law:

> The close tie between slaughter and sacrifice in the ancient mind made this regulation necessary. Yahweh wished to make sure that the profane slaughter of clean animals without defect in an open field was not turned into a sacrificial ritual, for such practice would be prone to becoming polluted with pagan customs, such as believing that these quasi sacrifices placated the spirits of the field. The tendency to follow syncretic [*sic*] practice would have been greater in the absence of any priest to officiate. Yahweh definitely wished to prevent the people from thinking that they were making a legitimate sacrifice any time they slaughtered an animal at any place other than a consecrated altar.[66]

If the law of Lev 17:3-7 is taken this way, vv. 8-9 are then best taken as recapitulating and expanding the prohibition of vv. 3-7, both in the scope of the sacrifices (*olah* is included) and the persons

---

[64] Also, based on the general meaning of the word זבח in the Priestly material, זבח should most naturally be taken to refer to *shelamim* in v. 5 (and in v. 7). (Also, if v. 5 was about any other offering, it would mean that this would from now on have to be offered as *shelamim* as well, which would not make good sense, either from the context of vv. 8-9 or the rest of the Priestly legislation.)

[65] Note that all this assumes that Lev 17:3-7 knows the regulations of Lev 1 and 3. At least, it is easy to understand verses 5-6 from the context of Lev 3 (So Schwartz 1996, pp. 24-25). These considerations then tie Lev 17 to P (cf. our earlier discussion concerning the relationship of Lev 17 with P and H).

[66] Hartley 1992, p. 271.

involved (*ger* is included).[67] One then has to conclude with Hartley that the laws of Lev 17:3-9 "do not address the issue of the ordinary slaughtering of domesticated animals",[68] and that Lev 17, read as its present narrative setting suggests, is about the centralization of the cult at the tent of meeting in the wilderness.

On the other hand, one may also read the law as limiting all profane slaughter to the tent of meeting. By limiting all slaughter to the tent of meeting and assigning it as *shelamim*, it is made certain that in practice, no *shelamim* offerings can be offered in the field. As Wenham states, "The motive underlying this severe law is spelled out in vv. 5-7. It is to prevent sacrifices to the *goat-demons* who inhabited the wilderness",[69] and, "Anyone involved in secret demon worship might claim that he merely killed the animal outside the camp. To plug this potential loophole it is enjoined that all animals must be killed in the tabernacle."[70] Also, Hartley's assertion, as quoted above,[71] that the law sought to prevent the profane slaughter of clean animals without defect in an open field from turning into a sacrificial ritual, would hold true in this case as well.

We should also note that according to Hartley, if Lev 17:3-7 were about profane slaughter, there would be a problem of what to do with animals which have a blemish, since such animals cannot be offered as *shelamim* (Lev 3:1, 6).[72] However, we may make the following logical deductions concerning this problem. First, one may conceive that the Israelites could also have been offering blemished animals as *shelamim* in the wilderness outside the context of the tent of meeting, or at least might have been tempted to do so. Then, if the law of Lev 17:3-7 were about the centralization of *shelamim* only, it would not make it clear what to do with these blemished *shelamim*, as only unblemished *shelamim* may be offered at the tent of meeting according to Lev 3. In other words, if

---

[67] Note however that Greek includes *ger* (προσήλυτος) in Lev 17:3.

[68] Hartley 1992, p. 271.

[69] Wenham 1979, p. 243.

[70] Ibid.

[71] See above, p. 84.

[72] Hartley 1992, p. 271. Note however that Lev 22:23 allows certain blemishes for a freewill offering (נדבה), and we will treat such animals in the following discussion as if they were unblemished.

blemished animals could be offered as *shelamim* outside the context of the tent of meeting, whichever way one takes the law, there are cases which it does not cover. Secondly, if one can on the other hand conceive that blemished animals were never sacrificed as *shelamim* outside the context of the tent of meeting (which is by no means certain, especially if the practice was idolatrous!), the law covers all cases if one takes it to mean *shelamim* only. However, in this case, we may still point out that there would be no need to legislate for blemished animals, as there would in any case be no danger that they could be offered to goat-demons. Thus, one may think that there would have been no need to prevent the profane slaughter of blemished animals.

Moreover, we may point out that if the law of Lev 17:3-7 is taken in its wider meaning, it covers all cases which are covered by the interpretation of the law as relating to *shelamim* only, plus such cases in which the animal was previously slaughtered only for food even though it could also have been brought to the tent of meeting to be sacrificed. In other words, the interpretation of the law as about *shelamim* only is a subset of the interpretation of the law to include profane slaughter of all animals which can be sacrificed at the tent of meeting. Yet in other words, the law covers more cases if it is taken in its wider meaning. The following diagram illustrates the matter.

Figure 2: Scope of the law of Lev 17:3-7

Finally, it has to be noted that if one takes the law of Lev 17:3-7 in its wider meaning (to include profane slaughter), vv. 8-9 fit with vv. 3-7 in that they state that all sacrifices, including *olot* must be brought to the tent of meeting, and that not only the Israelites, but also *gerim* must do so.[73]

Then, we must ask ourselves: which case was the law intended to cover, as it can legitimately be interpreted in two ways? It seems that it is best to think that the answer must ultimately lie in the way the Old Testament itself interprets it, provided that it is possible to detect this interpretation. If we look at the problem from this standpoint, the wider interpretation fits perfectly with the book of Deuteronomy,[74] at least at first sight. As the Jewish commentator Bamberger puts it,

> Now Deuteronomy (12:20ff.) provides that, after Israel has conquered and occupied the land, animals may be killed for food without sacrificial formalities, as long as the carcasses are drained of blood. The simplest explanation of this chapter [Lev 17], then, is that it was a temporary rule for the period of desert wandering; the Israelites were traveling in constant proximity to the Tabernacle and could easily bring their animals there and present them as sacrifices of well-being. But, after they settled in Canaan and spread over the country, frequent trips to a central shrine (such as Shiloh and later Jerusalem) would have been burdensome; and secular slaughter was therefore permitted. This explanation was given by Rabbi Ishmael in the second century and was adopted by later legal authorities. It makes excellent sense, on the assumption that the Torah was all given through Moses, that the present chapter dates from the time of encampment at Sinai and Deuteronomy from the end of the desert period, just before the invasion of the land.[75]

In other words, at least from the standpoint of its present narrative setting and in relation to the rest of the Pentateuch in its

---

[73] This would then mean that based on Lev 17:3-7, strictly speaking, a *ger* could slaughter any animals outside the context of the tent of meeting as long as such slaughtering would not be sacrificial (However, note again that LXX includes *ger* [προσήλυτος] in Lev 17:3; cf. above, p. 85, incl. n67). I will however not attempt to explore the significance of this seeming allowance further.

[74] We will discuss the matter in more detail below when dealing with centralization in Deuteronomy.

[75] Bamberger 1979, p. 177.

narrative setting, the wider interpretation of the law makes good sense. On the other hand, if the law of Lev 17:3-7 is taken in its narrower meaning, it is difficult to think why the laws in Deuteronomy which allow profane slaughter were necessary, at least if one reads them from the standpoint of their narrative setting in the Pentateuch. Also, it must be noted that Hartley, who interprets the verb שחט in its narrower meaning, concedes that, "the tone of the context suggests that it [the law] covers all slaughter as sacrifice".[76]

The major reason why commentators opt for the narrower interpretation is the statement חקת עולם תהיה-זאת להם לדרתם in v. 7.[77] Without this expression, it would be possible to say that the laws of Lev 17 were valid only for the wilderness period. However, the expression clearly seems to carry the meaning over beyond the wilderness period, constituting a major problem of interpretation for those who wish to take the wider meaning of the verb שחט. A number of conservative commentators have tried to solve this problem by saying that the phrase חקת עולם תהיה-זאת להם לדרתם concerns only the prohibition of satyr worship earlier in v. 7.[78] Yet, as Hartley notes, "it is structurally defensible that v. 7b applies to vv. 3-7a".[79]

On the other hand, most critical scholars see the law as a product of either the exilic or the post-exilic community. According to this view, the Jewish community was centred around Jerusalem during or after the exile and was so small and closely knit that the command was feasible.[80] However, Noth who thinks that the law arose right after 587 BC "in the still remaining cultic circles round about Jerusalem", doubts if the law could have been carried out even then.[81] Also, Ezra 2:70 (cf. Neh 11:20-36) implies that

---

[76] Hartley 1992, pp. 270-271.

[77] See Hartley 1992, p. 270.

[78] E.g. Keil and Delitzsch 1983/1861-1865, The Pentateuch, vol II, p. 409.

[79] Hartley 1992, p. 270.

[80] See Noth 1965, p. 130; Elliger 1966, p. 224 for a view of exilic origins, and Bamberger 1979, p. 179 for an exposition of a view for early post-exilic origins.

[81] Noth 1965, p. 130. Also, as is well known, not all of the population of Judea was carried into exile.

when the population returned, many of them settled in other places than Jerusalem. In fact, according to the book of Nehemiah, it was difficult to get people to live in Jerusalem during the time of Nehemiah (Neh 7:4-5; 11:1-2). Moreover, as Hartley points out, "Even during the post-exilic period the implementation of this decree would have placed severe hardship on pockets of Israelites scattered throughout Palestine who looked to the Temple as their worship center, the very people the small struggling community at Jerusalem needed for moral and financial support in their adventure to rebuild the capital city. The Jewish population scattered throughout the land could hardly bring all their animals to Jerusalem for slaughter."[82] Furthermore, there were many Jews living in Babylonia during the postexilic time. How could the law be binding on them?[83] And, as Schwartz observes, there is no evidence that a prohibition of common slaughter was observed in second temple times,[84] and one can quickly add that the same applies to the exilic time. Finally, one has to note that if the law was intended for the exilic, or early post-exilic community, it could have been in effect only for a short time,[85] and one thus cannot argue for the application of the law in exilic or early postexilic times based on an argument that the law could not have been given for the wilderness generation since it would have been valid only for a short time. In short, it is difficult to think that the law would have been made based on either the exilic or postexilic setting of Judah.

Then, how should we understand the expression חֻקַּת עוֹלָם לְדֹרֹתָם and the application of the law? In order to think about that, we must first remind ourselves that a major issue affecting the interpretation of the Priestly material is that many of the laws are set with Israel camped around the tent of meeting in the wilderness.[86] A number of cultic laws, such as Lev 1-10 have specifically been formulated from this viewpoint. In fact, there is no indication in Lev 1-10 how the law should be applied if the camp setting is no longer valid. On the other hand, there are a number of laws in the Priestly material which have been explicitly

---

[82] Hartley 1992, p. 270.
[83] So Brichto 1976, p. 45, quoting Y. Kaufmann.
[84] Schwartz 1996, p. 41.
[85] Cf. Hartley 1992, p. 270.
[86] Cf. above, p. 74.

formulated for conditions where Israel has come to the land of Canaan and settled in it. As far as P is concerned, such laws include leprosy laws (Lev 13-14) and the Passover law (Ex 12).[87] On the other hand, the land plays an even more important role in the Holiness Code. According to Joosten, who has investigated the matter extensively, "The notion of land is central to H, second in importance only to the notion of peoplehood. Time and again reference is made to 'the land' - the land of Canaan, the land of the Israelites, the land of YHWH."[88] In regard to this, it has to be stressed that in H, a number of laws have been given directly as applying to the land where the Israelites will settle in the future according to the narrative. These include Lev 19:23-25; 23:10-14; 15-22; Lev 25-26. Yet the camp is directly mentioned in H as well, and a number of laws such as especially Lev 17 (if it is to be taken as part of H) have been set in a camp in the wilderness. Thus, one has to note that in P, most laws have been set in the camp context, whereas in H, most laws already look forward to the promised land. This is also connected with the fact that the laws in P mainly concern cultic issues relating to the central sanctuary, whereas the laws in H include considerably more laws which do not at least directly relate to cultic issues or the central sanctuary (so at least Lev 18; most of Lev 19; Lev 20; Lev 25-26).[89]

Then, one must ask why most of the cultic laws, including Lev 17, have been set in a context of a camp in the wilderness. Surely such a formulation must have a purpose. If the camp setting was real, there must have been no doubt that the wilderness period would be short, and that the laws concerned would need to be applied later in the land. On the other hand, if the wilderness setting is later fiction, all the more there must have been a purpose for setting the laws in such a fictitious context.[90] For this reason,

---

[87] Even though the Passover law has been set in Egypt, as it speaks about houses, it must be taken from a context of having its direct (future from the standpoint of the narrative of Ex 12) application for settled conditions (see also Ex 12:25).

[88] Joosten 1996, p. 137.

[89] Note that in this respect, Lev 17 rather belongs to P than H.

[90] And, as discussed above (p. 88), there is no evidence that an exilic/postexilic situation in Judah was similar to the wilderness camp as regards the compactness of the community.

scholars have interpreted the wilderness camp as a paradigm for the land.[91] However, in what way is the camp paradigmatic for the land? According to Joosten, "One should be extremely cautious in using the picture of the camp to draw inferences with regard to the land as envisaged in H."[92] Joosten adds, "Thus it is sometimes supposed that H was written at a time when the Israelites' territory was small: otherwise, the prohibition of slaughter except at the central sanctuary would have been impractical (17:3-7)",[93] but, "Such an inference is unnecessary if we take account of the fictional nature of H."[94] What emerges from this is that the camp setting, whether one believes that it was real or imaginary, in some way sets out rules and principles which are applicable to the land which is different from the camp. Looking at this issue from another standpoint, if one reads the laws, as the laws have been given for the camp, strictly speaking, it is not immediately certain how they are to be applied when the camp setting is no longer valid.

To repeat, the law of Lev 17 has been given for a wilderness setting. First, self-evidently, the narrative context suggests this. Also, the mention of the tent of meeting (vv. 4, 5, 6) and the words על־פני השדה are fully compatible with the wilderness context, even though they could be used in other contexts as well.[95] However, the expressions במחנה and מחוץ למחנה in v. 3 explicitly and absolutely tie the narrative context of the law to the camp in the wilderness. Thus, any application of the law to settled conditions has to be indirect. If the law is to be חקת עולם להם לדרתם exactly in its current form, how will this be possible in a situation where no camp exists any more? Of course, one may think that the law was conceived so that the expression "in the camp or outside the camp" refers to the whole land (and beyond), and the tent of meeting refers to the Temple, and thus the law says that all slaughter in the land (and beyond) must be done at the temple.

---

[91] So Joosten 1996, pp. 145-148. Naturally, if one believes that the legislation is late, the Tent of Meeting has to be taken as paradigmatic for the temple.

[92] Joosten 1996, p. 148.

[93] Ibid., p. 148n45.

[94] Ibid.

[95] See Dt 28:3, 16 for a context of שדה vs עיר.

However, even though possible to envisage, it must be stressed that this would be interpretation.

If we think of the wilderness camp, it is an ideal setting for cultic matters from a spatial viewpoint. All Israel is together around the central sanctuary, the tent of meeting, and all the people may access the tent of meeting at any time. Thus, the picture the Priestly material gives is of a setting which is ideal as an outward arrangement of a nation in perfect unity and order, with God dwelling in their midst, present on the throne of cherubim[96] in the tent of meeting (Ex 25:22; 40:34-35). Whenever an Israelite wishes to offer, he can just come to the tent of meeting. Whenever there is any problem, it can quickly be resolved through an inquiry to God (e.g. Lev 24:10-16). The wilderness camp is a setting of one God, one nation, one place, one sanctuary. Thus, we may think that *the Priestly law in many ways envisages and concerns an ideal Israel.*[97] For this ideal situation, it is possible to give a strict prohibition of profane slaughter as in Lev 17:3-7. In this context, it is possible to control even the slaughtering by the people, so that all of their animals which can be slaughtered as *shelamim* are brought to the central altar and sacrificed as *shelamim*. Thus, it is possible to make sure that people will not sacrifice to idols instead. However, the law probably has another thrust as well. If we look at Lev 7:31-34, the priests are to receive a portion of *shelamim* offered at the central altar. The right thigh and the breast are to be their share. Thus, any *shelamim* offering brought to the tent of meeting would contribute to the upkeep of the priests. If then all possible slaughtering were done in the tent of meeting, it would serve both to avoid idolatry and to support the cultic personnel. And, of course, there would be the added benefit for the person concerned that he would be in the presence of Yahweh in the central sanctuary while making the *shelamim* offering.

Thus, we may think that it is better to take Lev 17:3-7, and many of the cultic regulations as paradigmatic and as an expression of ideal conditions. The law would be valid *paradigmatically* for the

---

[96] Cf. above, Chapter 2.2.1 for considerations of Yahweh's exact localization regarding the ark.

[97] We will compare this ideal with the ideal of Deuteronomy below.

coming generations.[98] If possible, it would be best to bring all animals that are slaughtered to the altar of the central sanctuary and offer them as *shelamim* there. Without going into too much detail at this point,[99] it is possible to think that Deuteronomy 12 relaxes the prohibition of profane slaughter, but still respects the Priestly ideal. According to Dt 12:20-22, if the central sanctuary is far, one may slaughter at will. However, Dt 12:20-22 nevertheless says: If the central sanctuary is close, come and offer your meat as *shelamim* at the central altar, and eat after that!

Also, the expression חקת עולם להם לדרתם may not be as binding as we would interpret it from our cultural standpoint which is removed from ancient Israel (and the Ancient Near East). For instance, according to 1 Sam 2:30, Eli loses his priesthood due to disobedience, even though the promise given to him and his father's family was עד־עולם.[100] Similarly, King Saul would have received an eternal kingship, but lost it due to his disobedience (1 Sam 13:13).[101] In other words, from the standpoint of the Bible's self-presentation, God may change his mind. Thus, there is no problem in thinking that the law of Lev 17:3-7 could have been repealed by Deuteronomy 12. One may in any case think that the principle of the law would remain valid later as well, both from the standpoint of the expression חקת עולם להם לדרתם and from the standpoint of Dt 12:20-22.

All this fits perfectly with Milgrom's observations that P "presumes a central but not a single sanctuary".[102] Bringing everything to a central sanctuary is an ideal for which the cultic laws have been geared, but there is no need to think that it was

---

[98] Note also that it is generally known that no court cases exist for the laws of Hammurabi (see Otto 1994, p. 161). Thus it is not certain what the role of the law codes was in the ancient Near East, whether they were created as paradigmatic from the start or whether they were made to be binding in practice as well. In fact, they may rather rather have been paradigmatic (see Kraus 1984, esp. pp. 111-123; Westbrook 1994, pp. 24-25). Thus, it is possible that Israelite legislation would at least have included paradigmatic aspects.

[99] See below in the section of Dt 12 for comprehensive details.

[100] Cf. A. Tomasino, *NIDOTTE* 3, p. 349.

[101] A. Tomasino, *NIDOTTE* 3, p. 349.

[102] Milgrom 1991, p. 34; cf. above, p. 78.

ever envisaged in the Priestly material that the ideal could actually be attained in the land. Thus, we may say that *in many ways the Priestly material argues for a central sanctuary as an ideal in the strongest possible way, but more or less tacitly allows other options as well.* Specifically, detailed cultic proceedings in relation to the tent of meeting have the camp in the wilderness as their setting, and this serves to argue for the importance of the central sanctuary. On the other hand, the Passover is not centralized, but is sacrificed in private homes (Ex 12). Moreover, the injunctions in Lev 23; Num 28-29 concerning the three national feasts (including the Passover) are more or less ambiguous as regards centralization even though according to these passages sacrifices are to be brought forward during feasts.[103]

It is also logical to think that, besides Lev 17:3-7, the rhetoric for arguing for the central sanctuary in the Priestly material applies to Lev 17:8-9 as well. The law of Lev 17:8-9 is strictly speaking valid only for the wilderness period, but when a later Israelite would read/hear the law, it would make him strongly appreciate the importance of the central sanctuary.

If one then compares the Priestly material with the Covenant Code, as far as centralization is concerned, the two complement each other well. The Priestly material strongly argues for the importance of the central sanctuary, but does not forbid local altars for which the Covenant Code legislates. This is perfectly in agreement with the contrast between the elaborate cult and priesthood of the Priestly material at the tent of meeting as compared to the simplicity of the cult at local altars as legislated by the Covenant Code. Furthermore, the tent of meeting in the Priestly material is the place where Yahweh dwells among his people Israel, whereas Yahweh "comes" to meet the worshippers at the local altars.[104] Thus, the tent of meeting and its cult is in every way more prominent than that of the local altars, and yet both have their function and purpose.

---

[103] Cf. also above, p. 78.

[104] As discussed in Chapter 2.2.2.

3.3. The Chosen Place and Centralization in Deuteronomy

Our next task is to investigate how Deuteronomy sees centralization and the relationship of the central sanctuary and local altars. We will also seek to relate the view of Deuteronomy to the views of the rest of the legal material of the Pentateuch which we have studied above. Above all, as Deuteronomy 12 contains the most explicit injunctions for the centralization of sacrifices, it will be the main focus of our discussion. Again, in order to interpret the message of Dt 12, it will be helpful to start by taking a brief look at some of the critical issues surrounding the chapter and how the chapter relates to the rest of the book of Deuteronomy.

As far as the narrative setting of Dt 12 is concerned, the chapter begins the central part of Deuteronomy, Chapters 12-26, which contain most of the laws of the book. Chapters 12-26 are surrounded by a memorial and a hortatory speech by Moses in chapters 1-11 and various admonitory speeches of Moses in chapters 27-34, including an instruction to build an altar on Mt Ebal (Dt 27), blessings and curses (Dt 27-28), a song (Dt 32) and a blessing (Dt 33) of Moses, and a historical epilogue (Dt 34).[105] It seems clear that the positioning of chapter 12 at the beginning of the central block of laws of the book serves to emphasize the significance of the chapter.[106] Also, as discussed above, that Dt 12 which concerns cultic matters starts the code of Deuteronomy is comparable to at least the Covenant Code which is commenced by the altar law of Ex 20:22-26.[107] There are several features which tie Dt 12 to the rest of the book. The centralization formula המקום אשר־יבחר יהוה אלהיכם and its variations occur in many places in chapters 12-26, and once in 31:11.[108] Also, McConville points out that the word המקום occurs several times in Dt 1-11, and once after Dt 26 (at 29:6) outside the centralization formula.[109] Especially, when המקום is combined with בוא, the expression is

---

[105] Cf. Clements 1989, p. 14.

[106] Cf. Miller 1990, p. 129.

[107] See above, p. 77.

[108] For all occurrences of the formula in its various forms, see Lohfink 1991, p. 151, Table 1.

[109] McConville 1984, p. 33.

clearly comparable to Dt 12 (Compare Dt 1:31; 9:7; 11:5; 29:6 with Dt 12:5-6, 11). According to McConville, outside chapters 12-26, these expressions speak about what Yahweh has done for Israel, whereas in chapter 12 they describe what Israel is to do in response to Yahweh's gracious action.[110] Also, McConville has noted structural similarity between Dt 7 and Dt 12.[111] Thus, we may conclude that there are enough reasons to consider Dt 12 as an integral part of the book of Deuteronomy as a whole, at least in general terms.

The structure of Dt 12 is tied to the question of the unity of the chapter. As is well known, there have been many attempts to see the chapter as having emerged in various stages and from various parts.[112] However, none of the proposed schemes for the prehistory of the chapter have been entirely convincing.[113] In view of this, one might as well take the chapter in its present form, and that is the approach we will follow here. On the other hand, there is no doubt that the chapter, besides commencing (v. 1) and ending (12:28-13:1) with exhortations, consists of various repetitions of centralization requirements or 'laws'. It seems that these centralization laws may best be divided into vv. 2-7; 8-12; 13-16; 17-19; 20-27.[114] If one takes Dt 12 as a unity, the different versions of the law may be part of the rhetorical scheme of the chapter. As McConville suggests, "The frequent repetitions are a matter of style, and serve the didactic purpose of the writer."[115] And, seeing

---

[110] McConville 1984, pp. 33-35.

[111] For details, see ibid., pp. 59-64.

[112] See Reuter 1993, pp. 29-41; McConville 1984, pp. 40-42; Lohfink 1996, pp. 127-148.

[113] See e.g. McConville 1984, pp. 40-42 for an evaluation and criticism of Steuernagel's and Horst's approaches, and ibid., pp. 56-57 for an evaluation and criticism of von Rad's approach. Cf. also Lohfink 1991 for a criticism of attempts to see diachronic development in Deuteronomy's centralization formula. Also, it is reasonable to think that there is no need to take *Numeruswechsel* as an indication of sources (cf. McConville 1984, p. 56).

[114] So von Rad 1966, p. 89, even though he puts vv. 20-28 into parentheses, seemingly as secondary to vv. 2-7; 8-12; 13-16 which he takes as the "triple form" of the centralizing law.

[115] McConville 1984, p. 64. Cf. also McConville's analysis of the structure of Dt 12 in ibid., pp. 64-65, 67.

Dt 12 as didactic fits well with the rest of the book of Deuteronomy.[116]

If one looks at the narrative setting of Dt 12, the chapter presents itself as an injunction of Moses, in line with most of the book as a whole.[117] Moreover, the speeches and injunctions of Moses have their narrative setting at the other side of Jordan, in the land of Moab (בעבר הירדן בארץ מואב; Dt 1:5). From a narrative viewpoint, the hearers of the speeches and laws of Deuteronomy have not yet crossed the Jordan to the promised land. They are the post-Sinai generation, camped at the plains of Moab, just about to enter the promised land.[118] The book of Deuteronomy ends with the death of Moses at Mount Nebo, after Moses has viewed the promised land from the Moabite side. It is only in the book of Joshua that the Israelites cross the Jordan into the promised land.

This narrative setting is explicit also in Dt 12. According to Dt 12:1, the laws will be valid in the promised land:

אלה החקים והמשפטים אשר תשמרון לעשות בארץ
אשר נתן יהוה אלהי אבתיך לך לרשתה[119] כל־הימים
אשר־אתם חיים על־האדמה:

These are the statutes and ordinances that you are to be careful to keep in the land which Yahweh, the God of your fathers, has given you to possess, all the days that you will live on the earth.

Moreover, Dt 12:10 states:

ועברתם את־הירדן וישבתם בארץ אשר־יהוה אלהיכם
מנחיל אתכם והניח לכם מכל־איביכם מסביב
וישבתם־בטח:

And you will cross over Jordan and settle in the land that Yahweh your God will give you as an inheritance, and he will give you rest from all your enemies round about, and you will live in safety.

---

[116] Cf. von Rad 1966, p. 91: "Deuteronomy is essentially strongly didactic."

[117] As von Rad (1953/1948, p. 12, referring to Klostermann) notes, only 7:4; 11:13-15; 17:3; 28:20; 29:4-5 indicate Yahweh as the speaker.

[118] Cf. Reuter 1993, pp. 224, 226; McConville and Millar 1994, pp. 123-124.

[119] Note however that בארץ אשר נתן יהוה אלהי אבתיך לך לרשתה is lacking in a number of manuscripts; see *BHS*.

From the standpoint of the narrative setting, the focus is on the future. The crossing of the Jordan is in the future. The giving of the inheritance is in the future. Rest and safety are in the future.[120]

These promises of settlement, rest and security contrast with the conditions of the present in Deuteronomy. According to Dt 12:8-9,

לא תעשׂון ככל אשר אנחנו עשׂים פה היום איש
כל־הישׁר בעיניו:
כי לא־באתם עד־עתה אל־המנוחה ואל־הנחלה
אשר־יהוה אלהיך נתן לך:

Do not do like we do today, each according to what is right in his own eyes since you have not yet come to the rest and the inheritance that Yahweh your God will give you.

At the moment, things are not yet as one would like them to be.

The emphasis on the future in v. 10 continues in v. 11, according to which the bringing of offerings to the "chosen" place is to occur in the future:

והיה המקום אשר־יבחר יהוה אלהיכם בו לשׁכן שׁמו
שׁם שׁמה תביאו את כל־אשר אנכי מצוה אתכם
עולתיכם וזבחיכם מעשׂרתיכם ותרומת ידכם וכל
מבחר נדריכם אשר תדרו ליהוה:

And may it be so as regards the place which Yahweh your God will choose for himself to make his name dwell there, that you shall bring there all that I have commanded you, your burnt offerings, your sacrifices, your tithes and the gifts of your hands and all the best of your votive offerings that you vow to Yahweh.

As the people are still at the land of Moab and the bringing of the offerings is in the future, similarly, one may suspect that the choice of the "place" is in the future as well. This is further suggested by the fact that the word בחר is in the imperfect tense (i.e. יבחר) in v. 11 and in the rest of the chapter (see vv. 5, 14, 18,

---

[120] Cf. Reuter 1993, p. 59.

21, 26), and similarly in the rest of the book of Deuteronomy when it refers to the chosen place.[121]

Thus, the promise in v. 10 about settlement, rest and safety is followed by the commandment in v. 11 that the people go and bring their offerings to the place Yahweh will choose. This then clearly suggests that the choice of the place, or at least bringing offerings there is to happen *after* the people have settled, and have achieved rest and security. This also means that the choice will not necessarily happen immediately after the crossing of the Jordan, but only after the conditions of settlement, rest and security from enemies have been achieved.

Dt 26:1-2 attests the same thinking. According to Dt 26:1-2, the Israelites are to bring first fruits to the chosen place *after* they have taken possession of the land and settled there. According to Dt 26:1,

והיה כי־תבוא אל־הארץ אשר יהוה אלהיך נתן לך
נחלה וירשתה וישבת בה:

And it shall be that when you come to the land that Yahweh your God gives you as an inheritance and you take possession of it and settle in it ...

Dt 26:2 then continues,

ולקחת מראשית ... והלכת אל־המקום אשר יבחר
יהוה אלהיך לשכן שמו שם:

And take from the firstfruits ... and go to the place which Yahweh your God will choose for the dwelling of his name.

The firstfruits are to be brought *after* taking possession and settling, and the choice of the place is in the future (imperfect of בחר is used, as always).

Thus, we have seen that the choice of the "place" and the bringing of offerings there is in the future for Deuteronomy, to be effected only after the people have settled in the land and achieved rest from their enemies so that they live in security.[122] This is also understandable from a practical standpoint. Suppose the chosen

---

[121] Cf. Lohfink 1991, p. 151, Table 1 for all occurrences in Deuteronomy.

[122] Cf. Riley 1993, p. 82, according to whom "the Deuteronomist ... specifies that the granting of Israel's rest will signify that the central sanctuary must be used exclusively (Dt 12:8-11)".

place were in the central-northern part of the country, how could a person who lived in the southern fringe of the country go up to the chosen place, especially three times a year if the conditions were not peaceful, also remembering the general difficulties of travel in ancient times? If the country were at war, how could the whole nation, especially males, gather in the chosen place? Besides the difficulty of actual travel, surely the enemy would achieve an easy victory in the meantime. Thus, it is logical to infer that there are conditions to the choice of the place and going there. The conditions are: The people have settled, and there is rest and security.

This practical aspect is confirmed by Ex 34:23-24. According to Ex 34:23-24,

שלש פעמים בשנה יראה כל־זכורך את־פני האדן
יהוה אלהי ישראל:
כי־אוריש גוים מפניך והר חבתי את־גבולך ולא־יחמד
איש את־ארצך בעלתך לראות את־פני יהוה אלהיך
שלש פעמים בשנה:

> Three times a year shall all your males appear before
> the Lord, Yahweh the God of Israel. For I will
> dispossess nations from before you and will enlarge
> your territory and no one will desire your land when
> you appear before Yahweh your God three times a
> year.

The passage recognizes the danger of what will happen if the males leave their towns and dwellings and travel to a sanctuary, and promises that Yahweh will dispossess the enemies of Israel and give the security required for the enterprise. If the passage is about local sanctuaries,[123] surely the danger from enemies would be even greater with the central sanctuary when the distance would be larger and travelling would take longer. It is also interesting that whereas v. 23 is generally taken to belong to J, v. 24 is often seen as Deuteronomic.[124] Thus, and especially when one bears in mind that it has often been thought that Deuteronomy used the legislation of the Covenant Code as its basis,[125] it is quite logical to think that the

---

[123] See above, p. 71n13 on this.

[124] See Durham 1987, p. 458.

[125] So already Wellhausen (cf. above, p. 6), and the same applies for the present; see e.g. Levinson 1997. Cf. also above, pp. 55, 70.

thought world of the Covenant Code and Deuteronomy is similar in many aspects, and we therefore have good reason to suggest that Ex 34:23-24 confirms that Deuteronomy saw security as necessary for pilgrimage.[126]

Then, more specifically, how long would it take for the people to achieve rest after they would cross the river Jordan? According to Dt 7:22,

וְנָשַׁל יְהוָה אֱלֹהֶיךָ אֶת־הַגּוֹיִם הָאֵל מִפָּנֶיךָ מְעַט מְעָט
לֹא תוּכַל כַּלֹּתָם מַהֵר פֶּן־תִּרְבֶּה עָלֶיךָ חַיַּת הַשָּׂדֶה:

And Yahweh will cast out these nations from before you little by little. You cannot finish them in haste lest the beasts of the field increase on you.

In other words, the passage indicates that a reasonably long time will pass before the Israelites will drive away their enemies. The same thought is expressed in the Covenant Code almost verbatim. According to Ex 23:29-30,[127]

לֹא אֲגָרְשֶׁנּוּ מִפָּנֶיךָ בְּשָׁנָה אֶחָת פֶּן־תִּהְיֶה הָאָרֶץ שְׁמָמָה
וְרַבָּה עָלֶיךָ חַיַּת הַשָּׂדֶה:
מְעַט מְעַט אֲגָרְשֶׁנּוּ מִפָּנֶיךָ עַד אֲשֶׁר תִּפְרֶה וְנָחַלְתָּ
אֶת־הָאָרֶץ:

I will not drive them away from before you in one year lest the land become desolate and the bests of the field increase on you. Little by little I will drive them out

---

[126] Cf. Tigay 1996, pp. 122-123, according to whom two conditions are necessary for putting centralization into effect: "the Israelites must enter their allotted territory, and must hold it securely. Security is necessary so that pilgrims may travel safely to the chosen place and will not fear that their homes may be attacked by enemies in their absence (Ex 23:24 [*sic*])". Yet, on the other hand, as Haran (1978, p. 294) observes, a "mass exodus from the settlements" is difficult even in peaceful conditions. Also, it would have been difficult for the place of the central sanctuary to accommodate all the people who came (ibid., p. 294). Finally, as Haran (ibid., p. 294) notes, "Even in the latter part of the Second Temple period, long after the canonization of the Pentateuch, when pilgrimage on the three feasts was considered an explicit precept of the Law, and huge crowds would flock to Jerusalem, the total number of pilgrims constituted only a small part of the people. How much more this would have been the case in earlier ages."

[127] Ex 23:27-31 is generally assigned to E (Childs 1974, p. 460); cf. our comments above, p. 52 regarding Ex 20:22-23:33.

from before you, until you will increase and take possession of the land.

Thus, besides affirming the close links between Deuteronomy and the Covenant Code,[128] Dt 7:22 and Ex 23:29-30 affirm that the conquest would not happen all at once. Especially, according to Dt 7:22 and Ex 23:30, Yahweh would drive the nations out before the Israelites "little by little" (מעט מעט). In other words, the passages indicate that a reasonably long time will pass before the Israelites drive away their enemies and the conditions are secure enough for the choice of the place where Yahweh's name dwells *and* for travelling there three times a year.

Then, if one thinks about the rhetorical impact of Deuteronomy for people who are living in the land a long time after the conquest, the Deuteronomic legislation advocates an ideal Israel where the land has been conquered, there is rest and security, and all Israel goes three times a year to the place Yahweh will choose. On the other hand, Deuteronomy also sees a time when the conquest is not yet complete. In fact, for Deuteronomy, that is the present time. Prosperity and security are the promises of the future. Then, from a rhetorical viewpoint, Deuteronomy's view of the conquest could serve as paradigmatic exhortation for the later generation, regardless of what one thinks of the original date and provenance of the book.[129] The later generation may be under oppression and difficulties. But, if they trust in Yahweh and serve him, Yahweh will give them rest and security just as he promised to the generation at the plains of Moab (Dt 11:22-23):

כי אם־שמר תשמרון את־כל־המצוה הזאת אשר אנכי
מצוה אתכם לעשתה לאהבה את־יהוה אלהיכם
ללכת בכל־דרכיו ולדבקה־בו:
והוריש יהוה את־כל־הגוים האלה מלפניכם וירשתם
גוים גדלים ועצמים מכם:

---

[128] Note also that verses 23-25aα, 31b-33 of the "Epilogue" of the Covenant Code (Ex 23:20-33) of which Ex 23:27-31 is considered to be a part are generally thought to be Deuteronomic addition (Childs 1974, p. 460).

[129] Cf. Reuter 1993, p. 213 (who holds a critical consensus date), "Die Stilisierung (of Deuteronomy) beinhaltet also zwei Elemente: erstens die Mosefiktion, die Mose als Sprecher des Dtn versteht und zweitens die Historisierung in die Zeit vor der Landnahme".

> For if you will carefully listen to all these
> commandments which I command you to love Yahweh
> your God, to walk in all his ways and to cling to him,
> Yahweh will dispossess all these nations from before
> you, and you will drive away nations greater than you
> and more powerful than you.

The process may be long and difficult, but Yahweh will make
it happen, if the people only trust him. Whereas now, just like the
people of the generation at Moab, the people of the present
generation are doing איש כל־הישר בעיניו, "what is right in their
own eyes" (Dt 12:8), if they start following Yahweh
wholeheartedly, then, in ideal conditions which Yahweh promises
to give as a result, the whole of Israel is to travel to the central
sanctuary and rejoice before Yahweh as one nation. The Priestly
ideal of one nation camped around one sanctuary where Yahweh
dwells in their midst will thus be achieved as much as it is possible,
that is, on three festive occasions a year.

Thus, while ultimately driving towards centralization as an
ideal under peaceful and secure conditions, Deuteronomy also sees
a transitional time when this ideal has not yet been attained. For
Deuteronomy, from a narrative standpoint, this transitional time is
the time when Israel has not yet settled in the land and does not yet
dwell in peace and security. Seen from this viewpoint, it would not
be surprising if Deuteronomy legislates also for the time before the
attainment of complete settlement and peace and security. Then, it
would come as no surprise that Deuteronomy could also legislate
for local altars, and Dt 16:21-22 actually does so:

לא־תטע לך אשרה כל־עץ אצל מזבח יהוה אלהיך
אשר תעשה־לך:
ולא־תקים לך מצבה אשר שנא יהוה אלהיך:

> Do not set up for yourself any wooden Asherah beside
> an altar of Yahweh your God which you make for
> yourself, and do not set for yourself (such) a *massebah*
> which Yahweh your God hates.

Before the settlement is complete, one may erect an altar to
Yahweh.[130] However, one is not to erect an Ashera, a Canaanite

---

[130] In this context, it is interesting that the expression
מזבח יהוה אלהיך in Dt 16:21 occurs also in Dt 12:27, even twice.
According to Dt 12:27, one has to offer burnt offerings on the altar of

cult object, beside an altar of Yahweh. Moreover, one is not to set up for himself a *massebah*, seemingly especially beside an altar, and if one takes the word *massebah* in this context to refer to a cult object which is a locus of the presence of Yahweh (or a locus of the presence of another god, or, of course, even merely a symbol of another god), v. 22 is fully compatible with Ex 20:22-26 and the rest of the Old Testament in its attitude towards *masseboth*.[131]

Moreover, one may ask what is the meaning of Dt 16:21-22 for a later generation far removed from the events of conquest and settlement. Perhaps there is war. Perhaps there is oppression. Perhaps there is famine. Travelling is dangerous. It is very difficult in practice to go to the "place" at all, let alone three times a year. Then, the Israelites are to serve Yahweh and worship at the local altars. Yahweh will meet them there.[132] Then there is the promise: If the people will all serve Yahweh, there will be better times. Yahweh will give peace, prosperity and security, and the people can go up to the chosen place and rejoice at the presence of Yahweh as one nation encamped around the central sanctuary where Yahweh dwells in their midst.

Similarly, one may think that it *could* be that as the Dt 27 altar law (and its counterpart in Josh 8:30-35) refers to the early days of the conquest and settlement, there was not yet any centralization requirement. However, we will examine the matter carefully in Chapter 4.3 below as a part of the examination (in Chapter 1) of how the Old Testament material which portrays the actual history of the premonarchical time understands and interprets centralization.

Thus, both Deuteronomy and the Priestly material advocate a similar view of an ideal Israel. Both see a situation where the

---

Yahweh (מזבח יהוה אלהיך), and similarly one has to pour the blood of his sacrifices (זבחיך; probably referring to *shelamim*) on the altar of Yahweh (מזבח יהוה אלהיך). This then speaks for a common provenance of Dt 12:27 and 16:21. One might even think that the altar spoken in Dt 12:27 also speaks about altars outside the central sanctuary, as 16:21 does. Finally, note that according to Driver 1901, p. 203 (referring to Dillmann), Dt 16:21 "presupposes by its wording ('beside the altar of Jehovah thy God, which thou shalt make thee') the law of Ex 20:24".

[131] Cf. above, Chapter 2.2.2, including p. 63n252.

[132] Cf. above, Chapter 2.2.2.

people of Israel are encamped around the central sanctuary where Yahweh dwells in their midst. The Priestly material sees that, as far as outward conditions are concerned, this ideal was a reality in the camp in the wilderness, and legislates many of its its cultic procedures for the camp.[133] Yet, the Priestly material does not view the situation in the land after the wilderness period from a centralized perspective, but rather sees the land from a perspective where Yahweh is dwelling in the central sanctuary in the midst of the people. For the Priestly material, the central sanctuary is very important, and if possible, people should bring their offerings there at least during the festivals. The fact that even slaughtering had to be done at the tent of meeting in the wilderness enhances the rhetoric for the importance of the central sanctuary. On the other hand, Deuteronomy goes further than the Priestly material as regards centralization. This is clear also from the fact that in Deuteronomy we find as centralized a number of institutions which are not centralized in the Priestly material. Especially, all three yearly feasts are centralized in Deuteronomy (Dt 16). Among these, the most explicit change is attested in regard to the Passover. Whereas the Passover is explicitly decentralized in the Priestly material with accompanying specific legislation (Ex 12-13), the Passover is explicitly centralized in Deuteronomy (Dt 16:1-8). However, all of this is natural if one sees the Priestly material as strongly arguing for the importance of the central sanctuary without however *demanding* centralization, and sees Deuteronomy as advocating centralization as an ultimate goal and ideal. Then, we might describe the Priestly material as *acentralized* in comparison to Deuteronomy which is fully centralized.

The only ostensible exception where the Priestly material is more centralized than Deuteronomy is the matter of profane slaughter. We stated above[134] that it is easy to think that at least from the narrative perspective of the Pentateuch, Deuteronomy relaxes the demand of Lev 17 to slaughter at the central sanctuary all animals which could be offered as *shelamim*.

---

[133] See above, Chapter 3.2 for details.
[134] See above, Chapter 3.2.

In this respect, McConville suggests that "Dt 12.16, 23ff. are references to something already known".[135] According to McConville, "In vv. 15b, 22 (i.e. immediately preceding the regulations on blood prohibition) the law of profane slaughter is exemplified or clarified by reference to the manner of consuming the gazelle and the hart. 'The clean and the unclean may eat of it, *as of the gazelle and as of the hart*. This is clearly a reference to something already known (cf. again 15.22b)."[136] McConville adds, "it is possible that in its allusion to the gazelle and the hart, Deuteronomy has in mind a practice whose legal basis is found in Lev 17.13. Here it is commanded that any beast taken in hunting shall have its blood poured on the ground and covered with dust before consumption."[137]

On the other hand, we may also point out that whereas according to Dt 12:15, 22, both the unclean and the clean (הטמא והטהור) may eat the slaughtered animals, according to Lev 7, an unclean person may *not* eat of *zebah shelamim* (see Lev 7:20-21).[138] Then, with Deuteronomy's allowing profane slaughter, Deuteronomy 12:15, 22 indicates that from now on, the meat which is slaughtered profanely is no more a *zebah shelamim*, and thus both the clean and the unclean may eat it.

Also, if Deuteronomy 12 is based on Lev 17, the injunction of Dt 12:20-22 becomes completely intelligible, as was already indicated in the previous chapter.[139] According to Dt 12:20-22, if a person lived close to the central sanctuary, it would be recommended for him to bring even the animals he would eat profanely to the central sanctuary and to offer them there as *shelamim* before actually eating them. However, Deuteronomy acknowledges that bringing animals to the central sanctuary for slaughtering for food would not be practical for most of the population, as they would live too far away from the central sanctuary. Taken thus, Deuteronomy 12 is perfectly in line with

---

[135] McConville 1984, p. 50.

[136] Ibid. Cf. Milgrom 1991, pp. 9-10.

[137] McConville 1984, p. 50.

[138] Cf. Milgrom 1991, pp. 423-426, according to whom (p. 424; in regard to to Lev 7:20-21), "Once again, one can see that the focus of this pericope is sacred meat for the table".

[139] See above, Chapter 3.2.

Lev 17. If one would bring animals for slaughter to the central sanctuary, it would allow for sacrificing them in the presence of Yahweh, and help the upkeep of the priests.[140] The practice could also be thought to serve as a deterrent against idolatry.[141]

The priority of the Priestly material is supported by Milgrom, who gives a number of reasons for seeing the legislation of D as dependent on that of P (and H).[142] Even if one might contest a number of Milgrom's examples, it is difficult to argue against the idea that Dt 24:8 refers back to the regulations concerning skin disease in Lev 13-14.[143] One should also note that according to Milgrom, "Lev 11 deals with nonsacrificial animals; hence, it does not enumerate the sacrificial ones. D Lists them (Deut 14:4-5) because they no longer need to be sacrificed and must, therefore, be incorporated into P's diet list",[144] even though in this case it

---

[140] However, it has to be noted in this respect that in general, the emphasis on priests in the Priestly material has been transferred to an emphasis on Levites in Deuteronomy, including Deuteronomy 12 (Dt 12:12, 18; 16:11; 18:6-8; but see Dt 18:1-5 for also including priests for consideration).

[141] We should also add here that contrary to Wellhausen and his successors (see Wellhausen 1905/1878, pp. 69-70, 74-75; cf. the review in McConville 1984, pp. 42-44), there is no clear evidence to think that the Covenant Code or any of the historical books see that slaughter was sacrificial at any other time in Israel's history than during the wilderness period. The passage which has often been quoted for the support of such a concept, 1 Sam 14:31-34 (see originally Wellhausen 1905/1878, p. 62, and cf. McConville 1984, pp. 42-44), does not need to be interpreted from a premise that the associated slaughter was a sacrifice. As McConville (1984, p. 46; see also ibid., pp. 44-48) suggests, "the likeliest interpretation of Saul's action is simply that he ensured that a profane slaughter was properly carried out. Consequently, there would be no need to see a sacrifice in the passage." Millard also suggests that if the associated animal was raised above ground level, for which action a rock would have been well suited, this would have helped blood flow out more easily and would thus have helped in draining the blood (A.R. Millard, personal communication, July 1999).

[142] Milgrom 1991, pp. 9-10.

[143] See Milgrom 1991, p. 9.

[144] Milgrom 1991, p. 10; cf. ibid., p. 646. See also Schwartz 1996, pp. 32-35.

could of course also be argued that P does not list the animals in question because they can no more be eaten profanely.

Finally, we should mention that since the terminology of Deuteronomy is in general less exact than Priestly terminology and the amount of detail as to the particulars of sacrifice is less than in the Priestly material, it is often argued that the more refined and detailed material is a later product.[145] However, it is as well possible that, as McConville states, "The sacrificial terminology is used in Dt 12 in a way that could almost be described as non-technical",[146] and that the exact details of the cult are often not a main concern of Deuteronomy.[147]

Thus, we may conclude with Milgrom that, "D overturns the Priestly law (H) that all meat for the table must first be offered up on the altar (17:3-7)",[148] even though we may also add that in their application for life in the land, both legal materials are essentially in agreement in that both would at least be happy if a person slaughtered sacrificially if the central sanctuary were close, and would allow profane slaughter if the central sanctuary were far away.[149] Moreover, there are good grounds for seeing Deuteronomy as dependent on the Priestly material. Then, remembering also that it is entirely conceivable that Deuteronomy draws from the Covenant Code as well, this implies that Deuteronomy is the latest part of the Pentateuch. However, we must add that whereas Deuteronomy is generally seen to be verbally dependent upon the Covenant Code,[150] one cannot speak

---

[145] This is naturally based on the evolutionary view of Wellhausen concerning Israel's history. See Wellhausen 1905/1878.

[146] McConville 1984, p. 55.

[147] Ibid.

[148] Milgrom 1991, p. 9. Cf. Schwartz 1996, p. 27ff., who argues that the whole of the Priestly material prohibits profane slaughter.

[149] The Priestly material has the camp as its frame of reference and thus only implicitly allows profane slaughter in the land, whereas Deuteronomy explicitly allows profane slaughter in the land, with the land as its direct frame of reference. Also, it is necessary for Deuteronomy to explicitly allow profane slaughter because otherwise it would not be clear what to do with the Priestly injunction in conditions of settlement and security when all sacrifices must be brought to the central sanctuary.

[150] See e.g. Levinson 1997, and cf. above, Chapter 2.2.2.

of a verbal dependency between the Priestly material and Deuteronomy.[151]

The mutual order of the Covenant Code and the Priestly material is less clear. However, as we have seen above,[152] the Covenant Code and the Priestly material are complementary with each other as regards the centralization of sacrifices, and this suggests that their mutual order is not all that important.[153] Seeing the matter in this way, the chronological order of the Pentateuchal law codes basically corresponds to their narrative order in the Pentateuch. Moreover, seen from the standpoint of centralization of sacrifices, each of the law codes has its purpose, and the law codes are not mutually contradictory but are complementary with each other. One may think that the law codes have been placed intelligently into the Pentateuchal narrative as a whole. Decentralizing material has been set in the beginning in a form of a covenant (Ex 20-24; cf. Ex 12-13, 34), followed by the regulations concerning the priesthood and the official cult from a context of a wilderness setting (Ex 25-Num), and the whole is concluded by a covenant which looks to the future life in the promised land where the people ideally serve Yahweh, live in peace and prosperity and come together to Yahweh's presence at a central sanctuary (Dt).

---

[151] Cf. Milgrom 1991, p. 9; Milgrom 1976, p. 12.

[152] See above, Chapter 3.2.

[153] In this respect, it is also interesting to note that the Priestly Passover legislation in Ex 12-13 precedes the Covenant Code in narrative order, whereas the rest of the Priestly legislative material comes after the Covenant Code (note however the sandwiching of the renewal of the covenant legislation in Ex 34 between the tabernacle blueprints and the construction of the tabernacle in Ex 25-31; 35-40).

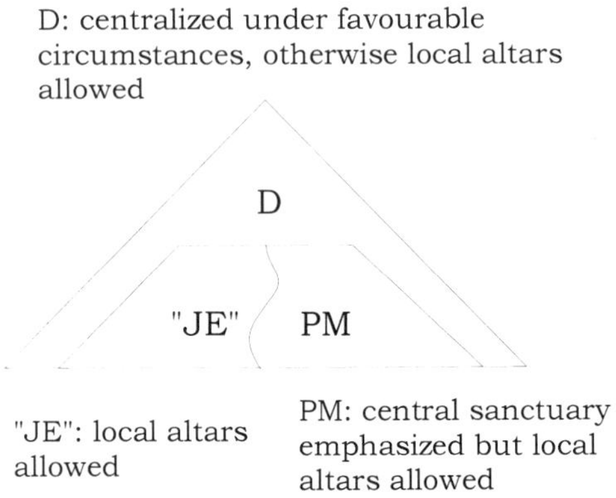

D: centralized under favourable
circumstances, otherwise local altars
allowed

D

"JE"   PM

"JE": local altars
allowed

PM: central sanctuary
emphasized but local
altars allowed

Figure 3: The relationship of pentateuchal altar laws

4. CENTRALIZATION AND THE PERIOD FROM THE SETTLEMENT TO THE BUILDING OF SOLOMON'S TEMPLE

4.1.   Jeremiah 7:12-15 and 26:4-6, 9 and the Role of Shiloh

We have now completed our investigation of general theological ideas which relate to the central sanctuary (Chapter 2) and centralization (Chapter 1). Our next task is to investigate how these ideas were actually reflected in Israel's historical experience of the period between the settlement and the building of Solomon's temple. As a number of Old Testament documents speak about Shiloh at least as an important sanctuary,[1] a central task for us is to clarify the role and significance of Shiloh in the past and its relationship to Jerusalem, the indisputable centre of Israel's religious and political life during the monarchy. As the book of Jeremiah contains a very explicit general theological-historical testimony concerning Shiloh (esp. Jer 7:12), we will start our investigation by an examinination of this testimony. We will also pay special attention to the question of whether the testimony can be considered as historically plausible.

We begin with a brief critical overview. Jeremiah 7:12-15; 26:4-6, 9, the passages in the book of Jeremiah which refer to the role of Shiloh and the relationship of Shiloh to Jerusalem, belong to the so-called temple sermons of Jeremiah, 7:1-15 and 26:1-19. As far as their form is concerned, the temple sermons are classified

---

[1] Cf. above, Introduction.

as belonging to the so-called prose-sermons of Jeremiah.[2] Practically all modern scholars think that the two temple sermons in Jeremiah 7 and 26 are separate accounts of a single event.[3] There is general agreement that 26:2-6 is an abbreviated version of 7:1-15,[4] and that the focus of 26:1-19 is on the reaction of the people to Jeremiah's message.[5]

A major issue with the passages, as with the book of Jeremiah as a whole, is the question of the provenance of the material. How much of the material stems from the prophet himself, and how much comes from later redaction?[6] If, and seemingly as, there is later redaction, what concerns does the later redaction express? The main issue which is relevant to our investigation in this respect

---

[2] Craigie 1991, p. xxxii summarizes and notes (cf. Holladay 1989, pp. 11-12): "There is a considerable variety in the literary forms of the various parts of the book that constitute the whole. Traditionally, three principal types of material have been distinguished, labelled Types A, B, and C, respectively. (The three types were recognized as early as B. Duhm, *Das Buch Jeremia*, 1901, and designated A, B, and C by S. Mowinckel, *Zur Komposition des Buches Jeremia* [Kristiania: J. Dybwad, 1914]). (i) The prophet's oracles, recorded in poetic form, are designated as *Type* A material. (ii) Prose narratives, which are essentially biographical and historical in character, written with references to Jeremiah in the third person, are designated *Type* B material. (iii) Speeches or discourses, which are in prose rather than poetic form, and which have a distinctive literary style, are designated *Type* C material. This threefold classification of the principal literary forms of Jeremiah is useful, though not comprehensive; some materials (e.g., so-called Confessions, commonly labeled Type A) do not easily fit into any of the classifications." Thus, according to this classification, Jer 7:1-15 and 26:1-19 belong to Type C material.

[3] See e.g. Bright 1965, p. 171; Holladay 1974, p. 62; Craigie 1991, p. 119; Scalise 1995, p. 6, McConville 1993a, p. 87. Of the older commentators, Keil and Delitzsch 1983/1861-1865, *Jeremiah*, p. 390 argues that 7:1-15 and 26:1-19 are based on two separate occasions.

[4] See Bright 1965, p. 171; Craigie 1991, p. 119; Scalise 1995, p. 6.

[5] Bright 1965, p. 171; McConville 1993a, p. 87. Carroll 1986, p. 515 however thinks that the "similarities between the edited version of 26 and the temple sermon as presented in 7:1-15" ... "represent strands added to 26 rather than another version of 7:1-15 giving occasion and response". See also Reventlow 1969 for a detailed attempt at a close examination and comparison of Chapters 7 and 26.

[6] See Holladay 1989, p. 10.

is that many passages in the book of Jeremiah attest a number of features which have close affinities with Deuteronomic style, language and theology,[7] and that for this reason they have often been seen to be the product of a Deuteronomistic redaction.[8] In fact, the book of Jeremiah, which portrays Jeremiah's ministry as starting from the 13th year of King Josiah (Jer 1:2), has often been seen as having connections with the reform of Josiah, or even as a mouthpiece of the reform.[9] This question of the relationship of the book of Jeremiah to the reform of Josiah is an important one, since according to de Wette and subsequent scholarship, the book of Deuteronomy was written to centralize all sacrifices to Jerusalem, and "the place which Yahweh will choose to let his name dwell there" is a veiled reference to Jerusalem.

However, although there are Deuteronomic features in the book of Jeremiah, and the problem of its relationship to the reform of Josiah is an important question, on the other hand it can be very quickly and unequivocally replied that there is no evidence that the book has *direct* connections with the reform of Josiah. As McConville points out,

> Indeed, when we begin to consider the Jeremiah prose on a broader canvas, and in the context of the whole book, it becomes apparent that serious problems attach to the view that Jeremiah is presented as a mouthpiece of the Josianic reform. First, Jeremiah is scarcely depicted as a believer in the need to centralize the worship of Israel in the Jerusalem temple.[10] At two prominent points in the book (though the reference

---

[7] See Holladay 1989, pp. 53-64; cf. Weinfeld 1972, pp. 359-361.

[8] Holladay 1989, p. 53.

[9] See McConville 1993a, pp. 11-26 for a detailed discussion of the issues involved.

[10] Cf. also the comment by Weinfeld (1964, p. 209n35): "Even Jeremiah does not make explicit mention of the centralization of the cult though he deeply admired Josiah (Jer 22:15-16) and had to all indications supported the reform (Jer 11:1-8). It seems that he did not regard the centralization of the cult as an end in itself but considered it only to be the means for purifying the cult. Thus Jeremiah does not speak of the sin of the high places but only of the sin of paganism and religious synchretism. In other words he considered the innovations affecting *Kultusreinheit* more important than those affecting *Kultuseinheit*."

may be to a single event) he boldly castigates the
practices there (7:1-15; 26:1-6). Second, there is no
explicit statement of his support for the reform. The
problem arising from the fact that his call to prophesy
is dated after the beginning of the reform,[11] and that he
is said to have prophesied continuously for twenty-
three years up to the fourth year of Jehoiakim (605
BC), with only scant praise at that for King Josiah, has
long been recognized. Conversely, there is no mention
of Jeremiah in Kings, though like *Jeremiah* it covers the
period up to the exile. This mutual coolness towards
the two major figures in the respective works, though
they treat the same theme and the same period, gives
pause to the supposition that they emanate from similar
or identical circles.[12]

In other words, if Deuteronomy was written to centralize all
worship to Jerusalem, the book of Jeremiah does not share such
concerns.

Moreover, the book of Jeremiah even explicitly states that
Shiloh was formerly the place where Yahweh let his name dwell:

כי לכו־נא אל־מקומי אשר בשילו אשר שכנתי שמי
שם בראשונה

But go now to my place in Shiloh where I formerly set
my name to dwell (Jer 7:12)

Thus, according to Jeremiah, there already existed a place
where Yahweh's name dwelt before Jerusalem. In other words,
Jeremiah did not think that the 'chosen place' refers to Jerusalem
only, and this provides further corroboration that the book of
Deuteronomy could refer to other places than Jerusalem as the

---

[11] Provided that, as McConville (1993a) notes in backnote 32, p. 184,
one follows the Chronicler's dating of the events. (Josiah started reform in
his eight year [2 Chr 34:3], Jeremiah started prophesying in the 13th year
of Josiah [Jer 1:2])

[12] McConville 1993a, p. 19. McConville also points out that the hope
for future for Judah is different in Jeremiah from that in DtH (ibid., pp.
19-20; see his book elsewhere as well for more details of this complex
question of hope, even though according to McConville, one can broadly
say that there is more hope expressed in Jeremiah than in DtH).

chosen place, and thus undermines the idea that Deuteronomy was written to centralize worship to Jerusalem.[13]

In this respect, practically all scholars who comment on Jer 7:12-15 and 26:4-6, 9 agree that Shiloh was an important sanctuary in the premonarchic period, and that Jeremiah's speech refers to the premonarchic sanctuary.[14] This conclusion is based on the presentation of Shiloh in 1 Sam 1-4, Judges 18:31, and Josh 18:1; 19:51; 22:9-34 which portray Shiloh at least as an important sanctuary, if not the central sanctuary of all Israel during the premonarchical period, and on the other hand the fact that the books of Kings indicate that Jerusalem became the chosen place after the building of the temple of Solomon (1 Ki 8:16, 29, 44).

That Jeremiah's speech refers to the premonarchic sanctuary is also consistent with archaeological finds at Tell Seilun[15] which

---

[13] Cf above, Introduction, p. 10. Schley goes as far as to say that, "Indeed, the tradition that Shiloh had been 'the place where Yahweh caused his name to dwell' appears to have been an important ingredient of the theology of the cultic community in Jerusalem" (Schley 1989, p. 173)

[14] See e.g. Holladay 1986, p. 248; Haag 1990, p. 99n20; McConville 1993, p. 45; Craigie 1991, pp. 121-122; Scalise 1995, pp. 16-18; Eissfeldt 1956, p. 146; Schley 1989, p. 173; Bright 1965, p. 171; Carroll 1986, p. 210; Day 1979, p 89; Eichrodt 1950, p. 19; Pearce 1973, p. 107. Day (1979, pp. 90-91) gives good reasons why a monarchic date as the frame of reference for Jeremiah (and Ps 78) cannot be maintained (arguing against van Rossum). Cf. also above, Introduction, p. 11.

[15] See Finkelstein 1986; Finkelstein 1988, pp. 205-234; I. Finkelstein, ed., *Shiloh: The Archaeology of a Biblical Site*, Tel Aviv: Institute of Archaeology of Tel Aviv University, 1993. According to Finkelstein (1988, p. 206; cf. Finkelstein 1993a, pp. 1-4), the identification of Tell Seilun with Shiloh is very plausible because of the directions in Jdg 21:19, because of a reference to the location by the 4th century AD *Onomasticon* of Eusebius and because of the name Seilun of the village which stood at the site until 16th century AD and of the adjacent spring. Also, according to Finkelstein (1988, p. 206), "the excavated remains accord with the history of Shiloh as reflected in the written sources". One should however note that Richardson (Richardson 1927) intriguingly suggested based on the variation of spelling in the name Shiloh in the Old Testament that there were originally two Shilohs, Tell Seilun and Beit Sila, and that Beit Sila which is located in the territory of Benjamin fairly close to Jerusalem was the location of the tent of meeting. Richardson was bluntly rejected by Albright (Albright 1927 in the same issue of *PEFQS* as Richardson), and

indicate that Shiloh was an important centre in Iron Age I. As Finkelstein describes:

> We found remains from Iron Age I virtually everywhere we dug. From this period we discovered buildings, stone-lined silos and other remains.[16]

Moreover,

> As for the regional settlement pattern, our survey indicates that population density in the immediate vicinity of Shiloh was two and even three times greater than at other places in the territory of Ephraim. Some 100 sites of Israelite settlement have been found so far in our survey, of which 22 are apparently within a radius of about three to four miles of Shiloh. By comparison, in a similar radius around Bethel, only 12 sites from this period were discovered; moreover, as far as we can tell, at least half of these settlements near Shiloh began at a later phase of Iron Age I, when the site reached its zenith. It is clear, then, that the density of population in the region was influenced by the cultic and economic center of Shiloh.[17]

Furthermore, based on archaeological finds, Shiloh was seemingly at least a religious centre in the Late Bronze Age. According to Finkelstein,

> Data from all over the tell indicate that there was no real settlement at Shiloh during the Late Bronze Age. Instead, on the summit of the tell, there was probably an isolated cultic place to which offerings were brought by people from various places in the region. The fact that there were very few permanent Late Bronze sites anywhere in the vicinity of Shiloh may indicate that many of these people lived in pastoral groups, in temporary dwellings. It is probable that these offerings, many of them Late Bronze I (15th century B.C.) in date, were brought to the site of the destroyed Middle Bronze Age sanctuary, which may even have been reconstructed. The steadily declining amount of pottery indicates a decrease in activity at the site, and then a

---

the matter has not been raised since (see Schley 1989, pp. 67-68; cf. Finkelstein 1993a, p. 4).

[16] Finkelstein 1986, p. 36.

[17] Ibid., p. 40.

complete cessation, apparently before the end of the Late Bronze Age.[18]

On the other hand, Iron II remains from Shiloh are less prominent. According to Finkelstein, "Following a period of abandonment, a small village, the poor remains of which were found in several places, occupied the site in Iron Age II (tenth to eighth centuries B.C.)".[19] Moreover, according to Finkelstein, a few structures have also been found on the flat area immediately to the north of the tell from the end of the Iron Age.[20]

Thus, according to Jer 7:12, Shiloh was the central sanctuary where Yahweh's name dwelt in the premonarchical period, and the reference is backed up by archaeological finds. On the other hand, as the reference to Shiloh in the book of Jeremiah as the place where Yahweh's name dwelt is very late in comparison with the premonarchical period (some 500 years), one could easily claim that even though Shiloh was an important sanctuary in the premonarchical time, the concept of the dwelling of the name of Yahweh itself is much later, especially as a part of the book of Deuteronomy.[21] However, there are reasons to think that the expression of the dwelling of one's name *may* date from much earlier than the time of Jeremiah. As has often been pointed out, the Akkadian expression *sakan sumsu* occurs in the Amarna letters. According to EA 287:60-63, "Behold, the king has set his name in the land of Jerusalem; so he cannot abandon the lands of Jerusalem."[22] According to Wenham,

> The phrase also occurs in other texts dealing with conquests, and is often associated with the erection of a stele or other victory monument. An inscription of

---

[18] Ibid., pp. 35-36.

[19] Ibid., p. 41.

[20] Finkelstein 1988, p. 228. According to Finkelstein (ibid.), these were excavated by Yeivin. Note also that Hellenistic, Roman and Byzantine remains were found in the Shiloh excavations (see Finkelstein 1986; Finkelstein 1988; Finkelstein, ed. [1993], *Shiloh* [see above, p. 115n15 for the reference]).

[21] Thus critical consensus.

[22] Wenham 1971a, p. 113; repeated in Wenham 1993, p. 103, also pointing out EA 288:5-7 for comparison (English translation of both also in *ANET*, p. 488; see KNUDTZON, pp. 866, 868 for the Akkadian).

Shamshi-Adad I of Assyria[23] reads: 'Thus I placed my great name and my (victory) stele in the land of Lebanon on the shore of the Great Sea.' Likewise Yahdunlim of Mari describes himself as 'one who erects stelae, mentioning (his) name' (*mu-re-ti na-re-e na-bi šu-mi* 1:22). Later in the same inscription in the context of reducing his enemies to vassalship, he says 'he established his name' (*šu-mi-šu iš-ta-ka-an* 2:20). Shalmaneser III on his expeditions to the West also erected stelae probably near the sanctuaries on Mounts Carmel and Lebanon.[24]

Wenham continues:

> More recently it has been pointed out that this phraseology is often associated with the inscribing of a name on the foundation stones of sanctuaries. The inscription of the name was essential to the validity of a temple. If this is the background of the Hebrew phrase, we could regard 'to make his name to dwell there' as the etymological equivalent of Akkadian (*šakānum šumam*) and 'to put his name there' as the semantic equivalent.[25]

Moreover, there are good reasons to think that Deuteronomic tradition could have spanned a much longer time than is often thought. If one looks at the ancient Near Eastern literary tradition outside Israel, there are many well-known cases where on one hand, literary style has demonstrably been maintained for many hundreds of years, and on the other hand, literary products have been transmitted for well over a millennium. As Niehaus summarizes,

> In Assyria one can now see a literary tradition which used the same stock phrasing from the time of Shamshi-Adad I to that of Ashurbanipal, a span of some 1200 years which included some 1100 years during which Akkadian had not been supplanted as a living language. Some of the stock phrasing was

---

[23] Dated 19th-18th centuries BC.

[24] Wenham 1971a, p. 113; repeated in Wenham 1993, pp. 103-104.

[25] Wenham 1971a, pp. 113-114; repeated in Wenham 1993, p. 104. Cf. Weinfeld 1972, pp. 193-195, who thinks that the phrase שם שכן in Deuteronomy was taken in by the Deuteronomist and applied by him for his specific theological purposes.

employed even several centuries earlier than Shamshi-Adad I, as has been shown. Moreover, it is fair to say that the Assyrian royal literary tradition got a start with the inscriptions of this king. It achieved a more complete crystallization with the annals of Tiglath-pileser I, in which a style was established and a precedent set for Assyrian annals from that time on, to the end of the Assyrian empire. Every indication is that that style would have continued for many centuries more had the empire itself not collapsed, since many of the stock phrases continued in use in Babylonian and Persian inscriptions of later date.[26]

Niehaus points out a further related example. According to Niehaus, "There is good evidence from the ancient Near East for the practice of depositing written materials in temples, as well as evidence for their rediscovery, and the re-use of stock phraseology stimulated by that rediscovery."[27] Niehaus presents evidence which suggests that Arik-din-ili (1319-1308) quotes almost verbatim phraseology deposited by Shamshi-Adad I (1814-1782). Shamshi-Adad I states, "When the temple becomes delapidated and any of the kings, my offspring, renovates the temple, may he anoint my clay inscriptions and steles with oil, offer sacrifice, and return them to their place".[28] Arik-din-ili, after some 500 years, says correspondingly, "May a future prince, when this temple becomes dilapidated and he renovates it, - may he anoint my steles with oil, bring a sacrifice, and return them to their place".[29] According to Niehaus, the phraseology does not occur in any of the inscriptions of the Assyrian kings between Shamshi-Adad I and Arik-din-ili,[30] and further, according to Niehaus, "Borger remarks that this inscription contains other elements that only appeared previously in the Shamshi-Adad inscription, which suggests that Arik-din-ili discovered the earlier king's inscription and adopted its formulaic

---

[26] Niehaus 1985, p. 413. It has to be stressed that the campaign reports of the Assyrian kings are stylistically very similar from the time of Tiglath-pileser I (ca. 1115-1077 BC) till the 7th century BC (see Niehaus 1985, *passim*; Younger 1990, pp. 79-115).

[27] Niehaus 1992, p. 27.

[28] Quoted by Niehaus (1992, p. 27).

[29] Quoted by Niehaus (1992, p. 28).

[30] Niehaus 1992, p. 28.

phrasing for his own."[31] Furthermore, Niehaus points out that Arik-din-ili adds the phrase "Shamash will then hear his prayers" to the stock phrase.[32] Finally, Niehaus gives examples of how two subsequent kings, Adad-Nirari I (1307-1275) and Shalmaneser I (1274-1245) themselves use and further modify as needed the phraseology of their predecessors.[33]

Thus, these Assyrian examples, besides showing that stock phraseology and literary style could stay alive for centuries and that stock phraseology could reappear even if it had been lost for centuries, also show that a stock phrase does not have to be reproduced verbatim, but it can be modified, expanded, or abridged.[34] On the other hand, we must add that if one examines the annals of Tiglath-pileser I and compares the Prism Inscription of Tiglath-pileser I with the Tenth Regnal Year Inscription of Tiglath-pileser I, one can see that there can also be reasonable variation of style within a single literary work, or between two literary works which are contemporaneous and mutually related.[35]

It is also well known in the ancient Near East that literary products themselves can generally be copied and and thus maintained for centuries. One parade example of this is the congregational lament 'Oh Angry Sea' quoted above, whose text has been reconstructed from various tablets dating from Old Babylonian to Seleucid times.[36] Also, Hallo points out that a number of *ershemmas* (tambourine laments) which were "probably" composed under the first dynasty of Babylon (early second millennium BC) still recur in copies of the first millennium.[37] Hallo

---

[31] Ibid.

[32] Ibid.

[33] Ibid., pp. 28-29.

[34] Cf. Niehaus 1992, p. 28.

[35] See Niehaus 1985, pp. 156-158, 165-190. Variations between the Prism Inscription of Tiglath-pileser I and the Tenth Regnal Year Inscription of Tiglath-pileser I also include additions, omissions, not following strict chronology, prolepsis, and numerical and factual discrepancies (see ibid., pp. 158-161, 191-201).

[36] Some 30 tablets and fragments; see Kutscher 1975, esp. pp. 8-14. Lines 62-72 quoted above, p. 49. See also e.g. Hallo 1996a, pp. 224-228 for more examples.

[37] Hallo 1996a, pp. 225-226; 1996b, pp. 1872-1873.

adds that new compositions of the genre of *ershemmas* appeared in the first millennium with copying, and perhaps even composition of these new *ershemmas* extending to the first century BC.[38] More examples could be cited.[39]

Then, the significance of the above examples is obvious as regards the relationship of the book of Jeremiah to the book of Deuteronomy. First of all, even though there is variation in the centralization formula,[40] it does not have to be taken as an indication of an evolutionary prehistory for the formula. Rather, it could simply be due to stylistic, and even chance variation.[41] Secondly, it could well be that even if Deuteronomic phraseology, including a reference to the chosen place, was not much used for a

---

[38] Hallo 1996a, p. 226; 1996b, p. 1873. Hallo (1996a, 1996b loc. cit.) also points out that the first millennium compositions often include an interlinear translation into Akkadian. Cf. also Cooper 1983, pp. 11-12, "The discovery of Abu Salabikh versions of compositions otherwise attested only in manuscripts written 700 years later, in the Old Babylonian period, has shaken the confidence of scholars in the common-sense approach to Sumerian literary history that for so long dominated Assyriological studies: 'Die archaische fassung ... zeigt überdies, dass gerade ein Passus, der zunächst einen terminus post quem für die Datierung zu bieten schien, entweder selbst eine Modernisierung und also für die Datierung unerheblich sein kann, oder dass vielmehr eine Wendung, die erstmalig in einem Überlieferungsbereich der Periode X bezeugt und da offenbar beliebt ist, sehr wohl schon vor der Periode X, nur eben in einem anderen Überlieferungsbereich, existiert sein kann.'" (quoting Krecher).

[39] See e.g. Hallo 1996b; cf. also K.A. Kitchen, *NBD*, pp. 349-350 regarding the transmission of Egyptian literary works through the centuries, including noting that, demonstrably, revision of the grammar, spelling and/or vocabulary of an ancient text occasionally took place during copying, reflecting the usage of the later generation.

[40] See esp. Lohfink 1991, p. 151, Table 1 for the various forms of the formula in Deuteronomy.

[41] Cf. also Lohfink 1991 for a criticism from another angle of attempts to see diachronic development in Deuteronomy's centralization formula, and Weippert 1980, p. 79: "Die Schwierigkeiten beginnen, sobald man versucht, die einzelnen Stufen der Formel auf die sukzessiven Etappen der Entstehungsgeschichte des Deuteronomiums zu verteilen, um so ihnen jeweiligen Ort in der altisraelitischen Glaubensgeschichte zu ermitteln."

couple of centuries before Josiah when many prophetic books were written,[42] and on the other hand, the seventh-sixth centuries BC which coincided with the time of the finding of the law-book by king Josiah were a time of a great popularity of Deuteronomic phraseology, the book of Deuteronomy goes back to an earlier time. In this respect, if the hypothesis of the Deuteronomistic history were seen to not be correct, but the books of Deuteronomy-Joshua are rather individual compositions,[43] it is conceptually possible, and in fact logical to think that the individual books may have been composed at different times in a Deuteronomic style, a style which was current in Israelite historiography even for centuries.[44] Moreover, as the historical books Joshua-Kings are centred around the theme of how Israel fared in respect to their relationship with Yahweh, the theme of the covenant is very important in them,[45] and this would naturally point to the book of Deuteronomy, and thus similarly, it would be natural to use Deuteronomic expressions and style in Israelite historical writing.[46]

Thus, there are good reasons for why the late reference in Jeremiah *could* be based on an early tradition about Shiloh as the place where Yahweh's name dwelt. Naturally, the question of how far back the tradition *actually* goes about Shiloh as the place where Yahweh's name dwelt must be left open based on the testimony of the book of Jeremiah. In this respect, one should also note that the questions of the relationship between Chapters 7 and 26 and their possible redactional history do not much affect the interpretation

---

[42] Note however especially that the Deuteronomic name formula occurs in Isa 18:7, even if the verse and the formula are often seen as a later addition (see Wildberger 1997, pp. 223-225; Kaiser 1974, pp. 96-97; Gray 1912, p. 316).

[43] See Westermann 1994 for this; see also below, Chapters 4.5 and 4.6.

[44] Cf. Niehaus 1985, pp. 414-415.

[45] Cf. also the Tukulti-Ninurta Epic for an Ancient Near Eastern text which interprets history through a covenant (see FOSTER, pp. 211-229 for the text of the epic; cf. also above, p. 33 for a quotation from the epic; cf. also Niehaus 1985, p. 336).

[46] So Niehaus 1985, pp. 339-341. See below, Chapter 4.2f. for special considerations of the relationship of the Priestly style and Priestly material with Joshua-Kings.

of the tradition of the "place" in Jer 7:12. Even if the tradition of the dwelling of Yahweh's name at Shiloh is part of, say, a separate Deuteronomistic redaction, it does not make much difference to the interpretation of the tradition, as the Deuteronomistic redaction may rely on a tradition which originates from an earlier time. Moreover, since the references to Shiloh in the book of Jeremiah are very late in comparison with the premonarchical time, putting the writing of the Shiloh tradition in Jeremiah or parts of it, say, a hundred years later does not make much difference.

Then, besides stating that it was formerly the place where Yahweh let his name dwell, what does the book of Jeremiah actually say about Shiloh to its exilic audience? According to Jer 7:12-15,

כִּי לְכוּ־נָא אֶל־מְקוֹמִי אֲשֶׁר בְּשִׁילוֹ אֲשֶׁר שִׁכַּנְתִּי שְׁמִי
שָׁם בָּרִאשׁוֹנָה וּרְאוּ אֵת אֲשֶׁר־עָשִׂיתִי לוֹ מִפְּנֵי רָעַת עַמִּי
יִשְׂרָאֵל:
וְעַתָּה יַעַן עֲשׂוֹתְכֶם אֶת־כָּל־הַמַּעֲשִׂים הָאֵלֶּה נְאֻם־יְהוָה
וָאֲדַבֵּר אֲלֵיכֶם הַשְׁכֵּם וְדַבֵּר וְלֹא שְׁמַעְתֶּם וָאֶקְרָא
אֶתְכֶם וְלֹא עֲנִיתֶם:
וְעָשִׂיתִי לַבַּיִת אֲשֶׁר נִקְרָא־שְׁמִי עָלָיו אֲשֶׁר אַתֶּם בֹּטְחִים
בּוֹ וְלַמָּקוֹם אֲשֶׁר־נָתַתִּי לָכֶם וְלַאֲבוֹתֵיכֶם כַּאֲשֶׁר עָשִׂיתִי
לְשִׁלוֹ:
וְהִשְׁלַכְתִּי אֶתְכֶם מֵעַל פָּנָי כַּאֲשֶׁר הִשְׁלַכְתִּי
אֶת־כָּל־אֲחֵיכֶם אֵת כָּל־זֶרַע אֶפְרָיִם:

(7:12) But walk now to my place in Shiloh where I formerly set my name to dwell and see what I did to it because of the evil of my people Israel. (7:13) And now, because you have been doing all these things, says the Lord, and I have spoken to you from early on and you have not listened, and I called to you but you did not answer, (7:14) I will do to the house which is called by my name and in which you trust and to the place which I gave to you and your fathers as I did to Shiloh (7:15) And I will send you away from my presence as I sent away all your brothers, the whole people of Ephraim.

Moreover, according to Jer 26:9 (from the standpoint of our purposes, Jer 26:4-6 essentially reproduces Jer 7:12-15),

מַדּוּעַ נִבֵּיתָ בְשֵׁם־יְהוָה לֵאמֹר כְּשִׁלוֹ יִהְיֶה הַבַּיִת הַזֶּה
וְהָעִיר הַזֹּאת תֶּחֱרַב מֵאֵין יוֹשֵׁב וַיִּקָּהֵל כָּל־הָעָם
אֶל־יִרְמְיָהוּ בְּבֵית יְהוָה:

> Why do you prophesy in the name of the Lord saying:
> This house will become like Shiloh and this city will
> become desolate, without inhabitants? And all people
> gathered around Jeremiah in the house of Yahweh.

Scholars agree that, in the book of Jeremiah, Shiloh is an object lesson of what will happen to Jerusalem. Just as Shiloh or at least its sanctuary lies in ruins, Jerusalem will be destroyed.[47] The temple by itself (Jer 7:4) and the status of Jerusalem as Yahweh's chosen place is not a guarantee of safety and prosperity.[48] The words which were essentially rejected by Jeremiah's contemporaries (see Jer 26:10-24) must on the other hand have been especially poignant to the exilic audience of the book of Jeremiah for whom the destruction of the temple was an experienced reality.

Then, if Jeremiah refers to the ruins of Shiloh, was there a specific event which produced these ruins and to which Jeremiah refers or alludes? A number of scholars think that the reference is to a destruction of Shiloh or its sanctuary in association with the loss of the ark at Aphek in about 1050 during the premonarchical time as depicted in 1 Sam 4, or at least to a destruction otherwise in the 11th century.[49] On the other hand, some scholars think that there was no destruction of Shiloh in the eleventh century, or at least the reference is to the destruction of Shiloh at the time of the fall of the Northern Kingdom by the Assyrians in 721 BC.[50] Some think that there is a double reference to two destructions, in the eleventh and in the seventh century.[51] It also has to be added that the texts outside the Jeremiah passages under consideration in fact do not mention directly a destruction of Shiloh either in the 11th or 8th century BC.

However, archaeological evidence is suggestive of an 11th century date of destruction. According to Finkelstein, in area C (in

---

[47] Pearce 1973, pp. 107-108; Holt 1986, p. 75; Schley 1989, p. 200; Day 1979, p. 94; Eissfeldt 1956, p. 139; Carroll 1986, p. 210; Bright 1965, p. 170; Holladay 1974, p. 66; Scalise 1995, p. 18.

[48] So practically all commentators.

[49] Day 1979, p. 94; Bright 1965, p. 170; Holladay 1974, p. 66; Eissfeldt 1956, p. 139; Carroll 1986, p. 210. Note also that this would fit with the idea that the Elide priesthood and the tent of meeting are later found at Nob (1 Sam 21-22; cf. above, p. 64).

[50] Pearce 1973, pp. 107-108; Schley 1989, pp. 200-201.

[51] Craigie 1991, p. 122; Haag 1990, p. 99n20.

the western part of the tell) where the Danish excavations already had discovered a destruction layer,[52] further excavations uncovered more evidence of a destruction of a building complex (Buildings 312 and 335) from Iron Age I.[53] Finkelstein describes, "These buildings were destroyed in a fierce conflagration. Burnt floors were found all over. Collapsed burnt bricks accumulated on these floors to a height of more than three feet. Some of the bricks had been baked by the blaze that had raged here. Roof collapse was discernible in many places."[54] Finkelstein also found carbonized raisins in one of the rooms of Building 335 and interpreted these as further evidence of a destruction.[55] Moreover, according to Finkelstein, "The accumulated debris on top of the brick collapse in the northern part of Building 335 contained a large quantity of animal bones and Iron I pottery."[56]

As far as pottery is concerned, Finkelstein describes,

> Chronologically the Shiloh assemblage falls between the early Iron I strata of 'Izbeth Sartah III, Giloh and Mt Ebal and the late 11th-10th century strata of 'Izbeth Sartah II-I and Kh. ed-Dawwara. It still has some of the features of the 12th century sites, such as cooking-pots with everted rims and the 'Canaanite jar', but the proportion of the early types in the assemblage is relatively small compared to the early Iron I sites. In dating the Shiloh assemblage one should consider both the existence of late Iron I vessels and the absence (or limited number) of typical late 11th-10th century types, such as cooking pots with thickened ridge, Philistine

---

[52] For the history of these, see Finkelstein 1988, pp. 207-210. However, the Danish excavations left the stratigraphy of the site ambiguous (see ibid., p. 208; Schley 1989, p. 77).

[53] See Finkelstein 1988, pp. 207-212, 220-225; Finkelstein 1986, pp. 36-38, including Finkelstein 1988, p. 209 for a map of the mound, and Finkelstein 1986, p. 37 for a drawing of the layout of the buildings 312 and 335.

[54] Finkelstein 1986, p. 39. Cf. Bunimovitz 1993, p. 24, Fig. 2.10. for a photograph of the destruction debris in Building 335, and ibid., p. 22, Fig. 2.7 for Building 312.

[55] See Finkelstein 1988, p. 226 Fig. 74; Finkelstein 1986, pp. 38-39.

[56] Finkelstein 1988, p. 226. Note that on the other hand, very few pottery were found in the debris of Building 312 (Bunimovitz 1993, p. 21).

sherds, slipped and burnished material, baseless round
cooking jugs [of a certain type], etc.[57]

Moreover:

> Within the Iron I material in Shiloh, Debris 623
> [overlaying building 335] seems to be slightly later than
> the assemblage found in the pillared buildings.
> Stratigraphically this is clear, although one could claim
> that the material which was dumped on the slope [area
> C, and thus building 335 is located on a slope] came
> from an earlier source, such as a *favissa* of offerings
> which were dumped to a temple. However, the
> somewhat later date for debris 623 seems to be
> confirmed by the quantitative analysis of the Shiloh
> material. Especially important is the proportion of
> cooking-pots with everted rim, and the fact that the
> two types of later pithoi and slipped sherds were found
> only in this debris. Nevertheless, the time difference
> between the two assemblages seems to be very limited
> and neither has the types typical of the 10th century
> BC.[58]

Finkelstein interpreted these finds as fitting with the
destruction of Shiloh by the Philistines in the eleventh century, in
association with the events of 1 Sam 4-6.[59] Of course, one might
object that it is difficult to pinpoint evidence to a specific date, and,
on the other hand, that no evidence exists which could indicate
who might have caused the destruction. However, the evidence
provided by Finkelstein (et al.) makes the idea of an 11th century
destruction of Shiloh, or at least parts of it, by the Philistines in
connection to the events of 1 Sam 4-6 very possible. In this
respect, we should also note that no destruction layers which could
be attributed to Iron Age II have been found from the poor
remains of Iron Age II.[60]

In any case, judging from Jer 7:12-15; 26:6, 9 and the
archaeological evidence, the city apparently was in ruins or at least
in a poor condition in Jeremiah's time. Also, whatever the total

---

[57] Bunimovitz and Finkelstein 1993, p. 162.

[58] Ibid.

[59] Bunimovitz and Finkelstein 1993, p. 162; cf. Finkelstein 1986, p. 39;
Finkelstein 1988, p. 226.

[60] See Bunimovitz 1993, p. 31; Finkelstein 1993b; Finkelstein 1988, p.
228; Finkelstein 1986, p. 41.

process which resulted in the state of affairs during Jeremiah's time, the book of Jeremiah states at least that the same end result would befall Jerusalem unless the people mend their ways.

Then, if Shiloh was formerly an important centre and sanctuary and the place where Yahweh's name dwelt but suffered destruction and decline due to the sins of the people of Israel (וראו את אשר־עשיתי לו מפני רעת עמי ישראל; Jer 7:12), this suggests that Yahweh had abandoned Shiloh.[61] On the other hand, as Jerusalem was the place where Yahweh's name dwelt at the time of Jeremiah, this suggests that, more specifically, Shiloh had been rejected and Jerusalem had taken its place. To this matter and its implications we will now turn.

4.2. Psalm 78:56-72 and the Intermediate Period from the Disaster of Aphek to the Building of Solomon's Temple

In this chapter, our primary aim is to understand what Ps 78:56-72 says about the mutual historical and theological relationship of Shiloh and Jerusalem, especially for the reason that Psalm 78:56-72 at least at first sight seems to speak about a rejection of Shiloh (vv. 60, 67) and a choice of Jerusalem (v. 68), and on the other hand clearly refers to historical events. In order to understand the message of Ps 78:56-72, we will make a detailed exegesis of the passage, comparing and correlating the events which are described in it and their interpretation with available parallel sources of Israelite historiography. As a preliminary for a verse-by-verse exegesis, we will examine such issues as the genre, structure, date and provenance of the psalm and their implications for the message and historical plausibility of the psalm.

Overall, Psalm 78 recounts the events of Israel's history from the Exodus until the reigns of David and Solomon. It is similar in content to Psalms 105 and 106, and can most conveniently be classified as a historical psalm along with these psalms.[62] Above all, the purpose of the psalm is to present a theological interpretation

---

[61] Cf. above, Chapter 2.1 for the concepts of divine temple abandonment in the ancient Near East.

[62] Westermann 1981a/1961-1977, p. 236 sees Exod 15, Deut 32, and Isa 63:7-14 as historical psalms as well.

of Israel's history where God is working in that history.[63]
Moreover, for Ps 78, this theological presentation of history has an
expressly didactic purpose.[64] The psalmist mixes an account of
God's wonders and Israel's faithlessness so that his hearers and the
future generation would trust God and follow God's ways and not
make the same mistakes as their ancestors have (vv. 3-8). The title
maskil (מַשְׂכִּיל)[65] of the psalm and the expression אֶפְתְּחָה בְמָשָׁל פִּי,
"Let me open my mouth in proverbs" in v. 2 suggest a clear
connection of the psalm with wisdom motifs.[66] The psalm also has
hymnic and meditative features in it.[67]

The expressly didactic aim of the psalm and its use of wisdom
motifs are the main reason why there has been much disagreement
among scholars as to what is its exact genre. However, as Tate
expresses it, "Most commentators agree on the general nature of Ps
78, although they use different terms to identify its form".[68]

The structure of the psalm has slightly puzzled scholars, and
various alternatives have been set forth.[69] However, it is clear that
vv. 1-11 are a "wisdom" introduction,[70] and commentators agree
that verses 65-72 are a coherent section.[71] Also, most
commentators take the psalm as a unity, even though there are
exceptions.[72] One peculiarity of the psalm is that the events it

---

[63] Cf. Westermann 1981a/1961-1977, pp. 214-249.

[64] See e.g. Carroll 1971, p. 133, Westermann 1981a/1961-1977, pp. 237-238.

[65] Even though this title might be a later addition. Even if so, this would confirm that the later readers of the psalm saw it as incorporating wisdom motifs.

[66] Kidner (1975, p. 281) reminds that "the word for *parable* (*māšāl*) gives the book of Proverbs its title".

[67] Campbell 1979, p. 51; Tate 1990, p. 284.

[68] Tate 1990, p. 284.

[69] See Clifford 1981, pp. 127-129 (esp. p. 127n7) and Tate 1990, pp. 287-288.

[70] See Clifford 1981, p. 127.

[71] See Clifford 1981, p. 129.

[72] Schreiner distinguishes an original psalm of praise for Yahweh which has been later reworked by adding the introductory section and the parts which criticize the faithless conduct of the people (Schreiner 1990, pp. 312-321). Haag divides Ps 78 into a core ("Grundschicht") and later addition ("Bearbeitung"), where the *Grundschicht* refers back to the

recounts are not in a strict chronological order. However, this feature can most naturally be taken as a rhetorical device, and if one distinguishes two cycles of historical recitals in the psalm, the structure of the poem starts to emerge. Then, according to Clifford, whose opinion seems most judicious,[73] the psalm can be structured as follows.[74]

Introduction: vv. 1-11

First Recital:	*Second Recital:*
Wilderness Events vv. 12-32	*From Egypt to Canaan* vv. 40-64
Gracious act (vv. 12-16)	Gracious act (vv. 44-55)
Rebellion (vv. 17-20)	Rebellion (vv. 56-58)
Divine anger and	Divine anger and
punishment (vv. 21-32)	punishment (vv. 59-64)
(manna and quail)	(destruction of Shiloh)
Sequel vv. 33-39	*Sequel* vv. 65-72

Figure 4: The structure of Ps 78 (Clifford)

As far as the date of the psalm is concerned, there exists a great range of differing opinions among scholars. Based on internal considerations, the *terminus a quo* for the psalm is the reign of Solomon, as the story cuts off at the time of Solomon and no later events such as the destruction of Israel and the exile of Judah are mentioned.[75] Then, those scholars who date the psalm to the tenth century include Eissfeldt and Campbell.[76] The next frame of dating is the time of the divided monarchy before the fall of the Northern Kingdom, with advocates including Dahood and Wright.[77] Moving

---

experiences of the Davidic-Solomonic era and its prehistory, and the *Bearbeitung* consists of exhortation to repentance and mending ones ways (Haag 1990, pp. 109-112). Moreover, Campbell thinks that there was a slight Deuteronomistic revision of an original tenth-century psalm (Campbell 1979, p. 75).

[73] Cf. McCann 1996, p. 990.

[74] Clifford 1981, p. 129.

[75] If however the reference to the sanctuary (מקדשו) in v. 69 could be taken as a reference to a heavenly temple rather than to Solomon's temple (see Tate 1990, p. 283), a slightly earlier date would be possible, even though this seems unlikely to us.

[76] Eissfeldt 1958, Campbell 1975, 1979. See Clifford 1981 p. 125n1 and Day 1986 p. 10n25 for a more comprehensive list.

[77] See Day 1986, p. 10n25 for a more comprehensive list.

forward in time, the next possibility is a date between the fall of the
Northern Kingdom and the exile of Judah, with advocates such as
Clifford, Weiser and Junker.[78] Finally, such scholars as Gunkel and
Kraus advocate a post-exilic composition,[79] and Westermann
thinks that the psalm is "probably a late psalm".[80]

A major issue in determining the date of the psalm is the
interpretation of the references to Ephraim in vv. 9 and 67.
Looking at the verses, one could naturally understand that the
references to Judah and Ephraim are references to the respective
premonarchic tribes, and this is the interpretation taken by those
who advocate an early date for the psalm during the reigns of
David and Solomon. However, a number of those who advocate a
date between the division of the monarchy and the exile of Judah
generally see the references to Ephraim as references to the
Northern Kingdom in general, especially in v. 9,[81] and the contrast
between Judah and Ephraim as theological legitimation of the
Southern Kingdom against the claims of the Northern Kingdom
(in case of a date before the Assyrian deportation) or as an
explanation of why the Northern Kingdom fell (in case of a date
before the Assyrian deportation).[82] On the other hand, even
though a number of those who advocate a postexilic date for the
psalm think that the psalm may reflect the anti-Samaritanism of the
Judean community,[83] they do not seem to think that either of vv. 9,
67 refers to the postexilic period,[84] and this may be partly due to
the fact that it is difficult to think of an event in the postexilic
period to which either of the verses might refer.

---

[78] See Clifford 1981, p. 125n2 for a more comprehensive list.

[79] See Day 1986 p. 9n23 and Carroll 1971, p. 144n6 for a more
comprehensive list. See also Clifford 1981, p. 125n3.

[80] Westermann 1981a/1961-1977, p. 238.

[81] See Junker 1953, pp. 492-493, Dahood 1968, p. 239; cf. Tate 1990,
pp. 289-290.

[82] See Tate 1990, p. 285, and the works of respective scholars.

[83] So Duhm 1899, pp. 202-203, and possibly Kraus (Kraus
1989/1961-1978, p. 124).

[84] See Duhm 1899, p. 202; Gunkel 1925-1926, pp. 343, 347; Kraus
1989/1961-1978, p. 130 (Note that Gunkel [1925-1926, p. 343] emends v.
9 and the result does not contain the mention of Ephraim and that Kraus
[1989/1961-1978, p. 121] dispenses with v. 9 altogether).

Moreover, we should point out that, first of all, even though the two main suggestions for what v. 9 refers to are the battle with the Philistines in 1 Sam 4[85] and the fall of the Northern Kingdom,[86] the reference is ambiguous, and might even be to an event which is not mentioned elsewhere in the Old Testament.[87] Secondly, and most importantly, none of those who advocate the term Ephraim as an epithet for the Northern Kingdom have satisfactorily explained exactly how the mention of Ephraim in v. 67 could refer to the Northern Kingdom. Rather, all seem to assume at least tacitly that Ephraim in v. 67 conveys the idea that the northern tribes had the leadership of Israel before the time of David.[88] Thus, even if one might somehow try to argue that the reference to Ephraim in v. 9 is to the Northern kingdom, there exist no reasons to see v. 67 to refer to anything else than the tribe of Ephraim, also remembering that v. 67 explicitly reads "the tribe of Ephraim" (שבט אפרים) and that vv. 56-72, and thus also v. 67 can naturally be read to describe the period before the division of the kingdom after David and Solomon. On the other hand, this is not to deny that Ephraim could have been used as an epithet for the Northern Kingdom after the division of the United Kingdom. On the contrary, it is very reasonable to suppose that, as Carroll suggests,

---

[85] E.g. Campbell 1979, pp. 60-61.

[86] E.g. Junker 1953, pp. 492-493. The battle at Gilboa where Saul died (1 Sam 31) has also been suggested (Tate 1990, p. 289, referring to Weiser 1962/1959).

[87] Cf. Tate 1990, p. 290.

[88] Carroll 1971, p. 145, after saying that, "The most obvious understanding of verses 59ff. is to relate them to the defeat of the Israelites by the Philistines and the capture of the ark at Aphek" adds that, "Another possible, though less feasible, view is the equation of the rejection of Ephraim with the disruption of the empire in the time of Rehoboam when Israel withdrew from participation in the southern monarchy." Besides singling out the late understanding of the rejection of Ephraim as a "less feasible" alternative, Carroll (op. cit.) makes no mention of how verses 56-72 should be exegeted in such a case. Note also that Gunkel (1925-1926, p. 347); Duhm (1899, p. 202) and Kraus (1989/1961-1978, p. 130), advocates of a postexilic date for the psalm, indicate that v. 67 refers to the time before the division of the kingdom.

"Eventually the term Ephraim became a synonym for the territory and people of Israel".[89]

Thus, we may in fact conclude that whatever the dating of the psalm, and whatever its intended hearers and its contemporary message to them, the historical references in verses 56-72 remain the same. In other words, verses 56-72 refer to the premonarchical and early monarchical period and their interpretation is not directly dependent on the date of the psalm. However, we may also add that as the reference is to the tribe of Ephraim, an earlier date for the psalm can be thought of as a more logical possibility than a later one.

Another issue for dating Ps 78 is its relationship to the Pentateuchal sources. The plagues of Egypt which are spoken of in the psalm occur in the Pentateuch in Ex 7-12,[90] generally seen to be composed of JE and P material.[91] Thus, a comparison of Ps 78 with Ex 7-12 might reveal a literary dependence and thus help to establish relative dating. However, only seven plagues are named in Ps 78 and they occur in a different order in the psalm from the Pentateuch. Moreover, even though all the plagues mentioned in Ps 78 also occur in the putative JE tradition, most of them occur also in P.[92] Further, the way the plagues are recounted differs from either source. Thus, as Campbell points out, "A survey of the plagues and their sequence shows that it is impossible to claim that Psalm 78 must depend on the pentateuchal sources. It makes use of language that is absent from these sources, disregards material present in them, and presents the plagues in a sequence that is different. The differences of expression are marked enough, even in plagues that are common, to invalidate any linguistic argument for dependence of Psalm 78 on the traditions available to us in the Pentateuch or Psalm 105."[93] On the other hand, the plagues

---

[89] Carroll 1971, p. 140.

[90] The plagues are also described in Ps 105; cf. Lee 1990, p. 83.

[91] See e.g. Childs 1974, pp. 130-142, 184-186 for source division of Ex 7-12. Strictly speaking, Ex 7-12 are also seen to contain minor Deuteronomistic additions, but these are not relevant for the present discussion.

[92] See Lee 1990, p. 83, Tate 1990, p. 292 and Campbell 1979, p. 69, including comprehensive comparisons of Ps 78, Ex 7-12 and Ps 105.

[93] Campbell 1979, p. 69. Cf. Eissfeldt 1958, p. 34.

tradition in Ps 78 might nevertheless be a free poetic retelling of the already existing Pentateuchal materials.[94] In this respect, if one moves out from the context of the plagues tradition, the manna event referred to in Ps 78:24 echoes Ex 16:4,[95] a verse which has been ascribed to both P and J.[96] Also, in v. 60 (cf. also v. 28), as Schley points out, "The parallelism of *miškān/ʾōhel* reflects the terminology of the Priestly materials of the Pentateuch, where these two terms are used interchangeably for the tent sanctuary (cf. Josh 18-22)".[97] Yet, here again one might argue that P and Ps 78 draw from a common tradition. Thus, it is difficult to date the psalm conclusively, regardless of what one thinks of the date of P (and JE).

The psalm also has clear connections with Deuteronomic theology.[98] For example, the psalm speaks about the covenant and its breach by the Ephraimites (vv. 10, 37).[99] Moreover, according to Clifford, the historical review and warning in the beginning of Deut 32:1-43 (see esp. vv. 1-4) resembles the introduction of Psalm 78.[100] Yet, according to Clifford, "More significant than similarities of style is the general Deuteronomic picture of Moses as the authoritative speaker of ancient traditions, rebuking, exhorting,

---

[94] Tate (1990, p. 293) states, "It is much more probable that the plague traditions were relatively fluid and malleable enough to be fashioned in different ways for different contexts. The exact details of the plagues were not a matter of great concern. What mattered most was the impact of the account." See also Lee 1990, p. 85.

[95] Greenstein 1990, pp. 206; 215n88. Manna is mentioned also in Num 11 (generally attributed to JE; see Wenham 1981, p. 19). However, it is clear that the allusion in Ps 78:24 can be taken to refer most conspicuously to Ex 16:4.

[96] See Greenstein 1990, p. 215n88 for arguing for Priestly appropriation (including reference to Gray 1903, p. 101 who assigns the whole of Ex 16 to P), and Childs 1974, p. 275 for assigning Ex 16:4 to J. However, the source-critical problems of Ex 16 are acute, and there is not much agreement on exactly how the chapter as a whole should be divided into sources (see Childs 1974, pp. 274-276).

[97] Schley 1989, p. 169.

[98] Day 1986, Junker 1953, Kraus 1989/1961-1978, Clifford 1981 (see below). See also Greenstein 1990, p. 201 (and p. 213n 54).

[99] Day 1986, p. 8.

[100] Clifford 1981, p. 130.

promising".[101] Furthermore, the sin of the Israelites with *bamoth* (v. 58) may refer to the centralization of the cult,[102] even though it has been argued that it may also merely refer to idolatry at the *bamoth*.[103] Granted that affinities with Deuteronomic theology are acknowledged, there is no agreement as to exactly how the psalm relates to Deuteronomic theology. According to Day, Ps 78 is a pre-Deuteronomistic work,[104] whereas Junker thinks that the composer of the psalm "clearly knew and presumed Deuteronomy".[105] According to Campbell, "a certain number of characteristically dtr phrases are found side by side with others that, although akin to dtr phraseology, are in fact normally avoided within these circles".[106] Campbell thinks that there was a Deuteronomistic revision of the psalm, which "would not be earlier than Hezekiah, but it would precede the period where the dtr language had developed a certain fixity in its formulaic usages".[107] Thus, it is difficult to date the psalm conclusively based on Deuteronomic features in it, regardless of what one thinks of the date of Deuteronomy.

A further clue for dating could be the fact that wisdom motifs exist in the psalm. According to Kraus, "the connection between the Deuteronomistic view of history and wisdom poetry would suggest a postexilic dating".[108] On the other hand, Junker dates the psalm and the book of Deuteronomy to the reign of Hezekiah for the same reason.[109] Moreover, as wisdom literature is as old as the earliest written records of human history,[110] and was widespread in the ancient Near East long before Israel appeared on the scene of

---

[101] Ibid.

[102] Cf. Eissfeldt 1958, p. 38; Day 1986, p. 11.

[103] So Eissfeldt 1958, pp. 39-40; Day 1986, p. 11.

[104] Day 1986, p. 8.

[105] Junker 1953, p. 493.

[106] Campbell 1979, p. 73. He adds that, "It is perhaps for this reason that Weinfeld characterizes the occurrences in Psalm 78 as possibly 'deuteronomic prototypes'" (referring to Weinfeld 1972, p. 365)

[107] Campbell 1979, p. 75.

[108] Kraus 1989/1961-1978, p. 124.

[109] Junker 1953, p. 496f.

[110] See e.g. Kramer 1963, pp. 217-228 for Sumerian wisdom compositions.

history,[111] and the origin of wisdom in Israel is debated,[112] it is difficult to date this psalm based on the fact that it includes wisdom motifs.[113]

One important argument for a post-exilic dating of the psalm is that it is similar to Psalms 105 and 106, and at least Ps 106:47 can easily be understood to have been composed in the postexilic time.[114] According to Westermann, when one compares Psalms 78, 105 and 106, "Ps. 105 describes the history of Israel, from God's covenant with Abraham down to the giving of the land in Canaan, as an unbroken chain of God's gracious deeds without the slightest hint of Israel's response. But Ps. 106 sees the same history from the perspective of a comprehensive confession of penance."[115] Westermann then thinks that the insertion of the "penance" elements was probably the influence of prophetic proclamation, especially that of the post-exilic prophets.[116] According to Westermann, the "dating of Israel's sins back to the time of her origin is strikingly similar to the prophet Ezekiel, as chapters 16, 20, and 23 indicate: 'But the house of Israel rebelled against me in the wilderness' (20:13)".[117] Thus, it would seem that Ps 78 which includes "penance" elements is late. However, the JE sources already include indication of the sins of the people in the wilderness as portrayed by the book of Numbers.[118] Moreover, the concepts of sin and penance are much older, as is indicated by traditions from the ancient Near East in general.[119]

Also, as Psalms 105 and 106 are indicated to have been used in public worship in 1 Chr 16, a similar setting might be possible

---

[111] See e.g. Murphy 1992, pp. 928-930.

[112] Cf. Murphy 1992, esp. p. 921 for a note of the origin of wisdom in Israel.

[113] Eissfeldt (1958, p. 40) explicitly finds it surprising that despite ancient Near Eastern parallels, the view persists that the psalm should be dated late because it includes wisdom motifs.

[114] Note however that according to Dahood (1970, p. 67), the language of Psalm 106 contains archaic features.

[115] Westermann 1981a/1961-1977, p. 239.

[116] Ibid., pp. 239-241.

[117] Ibid., p. 241.

[118] Cf. Wenham 1981, p. 19, which quotes Gray's source analysis for Numbers (from Gray 1903).

[119] Cf. e.g. the plague prayers of Muršili II (see COS 1, pp. 156-160).

for Ps 78, especially as Ps 78:1 exhorts the people to listen to the speaker's teaching (האזינה עמי תורתי).[120] In fact, Kraus hints at seeing a Levitical priest as the speaker, noting the similarity of form and content to the sermons of the Levites in the Chronicler's history.[121] If so, this would of course hint towards a late provenance for the psalm. Yet, Kraus himself on the other hand admits that, "of course" the poetic form of the psalm differs from Levitical sermons,[122] and one might rather agree with Tate that, "Any one of the different functionaries in Israelite worship - kings, priests, prophets, teachers, and laypersons - could be the speaker in Ps 78, but we will probably be nearer its original design if we think of a prophet".[123]

We should also add that it is difficult to think that the psalm is anti- Samaritan. As Day points out, "for the Samaritans it was not Shiloh but Shechem that was God's chosen dwelling place and Shiloh was rather the site of the illegitimate sanctuary erected by Eli the Jew".[124]

Dahood has used linguistic evidence to date the psalm. According to Dahood, "No psalm, it would seem, employs as many *yqtl* forms to express past time, see vss. 15, 26, 29, 38 (thrice), 40 (twice), 45, 47, 49, 58, 64, 72. Since the *yqtl* was the normal form of expressing past events in Ugaritic poetry and, to a lesser extent, in early biblical poems, one may use this linguistic feature as a criterion for the early dating of the psalm."[125] Even though these considerations rather speak for the earliness of the psalm, dialectal variations and archaizing are possible.

Finally, Tate has argued that if the psalm originates from before the division of the kingdom, it is unlikely that a Northerner would "have accepted religious literature which claimed that Yahweh 'rejected the tent of Joseph and the tribe of Ephraim he did not choose. But he chose the tribe of Judah ...' (vv. 67-68). After all, Joseph was the honored progenitor of the Northern

---

[120] Cf. Tate 1990, pp. 286-287.

[121] Kraus 1989/1961-1978, p. 123.

[122] Ibid.

[123] Tate 1990, p. 287.

[124] Day 1986, p. 9, adding in footnote 9: "Cf. J. Macdonald, *The Samaritan Chronicle No. II* (BZAW 107; Berlin, 1969)".

[125] Dahood 1968, pp. 238-239.

tribes of Ephraim and Manasseh, and Ephraim was the largest tribe in the region. Tribal loyalties were strong in that period; it is worth remembering that the United Kingdom survived less than eighty years. No one trying to provide a theological basis for the new nation would word it in a way calculated to offend half the country."[126] However, we can also think that rather, it would have been more difficult for Ps 78 to glory about Judah's leadership after the split of the kingdom,[127] especially as 1 Ki 12 (esp. vv. 22-24) indicates that the contemporaries understood that the split was Yahweh's doing. Also, it is possible that one of the contributing reasons for the division of the country was that Ephraim was the traditional leader and that it, and seemingly other Northern tribes as well, did not like the fact that Judah had taken its place (cf. 2 Sam 2-3 [esp. 2:8-10]; 1 Ki 12 [esp. 12:16-17]). Then, Ps 78 could also be thought to be theological legitimation which tried to establish unity of politics and worship by emphasizing the leadership of Judah and Jerusalem, even if this may have been interpreted as offensive by others.

We may conclude that none of the criteria discussed above for dating Psalm 78 and determining its historical setting are unequivocal. On the other hand, a postexilic date seems least plausible, and there are good grounds for a date before the division of the monarchy, i.e. in the tenth century BC, and an early date would naturally make the historical plausibility of the psalm greater, even though we have seen in the previous chapter (4.1) that literary, and thus also historical, material could be transmitted reliably through centuries in the ancient Near East. We may also add that whatever the date of the psalm, its inclusion in the canonical psalter must have been aided by the fact that it had continuing relevance especially for the people of Judah in the various historical situations that they experienced after the division of the United Kingdom, after the fall of the Northern Kingdom, and even in postexilic times.[128]

Let us then move on to a detailed interpretation of verses 56-72, also keeping in mind that the verses refer to the premonarchical

---

[126] Tate 1990, p. 286.
[127] So Eissfeldt 1958, pp. 36-37.
[128] Cf. Tate 1990, p. 287; McCann 1996, p. 992.

and early monarchical period and that their interpretation is not directly dependent on the date of Psalm 78.[129] If one expands on the "*Sequel* vv. 65-72" in Clifford's chart (for which see above, p. 129) with more detail, the structure of verses 40-72 can be expressed as follows.

Second Recital:
From Egypt to Canaan vv. 40-64
>   God's gracious act of giving the land to the Israelites (vv. 44-55)
>   Rebellion (vv. 56-58)
>   Divine anger and punishment (vv. 59-64) (destruction of Shiloh)

Sequel vv. 65-72
>   Divine "awakening" after a period of inactivity (v. 65)
>   Smiting of enemies (v. 66)
>   Choice of Judah instead of Joseph and Ephraim (vv. 67-68)
>   Building of the temple (v. 69)
>   Choice of David (vv. 70-72)

Commentators generally agree that Psalm 78:56-72 says that Jerusalem succeeded Shiloh as the place of Yahweh's chosen sanctuary.[130] Clifford states, "the poem sees Shiloh and Zion as successive central shrines for all Israel",[131] and Tate, quoting Clifford, thinks that a Shiloh-Zion appropriation is "most likely".[132] Yahweh's choice of Zion is of course in line with the classic statements of Zion theology that we can read elsewhere in the Old Testament.[133] Also, it is easy to concur with such commentators as Kraus and Schreiner who say that the choice of Zion and Jerusalem[134] and even its exclusivity[135] are a major part of the

---

[129] See above, p. 130f.
[130] E.g. Tate 1990, pp. 294-295; Day 1986 pp. 8-9.
[131] Clifford 1981, p. 135.
[132] Tate 1990, p. 293.
[133] Cf. e.g. Tate 1990, p. 295, Kraus 1989/1961-1978, p. 131.
[134] Kraus 1989/1961-1978, p. 131.
[135] Schreiner 1990, p. 325.

solution to the riddle posed in v. 2, and thus to the whole message and aim of the psalm.

Looking at v. 55, the focus is on God's giving the land to the Israelites, in addition to all the good deeds that he has done to the Israelites in the Exodus and Wilderness events. Yet the Israelites continue to act faithlessly. They behave just as their fathers did in the wilderness (v. 57). They test God, rebel against him, and do not keep his commandments (v. 56). Moreover, once they have settled in the land, they build illegitimate places of worship (במות; v. 58) and worship idols. The portrayal in vv. 56-58 accords well with the tradition in the book of Judges, especially Judges 2, which portrays the Israelites as forsaking the covenant (v. 2) and serving Baals and Asherim (vv. 11-13), and not destroying the altars of the indigenous Canaanite inhabitants (v. 2). Similarly, 1 Sam 8:8 speaks about the apostasy of the people and their serving of other gods than Yahweh. The psalm expresses that the Israelites are useless like a slack bow with which one cannot shoot (v. 57). V. 58 does not actually directly state whether the reason for God's anger concerning the *bamoth* was that Israelites worshiped only Yahweh in multiple places or that they also worshiped there in a non-Yahwistic ways. The poetic parallelism of v. 58 suggests the latter, but there is no reason to deny that it could also imply the former.[136]

Moving on to verses 59-60, in verses 58-60 the psalm expresses that God utterly rejected Israel because of their idols and high places. An important part of this rejection was that God rejected his dwelling in Shiloh. Verse 60,

ויטש משכן שלו אהל שכן באדם:

clearly states that Yahweh dwelt in Shiloh before Jerusalem, and that the tent of meeting was his dwelling in Shiloh.[137] If we look at the books of Samuel, 1 Samuel starts with Shiloh being at least an

---

[136] Cf. the comments above, p. 134. One also has to remember that in the book of Jeremiah, which is often linked to Deuteronomic concerns, there is not a single allusion to a requirement of sacrificing in a single place, but only polemic against idolatry (cf. above, Chapter 4.1, esp. p. 113).

[137] According to Schley (1989, p. 169; also quoted above, p. 133), "The parallelism of *miškān/'ōhel* reflects the terminology of the Priestly materials of the Pentateuch, where these two terms are used interchangeably for the tent sanctuary (cf. Josh 18-22)."

important sanctuary. Certainly, at least the ark is portrayed to be in Shiloh (1 Sam 3:3; 4:4). Also, according to the Masoretic text of 1 Sam 2:22, the tent of meeting was in Shiloh during the time of Eli and Samuel.[138] Joshua 18:1 and 19:51 state that the tent of meeting was set up at Shiloh during the time of Joshua,[139] and according to 1 Ki 8:4, the tent of meeting was taken into the temple. The narrative of 1 Sam 21, and especially the mention of the showbread at Nob (1 Sam 21:5-7) hints that the tent of meeting was at Nob after Shiloh.[140] Also, according to the late testimony of Chronicles, the tent of meeting was at Gibeon before the building and consecration of the temple (1 Chr 16:39-42; 2 Chr 1:3-6). Moreover, 2 Sam 7:1-7 states that Yahweh had not dwelt in a house since he led the Israelites from Egypt, but had gone about in a tent (2 Sam 7:6):

כי לא ישבתי בבית למיום העלתי את־בני ישראל
ממצרים ועד היום הזה ואהיה מתהלך באהל
ובמשכן:

Finally, as the tent of meeting was a 'house' of Yahweh,[141] the mention in Judges 18:31 of "the house of God" (בית־האלהים) in Shiloh may be a reference to the tent of meeting. On the other hand, in 1 Sam 1-3, clearly a building of some kind is implied,[142] as the word היכל[143] is used in 1:9; 3:3, and there is a mention of a doorpost in 1:9 and "the doors of the house of Yahweh"

---

[138] Most Greek texts do not have the mention of the tent of meeting, and this gave Wellhausen a good added reason to doubt the authenticity of the reference (Wellhausen 1905/1878, p. 41; cf. above, p. 7). See Schley 1989, p. 232n10 for a full discussion of the verse, including the similarity of the verse to Ex 38:8; Num 25:6-10.

[139] See Schley 1989, pp. 110-118 for more details, including critical issues concerning the references.

[140] Cf. above, p. 63.

[141] See above, Chapter 2.2.1.

[142] Abinadab's house at Kiriath Jearim (1 Sam 7) needs not to be considered, as it (and similarly, the house of Obed-Edom in 2 Sam 6:10-11) is not to be considered as a cultic site at least in a proper sense, but rather provided temporary lodgings for the ark (cf. above, p. 41, incl. n174).

[143] Note that a number of Hebrew manuscripts use בית instead of היכל (see BHS).

(דלתות בית־יהוה) in 3:15. For this reason, Graf in the nineteenth century argued that there had been no tent of meeting at Shiloh, and consequently, in relation to this, that the tent of meeting was merely a late fictitious concept modelled on the Solomonic temple.[144] The view of the tent of meeting as late fiction was shared by Wellhausen.[145]

However, archaeological finds since the time of Wellhausen have demonstrated that a tent sanctuary could have been possible in Israel in the late second millennium BC. According to the Ugaritic texts, gods enter into tents,[146] and El evidently had a tent-shrine.[147] In Egypt, structures which are conceptually similar to the tent of meeting have been found from the second millennium BC and earlier.[148] Moreover, the excavations at Timna have indicated that there was a tent shrine in the Late Bronze - Early Iron Age Hathor temple.[149] As the excavator describes:

> Behind this rather impressive row of *mazzeboth* and all along the inside of wall 3 a considerable quantity of red and yellow cloth was found. The cloth was of a heavy kind, lying in a thick mass and in many folds, often with beads woven into it. A similar mass of folded cloth was found along the inside of wall 1, also outside the court in Locus 101, along and close to wall 1. The detailed study of these textiles, not yet concluded, shows that they consist of well-woven wool and flax of varying tints of yellow and red. The appearance of such large quantities of cloth, stratigraphically belonging to

---

[144] See Schley 1989, p. 29. In fact, according to Childs, the idea that the tent of meeting is fictitious and a late concept already dates to the early 19th century (see Childs 1974, pp. 549-550 for details).

[145] Wellhausen 1905/1878, pp. 39-46; cf. above, p. 7.

[146] Clifford 1971, p. 223.

[147] Clifford 1971, pp. 221-223. Cf. also D. Pardee, *COS* 1, p. 245n29 regarding the interpretation of the word *dd* as 'tent'. Clifford (1971, p. 222) also points out that there is an evident reference to the tent of El in a fragment of a Canaanite myth in Hittite (English edition of all legible fragments and bibliography in *COS* 1, p. 149, transl. & ed. G. Beckman; see also *ANET*, p. 519).

[148] See K.A. Kitchen, *ABD* II, p. 706; Millard 1985, p. 73.

[149] Date based on pottery, and cartouches of various Egyptian pharaohs (see Rothenberg 1972, pp. 142-143 (Plates 82-85); pp. 163-166 (incl. Figs. 48, 49).

the last phase of the temple, and their location, i.e. all along walls 1 and 3, was at first hard to understand. It was obvious that they must have been part of the temple-furniture, some kind of hangings that had fallen down and been left lying where they were found. Yet we could see no structure on to which these hangings could have been attached. The problem solved itself when, during the clearing of the floor in Loci 107-109, two stone-lined pole-holes were found, penetrating into the white floor, but obviously not contemporary with it. These were the holes made to secure the poles of a large tent which, during the final phase of the temple, had covered the temple court. The temple had been turned into a tent-covered shrine, the first of its kind ever discovered. There are convincing reasons to relate this tent-sanctuary to the Midianites who seem to have returned to Timna for a short time after the Egyptian copper mining expeditions no longer reached the area, and worked and worshipped in their own way.[150]

Finally, as at least some of the early Israelites can be thought of as nomadic or pastoral people,[151] with many of them living in tents, it is quite logical to think that the God of such people could also live in a tent,[152] albeit in a more grandiose one than that of ordinary people.[153] Thus, it is entirely possible that a tent shrine stood at Shiloh.[154] In fact, as Schley suggests, "The existence of a Shilonite temple, however, does not preclude the erection of the tent shrine at the same place, so that the tradition of the tent of

---

[150] Rothenberg 1972, p. 151. See ibid., pp. 134-136 (Plates 66-73) and p. 157 Plate XI for photographs of the remains of the shrine.

[151] See Finkelstein 1988, including pp. 336-351, and cf. e.g. Mazar 1990a, p. 337; Thompson 1992, pp. 226, 237-238, 323-326; Coote and Whitelam 1987, *passim.*; Lemche 1998, pp. 65-77.

[152] Cf. Haran 1978, p. 18, according to whom, "A portable temple in the form of a tabernacle is, in itself, quite feasible in a semi-nomadic group".

[153] Cf. Postgate 1992, p. 264, quoted above, p. 35 on ancient Near Eastern conceptions that the dwelling of a god should be grandiose.

[154] So also Haran 1978, pp. 201-202; Freedman 1992, p. 295; Milgrom 1991, p. 30. Cross 1981, p. 175, even though he himself favours a Jerusalemite basis for the description of the tent of meeting, states that, "it is not impossible that such a grand shrine stood at Shiloh".

meeting at Shiloh does not confute the presence of a temple there".[155] Moreover, if one visits Tell Seilun, one will notice that the mound is very susceptible to wind. Thus, a more solid structure in association to a tent would be a natural solution to mitigate this problem.

We should also note in regard to v. 60 that even if we cannot be certain that Shiloh or its sanctuary was destroyed in association with the disaster of Aphek (1 Sam 4),[156] this is not a crucial problem from the standpoint of Ps 78. What is important is that God rejected Shiloh.[157] If Shiloh was not destroyed immediately, one can compare the fate of Shiloh with the fate of Saul. Even though Saul was rejected after the battle with the Amalekites (1 Sam 15; esp. v. 23; cf. also 1 Sam 13; esp. v. 13), his actual death and accompanying loss of kingship happened considerably later at the battle of Gilboa (1 Sam 31).

Next, verse 61 states that,

ויתן לשבי עזו ותפארתו ביד־צר:

And he gave his strength to captivity, his splendour to the hand of the enemy.

The reference to the strength (עז) of Yahweh naturally refers to the ark, as the Philistines captured the ark in 1 Sam 4-6, and as Psalm 132:8 speaks of the ark as the strength (עז) of Yahweh.[158]

---

[155] Schley 1989, pp. 141; similarly Freedman 1992, p. 299; Milgrom 1991, p. 31.

[156] As discussed above, Chapter 4.1, there is strong evidence for an 11th century destruction at Shiloh.

[157] Cf. Campbell 1975, pp. 215-217. We should add that even though divine temple abandonment was always a sign of great trouble in the ancient Near East, it is not certain that a city in question would be destroyed at least immediately (cf. the curse of Agade, where the city had great trouble after Inanna had left, but was not destroyed immediately but only after Naramsin, the ruler of the city ransacked Ekur, the temple of Enlil in Nippur; see Cooper 1983, pp. 53-55 [lines 55-93]; cf. above, Chapter 2.1).

[158] So Tate 1990, p. 294; Davies 1963, pp. 51-52, and similarly Campbell (see Campbell 1975, pp. 215-216; 1979, p. 60). Davies (1963, p. 52) also points out that most commentators (see scholars list in ibid., p. 52n6) have interpreted v. 61 to refer to the capture of the ark (until his day). To contend, one might say that it is possible that the people are spoken of as the strength (עז) of Yahweh, in poetic parallelism of the

Then, if we look at the matter from an ancient Near Eastern perspective, as described before, the loss of a god image in the ancient Near East was a sign that the god had abandoned his sanctuary and city, perhaps even the whole land.[159] Thus, the capturing of the ark, the Israelite seat of Yahweh's presence, was a sign that Yahweh had abandoned his sanctuary in Shiloh (vv. 60, 61).[160] This abandonment is also expressed by the exclamation "glory has departed from Israel" (גלה כבוד מישראל; 1 Sam 4:21, 22) of Phinehas' wife, "because the ark of God had been taken" (כי נלקח ארון האלהים; 1 Sam 4:22). Thus, the departure of the ark was interpreted as a sign of Yahweh's rejection of both Shiloh and of Israel, and this is in line with ancient Near Eastern theology.[161] On the other hand, the sojourn of the ark at the temple of Dagon and the land of the Philistines (1 Sam 5-6) indicates that Yahweh is stronger than the Philistines and their gods, and thus Yahweh was not captive to the Philistines because of their prowess, but Yahweh is sojourning in the land of the Philistines because of his own volition. The whole matter is Yahweh's own making, and shows that his hand is controlling history.[162]

Moving forward to vv. 62-64, let us start by noting that according to vv. 56-58, the reason why Yahweh abandoned Shiloh was the sins of the people. This is well in accord with the Sumerian/Akkadian text K 4874, as quoted above:

---

following verse 62, and this could be supported by the fact that Syriac reads ʿmh = עמו instead of עזו in v. 61. Or, if one follows the Greek translation, one might say that the reference ἰσχὺν αὐτῶν, 'their strength' refers to the people. Then, the reference in v. 61 would be most naturally to the Philistines taking captives after the battle at Aphek (1 Sam 4), or to some other battle and Philistine domination in general. However, as v. 62 adds that Yahweh's people were delivered over to the sword, and vv. 63-64 speak about the death of the young men and of the priests of Israel, this interpretation fits less well. Finally, even if one followed the Greek reading ἰσχὺν αὐτῶν, the ark could perhaps still be referred to as the strength of the people.

[159] See above, Chapter 2.1, esp. p. 34.

[160] Note that even v. 60 by itself is enough to establish this point.

[161] See also Campbell 1975, p. 185; Miller and Roberts 1977, pp. 60-75.

[162] See Miller and Roberts 1977, pp. 60-75.

At that time, in the reign of a previous king, conditions changed. Good departed and evil was regular. The lord became angry and got furious, He gave the command and the gods of the land abandoned it [...] Its people were incited to commit crime. The guardians of peace became furious, and went up to the dome of heaven, The spirit of justice stood aside, ..., who guards living beings, prostrated the people; they all became like those who have no god. Evil demons filled the land, the namtar-demon [...]..., they penetrated the cult centres. The land diminished, its fortunes changed. The wicked Elamite, who did not hold (the land's) treasures in esteem, [...] his battle, his attack was swift, he devastated the habitations and made them into a ruin, he carried off the gods, he ruined the shrines.[163]

On the other hand, according to 1 Sam 2-3, the sons of Eli neglected the proper procedures of the offerings (1 Sam 2:12-17), and conducted themselves improperly with the women who were part of the service of the tent of meeting (1 Sam 2:22[164]). Then, according to 1 Sam 2:27-36 and 3:10-14, the disaster at Aphek was part of Yahweh's judgment against the House of Eli. This judgment would be started by the death of Hophni and Phinehas, which would also serve as a sign of it (1 Sam 2:34; 4:11). The judgment was continued by the slaughter of the priests at Nob (1 Sam 22; cf. 1 Sam 2:30-33) and completed by the expulsion of Abiathar by Solomon (1 Ki 2:26-27; cf. 1 Sam 2:36).[165] Then, vv. 62-64 refers to the start of this demise, the defeat at Aphek and the resulting casualties (vv. 62-63)[166] and the death of Hophni and Phinehas (v. 64), with the latter part of v. 64 according well with the plight of Phinehas' widow (1 Sam 4:19-22).[167]

---

[163] See above, p. 34.

[164] Remembering the textual issues surrounding this verse (see above, p. 140, incl. n138).

[165] So also Klein 1983, p. 27.

[166] Note also that according to 1 Sam 4:10, 30.000 foot soldiers fell from Israel during the battle.

[167] Cf. Tate 1990, p. 294; and see also Carroll 1971, p. 145. Note also that everything, including women, children and even animals were killed by Saul at Nob (1 Sam 22:19), and thus v. 64 cannot refer to the slaughter at Nob.

Then, Ps 78 and 1 Sam 2-3 have slightly differing viewpoints. In Ps 78, it is the sins of the people and their high places and idolatry which arouses Yahweh's anger. In 1 Sam 2-3 it is the sin of the priesthood which causes Yahweh's anger. However, the two are mutually compatible. The idea of sin of both the people and the priesthood is compatible with the description of both Ps 78 and 1 Sam 2-3, even if these texts emphasize only one part of the problem, respectively.[168] In this respect, it is good to remember that both Ps 78:56-58 and 1 Sam 2-3 indicate that the sins of the people and the priests Hophni and Phinehas were of cultic nature. Then, when we remember that in general, violation against cult was one of the worst things that the leaders or people could do against gods in the ancient Near East,[169] it is not surprising that Yahweh is portrayed as greatly angered (Ps 78:59; 1 Sam 3:11-14).

Next in Ps 78, Yahweh awakes as from sleep (v. 65) and restores Israel's fortunes (v. 66). The reference may, as some have proposed, be to the plagues in the land of the Philistines as portrayed in 1 Sam 5-6.[170] However, they may as well be a reference to the general victories over the Philistines as referred to in 1 Sam 7; 14; 2 Sam 5; 8. Moreover, as Tate notes, "The background of the idea of the deity sleeping in the Baal traditions should not be overlooked (see 1 Kgs 18:27)" when interpreting this verse.[171] Also, the return of the ark from the land of the Philistines (1 Sam 6) is part of the process of Yahweh's awakening and restoring the fortunes of Israel.

The ultimate part of the restoration of the fortunes of Israel is the election of David, and of Judah and Jerusalem (vv. 68-72). Verse 67 provides a recapitulation of the background of this election: the tribe of Ephraim which had been the leader during the premonarchical period has been rejected together with Shiloh and is not chosen again. As Tate describes:

---

[168] Cf. on the other hand 1 Sam 8:7-8.

[169] See above, p. 35, incl. n145.

[170] According to Greenstein 1990 (p. 217n115), the Targum reads, "He struck their oppressors with hemorrhoids on their behinds".

[171] Tate 1990, p. 294. Also, note Greenstein's (1990, p. 211n11) comment of how the idea of the comparison of Yahweh to a drunken warrior disturbed some medieval exegetes.

God rejects the Northern sanctuary and the tribe of Ephraim as the locus of his worship. This is different from the rejection of v. 59. When God "vehemently repudiated Israel" at the fall of Shiloh, he judged the whole people and removed himself from all of them for a period. Now he denies only the tent of Joseph and the tribe of Ephraim and chooses instead Zion and the tribe of Judah, upon whom he bestows the Davidic monarchy. The emphasis in this passage is not upon the rejection of the Northern tribes - indeed, Clifford (1981, p. 137) is probably correct to argue that the Northern tribes are not rejected at all. The issue is the location of Yahweh's chosen sanctuary and his establishment of the Davidic kingship. (Note the chiastic arrangement in vv. 67 and 68: repudiated - tent of Jacob [sic, should be tent of Joseph] - tribe of Ephraim - no longer chose - chose - tribe of Judah - Mount Zion - he loved: ABBAABBA.)[172]

The prominence of Joseph and Ephraim in the premonarchical period, and the change of focus from Ephraim to Judah is confirmed by the Old Testament record outside Ps 78 and 1-2 Sam, and is also suggested by the archaeological record. In Genesis 48, Jacob sets Ephraim before Manasseh, and according to Deut 33:16, Joseph is a "prince of his brothers" (נזיר אחיו), which accords with Gen 37-50 (see esp. Joseph's dreams in Gen 37:5-11). Moreover, judging from the tribal origin of the individual Judges, and from other internal considerations of the book of Judges, Ephraim and the northern and Transjordanian tribes seem to be strong for most part of the Judges period.[173] On the other hand, except for the initial period of the Judges, as Miller and Hayes point out, "The southern tribes do not play a prominent role in the Judges narratives which tend to focus attention on matters pertaining to Ephraim/Israel".[174] The lack of prominence of Judah is seemingly illustrated also by Judges 4-5 which do not mention Judah and Simeon, and where the action takes place in the Kedesh-Tabor area of Galilee. Also, as Carroll points out, Joshua and

---

[172] Tate 1990, pp. 294-295
[173] See Miller and Hayes 1986, pp. 94-98.
[174] Miller and Hayes 1986, p. 103.

Samuel were Ephraimites.[175] Finally, one should not lose sight of the fact that Shiloh was in the territory of Ephraim, and it is worth noting that Bethel where at least the ark was for a time according to Judges 20 was not in the territory of Judah.[176]

As far as the archaeological record is concerned, according to Finkelstein, surveys and excavations have shown that the number of settlements found in the Northern hill country was reasonably large, whereas not many settlements were found in the Southern hill country, reflecting the prominence of the North.[177] On the other hand, there was a considerable increase of settlements in Judah in the beginning of Iron Age II, reflecting the increase of the prominence of the South at the beginning of the monarchy.[178] Thus, the archaeological record speaks for the prominence of the North in the premonarchical period, and for a shift of prominence from North to South at the treshold of the monarchy.

However, we should add here that one must remember that the presence of a nomadic element in a population is archaeologically undetectable, and as the Old Testament itself suggests that the Israelites were nomadic, this tempers the results of Finkelstein's work.[179] Moreover, Millard points out that a lot of Finkelstein's work is based on *surveys*, and these do not necessarily find all evidence that exists.[180] Furthermore, it is possible that a part of the reason why Judah is not prominent in the narratives of Judges is because the book has been written from a Judahite perspective and most narratives describe the period as apostate, and thus the portrayal of the failures of the Northern tribes and the

---

[175] Carroll 1971, p. 140

[176] For the issues involved with Judges 20, see below, Chapter 4.6.

[177] Finkelstein 1988, esp. pp. 47-55, 121-204. See also Ottosson 1991, pp. 199-205 for the prominence of Northern cities in relevant extant Egyptian documents relating to Canaan.

[178] Finkelstein 1988, pp. 326-327.

[179] Cf. Schley 1989, pp. 78-79: "Indeed, the tradition of the Israelites as tent-dwellers in the land seems to have persisted until quite late, and is reflected in the cries 'Each to his tents, O Israel!' (2 Sam 20:1), and 'To your tents, O Israel!' (1 Ki 12:16). 1 Sam 4:10; 13:2 also assume that the Israelites still dwelt in tents." Cf. also Hoffmeier 1997, p. 33, "the Iron I villages tell us nothing about Israel's origin, only its sedentarization".

[180] A.R. Millard, personal communication, May 2000.

relative silence of the failures of the South[181] serves to strengthen the claims of the leadership of Judah for the monarchic audience of the book of Judges.[182] Thus, one has to be careful not to make conclusive judgments from the relative silence of the activities of Judah during the judges period, even though an overall northern leadership during the period seems clear from both textual and archaeological evidence.

Then, in verses 70-72, God's choice of David is affirmed. Moreover, whereas in vv. 52-53 it is God who guides his people Israel, in verses 71-72 it is David who guides the people of Israel. In this light, and also in view of the poetic parallelism Jacob-Israel in v. 71, it is quite clear that the reference to Israel in v. 71 is to the whole of Israel, and not to the Northern Kingdom or to Samaria. Furthermore, the change of thought from vv. 52-53 to vv. 71-72 accords well with the fundamental theology of the Israelite monarchy. In premonarchical times, it was Yahweh who was king (1 Sam 8:7; Ex 15:18; Jdg 8:22-23). With kingship, Israel had a human king, a change which was not seen only in a positive light (1 Sam 8:7). On the other hand, according to Ps 78, the fall of the old tribal order, including the abandonment of the leadership of Ephraim and the sanctuary at Shiloh in Ephraim's territory was God's judgment on Israel (Ps 78:56-64). Then, God in his grace set up a new order in Judah and Jerusalem, with the establishment of kingship and the temple in Jerusalem (Ps 78:67-72).

---

[181] Except perhaps a mild implication in Jdg 15:9-13, even though according to Amit (1999, p. 148), Judah rather is hurt as a result of the other tribes being punished in Jdg 15:9-13 (and in Jdg 10:9). Moreover, one also has to remember that the usage of term Israel in the book of Judges suggests that it encompasses all tribes and thus Judah as well (see Jdg 1:1-2; 3:7-11).

[182] Cf. Amit 1999, pp. 147-150, according to whom the silence is intentional and serves the concerns of the book of Judges as a whole. Note especially the following comment by Amit (ibid., p. 148), "the fashioning of Judah as one that, unlike the other tribes, made a decisive contribution to the driving out of the Canaanites, and is not to be enumerated among the sinning tribes, sets the foundation for its election during the period of the monarchy". See further below, Chapters 4.5 and 4.6 for the portrayal of the books of Joshua and Judges of Judah and Ephraim.

This view of the events fits very well with the contents of the books of Samuel. The narrative of 1 Samuel starts with the central sanctuary being in Shiloh and with the Elide priesthood in operation (1 Sam 1). Then comes the judgment on the Elide priesthood (1 Sam 2-3), followed by the loss of the ark (1 Sam 4) and its return to Israel and its storage at Kiriyath Jearim (1 Sam 6; 7:1-2). These events are followed by the transition to kingship (1 Sam 8ff.), including Saul's failed kingship (1 Sam 13-15). Next, David is anointed (1 Sam 16). The massacre of the Elide priests at Nob (1 Sam 22) takes place. David becomes king (2 Sam 2-5). David brings the ark to Jerusalem (2 Sam 6).[183]

Thus, the books of Samuel depict the changing the old order of Shiloh into a new order of Jerusalem. Above all, the main focus of the books of Samuel is on describing how the old system where judges ruled Israel ended and changed to a new system of kingship under David, Yahweh's chosen king.[184] However, it should not come as a surprise that describing the change of the cultic order constitutes a vital part of the portrayal of the events which result in the emergence of the Davidic monarchy, fully in line with the general ancient Near Eastern emphasis on cultic matters.[185] First of all, the place of worship changes. Whereas in the beginning of 1 Samuel, the central place of worship is in Shiloh, towards the end, the temple in Jerusalem is anticipated. The ark has been brought to Jerusalem in a joyous procession (2 Sam 6). Moreover, David wishes to build a temple for the ark (2 Sam 7), and the matter is fulfilled by his son Solomon, as the books of Kings describe (2 Sam 7:12-13; 1 Ki 5-8). Secondly, priesthood changes. Whereas in the beginning of 1 Samuel the Elide priesthood officiates, at the end of 2 Samuel only Abiathar is left of the Elide line (1 Sam

---

[183] Moreover, the last chapter of 2 Samuel (2 Sam 24) describes how David builds an altar to the threshing floor of Araunah, and the Chronicles describe this event as determining the place for the temple (see 1 Chr 22:1).

[184] Overall, the books of Samuel in general have been seen as a legitimation of the Davidic monarchy; see esp. Rost 1982/1926.

[185] For the importance of cult in the ancient Near East, cf. above, p. 35, incl. n145.

22:20),[186] and he too is banished in the beginning of the reign of Solomon in favour of Zadok (1 Ki 2:26-27).[187] Both Abiathar and Zadok officiate during the time of David (2 Sam 8:17; 20:25), a transitional time between the fall of Shiloh and the building of the temple in Jerusalem.

Thus, as Campbell notes,

> Psalm 78 provides support from within the biblical tradition for understanding the Ark Narrative[188] as a theological narrative of rejection and election, straddling *a revolution of epochs*. Ps 78 supplies what is totally lacking in the Ark Narrative, a reason and justification for this rejection.[189]

Moreover, as Campbell continues,

---

[186] Cf. Cody 1969, p. 89; Schley 1989, pp. 142-143 and *passim* for issues involved in scholarly discussion in the connection of Abiathar to Eli. The perceived problem is that according to 2 Sam 8:17, Ahimelech is the son of Abiathar, whereas on the other hand, according to 1 Sam 22:20, Abiathar is the son of Abimelech. Also, according to 2 Sam 8:17, Ahitub is the father of Zadok, whereas according to 1 Sam 14:3, Ahitub is Phinehas' son. However, it is most logical to think that there were two Ahimelechs, one the father and the other the son of Ahitub (Youngblood 1992, p. 911), and thus descent from Eli could naturally be considered as follows: Eli - Phinehas - Ahitub (1 Sam 14:3) - Ahimelech - Abiathar - Ahimelech (1 Sam 22:20; 2 Sam 8:17). This would also fit chronologically, as Eli was a very old man at the time of the fall of Shiloh (1 Sam 4:15), and many decades passed from the time of the slain Ahimelech at Nob (1 Sam 21) till the time of Solomon (1 Ki 2:27). Moreover, the Ahitub in 2 Sam 8:17 who is the father of Zadok must be different from the Ahitub who was the brother of Ichabod (1 Sam 14:3), also for chronological reasons (see Youngblood 1992, p. 911; cf. 1 Chr 5:33).

[187] It seems reasonable to think that Abiathar has been taken to the list of 1 Ki 4:4 since he officiated during the time of Solomon before his banishment; cf. Patterson and Austel 1988, p. 50.

[188] Since Rost 1982/1926 (see esp. pp. 6-34; cf. Klein 1983, pp. 38-40; Campbell 1975; Miller and Roberts 1977), 1 Sam 4:1-7:1; 2 Sam 6 have been called as an 'Ark Narrative' and generally have been seen as a separate literary work which was integrated into the books of Samuel. Whether and how much this was the case is not relevant for our present concerns, rather we are interested here in the theological message of the material in its present form.

[189] Campbell 1975, p. 223; italics mine.

It must be understood that this is not merely "to show how and why the leadership of Israel passed from Ephraim and Shiloh to Judah and Zion" (Coats, *Rebellion in the Wilderness*, p. 219), but going beyond that to maintain that one era of Israel's history - an era which Ps 78 traces from Egypt to Shiloh - has been rejected, and a completely new era in Israel's history has been inaugurated.[190]

Finally, according to Campbell, "the coming of the ark to Jerusalem was understood as the sign of the renewed bestowal of Yahweh's favour and the inauguration by Yahweh of a new era after *a caesura in the saving history*".[191] Thus, while the books of Samuel describe a change of one era into another, this change involves an *intermediate* period in Israel's religious life. During this intermediate period, the old Shilonite order has collapsed, but the new Jerusalemite order has not yet been established. If one looks at the matter from the standpoint of chronology, the period from the disaster of Aphek till the building of the temple at Jerusalem lasted approximately 70 years. What is very important for our purposes is that *neither Ps 78 nor the books of Samuel and Kings in any way indicate that there existed a central sanctuary of the stature of Shiloh or later Jerusalem during this 70-year intermediate period.* As Tate notes, "After the destruction of Shiloh,[192] God had no dwelling among the people. The ark, which survived the battle, was returned by the Philistines and housed at Kiriath Jearim (1 Sam 6:1-7:2), but there was no shrine to take place of the one at Shiloh."[193] Also, Clifford's comment, "Zion in Judah is the successor to Shiloh and is the divine dwelling for all the children of Israel",[194] underlines that there was nothing significant between the rejection of Shiloh and the choice of Jerusalem.[195]

---

[190] Ibid., p. 223n1.

[191] Ibid., p. 244; italics mine.

[192] The essentials of Tate's comment do not change regardless of whether Shiloh was destroyed in association with the battle at Aphek or not.

[193] Tate 1990, p. 294

[194] Clifford 1981, p. 141

[195] Cf. Patterson and Austel 1988, p. 44, according to whom "the concept of the central sanctuary was, so to speak, in limbo" during this period.

Moreover, whereas according to Jer 7:12, Shiloh was the place where Yahweh's name dwelt,[196] there is no indication anywhere either in Ps 78 or in Samuel-Kings that Yahweh's name dwelt either at Kiriath Jearim, where the ark was (1 Sam 6:21-7:2),[197] or at Nob or Gibeon, where the tent of meeting was according to 1 Sam 21; 1 Chr 16:39-40; 21:29; 2 Chr 1:3-6.[198] That the ark was separate from the tent of meeting emphasizes that the period was a transitional period, and that Yahweh "rejected his dwelling at Shiloh, the tent which he had set among men" (Ps 78:60).[199] Yahweh took his dwelling in the temple at Jerusalem when the ark was taken in to the temple (1 Ki 8:4). At the same time, the tent of meeting was also taken into the temple to emphasize that the temple had superseded the tent of meeting,[200] and seemingly also as a historical relic. In this regard, that the tent of meeting was rejected as the "house" of Yahweh, whereas the ark continued as the object of Yahweh's presence provides a logical explanation of why the narratives of Samuel (and 1 Ki 1-8) see the ark as important, but make rare mention of the tent of meeting. The

---

[196] See above, Chapter 4.1. Note also the comment of Haag (1990, p. 85), "Die Tatsache, dass zwischen der sogenannten Tempelrede des Propheten in Jer 7, 1-15 und den Ausführungen in Ps 78 über die Verwerfung Efraims und die Vernichtung des Heiligtums von Schilo einerseits sowie über die Erwählung Judas und den Aufbau des Zionstempels anderseits ein traditionsgeschichtlicher Zusammenhang besteht, ist von der alttestamentlichen Forschung schon seit langem vermutet, jedoch wegen der exegetischen Unsicherheiten bei der Beurteilung beider Texte immer nur mit spürbarer Zurückhaltung behauptet worden." Note also Schley 1989, p. 173: "The belief that Jerusalem had succeeded to Shiloh's former status is precisely the substance of Ps 78:60-72, and the prophecy in Jeremiah 7:12-15 is a play upon this belief".

[197] Cf. also our comments above, p. 41, incl. n174.

[198] Cf. our considerations regarding Nob above, p. 64.

[199] Cf. Fretheim 1968, p. 9n49.

[200] So also Fretheim 1968, p. 9; similarly Hurowitz 1992, pp. 264-265. Note especially the following comment by Hurowitz (ibid., p. 265): "The idea of linking a new temple with an old one may be expressed in the Mesopotamian rite *libittu maḫrītu*, 'the former brick', by which a brick from a temple being restored is ritually removed and then placed in the foundations of the new temple".

Judean, Davidic writer of the books of Samuel (and 1 Ki 1-8) did not consider as important the tent of meeting which represented the old Shilonite order which had passed away. On the other hand, the vicissitudes of the ark and its bringing to Jerusalem were very important for him. However, the postexilic books of Chronicles see the Mosaic legislation and institutions as very important, and thus pay great attention to the tent of meeting as well.

Then, if we relate this all to Deuteronomic legislation, according to Deuteronomy 12, people are to bring their sacrifices to "the place Yahweh will choose from among all your tribes to put his name there for his dwelling" (Deut 12:5). However, during the intermediate period, as Yahweh had rejected Shiloh and had not yet chosen Jerusalem, there was no chosen place of Yahweh where he had set his name. Moreover, the conditions of the period were more or less chaotic and cataclysmic. There were wars with the Philistines (1 Sam 7-2 Sam 5), and a war between David's house and Saul's house after Saul's death (2 Sam 2-5). During the time of David, the time was not right to set a new place where Yahweh would make his name dwell (1 Ki 5:17-19; 2 Sam 7). It was only with Solomon and the peaceful conditions of his time that the temple was built and Jerusalem truly became the chosen place (1 Ki 5:4-5; 9:3).

Thus, during the intermediate period, there was no place to centralize worship to, and the situation of the nation was neither stable nor peaceful.[201] It was impossible to implement centralization of worship both from a theoretical and practical viewpoint. This state of affairs is also attested by the books of Samuel which give no clear condemnation of high places as long as

---

[201] Cf. Nathan's prophecy to David in 2 Sam 7:10-11,

ושמתי מקום לעמי לישראל ונטעתיו ושכן תחתיו ולא ירגז עוד ולא־יסיפו
בני־עולה לענותו כאשר בראשונה:
ולמן־היום אשר צויתי שפטים על־עמי ישראל והניחתי לך מכל־איביך והגיד
לך יהוה כי־בית יעשה־לך יהוה:

"And I will set a place for my people Israel and plant them and they will dwell in their place and they will be disturbed no more and wrongdoers will not continue to oppress them like before, from the days that I established judges for my people Israel, and I will give you rest from all your enemies. Moreover, Yahweh declares to you that he will establish you a house."

people worship only Yahweh (see 1 Sam 7:3-4). That Samuel sacrifices in a Yahwistic high place (e.g. 1 Sam 9:11-14) or at local altars (1 Sam 7:17; 10:8) is fully in accord with the conditions of the time.[202] As to the particulars of the cult in local places of worship, it is impossible to ascertain from the books of Samuel what shape the sanctuaries in Bethel, Gilgal or Mizpah (1 Sam 7:5-6; 7:16; 10:3; 10:25) were in the days of Samuel, and archaeological evidence does not give much help.[203] However, none of the places are described as *houses* of Yahweh at this time, and 2 Sam 7:5-7 explicitly denies that Yahweh had dwelt in a house between the exodus and the time of David. Moreover, 2 Sam 7:5-7 implicitly confirms that Yahweh dwells only where the ark is. Furthermore, the only cult object which could have served as a seat of Yahweh except the ark would have been a god image or a *massebah*, and we have seen that neither one was appropriate according to orthodox/canonical Yahwism.[204] A local altar would be enough to

---

[202] On the other hand, as regards the exilic time when Yahweh abandoned the temple of Jerusalem, it is quite possible to think that the synagogues or their forerunners (see Levenson 1981, p. 164; Meyers 1992, p. 252, according to whom the synagogue system is generally thought to have originated at around the time of the exile), started to replace local altars, with prayer and learning replacing sacrifice (see Levinson 1981, p. 165). Thus, synagogues would replace local cult centres, and consequently, as time moved on, the *bamoth*, and sacrifices outside the central sanctuary would not any more be such a central problem as they were before the exile, especially during the postexilic time (even if such cult centres as the Elephantine temple still existed during the postexilic time; cf. Meyers 1992, p. 252).

[203] This is illustrated by Gilmour (1995) who lists all archaeologically known possible cult sites in the Southern Levant during Iron Age I, but does not include Bethel, Gilgal or Mizpah. See also Haran 1978, pp. 30-33 for a summary of not finding any temples at Bethel, Gilgal and Mizpah. The archaeological problems also include site identification (cf. Haran 1978, loc. cit.), especially as regards the site of Gilgal which has not been positively identified (see W.R. Kotter, *ABD* II:1022-1024; cf. T. Noy, *ABD* II:1024 and *NEAEHL*, pp. 517-518 for the prehistoric sites of Gilgal). See also J.L. Kelso, *NEAEHL*, pp. 192-194 for Bethel and J.R. Zorn, *NEAEHL*, pp. 1098-1102 for Tell en-Nasbeh which is generally thought to be the site of Mizpah.

[204] See above, Chapter 2.2.2.

to secure Yahweh's presence and blessing.[205] Then, as Samuel is portrayed as an ardent Yahwist in the books that bear his name, and Bethel, Gilgal and Mizpah are portrayed as being under his control (1 Sam 7:16), it is entirely possible that the sanctuaries at Bethel, Gilgal and Mizpah were centered around a Yahwistic altar without a further cult object.[206]

In any case, sacrificing at local altars and high places could continue until the time of Solomon and the building of the temple. This is explicitly stated in the books of Kings. According to 1 Ki 3:2, "The people were still sacrificing at the high places, because a temple had not yet been built for the name of the Lord".[207] Thus, the books of Kings speak against high places only after the building and dedication of the temple (e.g. 1 Ki 15:14; 22:44; 2 Ki 12:3; 14:4;

---

[205] See above, Chapter 2.2.2.

[206] That this is conceivable is confirmed by Haran, according to whom, "by its basic character, the high-place was only a large altar" (Haran 1978, p. 28). Of course, one may still reply that Samuel did not mind about, say, *masseboth*, and/or the Exodus altar law may not yet have been in existence at the time of Samuel. However, especially bearing in mind the archaeological problems related to Bethel, Gilgal and Mizpah, the matter is completely unverifiable through empirical observation at these sites. As regards 1 Sam 10:25, if the book about kingship was set at a sanctuary at Mizpah, as seems most logical (cf. above, p. 37 for placing treaties in sanctuaries in ANE; could it however be possible that the ark had been brought to Mizpah for the occasion and the book about kingship deposited to the ark?), it is conceivable that a continuous presence of Yahweh at the site is not necessary to affirm that the book is *lipne YHWH*, but only Yahweh's intermittent presence during worship (cf. the showbread at the empty tent of meeting at Nob in 1 Sam 21:7 and the tent of meeting without the ark in 1 Chr 16:39-40; 2 Chr 1:5-6, as discussed above, p. 63).

[207] Cf. 1 Ki 12:27 which affirms that Jerusalem was a place which people sought in order to offer there after the building of the temple, and vv. 28-33 also suggest that people went there for at least for one yearly feast, if not more (cf. 1 Ki 9:25 [which Kraus 1966, p. 59 takes as evidence of three yearly festivals]) during the days just following Solomon. According to the book of Kings, that Jeroboam established an alternative system of worship in the Northern Kingdom was precisely to direct the northerners away from going to sacrifice in Jerusalem.

15:4, 35 etc.).[208] The only exception is Solomon (1 Ki 3:3), who in narrative sequence is castigated before the building of the temple. However, it is possible to think that the verse summarizes the reign of Solomon as a whole, and already anticipates Solomon's actions after the building of the temple, including Solomon's later idolatry in building *bamoth* to foreign gods (1 Ki 11:4-10).[209]

Thus, Ps 78 speaks about the rejection of Shiloh and Ephraim and the choice of Judah and Jerusalem. It implies that Shiloh and Jerusalem were successive sanctuaries in Israel. On the other hand, Ps 78 also implies that there was no sanctuary in Israel where worship should have been centralized between the disaster at Aphek (1 Sam 4) and the building of the temple in Jerusalem (1 Ki 8). This is emphasized by the fact that during that period, the ark and the tent of meeting were separated. The emphasis on the ark in the books of Samuel and 1 Ki 1-8, and on the other hand the silence concerning the tent of meeting is understandable since the ark was the object of Yahweh's presence, but the tent of meeting was seen as part of the old era of Shiloh which had been rejected. Whether or not the book of Deuteronomy existed, the books of Samuel (after 1 Sam 4) and the beginning chapters of 1 Kings portray a time during which there was no basis for a requirement of centralization of worship.

Also, we should add that especially if Ps 78 was written in the tenth century BC,[210] and in any case as the picture given in Ps

---

[208] Note also that these passages indicate reasonably clearly that each king in question had special responsibility for the existence of *bamoth* since he was the leader of the nation. Thus, we may also think that each king would have had special responsibility for enabling and implementing centralization.

[209] Cf. Provan 1995, pp. 44-45, who points out that Solomon's marriage to Pharaoh's daughter in 1 Ki 3:1 is already dubious (Dt 7:3-4), and the comment by House (1995, p. 109) concerning high places in the beginning of Solomon's reign: "For now this practice is excusable, but Solomon's long-term commitment to the high places is contrary to God's law...". Note also how DeVries 1985, pp. 48-51; Burney 1903, p. 28; Jones 1984, p. 122 find it difficult to see vv. 2 and 3 (of 1 Ki 3) together coherently.

[210] Cf. however also our comments in Chapter 4.1 regarding the transmission of literary material in the ancient Near East (and cf. above, p. 137).

78:56-72 is compatible with that known from the books of Samuel, Kings and Chronicles and the archaeology of Shiloh[211] and the Northern hill country,[212] there are good grounds to suspect that the picture that the biblical sources give about the period commencing with the disaster of Aphek (1 Sam 4) and ending with the building of Solomon's temple (1 Ki 8) is at least basically historically reliable.[213]

4.3.   The Covenant Ceremony at Mount Ebal (Dtr 27 and Josh 8:30-35) and the Early Period of Joshua

We have now clarified the general role of Shiloh in the premonarchical period and the relationship between Shiloh and Jerusalem in the period between the disaster of Aphek as described in 1 Sam 4 and the building of Solomon's temple, establishing that Shiloh and Jerusalem were successive central sanctuaries in Israel (with a period without such a sanctuary in between), and also suggesting that both Shiloh and Jerusalem were places where Yahweh's name dwelt in the sense described by the book of Deuteronomy. However, we have not yet dealt with the period before the rejection of Shiloh. For that, we will start from the earliest period of the settlement, working our way forward in time. The first passage which describes specific sacrificial activity in the land of Canaan by the incoming Israelites is Deuteronomy 27 and its parallel Joshua 8:30-35. Therefore, let us proceed by looking at these passages and their implications.[214]

Deuteronomy 27 describes a command of Moses to the Israelites to build an altar on Mt Ebal and to offer *oloth* and *shelamim* on it, and Joshua 8:30-35 records the fulfilment of this command by the Israelites under the leadership of Joshua.[215] As regards the literary setting of the passages, in general it has been

---

[211] Cf. above, Chapter 4.1.

[212] Cf. above, p. 148.

[213] Note that these comments do not really hinge on the nature and extent of the kingdoms of David and Solomon at large, or on the grandeur of the temple.

[214] Cf. our preliminary comments regarding these passages above in Chapter 3.3, p. 104.

[215] As regards to Dt 11:26-30 which refers to the blessings and curses of Dt 27 and Josh 8:30-35, see below.

thought that Dt 27 and Josh 8:30-35 do not fit well in their respective books. First of all, it is often felt that Dt 27 "disrupts the natural flow of thought and language between the concluding stipulations of chap. 26 and the introduction of the blessing/curse theology of chap. 28".[216] Also, as Barker summarizes, "Verse 1 seems abruptly to introduce Moses in the third person, suggesting a break with chapter 26. Despite a common overall theme with chapter 28, there are difficulties in relating the two chapters. Chapter 27 lists curses but not blessings and is concerned with the nature of the offense which provokes the curse whereas chapter 28 deals with the nature of the curse itself."[217] Secondly, as Anbar describes regarding Josh 8:30-35, "The victory over Ai is followed abruptly with *'az* 'at that time' (8,30) by the account of the building of an altar on Mount Ebal and the ceremony of the blessing and curse between Mount Gerizim and Mount Ebal in the presence of 'the whole congregation of Israel' (8,35). However, further on, in the account of the covenant with the Gibeonites, we learn that, in effect, the Israelites are still at Gilgal (9,6)."[218] Moreover, a Dead Sea scroll fragment places the text of Josh 8:30-34 before 5:2,[219] and LXX places Joshua 8:30-35 after 9:2.[220] Finally, as was already discussed before,[221] whereas according to the Wellhausenian consensus, Deuteronomy was written to centralize all worship at Jerusalem, the Ebal narratives explicitly command the building of a sacrificial altar elsewhere than in Jerusalem. Thus, the conclusion is often drawn that Dt 27 and Josh 8:30-35 are intrusions to their respective books. Specifically, many scholars have seen the passages either as predeuteronomic or postdeuteronomic addition, with the majority adopting the idea of postdeuteronomic addition.[222]

---

[216] Described by Hill 1988, p. 399.

[217] Barker 1998, pp. 277-278.

[218] Anbar 1985, p. 304.

[219] See Hess 1996, pp. 171, 19-20.

[220] Cf. Woudstra 1981, p. 146.

[221] See above, Introduction, p. 11.

[222] Those seeing the passages (or one of them; a number of the following commentators treat only one of the passages) as predeuteronomic addition include von Rad (1966, p. 165; Dt 27). Those seeing the passages as postdeuteronomic addition include Driver (1901,

There are also seeming difficulties as regards the internal arrangement of Dt 27. As Barker summarizes, "In v. 1, Moses and the elders address the people, though they do so in the first person singular; in v. 9 Moses is joined by the Levitical priests; in v. 11, Moses addresses the people alone. The instructions about the altar and sacrifices in vv. 5-7 are often regarded as an intrusion within the instructions about the stones and law of vv. 2-4, 8. Even within vv. 2-4, there seems to be an inconsistency with when the stones are to be erected. Verse 2 suggests immediately on crossing the Jordan; v. 4 is vaguer in time though; because it specifically names the place as Mount Ebal, near Shechem, it seems to preclude the actual day of crossing the Jordan."[223] Moreover, "In addition, there is uncertainty about whether the stones of the altar are the same as the stones on which the law was to be inscribed. Joshua 8:30-32 seems to imply they are though most interpreters of Deuteronomy 27 argue otherwise."[224]

As might be expected, the solutions to the problems of internal consistency have in general been sought diachronically, with the idea that more or less disparate traditions have been brought together and redacted further.[225] Some even think that there is a mixing of Gilgal and Shechem traditions in the passages, especially as the place reference to Gerizim and Ebal in Dt 11:29-30 is deemed difficult, and because the time reference ביום ("on the day") in Dt 27:2 apparently requires that the covenant ceremony be performed on the same day as the crossing of the Jordan, but Shechem is too far to be reached from the river Jordan in one day.[226]

---

pp. 294-295; Dt 27); Mayes (1979, p. 337; Dt 27); Miller (1990, p. 190; Dt 27); Cf. Anbar 1985, p. 309n27: "Josh 8,30-35 was composed in a late period, when striving for the centralization of the cult was already superfluous, and the central issue in community life was the demand to fulfil *all* the words of the Torah." According to Eissfeldt 1970, p. 95, Dt 27 and Josh 8:30-35 were put into their place by a postdeuteronomic editor who "considered Deuteronomy as the standard law to link the originally independent Deuteronomy with the older Hexateuch".

[223] Barker 1998, p. 278.

[224] Ibid.

[225] Cf. Barker 1998, p. 279; Hill, p. 400.

[226] See Eissfeldt 1970; von Rad 1966, p. 86.

However, none of the internal difficulties of the narratives are overwhelming. As regards the problem of the word ביום in Dt 27:2, it does not need to be taken to mean "on the day", but can as well be translated as "at the time".[227] As regards whether the words were written on the altar stones or on other stones, one may point out that Josh 8:32 allows for the possibility that the stones were not the altar stones.[228] If the writer of Josh 8:30-35 assumed that the reader was familiar with Dt 27, he could have changed the topic from the altar in Josh 8:31 to the stones of Dt 27 in Josh 8:32. Also, it is entirely logical to think that Dt 27:4 may recapitulate vv. 1-3 (note the expression את־האבנים האלה אשר אנכי מצוה אתכם היום 'these stones of which I command you today' in v. 4), and thus all these verses may speak about the same stones. Further, that vv. 5-7 of Dt 27 are bracketed by vv. 2-4, 8, can be taken as part of the literary strategy of the author. Finally, it is evident that the perceived difficulties in regard to changes of person and the variation between Moses, the Levites and the elders as speakers need not be real difficulties.

Also, there is reason to think that both Dt 27 and Josh 8:30-35 belong to their literary context. First of all, there is good reason to think that Dt 27 is an integral part of the book of Deuteronomy. That Dt 27 forms a bracket with 11:26-30 around chapters 12-26, the central law code of Deuteronomy,[229] rather shows careful design from the context of the book of Deuteronomy. Also, a number of the expressions in Dt 27 are very much in line with the rest of the book of Deuteronomy. The reference to "eating and rejoicing" before Yahweh (Dt 27:7) is a very Deuteronomic expression (cf. Dt 12:7, 18; 14:26). Similarly, the expression "land flowing with milk and honey" (Dt 27:3) is found elsewhere in the book of Deuteronomy (Dt 6:7; 8:8; 11:9; 26:9, 15; 31:20).[230]

---

[227] Barker 1998, p. 298, also pointing out Gen 2:4 for comparison.

[228] Note also that the writing on plaster is conceived rather as an Egyptian custom than Palestinian or Mesopotamian (Driver 1901, p. 296; Craigie 1976, p. 328). However, if the Israelites or at least part of them came from Egypt, there is nothing peculiar about the matter.

[229] Barker 1998, p. 293; Hill 1988, p. 400; Craigie 1976, pp. 212, 327.

[230] Cf. also Wenham 1993, p. 95, who points out that M.G. Kline (*WTJ* 23 [1960-1961], pp. 1-15), D.J. McCarthy (*Treaty and Covenant*, Pontifical Biblical Institute, Rome, 1963, pp. 109ff.) and N. Lohfink (*Das*

Second, the position of Josh 8:30-35 generally fits very well with the early days and events of the conquest, even though the chapter may not be in a strict chronological position in regard to the events. That all manuscripts, even though they do not place the passage in exactly the same place, nevertheless place it within the early chapters of Joshua is perfectly compatible with this idea. Moreover, the expression אז in Josh 8:30 can be taken loosely, and not as claiming that Josh 8:30-35 follows strict chronology,[231] and Josh 8:30-35 can be taken to form a flashback of what happened during the days of the early conquest after Joshua and the Israelites had crossed the Jordan, especially when there is evidence of comparable literary devices elsewhere in the ancient Near East.[232] Thus, there is no need to take Josh 8:30-35 as an addition from a narrative standpoint, but the passage can be taken as an integral part of the design of the book of Joshua as a whole.[233]

Hauptgebot. Eine Untersuchung literarischer Einleitungsfragen zu Deuteronomium 5-11, Pontifical Biblical Institute, Rome, 1963, pp. 111f., 234) see Dt 27 as carefully integrated into the overall structure of the book of Deuteronomy.

[231] So Anbar 1985, p. 304.

[232] Younger's (1990, p. 211) comments on Josh 10:12-15 are directly applicable to Josh 8:30-35 as well: "The text of Joshua 10:12-14/15 is very often seen by biblical scholars as a type of separate alternate tradition to the narrative of 10:1-11. However, the use of אז and the preterite (ידבר) should be understood as a type of flashback - simply introducing a section of the text which narrates material which chronologically belongs between verse 9 and 10. אז functions very much like its Assyrian semantic counterpart *ina ūmīšuma* in the Assyrian royal annalistic inscriptions where it lacks strict chronological significance. Hence, the biblical writer relates the principal incident which is connected to the battle (namely, the hailstones) first, before he then proceeds to the special point to be cited from the book of Yashar."

[233] One may even argue that Josh 8:30-35 belongs to its present place by a comparison of Josh 3-8 with Ex 12-17, as follows (table by Ottosson 1991, p. 79),

Ex 12-17		*Josh 3-8*
Ch 12-14	Passover celebrations	Ch 3-6 Crossing of Jordan
	Crossing of Sea of Reeds	Passover celebrations
Ex 14:26	Obliteration of Egyptians	Destruction of Jericho
Ch 15-17	Waters of Marah, Elim	Defeat at Ai

Moreover, as Sprinkle observes,

> It will not do to say that Deuteronomy 27 is a late addition, because Joshua 8 records the continuation of the story at Ebal. Such a double 'insertion' shows careful, deliberate editing. If such editing occurred, the person adding this material could be expected to delete the contradictory material in Deuteronomy 12 if he considered it contradictory. Furthermore, subsequent editors, if they wanted to stress the Jerusalem sanctuary, would be expected to eliminate these embarrassing additions. The fact that it was not deleted implies either that the person adding this material (along with any editor who followed him) was so incompetent that he did not notice or correct the contradictions between the texts, or else that the contradiction is in our minds rather than in the minds of the transmitters of the tradition.[234]

We may also point out here that it is clear that the Ebal ceremony should be understood as a covenant renewal ceremony.[235] It is natural to think that the purpose of the covenant ceremony on Mt Ebal is to renew and ratify in the promised land the covenantal relationship which had been made between Yahweh and the people of Israel before crossing the Jordan to the promised

---

(apostasy)	& Ch 7-8 [sic] with Massah-Meribah	Break of covenant
	Loss and victory at Rephidim	Victory at Ai
	Moses' staff of God (hands)	Joshua's כידון
	Building of an altar	Building of an altar at Ebal

In any case, one must note that at least the crossing of Jordan narrative in Josh 3-4 clearly refers back to the crossing of the Sea of Reeds (cf. Ottosson 1991, pp. 54-57 for connections, including the explicit Josh 4:23).

[234] Sprinkle 1994, p. 43.

[235] So Barker 1998, p. 277; Craigie 1976, pp. 326-329; Hill 1988, pp. 405-406; Tigay 1996, p. 246; Soggin 1972, p. 240; cf. Driver 1901, p. 294; Anbar 1985, p. 306; Butler 1983, p. 95.

land.[236] That the Ebal ceremony is to be taken as a covenant is confirmed by a number of similarities between the Ebal ceremony and the Sinai covenant ceremony as described in Ex 24:4-8.[237] In both cases, stones were set up (Ex 24:4 vs Dt 27:2-4),[238] and an altar built and *oloth* and *shelamim* offered (Ex 24:5 vs Dt 27:5-7; Josh 8:30-31).[239] Also, in the Exodus account Moses reads the book of the covenant to the people (Ex 24:7), and in Dt 27, blessings and curses are announced which according to Joshua 8:34 then come from the book of the law.[240] Another matter which ties Dt 27 and Josh 8:30-35 to the book of Exodus is that according to Dt 27:5-6 and Josh 8:31, the Israelites are to build the altar from unhewn stones, which is perfectly in line with the altar law of Ex 20:24-26.[241] Then, the similarity of the Mount Ebal tradition to the tradition in the book of Exodus rather speaks for the earliness than the lateness of the Mount Ebal tradition.[242] Moreover, that Deuteronomy 27 refers to the Exodus altar law is analogous to the rest of the book of Deuteronomy, as scholars often think that the book of Deuteronomy used the Covenant Code, including the altar

---

[236] Cf. Barker 1998, p. 301. Also, since sacrifices were involved, Weinfeld's assertion that "In the deuteronomic covenant ... the sacrificial element is *completely* absent" (Weinfeld 1972, p. 103; italics mine) is rather odd. Note also the interesting comment by Levine (1974, p. 52) that the Deuteronomist associated the Ebal ceremony with the initiation of Yahwistic worship in Canaan.

[237] See Tigay 1996, p. 247; note that according to Childs (1974, pp. 500-501), Ex 24:4-8 generally have been assigned to E (in spite of the divine name Yahweh in the verses).

[238] Cf Tigay 1996, p. 487.

[239] Cf. Anbar 1985, p. 306; Tigay 1996, p. 247.

[240] Cf. Tigay 1996, p. 247.

[241] See Anbar 1985, p. 306 for a detailed verse comparison of Dt 27:5-7 and Ex 20:24-25. Note also that the word ברזל, iron, is used in Dt 27:5 and Josh 8:31 in regard to the prohibited tool, whereas Ex 20:25 uses חרב. See also Millard 1988 for the use of iron before the Iron Age proper, including finds of artefacts which contain iron and many literary examples which mention iron, the oldest of which come from the Middle Bronze Age.

[242] Cf. also our comments regarding the dating of the Ex 20:22-26 altar law and the Covenant Code above, p. 53.

law of Ex 20, as a basis for its legislation.[243] Seen this way, the connection of Dt 27 with the book of Exodus is fully in accord with the idea that the chapter belongs to the book of Deuteronomy as much as the rest of the material, and this of course also strengthens the idea that Josh 8:30-35 should be seen as a part of the book of Joshua as well.

Then, that Dt 27 can be considered as an integral part of the book of Deuteronomy and that Josh 8:30-35 fits to its place in the Deuteronomic book of Joshua[244] implies that the events described by the chapter were seen as fully legitimate from the standpoint of centralization by both the writer of Deuteronomy and the writer of Joshua. The most natural explanation for the events from the standpoint of centralization is that *neither the author of Deuteronomy nor the author of Joshua thought that the centralization requirement was in force in the early days of Joshua to which the events portrayed by Dt 27 and Josh 8:30-35 belong.*[245] The time after the crossing of Jordan was a time of a war of conquest. The Israelites were not yet in the possession of the land. It would have been out of the question to talk about peace and security. First, the land would have to be conquered and the people would have to settle, and only after that it would be possible to speak about conditions which would allow pilgrimage to a central sanctuary.[246] That the writer of Joshua thought that the chosen place would be set only in the future may also be suggested by Josh 9:27. No place is mentioned as the place where the Gibeonites would serve, and the future form of יבחר in Josh 9:27 implies that the choice of the place[247] is to happen in the future.[248]

---

[243] See Levinson 1997, Otto 1994 and Lohfink 1991, p. 175; cf. above, pp. 6, 55.

[244] Cf. Wenham 1971b for the Deuteronomic character of Joshua; cf. also below, p. 212.

[245] According to Noth (1930, p. 149), Dt 27:5-7 was not seen as contradictory to the rest of Deuteronomy by its incorporator, as the Ebal tradition refers to a time before the Jerusalemite central sanctuary. Similarly Tigay, who also suggests that the sacrifices described in Dt 27 and Josh 8:30-35 are part of a one-time ceremony (Tigay 1996, p. 249).

[246] See above, Chapter 3.3.

[247] Greek versions add κύριος to יבחר, which, if not indicating an underlying text variant which contained the word יהוה, at least indicates

Also, it is difficult to think that either the author of Deuteronomy or Joshua considered that the wilderness paradigm was valid any more after the crossing of the river Jordan.[249] That the manna had ceased to fall after eating of the produce of the land after the crossing indicates that a new era had begun (Josh 5:10-12). Moreover, the close proximity of the people to the tent of meeting was to be broken by the start of the conquest and the dispersion of each tribe to conquer his inheritance. Thus, there is no need to think that either the author of Deuteronomy or the author of Joshua thought that there existed a centralization requirement during the early days of the conquest, and therefore both Dt 27 and Josh 8:30-35 can describe the building of an altar on Mount Ebal during the early days of the conquest.

On the other hand, according to the book of Joshua, the events at the end of the book are temporally distinct from events at the beginning. Whereas the first chapters take place right after the crossing of the Jordan, the last chapters at least essentially portray a later time when Joshua is "old and advanced in years" (זקן בא בימים; Josh 13:1; 23:1, 2). Consequently, we may suspect that the situation as regards centralization might be different for the later days of the conquest as described by the latter part of the book of Joshua, and that is the subject we will turn to next. However, we will first make an excursus on Mount Ebal archaeology.

---

that the Greek translator of the verse thought that the expression refers to the chosen place.

[248] It is also possible that the choice spoken of in Josh 9:27 means choice from the perspective of the narrator rather than from the perspective of the narrated events. In that case, the narrator of Josh 9:27 would be speaking in a time when the chosen place was not set. However, we will not explore that possibility and its implications further here, also for the reason that we will make detailed considerations of the date of the book of Joshua in Chapter 4.5 below based on more comprehensive criteria.

[249] Cf. above, especially Chapter 3.3 for reasons to see P as earlier than D, and D as dependent on P.

4.4.   Excursus: Mount Ebal Archaeology

In April 1980, the only known Iron Age site was discovered on Mount Ebal.[250] Excavations were then carried out between 1982-1987 under the direction of A. Zertal.[251] A preliminary report of these excavations was published in *Tel Aviv* 1986-1987, and this preliminary report is the basis for the following discussion. Excavations were continued also after 1987, but had to be discontinued in 1989, and the whole site has not been excavated.[252] A final report is due soon.[253]

The excavations uncovered a site with two chronological strata, labelled Stratum I and II, of which Stratum I was subdivided into Phase B (the main phase) and Phase A (post-occupational phase).[254] According to Zertal, "Both strata belong to the beginning of Iron Age I, reflecting the material culture of the Israelite settlement period in the central hill country. Both strata were short lived, and the entire lifespan of the site did not exceed 100-200 years. No signs of destruction or fire were discerned in the transition between the strata nor at the time of abandoning the site."[255] Furthermore, according to Zertal, "According to the two Egyptianized scarabs unearthed, the seal and the pottery, Stratum II was founded in the middle of the 13th century B.C.E. or slightly later (ca. 1240) and ended around 1200 B.C.E. Stratum IB followed immediately and was abandoned in the middle of the 12th century (ca. 1130), and the site was never resettled."[256]

Stratum II is divided between two separate areas, named Areas A and B.[257] Area B was interpreted as a four-room house.[258]

---

[250] Zertal 1986-1987, p. 105. According to Zertal (ibid.), "Of the 12 sites discovered, one belonged to Middle Bronze Age IIB and the rest dated to much later periods, beginning with the Persian period."

[251] Zertal 1986-1987, p. 108.

[252] A. Zertal, personal communication, December 1999.

[253] Ibid.

[254] Zertal 1986-1987, p. 109.

[255] Ibid.

[256] Ibid.

[257] See Zertal 1986-1987, p. 110 Fig. 3. According to Zertal (ibid., p. 112), even though there is no direct stratigraphical connection between Area A and Area B, since both Area A and Area B were covered by

The remains of Area A are small, including a surface (Surface 61), two short pieces of wall (Walls 18 and 36), a pit (Pit 250) and a round structure, called Installation 94.[259] According to Zertal, "A large collar-rimmed jar was uncovered near Wall 18."[260] Also, according to Zertal,

> "Installation 94, which is an integral part of Surface 61, was unearthed in the eastern part of this surface. It is 2 m. in diameter and built of medium-size stones, some of them charred, protruding 20-25 cm. above the surface. Its southern side is covered by Wall 13 of Stratum IB, which effectively cancelled its use. It was found covered with stones, beneath which was a 10 cm. layer of clean ash containing many animal bones, some burnt. The installation is located in the exact centre of the overlying building, and in the middle of the opening between its inner Walls 13 and 16, creating an obstacle for passage between the two spaces. A similar round structure, 1.45 m. in diameter, discovered in Courtyard 103 of Stratum XI in the Philistine temple at Tell Qasile, was interpreted by the excavator as a sacrificial altar."[261]

Also, Pit 250, which is located close to Installation 94, contained "two large hammerstones, pottery sherds of restorable vessels and a chalice made of light volcanic material, probably pumice".[262] According to Zertal, "According to these findings, Pit 250 may have been used as a *favissa*, just before it was sealed by the fill of stratum IB."[263]

Furthermore (in Area A), "A trial probe (Locus 81) was made along Wall 5 under the southern courtyard of Stratum IB to examine the remnants beneath its stone paving. Sizeable quantities of ash, coals, burnt wood and animal bones were found on the

---

structures of Stratum IB, it may be assumed that they were all part of the same system.

[258] See ibid., pp. 111-112.

[259] Ibid., p. 109, and ibid., Fig. 3, p. 110.

[260] Ibid., pp. 109-110.

[261] Ibid., pp. 110-111. The stones of Installation 94 are unhewn, and the structure was hollow (A. Zertal, personal communication, December 1999).

[262] Zertal 1986-1987, p. 111.

[263] Ibid.

bedrock. There were also some dispersed hearthstones. Restorable pottery vessels found in and around these stones included two jars, a krater and a bowl. Some querns were also recovered."[264] According to Zertal, "The picture, as suggested by the burnt bones, is one of cooking, roasting and/or sacrificing, which apparently took place on bedrock in the open."[265]

Stratum IB was divided into three main areas, A, B and C. According to Zertal, "In stratum IB the character of Area B underwent a radical change. In Stratum II it was a domestic quarter, whereas now the architecture took on monumental dimensions, creating a large courtyard, a kind of platform in front of the main complex (Wall 32) and a broad staircase entrance to the enclosure."[266] According to Zertal, the Stratum II structure "was filled up with stones and earth containing pottery sherds of the Stratum II horizon. All the 1.5 m.-high space above the Stratum II floor was thus raised to the height of the upper terrace level. The new levelled unit was paved with stones."[267] Also, "On this stony pavement some hearths and installations were unearthed together with a large quantity of Stratum IB potsherds stuck between the stones, and many animal bones."[268] As regards the entrance, according to Zertal, "The Iron Age I-II entrances known so far are generally fortified and as narrow as possible. The entrance to the site at mount Ebal has a different concept. Its unusual width and lack of surrounding defensive walls suggests a ceremonial function."[269]

According to Zertal, Area C of Stratum IB, "consists of the northern open ground surrounded by outer enclosure walls 78 and 99 and inner enclosure Wall 77."[270] Zertal has interpreted these walls "as enclosure walls rather than defensive walls because of the unusual entrance structure, the limited height of the walls and the

---

[264] Ibid.

[265] Ibid.

[266] Ibid., p. 119. According to Zertal, the staircase had three steps (ibid., p. 121).

[267] Ibid., p. 119.

[268] Ibid.

[269] Ibid., p. 121.

[270] Ibid., p. 121; see also ibid., p. 122 Fig. 10.

fact that the weakest wall was built on the weakest line".[271] Also, "The area C excavations showed that the enclosure walls belong to the main phase of the site, Stratum IB, and that no regular structures were built inside. In all other Iron Age I sites (with the exception of the 'Bull Site'), domestic structures are either part of the wall or located inside it."[272]

Area A of stratum IB contained the central complex of Stratum IB. According to Zertal, "The central complex of this stratum has five architectural elements: the main structure, the surrounding complex of walls, the courtyards, the double wall between the courtyards (the 'ramps') and the installations around the structure. Some of the latter belong to Stratum II."[273] Regarding the main structure,

> Built of large unhewn stones, this rectangular structure is located on a rocky spine of the ridge in Area A. Erected on bedrock, it rises 3.27 m. above it. Its corners are oriented towards the four points of the compass, the south and north corners with an error of less than 1 degree.[274]

Moreover, "The structure is relatively well preserved, perhaps due to the support of the surrounding walls and courtyards. However, it suffered from an earthquake that partially destroyed its eastern and northern corners."[275] Furthermore, "The structure was found to be artificially filled with layers containing various combinations of earth, stones, ashes, animal bones and potsherds. Four distinct layers (A-D, from bottom to top) were recognized (Fig. 8, p. 118). Layer A, which consisted of pure black ash containing many animal bones and sherds, was laid thinly and evenly over the floor of Stratum II in the western and eastern parts of the structure. Layer B, about 60 cm. thick, contained mostly stones and earth with a few bones and sherds. Layer C, consisting of 60 cm. of pure black ash, had the largest concentration of animal bones and pottery. The layers sloped diagonally downwards from

---

[271] Ibid., p. 123.

[272] Ibid.

[273] Ibid., p. 113.

[274] Ibid. See also ibid., p. 114, Fig. 5 for a drawing of the structure. The outer measurements of the main structure are 9 m by 7m.

[275] Ibid., p. 113.

inner Walls 13 and 16, indicating directions from which they were poured."[276] Moreover, "In the middle of the northern part of the fill [Layer C] some 20 pieces of white plaster about 3 cm. thick were neatly arranged in layers. These plaster chunks must have originated in Stratum II, and similar traces of plaster were found in Area B in both strata."[277] Says Zertal, "To the best of my knowledge, no plaster of any sort has been recovered from any other Iron Age I site."[278] Moreover, "The final layer [Layer D] of the fill consisted mainly of stones. This may have been the remains of a rough paving intended to seal the fill inside."[279] Finally, "The layers inside the structure were apparently all laid at the same time, since they are evenly spread throughout (except at the sides from which they were poured), and the sherds in all of them are homogeneous. Since none of the sherds could be fitted together, it is unlikely that this was debris from an upper storey, because such debris usually contains at least partially restorable vessels."[280]

Furthermore, "An accumulation of material identical in nature to Layer C of the fill inside the structure, and likewise containing many cattle bones, was found outside near its eastern corner (Loci 101, 131). We assume that this deposit originated from the fill material inside the structure and spilled out when its eastern corner collapsed. If this assumption is correct, Scarab No. 1, dated to the second half of the reign of Ramesses II (Brandl 1986-1987), which came from Locus 101, would give the structure a *terminus post quem* of the mid-thirteenth century B.C.E. The stone seal, also dated to the 13th century, found deep down in the northern part of Layer C of the fill (Locus 249) corroborates this date."[281]

According to Zertal, "In our opinion, this structure was never used as an ordinary building. It has no entrance and no floor. The stratum II surface could not be used as a floor either, because its western side is partitioned into cells and eastern part of the structure stands on irregular bedrock, 50 cm. lower than surface 61. Finally, installation 94 of Stratum II juts up in the direct center of

---

[276] Ibid.

[277] Ibid.

[278] Ibid., pp. 113-114.

[279] Ibid., p. 114.

[280] Ibid.

[281] Ibid., p. 115; see also Brandl 1986-1987, pp. 166-169, 170-171.

the gap between inner Walls 13 and 16, creating an insurmountable obstacle for any movement inside the structure. We therefore assume that it was constructed as a high platform, filled with stratum II deposits from elsewhere on the site, such as the bone and ash material found among the hearths of Locus 81."[282]

Furthermore, "The main structure was bounded on three sides by a number of additional walls, all equal in height and all about 80 cm. lower than the top of it."[283] The walls also created two courtyards. According to Zertal, these courtyards "are open, squarish, paved architectural units attached to the main structure. Although they differ slightly in plan, they both seem to be part of the overall design."[284]

Furthermore, according to Zertal, "Two parallel and adjacent walls (Walls 2 and 7) rise from the southwest to the top of the main structure (Figs 5, 6). Wall 2 is 7 m. long and 1.2 m. wide like a triangular wedge, with its base adjoining Wall 9 of the main structure and its apex on ground level perpendicular to Walls 3 and 5 of the courtyards (Fig. 6). Its gradient has been calculated as 22 degrees. At its highest preserved point (not far from the spot where it joins Wall 9), it is one course higher than the main structure, from which we assume that the structure is missing about one course of its stones. Since Wall 2 is an integral part of Walls 3 and 5, which in turn are part of the surrounding wall complex, it appears that all these elements were built in the same phase."[285]

In this regard, according to Zertal, "We have interpreted Wall 2 as a ramp rather than as an ordinary dividing wall on the following grounds: (1) It is the only means of ascent to the top of the main structure; (2) were it an ordinary wall, its outer end would have joined walls of approximately the same height as the main structure, whereas Walls 3 and 5 are low 'framewalls', whose function was to retain the floors of the open courtyards. If the courtyards had been walled and roofed, their walls would have left some evidence, at least at the points where they joined the main structure. Not only is such evidence lacking, but the entrance into the northern courtyard (and possibly the southern one as well) was

---

[282] Zertal 1986-1987, p. 115.
[283] Ibid.
[284] Ibid., p. 116.
[285] Ibid., p. 117.

by three steps, built along the width of the courtyard. Thus Wall 3 is the top step of a broad stairway on the same level as the paving of the northern courtyard."[286] Finally, "The purpose of Wall 7 described above is unclear, since it did not serve any constructional purpose. It may have served as a secondary ramp leading up to the ledges of the main structure."[287]

According to Zertal, "About 70 to 80 installations were uncovered to the north, south and east of the central complex. These consisted of crudely arranged stone-bordered circles, squares, or rectangles (and many irregular shapes) with an average diameter or width of 30 cm. to 70 cm. They are intermixed and built one upon the other in some cases. They probably represent at least two stages of use (Strata II and IB), but their stratigraphic relation to each other is not always clear. The upper layer was in turn covered by the stone mantle of Stratum IA."[288] According to Zertal, "In view of their great number, their concentration around the main structure and the presence of votive vessels, we interpret these installations as places for visitors to a sacred site to leave their offering vessels."[289]

Finally, Zertal describes Stratum IA. According to Zertal, as regards Area A, "When excavating the main structure, parts of it were found covered with stones."[290] In Zertal's judgment, "These may have been an accumulation due to field cleaning in later periods, but we think it is more likely that they were deliberately placed there."[291] Further, "If these rocks were indeed intended to cover the structure, then what we may have here is an artificial 'burial' of the place, presumably at the time of its abandonment. However, it should be noted that the courtyards were apparently not covered by stones but left exposed to the erosional elements

---

[286] Ibid.

[287] Ibid.

[288] Ibid., pp. 117-118.

[289] Ibid., p. 118, referring on p. 119 also to 1 Sam 1:24; 10:3 for the attestation of the custom of bringing vessels to a sacred site. Note also that about half of the installations contained vessels or parts of vessels (Zertal 1986-1987, p. 118).

[290] Zertal 1986-1987, p. 123.

[291] Ibid.

that carried away their beaten earth floors."[292] In Area B, according to Zertal, covering the courtyard paving of Stratum IB and 80 cm. higher there was another layer of well arranged medium-sized stones "whose purpose was apparently to cover the courtyard or to raise its level".[293] Furthermore, "The external part of the western courtyard, mainly above Walls 29 and 28, was found to be in its covered state, showing the post-occupational phase at the site. In the inner part however, it seems that some of this cover was removed by later cultivation."[294] Overall, Zertal makes the conclusion that, "before the final abandonment the site was deliberately 'buried' by a layer of stones".[295]

Zertal has also made a careful pottery analysis of the site.[296] In summary, according to Zertal, "The ceramic inventory at Mt Ebal is a homogeneous, well dated and short-lived assemblage."[297] The following material should be noted among those points which Zertal emphasizes (quoted selectively from Zertal 1986-1987, pp. 142-144):

> 1) The pottery of Stratum II is different from that of the 31 Late Bronze Age sites explored in the survey of the Manasseh hill country or the published material of the four that have been excavated in the region (Shechem, Taanach, Tell el-Farah [N], Megiddo) and from the general LB assemblages in Canaan. Nonetheless, 3% of the total finds are in the Late Bronze Age tradition, including two Mycenaean IIIB-C sherds.

> 2) The assemblage of Stratum II also differs from that of other Iron Age sites by the types of pottery and their relative frequencies. Some new and unique types make their appearance: the three-handled jar-jug, the three-handled jug and the votive vessels. The fact that these types are not found at places such as Taanach, Tell el-Farah (N), Megiddo, Hazor, Giloh and Izbeth Sartah may be due to the cultic nature of the site at Mount

---

[292] Ibid., p. 124.
[293] Ibid.
[294] Ibid.
[295] Ibid., p. 124, which see for still more details.
[296] Ibid., pp. 124-147.
[297] Ibid., p. 140.

Ebal. This may also account for the rarity of the cooking pots.

3) Cooking pots Type A, in the Late Bronze Age tradition, appear in Stratum II as 41% of the total number of cooking pots. As we learned from the survey, the sites where there is a high percentage of cooking pots of this type (25% or more of the total number of cooking pots) are concentrated mainly in the eastern half of the Shechem syncline (east of a line drawn roughly from Jenin to Shechem).

6) The noticeable continuity between Strata II and I, both in vessel types and their relative frequencies, shows that the site continued to be occupied and/or visited by the same ethnic groups.

7) The date of the abandonment of the site or the *terminus ante quem* can be suggested by ceramic comparisons with Stratum IB. Because of the regionality of the Iron Age I culture, only sites in the general vicinity have been taken into account. The nearest relevant sites and levels related to Mount Ebal Stratum IB are Taanach Periods IA-IB, Afula Stratum IIIB and Megiddo Strata VIIA-B. All these terminate in the middle of the 12th century B.C.E. and do not enter into the 11th century.

8) The stratum IB inventory differs from and predates 11th century B.C.E. assemblages such as those of Taanach IIA, Megiddo VI and Tell el-Farah (N) VIIA-B. No painted or burnished material was recovered. As for the combination jar-jug from Tell Qasile Stratum X, we tend to see it as an exception at Tell Qasile, as suggested by the excavator.

9) The assemblages of both strata are basically similar to those of the surveyed sites in the Manasseh hill country. The pinched mouth jar, the thickened-rim ("Manassite") bowl and the vessels decorated with punctured designs are local and regional products.

10) There are several vessels, however, that also point towards the cultic use of the site, as the small juglets with pointed base and/or rounded body (Fig. 18:1-2) and the small carinated bowl (Fig. 14:11-12) are possibly votive vessels, perhaps produced at the site itself. The three-handled jar-jug, of which six restorable specimens were found at Mount Ebal and a parallel in

the Philistine temple at Tell Qasile, may also be a cultic vessel.

As far as stone and metal artefacts are concerned, according to Zertal, "Conspicuous by their absence are flint sickle blades, so typical of the agricultural Iron Age I sites."[298] Moreover, "On the other hand, a number of flint knives, which are very rare in Iron Age I sites, were recovered."[299] According to Zertal, "The site of Mount Ebal is rich in metal objects. Nearly fifty bronze, iron, silver and gold items were unearthed and registered in seven seasons."[300] These are typical of the Late Bronze-Early Iron Ages.[301]

As far as the interpretation of the finds is concerned, Zertal thinks that the Stratum II structure in area A is cultic. According to Zertal, Installation 94 and Surface 61 "point to ritual activities, related to burning and animal sacrifice".[302] Zertal interprets the four-roomed house in Area B to be of domestic nature. According to Zertal, "It may have served as a residence for the people who were in charge of the cultic place on the ridge above."[303]

Regarding Stratum IB, Zertal points out that "The most difficult obstacle in interpreting the finds of the main stage at Mount Ebal is the lack of any known parallels in Iron Age I."[304] Also, "Architecturally, four possible interpretations can be given to the main complex in Area A of this stratum: a domestic building (farmhouse), a storehouse, a tower, a cultic structure or a combination of the above."[305]

Zertal then notes that the main complex is completely different architecturally from that of any known domestic building from the same time.[306] Also, the following speak against an interpretation of the structure as a farmhouse: 1) Silos or storage bins are missing. 2) No dog or ass bones are included, in contrast to most Iron Age Sites. 3) Sickle blades, used to harvest winter

---

[298] Ibid., p 148.
[299] Ibid.
[300] Ibid., p 150.
[301] Ibid.
[302] Ibid., p. 151.
[303] Ibid.
[304] Ibid.
[305] Ibid.
[306] Ibid., pp. 151-152.

crops, are missing. 4) There is no evidence for processing of other food products, such as olive presses or winepresses.[307] As far as the possibility of a storehouse is concerned, Zertal notes that the storehouse at Shiloh was full of large storage jars and pithoi, whereas the Mount Ebal structure was not.[308]

According to Zertal, there are also good reasons for not taking the structure as a tower. First of all, "no tower dating to the Israelite settlement period is known so far".[309] Secondly, according to Zertal, watchtowers to guard crops appeared only during Iron Age II, when the small IA I settlement sites became bigger and fields expanded further away from the village centres.[310] Thirdly, "Mount Ebal has always been an obstacle to transportation and there is no road there for a watchtower to observe".[311] Fourthly, no security considerations were taken into account in choosing its location, and the site is not surrounded by a defensive wall.[312] Finally, the possibility of a tower in a religious context is precluded, since, according to Zertal known (seeming) examples at Megiddo and Shechem (from LBA) are architecturally "entirely different".[313] Also, according to Zertal, no evidence for any superstructure exists.[314] Moreover, the stone debris is insufficient for a second storey and no evidence of bricks or brick material exists.[315] Finally, "The fill of the main structure was poured in layers and is not the usual hodgepodge of destruction debris from an upper storey".[316]

Thus, according to Zertal, "By the process of elimination, we are therefore left with the concept of Mount Ebal as a cultic site".[317] Then, according to Zertal, "The absence of any building in the ordinary sense of the word in Stratum IB at Mount Ebal

---

[307] Ibid., p. 152.
[308] Ibid., p. 153.
[309] Ibid. (cf. however below, p. 179n327).
[310] Zertal 1986-1987, p. 153.
[311] Ibid.
[312] Ibid.
[313] Ibid.
[314] Ibid.
[315] Ibid.
[316] Ibid.
[317] Ibid., p. 154.

excludes its definition as a temple."[318] Zertal also notes that the covering of the site with stones in Stratum IA could have taken place because the site was still considered sacred after it was abandoned.[319]

Also, according to Zertal, "The limited range of the faunal remains, all conforming to Mosaic dietary laws, and all except the fallow deer mentioned in the Bible as suitable for burnt offerings, is probably significant, since the assemblage differs from that found in Bronze Age and Iron Age domestic sites and in Canaanite cultic sites."[320] Moreover, the structure in Stratum IB "seems to be designed for a large crowd".[321] According to Zertal, one has to note, though, that despite a large number of pottery offerings, "except for a few votive vessels, and perhaps the chalices, no cultic vessels were found, unless the unique jar-jug, which has a parallel in the Philistine temple at Tell Qasile, is indeed a cultic vessel. The stone basins, which are not found at any other site, may also have had some unknown cultic function."[322]

Finally, Zertal concludes, "The question must be raised as to whether there is a connection between the biblical tradition and the finds from the site. No conclusive answer can be given, but it should be noted that this is the only transitional Late Bronze Age / Iron Age site existing on the mountain. It correlates with the biblical tradition by the date of the events, the location and general character of the site."[323]

Archaeologists have generally been either cautious[324] or negative[325] towards a cultic interpretation of the site, let alone

---

[318] Ibid.

[319] Ibid., p. 156, referring to scholars who have interpreted certain other finds as cultic burials of sacred monuments or sites.

[320] Ibid., p. 157; cf. Horwitz 1986-1987, esp. p. 185 Table 8 and p. 187.

[321] Zertal 1986-1987, p. 157.

[322] Ibid.

[323] Ibid., p. 158. Ten years after the excavations, Zertal thinks that the site is most likely connected with Joshua's covenant ceremony (A. Zertal, personal communication, December 1999).

[324] See Mazar 1990a, p. 350; Finkelstein 1988, pp. 82-85; Hess 1993, pp. 135-137; Gilmour 1995, pp. 108-120.

[325] Kempinski 1986; Fritz 1993, p. 185; Ahlström 1993, p. 366; Ottosson 1991, p. 241.

about connecting it with Joshua. However, there has been no satisfactory answer to the problem of what the function of the structure is if it is a settlement building as parallels are lacking,[326] and on the other hand, to the problem that if the structure is a watchtower why there is no destruction debris, especially around the sloping 'ramp' which is supposed to have been formed by the collapse of the tower.[327] Further, one should add that when scholars object to the possibility of interpreting the site as Joshua's altar based on a reading of the book of Joshua, they are not proceeding on an archaeological basis, but replacing one literary reading of the biblical text with another.[328]

On the other hand, even if the cultic nature of the site is acknowledged, it is by no means certain that the site belonged to the Israelites at the time concerned.[329] Yet, if one were to assume a thirteenth century exodus/settlement as most scholars do, the impression given in the biblical sources is that the Shechem area

---

[326] Note however that Gilmour (1995, pp. 116-117) suggests that the installations (cf. above, p. 173) around the main structure should be interpreted as small silos (but cf. Zertal [1986-1987, p. 152], according to whom, "The installations surrounding the main structure were definitely not used for grain storage since neither their size nor construction is suitable for such a function").

[327] Cf. esp. Kempinski 1986, p. 45 vs Zertal 1986, pp. 50-51 concerning destruction debris. On the other hand, it has to be pointed out that an Iron I watchtower has been found at Giloh since Zertal's report on Mt Ebal and, moreover, this tower evidently was not located inside a defensive wall, even though evidence of a defensive wall exists elsewhere at the site (see Mazar 1990, incl. p. 78 Fig. 1; p. 92). It is also worth noting that the Iron I tower at Giloh was *not* located on the highest point of the hill (see Mazar 1990, incl p. 78 Fig. 1; pp. 83-84). Finally, the measurements of the tower, (roughly 11 m square; see ibid., p. 79) are fairly similar to the main structure at mount Ebal (7 m by 9 m), even though on the other hand, the Giloh structure has a solid foundation (the foundation IA II tower is similar to the main structure at Mt Ebal; see Mazar 1990, p. 97 Fig. 10), and nothing comparable to Installation 94, the fill of the main structure, and the surrounding wall complex exists at Giloh.

[328] See esp. Kempinski 1986, pp. 48-49, criticised by Zertal 1986, pp. 52-53.

[329] Cf. Hess 1993, p. 136.

was at least under a strong influence of the Israelites at the time. But here again, one comes back to the literary sources.

Also, Finkelstein has challenged the dating of Mount Ebal remains based on pottery analysis. According to Finkelstein, there are two similar specimens at Shiloh and one at Tell Qasile Stratum X (11th century) to the six storage jars with three handles found at Mount Ebal.[330] Due to the parallels, Finkelstein suggests a later date for Mount Ebal than Zertal.[331] However, if Late Bronze vessels were still attested at Mount Ebal, it is conceivable that the combination jar-jug in question had a reasonably long period of use even though it is rare among finds.

A clear difficulty about connecting the site with Joshua's covenant ceremony is that deer bones were found among the animal remains.[332] As deer evidently is not one of the sacrificial animals in the Bible, this makes it more difficult to associate the site with the biblical testimony (Ex 20:22-26; Josh 8:30-35).[333] To harmonize, one would have to be able to show that the deer remains could originate from the outside of the main structure itself,[334] and think that they are remains of ceremonial eating.[335]

---

[330] Bunimovitz and Finkelstein 1993, p. 158; Finkelstein 1988, p. 85.

[331] Bunimovitz and Finkelstein 1993, p. 158.

[332] Fallow deer comprised 10% of the total diagnostic bone sample (Horwitz 1986-1987, p. 174). Also, fallow deer forms 21% of the diagnostic material in the main structure, whereas it forms 5% of the of the diagnostic material in all the other areas combined (Horwitz 1986-1987, p. 174). Note also that deer bones were found even inside Installation 94 of Stratum II (A. Zertal, personal communication, December 1999).

[333] Cf. Horwitz 1986-1987, pp. 183, 186.

[334] I.e. the deer remains should be thought to be a part of an artificial fill which was inserted when the monumental structure of Stratum IB was constructed.

[335] Cf. also Dt 27:7; Dt 12:7, 17-18 concerning ceremonial eating, and note that Deuteronomy explicitly allows the eating of deer (Dt 14:5). On the other hand, according to Zertal, B. Mazar thought that deer was still accepted as a sacrificial animal at the time of the Ebal ritual, and was only in the process of being removed from that role at the time (A. Zertal, personal communication, December 1999). One might perhaps also try to ask/speculate whether Ex 20:22-26, Lev 17; Dt 27 and Josh 8:30-35 exclude the possibility that deer could be offered on a local altar (i.e.

Moreover, if one were to suppose that the site might be connected with Joshua, a number of further detailed questions would remain. A major problem is the relation of Strata II and I. The first issue to point out is that there is clear evidence that both Strata I and II may have involved cultic activity. In fact, Stratum II gives very strong evidence of burning, as the stones of Installation 94 were charred, and ash containing animal bones was found directly by it[336] and inside it,[337] and moreover, the fill of the main structure which contains ash originates from Stratum II.[338] Also, as there were hearths and installations on the stony pavement of the courtyard in area B in Stratum IB together with "a large quantity of Stratum IB potsherds stuck between the stones" and "many animal bones",[339] and burnt bones belonging to Stratum IB seem to have been found around the main structure,[340] there seems to have been cultic activity associated with Stratum IB as well. Also, it is interesting in this regard that the "ramp" leading to the top of the main structure of Stratum IB was only 1.2 meters wide,[341] and it would thus be difficult to bring animals up to the top of the main structure, as Kempinski observes.[342] Yet, on the other hand, if the structure was an altar, it is by no means certain that the killing of animals would have occurred on the top of the structure (cf. Lev 1:3-9 etc.).

Another important issue in regard to the relation of Strata II and I is that the main structure of Stratum IB has been built so that Installation 94 of Stratum II is at the exact centre of it.[343] This very strongly suggests that the two belong together. On the other hand, if we were to take at least reasonably at face value the biblical tradition of a conquest which included a programme to eliminate

outside the central sanctuary regulated by the Priestly offering rules) on a special occasion, even if this were not the normal practice.

[336] Zertal 1986-1987, p. 109.

[337] So A. Zertal, personal communication, December 1999.

[338] Zertal 1986-1987, p. 113, and A. Zertal, personal communication, December 1999.

[339] Zertal 1986-1987, p. 119.

[340] See Horwitz 1986-1987, p. 177 Fig. 3.

[341] Zertal 1986-1987, p. 117.

[342] Kempinski 1986, p. 45.

[343] Cf. Zertal 1986-1987, p. 110 (including Fig. 3 on that page).

Canaanite cultic practices, it would be hard to think that Joshua, the ardent Yahwist, would have built the altar on a Canaanite cultic structure so that the altar was left partly standing neatly in the centre (cf. also Dt 12:3). We would not expect either that he would fill the new structure with debris from the previous structure, nor leave the situation as it is until he would produce debris with which he could fill the structure. Rather, even if the structure were not a cultic one, we would expect that he would carefully destroy all of the structures of the previous place or build on a previously unused place.[344] And, the biblical tradition naturally indicates that it was the first time when the Israelites were at the site, since they had just crossed the Jordan. Thus, supposing that Stratum IB was Joshua's altar, it would be difficult to think that Stratum II could have been Israelite. In other words, it is hard to square the circumstances of Stratum IB so that it was the altar of Joshua's covenant ceremony.

On the other hand, as indicated above, there is very good reason to think that installation 94 in Stratum II was an altar.[345] Then, if we think that the exodus / early settlement happened in the thirteenth century, it should rather be this altar which should be associated with Joshua, if anything.[346] Then, why would the second structure have been built? The most natural possibility is that Stratum IB was an improved version of the altar, and has been built on top of Stratum II. If so, one could think of a possibility that the new construction was used also as a monument.[347] In this regard, we know that according to Josh 4, stones were to be set up at Gilgal as a monument for the future generations. We also know

---

[344] Note also the installations around the main structure which seem to have been used in both strata (Zertal 1986-1987, pp. 117-119; cf. above, p. 173).

[345] Cf. again Zertal 1986-1987, pp. 110-111.

[346] Zertal thinks that the older altar was part of a foundation ceremony before the building of the actual altar (A. Zertal, personal communication, December 1999). Also, except for the living quarters (for which see Zertal 1986-1987, pp. 111-112), it is not certain how long Stratum II lasted. According to Zertal, Stratum II could even have been very short-lived (A. Zertal, personal communication, December 1999). On the other hand, there was evidence of layering in Stratum IB, which indicates some time of use (ibid.).

[347] Cf. Zertal 1986-1987, p. 160.

that according to Josh 22:9-34, the Transjordanian altar was a big monument (Josh 22:10).[348] That the altar was a monument could be corroborated by the fact that no living quarters have been found for Stratum IB so far.[349] Rather, an entrance and a courtyard was built on top of Stratum II living quarters of area B.[350] Yet, that animal bones were found in Stratum IB may suggest cultic activity in association with Stratum IB as well.[351]

One also has to remember that the site as a whole was soon abandoned. Was the site buried intentionally? The matter is not certain, especially as the whole of the Stratum IA was not covered with stones. But if the site was buried intentionally, it is possible that the site was buried in order to avoid its abuse. One might even think that the site was abandoned in favour of Shiloh.[352]

Then, what about the plastered stones? First of all, no writing was found on them.[353] Yet, Zertal thinks that there could have been writing on them originally.[354] Also, one has to stress the fact that finding plaster at the site is extraordinary.[355] As the pieces of plaster seem to have been arranged neatly,[356] this suggests that they could have been set there ceremonially. One could even imagine

---

[348] See below, Chapter 4.5 for a detailed treatment of Josh 22:9-34.

[349] Cf. Zertal 1986-1987, p. 123.

[350] Cf. Zertal 1986-1987, pp. 119-121. Yet one has to remember that the whole site has not been excavated (A. Zertal, personal communication, December 1999).

[351] Cf. above, p. 181.

[352] Thus also Zertal (A. Zertal, personal communication, December 1999). For considerations of the role of Shiloh during the last days of Joshua and the period of Judges, see below, chapters 4.5 and 4.6.

[353] A. Zertal, personal communication, December 1999.

[354] Ibid.

[355] Cf. again Zertal 1986-1987, pp. 113-114: "To the best of my knowledge, no plaster of any sort has been recovered from any other Iron Age I site." Also, according to Zertal, only two other examples of plastered finds are known otherwise: Tell Deir Alla and Kuntillet Ajrud in Sinai (A. Zertal, personal communication, December 1999; cf. Tigay 1996, p. 248; Boling-Wright 1982, p. 248).

[356] Zertal 1986-1987, p. 113.

that the pieces are plaster from the first structure which had fallen off due to weathering.[357]

In this regard, if one thinks of the possibility of linking the structure with Joshua, one may ask the question of where the associated standing stones should be. No trace of such stones has been found. Yet, as the whole site has not been excavated, one might think of the possibility that they lie buried elsewhere nearby.[358] One might also think that the stones were carried off or otherwise eliminated when the site was abandoned.

Finally, Zertal suggests that it might be possible that the current location of Mt Gerizim is not the same as in Joshua's time. According to Zertal, it has been suggested that one of the mountains which faces the altar could be the Mt Gerizim of Joshua.[359] On the other hand, if the location of Mt Gerizim is what is currently thought, even though the structure excavated by Zertal is not visible from there, it would not necessarily preclude the possibility of a connection of the site at Mt Ebal with Joshua. The curses ceremony need not be thought to have taken place at the site of the altar.

We may conclude that Zertal has given good reasons to suggest that the Mt Ebal site as a whole could be of cultic nature, but on the other hand, the matter is by no means certain. It is also possible that the site could relate to the Israelites, and even the covenant ceremony of Joshua, even though it has to be emphasized that this is by no means certain, and specifically, a number of the details of the site are at least somewhat problematic when one compares them with the testimony of Dt 27 and Josh 8:30-35. Moreover, even if the archaeological and literary data could be made to fit, at times one has to at least somewhat try to stretch one's imagination in order to think how they could be correlated in detail. All in all, we may conclude that based on the available evidence, the interpretation of the structure found on Mount Ebal

---

[357] Note however that traces of plaster were also found in Area B in both Strata II and IB (cf. above, p. 171).

[358] So A. Zertal, personal communication, December 1999. In fact, Zertal notes that about 50 m West there is a big pile of rocks (30 long and 5 m high), and that a cut was made into the pile, revealing a beginning of walls underneath.

[359] A. Zertal, personal communication, December 1999.

cannot be considered as settled, and we must reserve final judgment, noting also that whether or not the site is "Joshua's altar" does not essentially affect the conclusions of this study. However, in any case, the uniqueness of the main structure with its surrounding wall complex and its possible connections with Joshua make the question of the nature of the site at Mount Ebal not less than intriguing. Also, the fact that no structure has been found from Mt Ebal during Iron Age II rather speaks for the antiquity of the Joshua tradition, as there is no evidence of a cultic centre at Mt Ebal during the time of the monarchy from which to draw the tradition.[360] Moreover, it is doubtful that a late writer would have created a story about an important ceremony outside Jerusalem in the territory of Joseph if he were promoting the centrality of Jerusalem, even if the story refers to a time before the building of Solomon's temple.[361]

4.5.   The Transjordanian altar (Josh 22:9-34) and the Last Days of Joshua

In order to appreciate how the book of Joshua portrays centralization of worship in the last days of Joshua, we will take Josh 22:9-34 as the basis of our discussion. We will then relate the passage and its view of centralization with the rest of the material in the latter part of the book of Joshua. The message and literary composition of Josh 22:9-34 will also lead us to take issue with such larger questions as the date and provenance of the book of Joshua as a whole and the relationship of the book of Joshua to the Pentateuch and to Judges-2 Kings.

Joshua 22:9-34 describes an incident regarding the Transjordanian tribes of Reuben, Gad and Half-Manasseh. When

---

[360] Note however also that based on Dt 27; Josh 8:30-35, it is possible to think that the altar was used only for the one-time event of covenant renewal (cf. Tigay 1996, p. 249; Levine 1974, p. 40), and consequently, one may think that it is entirely possible that no remains of the altar, which basically could have been located anywhere on the mountain, would have survived in any case. On the other hand, the erecting of stones (Dt 27:1-4; cf. above, p. 158f.) would suggest monumental usage, and thus an appropriation beyond a one-time ceremony.

[361] Cf. Zertal 1986-1987, p. 158; Soggin 1972, pp. 241, 243-244; Anbar 1985, p. 309; Gray 1986, pp. 94-95.

the Transjordanians return from the conquest to their allotted territory, they build a big altar at the side of Jordan (v. 10).[362] Upon hearing this, the rest of the Israelites see the matter as a cultic violation and send a delegation to confront the Transjordanians (vv. 11-20). However, the Transjordanians explain that the altar is not to be for sacrifice, but it is to serve only as a memorial and a reminder for proper worship in front of the altar of the Lord which is before his tabernacle (מִשְׁכָּן; vv. 21-29). The Israelite delegation, led by Phinehas *ben* Eleazar accepts this explanation and returns back home to Cisjordan (vv. 30-34).

According to J.S. Kloppenborg,

> The story of the departure of the two and one-half Transjordanian tribes following the completion of the conquest and the building of their altar remains a puzzle in spite of the attention which it has received. Viewed in the context of Joshua, chap 22 is anomalous on several counts. It relates action of the confederacy not against the Canaanite inhabitants of the land but against another Israelite group. In this it resembles the attack on Benjamin (and Jabesh-Gilead) in Jgs 19-21. The dispute does not appear to be primarily political or territorial but cultic, and it presupposes (anachronistically) the legitimacy of a single cult-center. Accordingly it is not Joshua, but a priest, Phinehas son of Eleazar who is the central actor. Equally remarkable is the solution to the dispute: the Transjordanian altar is no altar at all, but only a "witness stone". It is perhaps these and other problems that explain the general uneasiness felt with this chapter and the reluctance of the standard histories of Israel to treat it in any depth (or even to suggest an appropriate chronological framework for the events narrated).[363]

Considering these comments by Kloppenborg in regard to Joshua 22:9-34, it should come as no surprise that scholarly interpretation of the passage is very diverse. Various opinions exist as to the purpose and setting of the narrative and its traditio-

---

[362] Concerning the problems involved in determining the exact location (vv. 10-11) and the name (v. 34) of the altar, see Snaith 1978, pp. 330-335; Kloppenborg 1981, pp. 368-369.

[363] Kloppenborg 1981, p. 347.

historical formation. Kloppenborg summarizes Noth, Steuernagel, Herzberg and Möhlenbrink as follows:

> Noth sees an old aetiological legend explaining the now-missing name in v. 34, although he hesitates to say more in view of the thorough re-editing of the chapter. Steuernagel posits an old story of an altar named "witness" (עד) at a cultic city with a stone circle (גלילות), perhaps near Gilgal. To this Herzberg adds that behind the deuteronomistic theology of centralization of the cult lies an old story whose purpose it was to attest the unity in worship of the Trans- and Cis-Jordanian tribes. Möhlenbrink goes much beyond these reconstructions: Jos 22:9-34 is a cult-polemic legend from the period of the judges which reveals the conflict of two amphictyonic centers, Gilgal, the cult center for a Reubenite-Gadite-Benjaminite confederacy, and the Israelite (Ephraimite) sanctuary at Shiloh.[364]

Also,

> Perhaps the most radical thesis is that of J. Dus who recognizes both P and Dtr editing but dates both to the period of Judges! In his view, during the period of judges the ark was periodically placed upon a wagon pulled by cows and allowed to go wherever the cows took it. It was by this method that the "place which Yahweh himself shall choose among the tribes" (Dt 12:5) was determined. Since Jordan formed a barrier to the cows, Reuben and Gad felt it necessary to build their own sanctuary. This provoked hostilities and eventually led to the decision to keep the ark at Shiloh.[365]

Kloppenborg himself thinks that Josh 22:9-34 is based on an old tradition of a Yahwistic altar which a postexilic Priestly writer has changed into a nonsacrificial altar and added the elements of conflict in the story.[366] De Vaux writes that all that he would venture to say is that the story preserves the memory of conflicting cults.[367] According to Eissfeldt, Josh 22 presents "eine Erzählung

---

[364] Ibid., pp. 347-348.
[365] Ibid., pp. 348-349.
[366] Ibid., pp. 365-370.
[367] De Vaux 1978/1971, p. 583.

über einen Angriff auf das Kultmonopol des Heiligtums von Silo und seine Zurückschlagung".[368] Moreover, for Eissfeldt, "Die Erzählung Jos 22 betrifft wenigstens in ihrer Grundlage nicht kultische Strömungen der drei Jahrhunderte 700 bis 400 v.Chr., sondern Vorgänge des 12. Jahrhunderts v.Chr., die Silo zum Mittelpunkt haben und erst nachträglich zu den Kultproblemen jener drei Jahrhunderte in Beziehung gesetzt worden sind."[369] Butler thinks that the tradition originally restricted sacrificial worship to Shiloh, and was forbidden at Gilgal, the place where the rival altar stood. According to Butler, the original tradition which comes from the time prior to Samuel was taken up in the book of Joshua in the postexilic era to speak to the Babylonian exiles concerning worship outside the land of Israel. However, Butler leaves open the extent of editing of the ancient tradition in the postexilic period, noting: "Did the tradition as a whole gain its contours at the time of Shiloh's dominance?"[370] Finally, according to McConville, "at least the core of the present narrative belongs to a time before the period of the monarchy, when the centrality of Shiloh in Israel was in fact being asserted (cf. Jdg 21:21; 1 Sa 1-3)".[371]

All the above scholars think that Joshua 22:9-34 is based on an old tradition which has undergone more or less extensive editing to reach its present form. Yet, in Kloppenborg's words,

> While most critics admit either Deuteronomistic or Priestly editing of the passage (or both), some insist that Jos 22 is a retrojection of Priestly and post-exilic concerns into the period of the conquest. No early tradition is present at all. A. Menes, for example, sought to show that the passage is an aetiology for the synagogue ("an altar without sacrifice"). The exiles, for whom worship outside Israel was necessary (Ez 11:14-16), solved their dilemma by regarding the synagogue as a "copy" (Jos 22:28; cf. Ez 11:16) of the altar in Jerusalem, but they avoided sacrifice in accordance with the post-deuteronomistic understanding of the cult. Jos 22:9-34 was therefore to be regarded as a legitimation

---

[368] Eissfeldt 1962-1979b/1973, p. 14.
[369] Ibid.
[370] Butler 1983, pp. 243-244.
[371] McConville 1993, p. 100.

of the synagogue and an exilic creation. Likewise rejecting the presence of ancient tradition in this chapter, J.G. Vink believes that Jos 22 is a late post-exilic aetiology which, far from warning against illegitimate sanctuaries, actually legitimates limited cultic use of altars outside Palestine, such as the one at Yeb mentioned in the Elephantine Papyri (EP 32).[372]

Kloppenborg has argued well against the interpretation of Menes. In Kloppenborg's words,

> It seems most unlikely that an aetiology for the synagogue would involve an altar, since that was not a usual part of the synagogue furnishings. Had the tribes built a *bet el* not for sacrifice, or a place of assembly (*byt hknst*) or had the account mentioned "prayer" there would be more justification in seeing an aetiology for the synagogue.[373]

Against Vink, one may say that the priests at Yeb in their letter to Judah (EA 30, lines 24-28;[374] the letter dated 408 BC[375]), say that they would like to get the temple rebuilt as formerly[376] so that they could offer there on the altar (על מדבחא) meal-offering (מנחתא[377]), incense (לבונתא) and sacrifice (דבחן, עלותא [line 28]).[378] The answer from Judah (EA 32;[379] dated about 408 BC[380]) authorizes the building of a new temple in place of the former, and offering meal offering (מנחתא) and incense (לבונתא) on the altar (מדבחא) "as formerly was done" (זי לקדמין הוה מתעבד [lines 10-11]). Whatever one thinks of the disposition and knowledge of the

---

[372] Kloppenborg 1981, p. 349.

[373] Ibid., p. 363.

[374] See PORTEN-YARDENI, vol 1, pp. 68-69 for the text, including a copy of the original manuscript; cf. Cowley 1967/1923, pp. 111-113.

[375] See Cowley 1967/1923, p. 108.

[376] Lines 4-13 tell how the temple was destroyed by Egyptians three years earlier.

[377] According to Cowley 1967/1923, p. 117, "a mistake for מנחתא".

[378] Note also that lines 20-22 lament that meal-offering, incense or sacrifice had not been able to be offered since the temple was destroyed (cf. lines 4-6).

[379] Lines 8-11; see PORTEN-YARDENI, vol 1, pp. 76-77 for the text, including a copy of the original manuscript; cf. Cowley 1967/1923, p. 123.

[380] See Cowley 1967/1923, p. 122.

Judean writers as regards to the legal requirements of the Pentateuch,[381] especially bearing in mind that the correspondence is between the priests of Elephantine and the political establishment of Judah,[382] the disposition and knowledge are not the same as that indicated by Joshua 22:9-34. Based on Joshua 22:9-34, there should have been no cultic activity on the Elephantine altar whatsoever. In relation to this, Joshua 22:23, 29 specifically excludes meal offerings (מנחה) which the reply from Judah to Elephantine explicitly authorizes. Thus, it is hardly likely that Joshua 22 can be interpreted based on the evidence of the Elephantine papyri as an aetiology which legitimates the Elephantine temple.[383]

Another scholar who has argued for a purely post-exilic setting of the narrative is Fritz. According to Fritz, "Die Bildung paßt in die Auseinandersetzungen der nachexilischen Zeit, als der Tempel von Jerusalem zum Mittelpunkt des israelitischen Kultes geworden war und die Frage der Zugehörigkeit von Juden außerhalb Judäas zum rechtmäßigen Israel dringend wurde."[384]

However, Fritz's interpretation has immediate problems. Simply, why would the Jews outside Judea, either in Samaria, or more probably in Babylonia be addressed via the appellation of Reubenites, Gadites and Manassites? Moreover, for the Judeans of the postexilic time, the Transjordanians have been deported some 300 years earlier, and have not returned (1 Chr 5:26). Thus, to speak about the Transjordanians already suggests a historical reminiscence of past days, a matter which Fritz's approach excludes. Further, who would have thought that Babylonia or Egypt, where the Elephantine colony is, is a land which the Israelites have inherited (Josh 22:19)? What meaning would an altar at the side of Jordan have either for the Babylonians, for the people of Elephantine, or even for the Samaritans (Josh 22:10, 23-27)? Moreover, in Josh 22, it is only the land east of Jordan which may be unclean, not Samaria or Egypt (Josh 22:19; cf. the importance of the river Jordan in Josh 22:25). Why would a possible settlement to

---

[381] Cf. Cowley 1967/1923, pp. xix-xxii.

[382] EA 30 was addressed to Bigvai, (Persian) governor of Judah (EA 30, line 1), and the reply in EA 32 (line 1) is a memorandum from Bigvai, and Delaiah, son of Sanballat governor of Samaria (cf. EA 30, line 29).

[383] Cf. Kloppenborg 1981, p. 364.

[384] Fritz 1994, p. 222.

Judah be mentioned (Josh 22:19) if it were not in any way necessary for those Jews who live in Samaria, or even for those who live in Elephantine? There simply are too many things that do not make sense if one wishes to suggest that Josh 22 was composed to address Jews outside Judah in the postexilic era.

Thus, it is not easy to find a post-exilic *Sitz-im-Leben* for the narrative as a whole. As regards the views of those scholars who think that there was an original story which was substantially different from its present form, the fact that practically all of them disagree concerning what the original form of the story was underlines the problem of trying to discover one from the present form of the narrative. The problem is even more underlined especially when none of these scholars, except for Dus, have ventured even to do a source-critical analysis of the text, even if every one of them agrees that the passage has gone through either Deuteronomistic or Priestly editing, or both.[385] The problem of separating the passage into sources is also demonstrated by the fact that one can conveniently describe the passage by a palistrophic model, as indicated by Jobling:

(a) Transjordanians build the altar (v. 10)
  (b) Cisjordanians threaten war (v. 12)
    (c) Cisjordanians send an embassy (vv. 13-15)
      (d) Accusatory speech by the embassy (vv. 15b-20)
        (e) Transjordanians' reply (vv. 21-29)
      (d') Accepting speech by the embassy (vv. 30-31)
    (c') Return of the embassy to Cisjordan (v. 32)
  (b') Withdrawal of the Cisjordanian threat of war (v. 33)
(a') Transjordanians name the altar (v. 34)[386]

Figure 5: The structure of Josh 22:9-34 (Jobling)

In any case, those scholars who think that the original form of the account was at least reasonably similar to its present form all broadly agree that the passage is about the cultic hegemony of

---

[385] See Kloppenborg 1981, p. 349 (quoted above, p. 188); Eissfeldt 1962-1979b/1973, pp. 10-14; Dus 1964, pp. 539-545. Cf. Noth, according to whom the passage "cannot be divided into sources" (Noth 1953, p. 134).

[386] Jobling 1980, p. 191.

Shiloh in the premonarchic period.[387] Especially, it is notable that according to Eissfeldt,

> Die Erzählung Jos 22 betrifft wenigstens in ihrer Grundlage nicht kultische Strömungen der drei Jahrhunderte 700 bis 400 v.Chr., sondern Vorgänge des 12. Jahrhunderts v.Chr., die Silo zum Mittelpunkt haben und erst nachträglich zu den Kultproblemen jener drei Jahrhunderte in Beziehung gesetzt worden sind.[388]

Thus, it is not at all unnatural or unreasonable to see at least the basic form of Joshua 22:9-34 to concern the premonarchic period, in line with the narrative's self-presentation. Then, a major issue is the Priestly and Deuteronomic features of the narrative and their implications on the dating, provenance and the interpretation of the narrative.

Even though critical scholars have not been able to divide the chapter into sources, D.G. Schley has listed the following Priestly expressions in Josh 22:9-34:

אֶרֶץ כְּנַעַן: vv. 9a, 10a,11, 32

שִׁלֹה: vv. 9a, 12b

אֲחֻזָּה: vv. 9, 19 (with verb אחז)

עַל־פִּי יהוה בְּיַד־מֹשֶׁה: v. 9

וַיִּקָּהֲלוּ כָּל־עֲדַת בְּנֵי־יִשְׂרָאֵל: v. 12 (cf. Josh 18:2 [sic; actually 18:1])

כָּל עֲדַת יהוה: v. 15b [sic; actually v. 16]

פִּינְחָס בֶּן־אֶלְעָזָר הַכֹּהֵן: vv. 13b, 31a, 32a

פִּינְחָס הַכֹּהֵן: v. 30a

לַעֲבֹד אֶת־עֲבֹדַת יהוה: v. 27

טְמֵאָה אֶרֶץ אֲחֻזַּתְכֶם: v. 19a

זִבְחֵי שְׁלָמִים: v. 23

מֶרֶד: v. 22

מָרַד: vv. 16, 18, 19, 29

---

[387] Eissfeldt (1962-1979b/1973, p. 14), Butler (1983, p. 243) and McConville (1993, p. 100). Dus and Möhlenbrink can also be included in this group.

[388] Eissfeldt 1962-1979b/1973, p. 14 (also quoted above, p. 188). Cf. Ottosson 1991, p. 35: "Det rör sig här om gammalt material, som kanske rent av går tillbaka på Sauls tid (There is old material included here which perhaps even goes back to the time of Saul)."

מַעַל ... מָעַל: vv. 16, 20, 31

נשׂאים: vv. 14 (3x), 30a, 32a (cf. Num 17:17, 21; Josh
   22:14a; Num 4:34; Josh 22:30a)

הטהרנו: v. 17

מִשְׁכַּן [יהוה]: vv. 19, 29[389]

Figure 6: Priestly expressions in Josh 22:9-34 (Schley)

It is clear from Schley's list that the passage has many affinities with Priestly language and ideas.[390] Deuteronomic features are more difficult to find. However, McConville has pointed out that the unity of Israel, which is one of the great themes of Deuteronomy, is affirmed in Joshua 22:9-34.[391] Clearly a main thrust of the narrative is to affirm the unity of the Transjordanians with the rest of Israel.[392]

As regards the unity of worship in the passage, all commentators agree that such a concept is advocated by the narrative in its final form. On the other hand, even though Wellhausen thought that the passage attests Priestly concerns of the unity of worship,[393] later commentators have not agreed whether a Priestly or a Deuteronomistic conception of unity of worship underlies the passage. A number of commentators think that the conception of the unity of worship is Deuteronomistic.[394] Others think that it is Priestly.[395] Some do not indicate either way

---

[389] Schley 1989, p. 205, Table 5.

[390] Se also Noth 1987/1943, p. 118; 1953, p. 133; Eissfeldt 1962-1979b/1973, pp. 10-12; Kloppenborg 1981, pp. 356, 361; Dus 1964, pp. 542-544; de Vaux 1978/1971, pp. 581-582; Weinfeld, 1972, p. 181; Gray 1986, pp. 52, 171-172; Wellhausen 1905/1878, pp. 37-38.

[391] McConville 1993, pp. 99-100. Cf. McConville's reference to von Rad on the concept of unity of Israel as a great concept of Deuteronomy in ibid., p. 99n84. Cf also Wenham 1971b, pp. 144-145.

[392] We have also indicated above, Chapter 3.2 that the unity of Israel is part of Priestly concerns as well. However, the Priestly concept is rather implicit, whereas the Deuteronomic concept is rather explicit.

[393] See Wellhausen 1905/1878, pp. 37-38.

[394] See esp. Snaith 1978, p. 330; Soggin 1972, p. 214; de Vaux 1978/1971, p. 581.

[395] Schley 1989, p. 125; Weinfeld 1972, p. 181; Dus 1964, p. 542; Kloppenborg 1981, p. 359.

or do not at least make the matter clear.[396] The reason for this uncertainty is undoubtedly the fact that on the one hand, the passage contains many Priestly features, and Josh 22:29 explicitly states that,

חלילה לנו ממנו למרד ביהוה ולשוב היום מאחרי
יהוה לבנות מזבח לעלה למנחה ולזבח מלבד מזבח
יהוה אלהינו אשר לפני משכנו:

> Far be it from us that we would rebel against Yahweh
> and turn away from following Yahweh to build an altar
> for burnt offering, meal offering, or sacrifice in
> addition to the altar of Yahweh our God which is in
> front of his tabernacle.

In other words, the passage clearly seems to affirm that all sacrifices should be centralized to the tent of meeting. Then, if one follows the Wellhausenian interpretation of Lev 17,[397] one can naturally think that the concept of worship in the passage is Priestly. On the other hand, as the passage as a whole attests the unity of Israel, a great Deuteronomic theme, it is also easy to think that the centralization requirement is Deuteronomic.[398]

However, this problem is easily solved based on our previous considerations. We have suggested that the centralization requirement of Lev 17 was only paradigmatically valid after the wilderness period.[399] Thus, the centralization requirement in Josh 22:9-34 is not Priestly. On the other hand, if we look at the narrative in the book of Joshua which surrounds Josh 22:9-34, according to Josh 21:43-45,

ויתן יהוה לישראל את־כל־הארץ אשר נשבע לתת

---

[396] Eissfeldt 1962-1979b/1973, p. 14. Also, Eissfeldt thinks that the concept was originally neither Priestly nor Deuteronomistic, even though he states that, "Gewiß ist unsere Erzählung im Sinne von D und P ausgelegt, wie sie denn Elemente der Vorstellungswelt und des Sprachgebrauchs von D und P aufweist." (ibid.). Noth 1953, p. 133 seems to indicate a Deuteronomistic concept, but one cannot be absolutely certain. Gray 1986, p. 52 seems to lean on a Priestly appropriation.

[397] Cf. above, Introduction, p. 8, incl. n37.

[398] According to McConville 1993, p. 100, "The 'Deuteronomic' character of the issues here are beyond dispute."

[399] See above, Chapter 3.2; cf also the early period of Joshua, as discussed above, Chapter 4.3.

לאבותם וירשוה וישבו בה:
ויגח יהוה להם מסביב ככל אשר־נשבע לאבותם
ולא־עמד איש בפניהם מכל־איביהם את כל־איביהם
נתן יהוה בידם:
לא־נפל דבר מכל הדבר הטוב אשר־דבר יהוה
אל־בית ישראל הכל בא:

And Yahweh gave to Israel all the land which he swore
to their fathers to give, and they took possession of it
and settled in it. And Yahweh gave rest to them all
around as he swore to their fathers and not one of their
enemies could stand before them, Yahweh gave all
their enemies to their hands. Nothing failed of all the
good words which Yahweh had said to the house of
Israel, all came to pass.

Moreover, according to Josh 22:4, when Joshua lets the
Transjordanians back, just before the incident of Josh 22:9-34,

ועתה הניח יהוה אלהיכם לאחיכם כאשר דבר להם
ועתה פנו ולכו לכם לאהליכם אל־ארץ אחזתכם
אשר נתן לכם משה עבד יהוה בעבר הירדן:

And now, Yahweh your God has given rest to your
brothers as he spoke to them, and now, turn and go to
your dwellings to the land of your inheritance which
Moses the servant of Yahweh gave to you on the other
side of Jordan.

Furthermore, according to Josh 23:1,

ויהי מימים רבים אחרי אשר־הניח יהוה לישראל
מכל־איביהם מסביב ויהושע זקן בא בימים:

And it happened after many days after Yahweh had
given rest to Israel from all their enemies and Joshua
had become old in years...

Moreover, if one looks at the book of Deuteronomy,
according to Dt 12:9-11,[400]

כי לא־באתם עד־עתה אל־המנוחה ואל־הנחלה
אשר־יהוה אלהיך נתן לך:
ועברתם את־הירדן וישבתם בארץ אשר־יהוה אלהיכם
מנחיל אתכם והניח לכם מכל־איביכם מסביב
וישבתם־בטח:
והיה המקום אשר־יבחר יהוה אלהיכם בו לשכן שמו

---

[400] Recall above, Chapter 3.3.

שם שמה תביאו את כל־אשר אנכי מצבה אתכם
עולתיכם וזבחיכם מעשרתיכם ותרומת ידכם וכל
מבחר נדריכם אשר תדרו ליהוה:

... since you have not yet come to the rest and the
inheritance that Yahweh your God will give to you.
And you will cross over Jordan and settle in the land
that Yahweh your God will give you as an inheritance,
and he will give you rest from all your enemies round
about, and you will live in safety. And may it be so that
you bring all that I have commanded you, your burnt
offerings, your sacrifices, your tithes and the gifts of
your hands and all the best of your votive offerings that
you have vowed to Yahweh to the place that Yahweh
your God will choose for himself to make his name
dwell there.

Furthermore, according to Dt 26:1,[401]

והיה כי־תבוא אל־הארץ אשר יהוה אלהיך נתן לך
נחלה וירשתה וישבת בה:

And it shall be that when you come to the land that
Yahweh your God gives you as an inheritance and you
take possession of it and settle in it ...

Thus, Dt 12:10 contains a promise that the Israelites will cross
the Jordan and settle (ישב) in the land, and that Yahweh will also
give them rest from all their enemies (והניח לכם מכל־איביכם
מסביב). Moreover, according to Dt 26:1, Yahweh will give the land
to the Israelites as an inheritance and they will take possession of it
(ירש) and settle (ישב) in it. On the other hand, according to the
book of Joshua, this promise is actually fulfilled. According to Josh
21:43, the Israelites had taken possession (ירש) of the land and had
settled (ישב) in it, and Yahweh had given them rest all around (v.
44) (וינח יהוה להם מסביב) from all their enemies (מכל־איביהם) so
that the enemies could not stand before the Israelites. This rest is
also referred to in Josh 22:4 and Josh 23:1. Thus, Joshua 21:43-45;
22:4; 23:1 refer back to concepts expressed by Dt 12:10 and Dt
26:1,[402] and Josh 21:45 indicates that the settlement, rest and

---

[401] Recall above, Chapter 3.3.
[402] Cf. also Josh 21:44 vs Dt 7:24.

inheritance[403] promised by Yahweh in the book of Deuteronomy has now come to pass. Moreover, everything in the book of Joshua indicates that Josh 21:43-45; Josh 22-24 occur many days after the events portrayed in the beginning of the book of Joshua (see esp. Josh 11:18; 13:1; 22:3; 23:1),[404] and one should also compare this self-presentation of the book of Joshua with Dt 7:22-23 (cf. Ex 23:27-30), according to which the conquest would not happen all at once but gradually.[405]

Then, Josh 21:43-45; 22:4; 23:1 affirm that *the Deuteronomic conditions required for the centralization of worship were achieved during the last days of Joshua*.[406] This fits perfectly with the portrayal of the events of Josh 22:9-34. The Transjordanian altar threatened to be a violation of the injunctions in Deuteronomy to centralize worship to a place which Yahweh would choose. On the other hand, as the book of Joshua indicates that the tent of meeting was in Shiloh during the time (Josh 18:1; 19:51; 22:9), it follows that *the author of Joshua indicates that during the last days of Joshua, Shiloh was the place where Yahweh's name dwelt* in the way expressed by Dt 12, and that consequently, all worship should have been centralized to Shiloh.

---

[403] Note the correspondence of נחלה in Dt 12:10; 26:1 and the distribution of the land in Joshua 13-19 etc., including Josh 23:4.

[404] See below for special considerations of Josh 24.

[405] Cf. above, Chapter 3.3.

[406] Cf. Riley 1993, p. 82, "The Deuteronomist ... specifies that the granting of Israel's rest will signify that the central sanctuary must be used exclusively. This rest is actually granted to Israel under Joshua (Josh 21:44; 22:4; 23:1)". Similarly Tigay 1996, p. 123; cf. Kaufmann 1985/1953, p. 18. As regards the problem of complete vs. incomplete conquest (for the problem and suggested solutions, see Hess 1996, pp. 284-286; Younger 1990, pp. 241-243; cf. Kaufmann 1985/1953, pp. 91-95), the main point for us is that the author of Joshua indicates that the conditions required for centralization have been obtained. In this respect, nations have been dispossessed, but not necessarily *all* nations in the land (see esp. Josh 23:9; 24:11-12 vs esp. Josh 23:5, 13, and compare these with Ex 23:28; 34:24), and note that Ex 34:24 does not necessarily need to be taken to indicate that *all* nations must be dispossessed before conditions can be considered peaceful enough for pilgrimage, even though, undoubtedly, the dispossessing of all nations is the ultimate promise and goal.

We should also take note of von Rad's study of the biblical conception of rest here.[407] Von Rad notes that in the Deuteronomistic History, there are three major times when it is expressed that the Israelites achieved rest. First, rest is achieved in the time of Joshua (Josh 21:43-45; cf. Josh 1:13, 15; 22:4; 23:1).[408] The second occasion is in the time of David (2 Sam 7:1, 11).[409] The third time is during Solomon's reign (1 Ki 8:56).[410] Von Rad also notes that in Chronicles, it is expressed that God gave rest to kings Asa (2 Chr 15:15) and Jehosaphat (2 Chr 20:30) as well.[411] However, according to von Rad, the Chronicler's concept of rest differs from that expressed in the Deuteronomistic History.[412]

All this fits very well with our considerations. The times of rest are connected with the choice of a chosen place and centralization. In the last days of Joshua, people achieved rest and Shiloh became the chosen place, as suggested by Josh 21:43-45; 22:4; 23:1 and the incident of the Transjordanian altar (Josh 22:9-34). On the other hand, David achieved rest, but only his son Solomon could build the temple since according to the Bible, David still had the "stamp" of war on him (1 Ki 5:17-19; 1 Chr 22:7-10; 28:2-6). Rest was continued during the days of Solomon (1 Ki 5:4-5) and the temple built (1 Ki 6-8). However, even though, as von Rad suggests, it might be true that, "Actually, the state of rest may be more truly ascribed to the time of Solomon than to any other",[413] the picture from biblical sources is that centralization was better achieved during the last days of Joshua than in the days of Solomon. Whereas according to Josh 22:9-34, centralization was imposed on the Transjordanians during the days of Joshua,

---

[407] Von Rad 1965b/1933.

[408] Von Rad 1965b/1933, p. 96.

[409] Ibid.

[410] Ibid.

[411] Ibid., p. 97.

[412] Ibid. Note also the connection in the ancient Near East between divine rest and temple-building, as summarized by Hurowitz (1992, pp. 330-331), and how the books of Chronicles speak also of the rest of Yahweh in relation to the building of the temple (1 Chr 6:16; 28:2; 2 Chr 6:41; cf. Ps 132:8; see Riley 1993, pp. 64-66, 71).

[413] Von Rad 1965b/1933, p. 96.

Solomon the king is explicitly castigated by 1 Ki 3:2-3 for sacrificing at *bamoth*.[414]

Having said all of the above, we must however note that there still exists a passage which raises problems as regards to centralization during the last days of Joshua and needs treatment before we can say that our interpretation of the last days of Joshua is complete. If one looks at Josh 24,[415] it portrays a covenant renewal at Shechem. Joshua gathers the Israelites to Shechem and exhorts them to follow Yahweh. The passage undoubtedly belongs to the last days of Joshua in its literary context, judging both from its setting at the end of the book of Joshua and from the statement in Josh 24:18 (מפנינו ... ויגרש יהוה את־כל־העמים) that Yahweh has driven out all nations before Israel. Moreover, according to Josh 24:29, Joshua dies after the events portrayed in Josh 24, or at least after the events portrayed at the latter part of the book of Joshua. Then, it is logical to think that, seen from the context of the book of Joshua as a whole, the occasion belongs to a time when all worship should be centralized. However, according to Josh 24:26, there is a sanctuary of Yahweh (מקדש יהוה) at Shechem where the events of Josh 24 which include making a covenant take place. What should be thought about the matter?

First of all, it has to be noted that sacrifices are not mentioned in the chapter, whereas both the covenant ceremony at Sinai (Ex 24:1-8) and the covenant ceremony at Mount Ebal (Dt 27; Josh 8:30-35) explicitly describe sacrifices as part of the proceedings.[416] Thus, keeping in mind that the Deuteronomic covenant *per se* does not include a sacrificial element (cf. esp. Dt 29),[417] that the language

---

[414] Cf. also above, p. 156.

[415] The literature on Josh 24 is immense. The most extensive treatment is Koopmans 1990 which covers all aspects of scholarship on the chapter, including an extensive review of past scholarship and bibliography.

[416] Cf. above, Chapter 4.3.

[417] Cf. Weinfeld 1972, p. 103. In fact, according to Levine (1974, p. 37), "As far as the enactment of covenants is concerned, the use of sacrifice, where attested, represented only one of several means available for the celebration of a covenant. A clear example is Genesis 31:54, where a זבח was offered to Yahweh in the course of enacting a covenant, but

of at least a number of verses of the passage have clear
Deuteronomic affinities,[418] and that the passage is set in its present
literary setting at the last days of Joshua, it is entirely possible that
sacrifices were not part of the ceremony, and that the author of
Joshua understood the matter to be so. Moreover, it is by no means
certain that the author of the book of Joshua thought that the
sanctuary in Josh 24:26 was in sacrificial use overall at the time
portrayed by Josh 24. That the concept of a nonsacrificial מקדש is

---

only subsequent to the treaty oath (verse 53), and to the erection of a stela
commemorating the occasion (verses 44-52)." Moreover, according to
Levine (ibid., p. 37n93), "In descriptions of covenants in the Bible where
some amount of detail is provided, it is most often the case that no
sacrificial activity is recorded. This allows for the conclusion that sacrifice
was not essential to the process of covenant enactment, itself. Cf. the
following records: a) Gen 21:27-32, the covenant between Abraham and
Abimelech, where only the (עדה 'proof' and the שבועה 'oath' are
mentioned. b) 1 Sam 18:3-5, the covenant between David and Jonathan,
where personal garments and weapons belonging to Jonathan were given
to David to symbolize the finalizing of the covenant. c) 1 Sam 20:16-17, a
further covenant between Jonathan and the house of David, where only
an oath is mentioned. d) 2 Kings 11:4, the covenant between Jehoiada and
officials in the temple on the matter of the legitimate heir, where only an
oath is mentioned. e) Josh 9:15, the covenant with the Gibeonites, under
Joshua's leadership, where only an oath is mentioned. f) Josh 24:25-27,
the covenant between Yahweh and Israel, negotiated by Joshua, where a
commemorative stela, oath, and written record are mentioned, but no
sacrifice. g) 2 Kings ch. 23, the covenant between Yahweh and Israel,
under Josiah's leadership, enacted 'in the presence of Yahweh', where an
oath is implied, and a written document mentioned, but no sacrifice. h)
Dt, ch. 29, the covenant between Yahweh and Israel, under Moses'
leadership, where a written document is mentioned (v. 19) and oaths (vs.
18, 26), but no sacrifice. i) Gen ch. 15, the covenant between Yahweh and
the family of Abraham. What was executed on that occasion bore definite
connections to sacrifice, but not in the accepted manner of Israelite
sacrifice." Levine also notes 2 Sam 3, "the covenant between Abner and
David, where we find the covenant oath followed by a feast (v. 20), but
no sacrifice, proper" (ibid., p. 38n94).

[418] See Koopmans 1990, pp. 1-83, 104-145 and *passim* (including the
views of commentators listed therein, including Wellhausen, Eissfeldt,
Noth, von Rad etc.); Ottosson 1991, pp. 147-155.

an entirely logical possibility is also suggested by Lohfink, according to whom,

> Ferner belegen die Ausgrabungen von Arad, so schwer die Zerstörungsschichten absolut zu datieren sind, vor der endgültigen Profanüberbauung des zerstörten Jahweheiligtums eine Zwischenphase, in der zwar noch das Heiligtum, aber nicht mehr die große 'Altar' stand.[419]

Moreover,

> die Ältere Schicht (des Deuteronomiums) noch nicht von Heiligtümern sprach und daß der Tempel von Jerusalem auch im definitiven Text für die Gestalt des Kultes Israels eher als einzige Opferstätte thematisiert wird, nicht als einziges Heiligtum.[420]

Furthermore, according to Lohfink,

> Mann kann sagen, das Deuteronomium formuliere von einem Standpunkt aus, der vor der Landnahme liegt. Es siehe also die Errichtung verschiedener Heiligtümer gar nicht vor.[421]

In other words, as Lohfink suggests, from the standpoint of Deuteronomy it would be possible to conceive that there could have existed a sanctuary (or sanctuaries) without a sacrificial altar in a situation where centralization of all sacrifices is required. This would then suggest the possibility of a "holy place" of Yahweh[422]

---

[419] Lohfink 1995, pp. 220-221. Naturally, Lohfink bases his deliberations essentially on a seventh-century date of Deuteronomy.

[420] Lohfink 1995, p. 221.

[421] Ibid.

[422] Cf. Haran 1978, p. 50, "the term מקדש of Yahweh mentioned in this narrative does not mean a temple, but only a 'holy place'". Haran (ibid., p. 50; 1981, p. 36) further suggests that the site of Josh 24 was a "cultic open area", and mentions other possible cultic open places, especially pointing out most of the places where the patriarchs worshipped, plus Gideon's altars in Jdg 6 (Haran 1978, pp. 48-57); As far as archaeology is concerned, cf. Mt Ebal (if cultic), and the "bull site" (see Mazar, *BASOR* 247 [1982], pp. 27-41; cf. Mazar 1990, pp. 350-352; Gilmour 1995, pp. 89-92; Mettinger 1995, pp. 153-155; Finkelstein 1988, pp. 86-87; cf. Fritz 1993, pp. 185-186 for a more critical view) which *may* have been a cultic open area. Cf. also Fritz 1993 on separate open-air altars and cult places found in prehistoric Europe and pre-classical Greece and Hägg 1993 for open cult places found in Bronze Age Aegean.

without an altar or even without much external paraphernalia. In other words, it is entirely possible that the author of Joshua thought that the sanctuary at Shechem in Josh 24 was a "holy place" without sacrifices,[423] at least during the time which it portrays,[424] and that the ceremony in Josh 24 did not involve sacrifices. Moreover, when one takes into account the fact that according to the testimony of the Old Testament, Yahweh is free to manifest his presence on earth at various places at his will and depending on the occasion outside the context of the ark, the central sanctuary, local altars, or a cult object,[425] it follows that it is entirely possible that the writer of Joshua indicates that Yahweh could manifest his presence at the sanctuary in Shechem even though no sacrifices were made and no altar or cult object as a seat of Yahweh[426] existed. Thus, Josh 24:1 could state that the people "stood before God" (ויתיצבו לפני האלהים). An expressly memorial function of the sanctuary at Shechem in the book of Joshua is also fully compatible with Josh 4 and Josh 22:9-34, as according to these passages the stones at Gilgal are expressly intended as memorials (אות; Josh 4:6) without mention of any accompanying structure let alone an altar in association with them,[427] and the Transjordanian altar expressly was to serve as a witness (עד; Josh

---

[423] In fact, if the אלון מצב (perhaps "the oak of the pillar"; cf. *HAL*, p. 587) in Jdg 9:6 refers to the same place as the האלה אשר במקדש יהוה in Josh 24:26, as is very possible (according to Ottosson 1991, p. 156, regarding Gen 12:6; 35:4; Josh 24:26; Jdg 9:6, "Det torde knappast råda någon tvekan om att samma träd avses [there should hardly be any doubt that the same tree is meant]"; similarly Koopmans 1990, p. 379; Cundall 1968, p. 127, who also points out the similarity of Jdg 9:6 with 1 Ki 12:1; Keil 1983/1861-1865, *Joshua*, p. 233), both the books of Joshua and Judges suggest that the place was both intended and kept rather as a monument during the premonarchical time.

[424] So Keil 1983/1861-1865, *Joshua*, p. 233.

[425] E.g. Gen 18; 1 Ki 19:9-18. For the stone of witness in vv. 26-27 from the context of its role in contrast to *masseboth*, cf. above, Chapter 2.2.2 (p. 63).

[426] Cf. above, Chapter 2.2.2.

[427] The problems of the narrative of Josh 4 as to where (perhaps even to more than one place) the stones were actually erected nonwithstanding (see e.g. Butler 1983, pp. 41-44 for a description of the difficulties in making sense of the exact flow of the narrative of Josh 3-4).

22:27, 28, 34) for later generations.[428] Thus, we may conclude that from the narrative standpoint, Joshua essentially gathered the people to an ancient memorial which commemorated the act of Jacob making his family put away their gods (Gen 35:1-4), and Joshua exhorted the people of his generation to do basically the same as Jacob's family did.[429]

In this respect, if we look at the Exodus altar law, according to Ex 20:24b, Yahweh says that, "In every place where I will cause my name to be remembered, I will come to you and bless you". Then, it would be logical to think that Shechem and Gilgal where important events occurred and monuments commemorating them were set in place would be places where Yahweh had caused his name to be remembered. Furthermore, especially as Ex 20:24b follows v. 24a somewhat abruptly and fits to the context slightly loosely,[430] one may even think that the passage might transcend the altar law, and thus it could be taken to mean that in conditions where all sacrifices are centralized, a place where Yahweh has caused his "name to be remembered" could still continue as a "holy place" where Yahweh might continue to manifest his presence on occasions.[431] This would reinforce the idea that Yahweh could manifest himself at Shechem and Gilgal, and perhaps even at the site of the Transjordanian altar even if

---

[428] Ottosson (1991, p. 155) makes a connection between Josh 24:27 and Josh 22:9-34 (esp. v. 34).

[429] It also has to be noted that the text implies that the covenant ceremony was a one-off occasion; cf. Levine 1974, p. 40, "There is really no evidence in biblical literature for regularly scheduled covenant renewals, as part of the ongoing cult. Those occasions of covenant renewal, or the reaffirmation of earlier covenants through entering into a new one, relate to particular moments of transition, crisis, or radical change in Israel's history, and are always portrayed as one-time events necessitated or warranted by particular circumstances." Comparative material of covenants from the rest of the ancient Near East also makes this point clear, as Levine notes (ibid., pp. 39-40).

[430] So also Robertson 1948, pp. 13, 20.

[431] A later synagogue could perhaps be imagined to fit to this category (cf. also above, p. 155n202).

sacrifices were not offered at these places.[432] In fact, one may think that an association with an important event in Israel's history which generally would also include an original self-manifestation of Yahweh could warrant calling a place a מִקְדָשׁ in its own right.

We have now interpreted Josh 22:9-34 in its context as a part of the final form of the book of Joshua based on its view of centralization, concentrating on what the text says in itself, with the exception of suggesting that it is difficult to deny that the passage is at least derived from ancient tradition. However, let us next look at the question of the possible date and provenance of the passage in detail. An important part of our considerations will also be to confirm that Josh 22:9-34 can be thought to be an integral part of the book of Joshua from a literary standpoint. Moreover, we will see if the considerations of the date and provenance of Josh 22:9-34 might conveniently bring about special implications to at least some of the critical questions surrounding the book of Joshua as a whole and even beyond. In this, we will also draw on the results of our exegesis of Josh 22:9-34 and other results we have obtained so far in this study, especially those relating to the mutual relationship of Shiloh and Jerusalem and North and South as discussed in Chapter 4.2. To begin with, the first issue concerning the provenance of Josh 22:9-34 is that the passage overall attests Deuteronomic concerns, including a Deuteronomic requirement of centralization of worship. On the other hand, the passage has strong Priestly features as well. Then, if one thinks that the Priestly features were simply taken in as part of the narrative and the book of Joshua by a Deuteronomic editor, it is very natural to imagine how the passage came into being. In this respect, as we have seen above, the passage fits perfectly with the Deuteronomic portrayal of the conditions of conquest and settlement which the latter part of the book of Joshua attests. Also, that the Priestly material in Josh 22:9-34 has been used to support a Deuteronomic purpose

---

[432] Cf. again esp. 1 Ki 19:9-18 where Yahweh comes to be present with Elijah at Horeb even though the narrative implies that no altar is involved and no sacrifices are offered.

fits perfectly with our earlier considerations of the altar laws, according to which Deuteronomy draws on Priestly material.[433]

On the other hand, if one thinks that Priestly material in general is later than Deuteronomy, one runs into formidable difficulties. As we have indicated above, scholars have found it very difficult to divide the passage into sources.[434] Moreover, the view of worship in the passage is Deuteronomic. Thus, one will have to postulate a later Priestly redaction of the passage which is difficult to separate from the overall narrative and for which it is difficult to give a good motivation as the earlier version already basically includes all the information necessary to argue for the centralization of worship, the main thrust of the narrative.

To confirm further the idea that Priestly material has been taken in to support a Deuteronomic purpose, it is also useful to look at how the passage relates to its literary environment, both in the book of Joshua and outside of it. Then, except for the Deuteronomic concern of centralization during the last days of Joshua with which Josh 22:9-34 perfectly fits, let us start by observing that if one reads Josh 22 as a whole, vv. 9-34 naturally continue the story of vv. 1-8, and both narratives fit together very well, even though there are differences between them. Even though Josh 22:1-8 is Deuteronomic both in language and content,[435] and Josh 22:9-34 includes a number of Priestly features, both narratives at least can be thought to be Deuteronomic as a whole. Moreover, even though both narratives are intelligible on their own,[436] they nevertheless make a perfectly connected and intelligible story together. Finally, even though, as Kloppenborg

---

[433] See above, Chapter 1.

[434] See above, p. 191.

[435] See Noth 1953, p. 133; de Vaux 1978/1971, p. 581; Gray 1986, p. 169; Soggin 1972, p. 212; Kloppenborg 1981, p. 351. To be precise, verses 1-6 would be enough to be taken as a unit. According to Noth (1953, p. 133), Joshua 22:1-6, together with Josh 21:43-45 and Josh 23:1-16 forms the Deuteronomistic conclusion of the occupation tradition, and vv. 7-8 are a "redactional link".

[436] According to Kloppenborg (1981, p. 351), "Vv. 1-8, while in their present state serving as an introduction to 9-34, anticipate none of the hostilities of the latter. On the other hand, 9-34 are completely intelligible without 1-8."

points out, "The central character in 1-8 is Joshua but Phinehas and the *nesiᵓim* in 9-34",[437] this does not mean that the two do not fit together.

Also, Josh 22:20 directly refers back to Joshua 7, the narrative about the Achan incident in association with the conquest of Ai.[438] It is especially noteworthy that the Priestly word מעל used to describe Achan in Josh 7:1 occurs also in Joshua 22:20 (cf. also Josh 22:31). Moreover, the concept of divine retribution based on מעל is similar in Josh 22 and Josh 7. In both cases, the whole congregation of the Israelites would suffer because of a sin of an individual or a part of the community. As Joosten points out, this concept of divine retribution is Priestly.[439] Then, this in fact suggests that both Josh 22:9-34 and Josh 7 draw on Priestly concepts.[440]

It is also interesting to compare this concept of divine retribution in Joshua 22:9-34 and Josh 7 with 1 Chr 5. In 1 Chr 5:25 it is said that the Transjordanians "became faithless (מעל) against the God of their fathers and played the harlot after the gods of the nations which God destroyed before them". However, whereas in Joshua 22:31 it would have been the *Israelites* who would have suffered because of the sin of the Transjordanians, in 1 Chr

---

[437] Kloppenborg 1981, p. 351.

[438] According to Noth 1991/1943, p. 63, Dtr (who of course wrote before the postexilic time) received the Ai story (Josh 7-8) as such, making only a very minor modification in Josh 8:1.

[439] Joosten 1996, pp. 41-42; 86-87.

[440] Cf. Ottosson 1991, p. 26, "Jos 7 är klart icke-deuteronomistiskt stilistiskt sett. Det originella i sammanhanget är, att man kan känna igen 'P-språk' i 7:1 och vv. 6 ff. (Josh 7 is clearly arranged stylistically in a non-deuteronomistic way. In relation to this, it is remarkable that one can again recognize P-style in 7:1 and vv. 6 ff.)". Note in this respect that according to Noth 1991/1943, p. 63, Dtr received the Ai story (Josh 7-8) as such, making only a very minor modification in Josh 8:1. Noth (1953, p. 43) even stresses that Josh 7:1 is not a later addition but belongs to the original Ai story. Also, even though Fritz (1994, p. 79) thinks that there are a number of minor additions in Josh 7, such as the Priestly and thus postexilic addition of מעל in 7:1, he nevertheless thinks that these additions have not changed the character of the story of Joshua 7, which according to him is the composition of the Deuteronomistic historian as its structure, style and didactic character show.

5:25 it is the *Transjordanians themselves* who suffer because of their sin. Thus, the postexilic Chronicles emphasizes a different concept of divine retribution from the book of Joshua,[441] and when one couples this with the impression that around the time of the exile, the previously more dominant concept of collective guilt moved towards the concept of individual guilt (cf. Jer 31:29-30; Ez 18:2 ff.), this further suggests a pre-exilic setting for Josh 22:9-34.[442] Furthermore, whereas in Josh 22:31, the Transjordanians are cleared of faithlessness (מעל), according to 1 Chr 5:25, the Transjordanians were faithless, and went to exile for that reason.

Another passage which may attest the concept of divine retribution on the whole congregation is Josh 22:17. According to Josh 22:17, punishment fell on the congregation (בעדת יהוה) because of the Peor incident and moreover, the people have not yet purified themselves of it (לא הטהרנו ממנו). Whatever the case, what is clear is that the verse refers back to Num 25. On conventional source criticism, Num 25:1-5 belongs to JE, and Num 25:6-18 belong to P,[443] and the passage could thus refer back to either the JE or P version of the events. On the other hand, as Josh 22:9-34 contains many Priestly features and vv. 1-5 present nothing particular in themselves in addition to vv. 6-18, it is entirely possible to think that the passage refers to Num 25 as a whole.

A further feature which ties Joshua 22:9-34 to the rest of Joshua, and to the Pentateuch is the existence in Josh 22:24 of a variant of the "catechetical" formula which recurs several times in the Hexateuch, as follows:

Ex 12:26 (Passover rites):
והיה כי־יאמרו אליכם בניכם מה העבדה ...
Ex 13:14 (firstborn dedication):
והיה כי־ישאלך בנך מחר לאמר מה־זאת ...
Dt 6:20 (the law):
והיה כי־ישאלך בנך מחר לאמר מה־העדת ...

---

[441] Cf. Riley 1993, pp. 42-53, 147-148 for more use of מעל in Chronicles.

[442] Cf. Joosten 1996, pp. 121-122. Note that Tigay (1996, p. 227) suggests that Dt 24:16 refers rather to judicial than divine punishment; cf. 2 Ki 14:6; 2 Chr 25:4.

[443] See e.g. Wenham 1981, p. 19 for this.

Jos 4:6 (stones at Gilgal):

כי־ישאלון בניכם מחר לאמר מה האבנים

Jos 4:21 (stones at Gilgal):

אשר ישאלון בניכם את־אבותם לאמר מה האבנים

Jos 22:24 (altar of witness):

מחר יאמרו בניכם לבנינו לאמר מה־לכם וליהוה [444]

Figure 7: "Catechetical" formulas in Genesis-Joshua

Now, Ex 12:26 and 13:14 can be assigned to D,[445] and there is no doubt about the Deuteronomic character of Josh 4:6, 21.[446] This then suggests that Josh 22:24 is also a Deuteronomic feature, tying Joshua 22:9-34 to the rest of the book of Joshua.[447] Furthermore, the existence of this "catechetical" formula strongly implies that the altar of witness was intended to serve an important role in Israelite tradition, and this underlines the importance of the narrative of Josh 22:9-34 for the original audience of the book of Joshua. In this context we would also like to add that the existence of the catechetical formula in Josh 4:6, 21 makes it extremely unlikely that the Gilgal narratives (Josh 4-5) serve as an aetiology to legitimate a sanctuary[448] at Gilgal, at least if the author wrote from a Jerusalemite perspective, as the catechetical formula is part of the idea that the stones are to be signs "for ever" (עד־עולם; 4:7). It is hard to believe that a Jerusalemite Deuteronomic author would have promoted a rival sanctuary to be valid "for ever".[449] Thus, it is entirely possible, and in fact more logical that the author of Joshua understood the stones at Gilgal to act purely as signs, and yet as objects of religious pilgrimage.[450]

Joshua 22:9-34 also has similarities to Judges 19-21. In both cases the narratives involve an action taken by the Israelite

---

[444] See Kloppenborg 1981, p. 369, referring to Soggin, VT 10 (1960), pp. 341-347.

[445] So Childs 1974, p. 184.

[446] Cf. Noth 1987/1943, p. 111.

[447] Note also that, certainly, the usage of the formula in 22:24 serves to specifically emphasize the unity of Israel in Josh 22:9-34.

[448] I.e. a sacrificial sanctuary.

[449] Our considerations above, p. 93 regarding the meaning and validity of such an expression nonwithstanding.

[450] Cf. above, p. 202 on the stones at Gilgal.

confederacy against another Israelite group (Benjamin, Jabesh-Gilead).[451] In both narratives Phinehas *ben* Eleazar features. In both narratives there is a trip to Transjordan involved (Jdg 21:10-12). Shiloh features in both narratives (Josh 22:9, 12; Jdg 21:12), as does the expression כנען ארץ (Josh 22:9; Jdg 21:12; in both of these cases the expression is actually שלה אשר בארץ כנען).[452] And, both narratives purport to describe the period of conquest / early period of Judges. Then, this speaks against detaching Josh 22:9-34 from the rest of the book of Joshua.

Finally, there is yet another important issue to consider in the literary setting and provenance of Joshua 22:9-34. If one compares Josh 22:9-34 with Num 32, one can find a number of important similarities in the storylines of these two passages as follows, as pointed out by Jobling:

> (a) A transjordanian initiative sets the story in motion (Num 32:1-5; Jos 22:10).
>
> (b) Moses / the Cisjordanian embassy express anger at the initiative. Each (particularly in the second case) goes to some lengths of implausibility to put the worst possible construction upon it. And each makes allusions to the past to establish the case (and to help introduce Yahweh.)
>
> (c) The Transjordanians make a suggestion / response which is satisfactory, and in fact provides the substance of a bargain (Num 32:16-19; Jos 22:22-29)
>
> (d) Acceptance by Moses / the Cisjordanian embassy (Num 32:20-24, Jos 22:30-31).[453]

Furthermore,

(e) In both accounts there is hint of a possible settlement of the Transjordanians to the West as part of the argumentation (Num 32:30; Josh 22:19).[454]

(f) In both accounts the Transjordanians have a concern for their children (Num 32:16, 17, 26; Josh 22:24-28; cf. Num 32:11-13).[455]

---

[451] So also Kloppenborg 1981, p. 347 (quoted above, p. 186).

[452] Cf. Schley 1989, p. 132.

[453] Jobling 1980, p. 192.

[454] Ibid., p. 193.

[455] See ibid., p. 196.

(g) "In both stories, the Transjordanians undertake to cross the Jordan for the service of Yahweh."[456]

Moreover, one may arrange the passages which concern the Transjordanians in the Hexateuch in the following way:

A. Num 32: Intro to the Transjordanian issue with conflict-resolution
    B. Deut 3:12-16: obligation to the Transjordanians
    [Deut 29:6-8: review of Tranjordanian issue]
    B. Josh 1:12-18: repeat obligation to the Transjordanians
    [Josh 4:12: honouring of obligation by the Transjordanians]
    [Josh 13:8-31: review of allotment of territory to the Transjordanians]
    B' Josh 22:1-8: obligation to the Transjordanians fulfilled
A' Josh 22:9-34: Final story with conflict-resolution

Figure 8: Transjordanians in the Hexateuch

Even though everything does not fit neatly into to a chiasm, it is clear that in the final form of the "Hexateuch", A is the introduction to the Transjordanian issue and A' is its conclusion. Also, if one ignores AA' which contain Priestly material, BB' forms a bracket of a Deuteronomic introduction and conclusion.

That Josh 22:9-34 and Num 32 are connected is further confirmed by the following considerations. According to Noth, Numbers 32 can be divided to sources as follows: Verses 32:*1-5, 16a, 39-42 belong to older sources (J or E), 32:16, 17, 24, 33-38 belong to Deuteronomistic redaction, and the rest is Priestly redaction.[457] Moreover, Noth notes concerning the Priestly redaction: "These are admittedly reminiscent of the language and style of P but they do not represent this language and style in its pure form. Above all, they are so clearly dependent, from a literary point of view, on the older text that they cannot be regarded as elements of a once independent narrative tradition."[458] Other commentators, before and after Noth, have held similar, even if not exactly same opinions.[459] It is also worth noting that G.B. Gray

---

[456] Ibid., p. 196.
[457] Noth 1987/1943, pp. 128-129. See also Noth 1968, pp. 235-236.
[458] Noth 1987/1943, p. 129.
[459] Cf. the helpful summary in Budd 1984, pp. 337-342.

thought of Num 32 that "a strict analysis of the chapter as between JE and P cannot be satisfactorily carried through".[460]

Then, according to customary source division, "conflict-resolution" is missing in both JE and D versions of Numbers 32. In other words, the conflict-resolution plot is the creation of Priestly editing according to source-critical theory. Then, if the conflict-resolution plot is not the creation of Priestly editing in Joshua 22:9-34, it is most likely that Josh 22:9-34 is primary, and that Num 32 is based on it. On the other hand, if the conflict-resolution plot is the creation of Priestly editing in Joshua 22:9-34, it would be easy to postulate that both Josh 22:9-34 and Num 32 come from the same hand, or at least that their present arrangement has been carefully thought out. This then implies that the Priestly tradition deliberately connects Josh 22:9-34 and Num 32, and, remembering also the connection of Josh 22:17 to Num 25,[461] suggests that Josh 22:9-34 is aware of the conquest tradition of Numbers.

These issues then naturally bring us to the problem of the literary composition and provenance of the book of Joshua. Especially since Wellhausen it was generally thought that Joshua formed part of the Hexateuch, which meant that the book was to be seen together with the Pentateuch and as having been composed from the Pentateuchal sources. However, since Noth's *Überlieferungsgeschichtliche Studien*,[462] Joshua has generally been seen as a part of the Deuteronomistic History rather than as belonging to the Pentateuch. The major tantalizing issue concerning the theories of the Hexateuch and the Deuteronomistic history is that, on one hand, when one reads Joshua in its final form, it is quite natural to see Joshua as the fulfilment of the Exodus/Sinai tradition as depicted in Exodus-Numbers. Especially, it is clear that Numbers 32 links to Joshua 1:12-18; 4:12; 13:8-33; 22:1-8, 9-34, that Numbers 33:50-34:29 link to Joshua 13-19, and that Numbers 35 links to Joshua 20-21.[463] Furthermore, Numbers 32 and 33:50-56 are recognized to contain Priestly material, and Numbers 34 and 35

---

[460] Gray 1903, p. 426.

[461] See above, p. 207.

[462] Noth 1991/1943 and Noth 1987/1943.

[463] Cf. Ottosson 1991, pp. 11-37, esp pp. 29-31 for overall literary connections between Joshua and Numbers.

have often been assigned to P.[464] What is more, Joshua 13-19 contain at least some Priestly material, and, as we have seen, Joshua 22:9-34 are clearly influenced by Priestly material. There are also other connecting features between Numbers and Joshua. For instance, as Noth points out, in Numbers 14:24 (assigned to JE), "there is a reference forward to Caleb's occupation of the land".[465] Thus, it is easy to think that Joshua is firmly connected with Numbers. Then, if one would see those parts in Joshua which connect to Priestly material in Numbers as Priestly (esp. Josh 13-19 and 22:9-34), one would naturally lean towards a theory of a Hexateuch, with Joshua being a logical continuation of the conquest tradition(s) in Numbers.

On the other hand, as opposed to the theory of the Hexateuch, the overall theology of Joshua is clearly Deuteronomic. As Wenham has specifically pointed out, the theological concepts of holy war, the land and its distribution, the unity of Israel, the role of Joshua and the covenant and the law of Moses are the main conceptual links between Joshua and Deuteronomy.[466] In relation to these, Joshua includes much Deuteronomic vocabulary and phraseology, and we have also seen in this and the previous chapter that the Ebal account and Josh 22:9-34 are fully in accord with concepts advocated by the book of Deuteronomy. Moreover, Joshua is the direct continuation of Dt 31-34, and not of Numbers. Thus, seen from this angle, Joshua seems to be firmly connected with Deuteronomy rather than with Numbers. Furthermore, being Deuteronomic in its general character, Joshua is similar to the historical books Judges-Kings which from the narrative standpoint continue from where Joshua leaves off, and also, like Deuteronomy, seem to include little if any Priestly material.

Martin Noth, whose views are still largely followed at present,[467] suggested a solution to this problem by starting from the

---

[464] See e.g. Wenham 1981, p. 19. Note also that, according to Wenham (ibid.), "In chapters 32 and 33 G.B. Gray believes both JE and P are present, but he does not think they can be disentangled convincingly".

[465] Noth 1987/1943, p. 140.

[466] Wenham 1971b, pp. 141-148.

[467] Cf. Ottosson (1991, p. 13), according to whom "Fortfarande får Noth betraktas som exegetlikaren, ehuru det ibland skymtar tendenser att tidigarelägga P (Noth may continuously be considered as exegetical

premise that the conquest tradition was an independent unit in the beginning. The book of Joshua was built around this tradition. Noth also argued that there was originally no P account of the conquest, but P concluded his account with the death of Moses.[468] Noth based this argument on basically arguing as much as possible that those features which exist in Numbers and relate to the conquest are not Priestly. Noth succeeded in eliminating so much material which has commonly been attributed to P that he could argue that those parts which are indisputably Priestly are the result of secondary additions and do not stem from a P narrative.[469] On the other hand, Noth argued that the older literary sources J and E "culminated in the theme of the conquest".[470] However, according to Noth, "when they were fitted into the framework provided by the P narrative it was the Pentateuch which emerged, with the theme of the conquest of the land to the west of the Jordan dropping away completely. The conquest narrative in the book of Joshua, on the other hand, was part of the work of Dtr. from the start, and this developed completely independently of the Pentateuch."[471]   Finally, during the postexilic period, the Pentateuch and the Deuteronomistic history were joined together, and more connecting links were added between Numbers and Deuteronomy on one hand, and Numbers and Joshua on the other, and these connections were, as Noth seems to indicate, made in Priestly style.[472]

Noth did not have a very high regard for Joshua 22:9-34 as a part of the book of Joshua. According to Noth, the language and content of Josh 22:9-34 "are reminiscent of P", but on the other hand "there are such clear deviations in language and content from P, that this peculiar passage ... is no longer ascribed to the 'Hexateuchal' source P".[473] Joshua 22:9-34 "must obviously be a

---

standard, even though sometimes there are seen inclinations to put P earlier)".

[468] Noth 1987/1943, p. 135.
[469] Ibid., pp. 121-134.
[470] Ibid., p. 141.
[471] Ibid., p. 141.
[472] Ibid., pp. 143-148.
[473] Ibid., p. 118.

very late isolated supplement to the book of Joshua".[474] It is quite obvious why Noth thought this way. The existence of a Priestly account in Joshua, especially if it is well grafted into the book, would indicate that a Priestly author was interested in the conquest tradition, which in turn casts doubt on the validity of Noth's denial of Priestly material in the books of Numbers and Joshua.

However, we have seen that Josh 22:9-34 is an integral part of the book of Joshua, and that it is also explicitly connected to the Priestly parts of Num 32. Thus, it is difficult to believe Noth's theory of the Deuteronomistic history in its present form, especially when Noth has already been criticized for eliminating Priestly material from Numbers and Joshua in a way which has a stamp of dubiousness about it.[475] Moreover, Noth's theory is simply too complicated. Too many redactions, combinations and accretions are postulated, and Noth treats literary works in a piecemeal and mechanical way (but nevertheless cannot divide Josh 22:9-34 into sources). Also, it is hard to think that P would have concluded his account with the death of Moses without any regard to the wider context to which that death relates, that is, entering into the promised land. The idea of cutting off the conquest tradition of the older Pentateuchal sources, especially when the their accounts "culminated in the theme of the conquest", is also problematic.

On the other hand, if one sees the Priestly material of the Pentateuch as earlier than Deuteronomy,[476] and the Priestly material in Joshua as material which was taken over and used by the Deuteronomic editor of Joshua, all these problems disappear completely.[477] The author of Joshua drew both on Priestly and Deuteronomic tradition. This then naturally implies that all parts of

---

[474] Ibid., p. 118.

[475] See Weinfeld 1972, p. 182n1, according to whom Noth's "attempts to disprove the Priestly origin of Num 32-6 and Josh 14-22" are "unconvincing".

[476] Cf. above, Chapter 1 for reasons to see the Priestly altar law of Lev 17 as earlier than the altar law of Dt 12.

[477] Cf. Ottosson 1991, esp. pp. 11-37, for other reasons to see Priestly material in Joshua as prior to Deuteronomic material.

the book of Joshua are exilic at the latest.[478] Moreover, the connections from Joshua back to the Priestly tradition of Numbers and to the Exodus motif in the Pentateuch[479] imply that there was no "Deuteronomistic history" in the sense Noth has suggested. Furthermore, the literary composition of Joshua also implies that the reason why the books of Judges, Samuel and Kings do not include much Priestly material is not that Priestly material did not exist during the time these books were written, but that there must have been some other reason why they did not include much

---

[478] Cf. Ottosson 1991, who dates the book to the time of Josiah and states (pp. 36-37), "En exilsk eller efterexilsk avfattningstid, vilket i allmänhet antas, är jag mycket skeptisk till (I am very skeptical regarding the generally followed view of an exilic or postexilic time of composition)"; for Ottosson's specific reasons, see ibid., pp. 11-37.

[479] In this respect, according to Westermann (1994, p. 39), "Das Exodusmotiv kommt in den Geschichtsbüchern 27 mal vor, mit den Summarien in Dtn zusammen 30-32 mal." Westermann then lists major occurrences in speeches, including a comment on Josh 24:2-8, "In Jos 24:2-8 ist es ein ausführlicher Rückblick auf die Geschichte, eine Weiterbildung der kurzen Summarien in Dtn" (ibid.). After this, Westermann comments, "Alle diese Stellen werden übereinstimmend als dtr. angesehen. Das bedeutet aber, daß der Autor oder der abschließende Redaktor das Exodusmotiv gekannt haben muß; er selbst gebraucht es häufig. Damit wird die Frage, warum er dann sein Werk nicht mit dem Exodusgeschehen eingeleitet und angefangen hat, sehr schwierig zu beantworten. Ich kenne keinen einzigen Versuch in der Literatur. Eine Antwort auf diese Frage ist wohl kaum zu finden. Das Problem das sich hier stellt, ist gelöst, wenn man die Hypothese eines DtrG aufgibt. An seine Stelle tritt dann eine mit Ex + Num beginnende Reihe von Geschichtsbüchern, die an zwei Stellen von Gesetzsammlungen unterbrochen sind. In dieser Reihe beginnt die Geschichte Israels mit dem Buch Exodus und sie erstreckt sich bis zum Ende dieser Geschichte in 2 Könige. Die Reihe wird dadurch zusammengehalten, sie wird dadurch einheitlich, daß jedes einzelne Buch einen Abschnitt der Geschichte Israels behandelt, die beiden eingefügten Gesetzsammlungen nicht." (ibid., pp. 39-40) Westermann also points out Josh 2:8-11; 5:1; 9:9, speeches by non-Israelites which refer back to the Exodus motif (ibid., p. 40). Finally, one should also recall the connections of the narrative of the crossing of Jordan in Joshua as a whole with the crossing of the Sea of Reeds in Exodus (see above, p. 162n233).

Priestly material. As we have already suggested above,[480] it is possible to conceive that since the Priestly material is associated with the tent of meeting which is most at home in Shiloh, the Judahite and Jerusalemite writer of the books of Samuel did not wish to emphasize the role of the old order of Shiloh and Ephraim which had passed away, and the same would apply to the book of Judges as well, as it also attests Judahite concerns.[481] If Jerusalem wanted to emphasize its election over Shiloh, and the role of the temple over that of the tent of meeting as Ps 78 attests, it is difficult to think that the Priestly material would originate from Jerusalem.[482] Moreover, as the Priestly material directly concerns the tent of meeting and its cult, it cannot have been applied directly for the Jerusalemite temple and cult, but only indirectly.[483] Thus, the Priestly material does not fit well conceptually in the time of the Monarchy.[484]

---

[480] See above, Chapter 4.2.

[481] For more details regarding the book of Judges, see below, Chapter 4.6. Also, it has to be remembered that the motif of the covenant, and thus Deuteronomic material and style would be fitting for historical recollection in Israelite history (cf. above, p.122, incl. n45).

[482] Also, in view of Jeroboam's actions in the north, as described in 1 Ki 12:26-33, it is unlikely that the Priestly material has its provenance in the North after the division of the kingdom.

[483] The books of Chronicles explicitly describe how David rearranged the cult in Jerusalem (see esp. 1 Chr 16; 23-26; 28). To say that the Priestly material is historical fiction does not take away the incompatibility between the Priestly material and the monarchic situation.

[484] It would be logical to think that the Priestly material would come back into vogue with the priest Ezekiel and his vision of the restoration of the temple and its cult, and during the postexilic period when both the old order of Shiloh and the new order of Jerusalem had failed and the community had to reflect on and reinvent its identity. As far as the exilic book of Kings is concerned, the interest of the author (during whose time there is good reason to think that the Priestly material already was in existence) is not in the exact details of the Jerusalemite cult or other related technicalities, but on the failure of the Israelites to worship Yahweh which goes hand in hand with the Deuteronomic concerns about worship at *bamoth* after the building of Solomon's temple and the resulting historical catastrophes of the exile of the Northern and Southern kingdoms. It is also conceivable that the author is also influenced with a

For this reason, as the composition of the book of Joshua and the priority of Lev 17 to Dt 12[485] imply that the Priestly material is pre-exilic,[486] it is most logical to think that the Priestly material, or at least substantial parts of it, dates not from the time of the Monarchy, but from the premonarchical period, and as Shiloh was rejected and its importance taken away after the disaster at Aphek (1 Sam 4), this then naturally suggests a time before the disaster.[487]

When one couples these observations with the fact that Shiloh as the location of the tent of meeting plays a prominent part in the end part of the book of Joshua, both from a Priestly and a

---

Deuteronomic tradition current in Judah before the exile (cf. the considerations above in Chapter 4.1). The author then interprets his fairly nontechnical sources from a Deuteronomic viewpoint (note however that some Priestly features are nevertheless included in his sources as well, e.g. in 1 Ki 8:1-11; Deuteronomic sources may also be included). In this respect, a new style would then be reflected in Chronicles in the new situation of the community after the exile, including attesting both Priestly and Deuteronomic concerns of past history.

[485] Recall above, Chapters 3.2 and 3.3 for the priority of Lev 17 to Dt 12.

[486] Cf. also Haran 1978, pp. 5-12; Weinfeld 1972, pp. 179-189; and Hurvitz 1982 who argues on linguistic grounds that P predates Ezekiel.

[487] Cf. Milgrom 1991, pp. 30-35, who dates the origins of P to the premonarchical period during the prominence of Shiloh. Note also that according to Milgrom (1983a), the word עדה does not occur in postexilic texts, and on the other hand is replaced by קהל in postexilic texts (Milgrom 1983a, pp. 2-12; note that 2 Chr 5:6 is practically the same as 1 Ki 8:5, suggesting that it was directly copied from there), the word מטה in the sense of 'tribe' does not occur in postexilic documents, and not even in Deuteronomy, Jeremiah or Ezekiel (ibid., pp. 12-15; the occurrences in Chronicles are in texts copied from older sources), and that ראש in conjunction with אלפי ישראל "goes back to the time when the clan structure was fully operative" (ibid., pp. 15-17). Milgrom concludes that the temporal distribution of these Priestly terms supports "the view that the Priestly account of the wilderness sojourn has accurately preserved a host of institutions that accurately reflect the social and political realities of Israel's pre-monarchic age" (ibid.). It is also worth pointing out that these terms all occur in Josh 22:9-34 in their early meanings (22:12, 16 [עדה]; 22:14 [מטה]; 22:14 [ראש...לאלפי ישראל]), rather suggesting an early date for Josh 22:9-34.

Deuteronomic standpoint, this then suggests that it is logical to think that at least a substantial part of the book of Joshua dates from the premonarchic period when Shiloh was the main sanctuary in Israel.[488]

Koorevaar has come to a similar conclusion about the provenance of the book of Joshua based on a structural examination of the book as a whole.[489] According to Koorevaar, the book of Joshua as a whole divides into four sections:

1:1-5:12	5:13-12:24	13:1-21:45	22:1-24:33
cross	take	divide	serve
עבר	לקח	חלק	עבר[490]

Figure 9: Four sections of the book of Joshua (Koorevaar)

According to Koorevaar, "The structural-theological purpose is found in the third main section: cross+take=divide". Moreover, Koorevaar sees chapters 14:6-19:51 as a concentric-chiastic structure, as follows:[491]

1. 14:6-15   Beginning: Caleb's inheritance
2. 15:1-17:18   The lot for Judah and Joseph
3. 18:1-10   The tent of meeting taken to Shiloh and the apportioning of the land
4. 18:11-19:48   The lot for seven remaining tribes
5. 19:49-51   Ending: Joshua's inheritance[492]

Figure 10: The structure of Joshua 14:6-19:51 (Koorevaar)

Koorevaar explains the connection between Josh 14:6-15 and 19:49-51,

> The profane division by the lot is sandwiched between Caleb's inheritance and Joshua's inheritance. ... These

---

[488] Cf. also Ottosson 1991, p. 36, "Men det är ofrånkomligt, att lokalfärgen i det prästerliga materialet är nordlig i många fall. Hit hör inte minst Silo-traditionerna. (However, it is clear that the local colour in the Priestly material [of Joshua] is Northern in many cases. Here belong not the least the Shiloh traditions.)"

[489] Koorevaar 1990.

[490] Koorevaar 1990, p. 283.

[491] In fact, I have taken only the inner part of Koorevaar's larger chiasm which would cover 13:8-21:42.

[492] Koorevaar 1990, p. 289.

two men were the only ones from that (military) generation that entered the land of Canaan. Through their faithfulness the division of the land was made possible in every respect.[493]

Moreover, Koorevaar explains the linkage of Josh 15:1-17:18 and 18:11-19:48,

'The lot for Judah and Joseph' stands in contrast to 'The lot for the seven remaining tribes'. The profane designation by means of the lot took place in two phases and in two different places. Between those two portions one finds the portion 'The tent of meeting taken to Shiloh and the apportioning of the land'. In this way the two 'head' tribes are separated from the other seven.[494]

Regarding the central section Josh 18:1-10,

The portion 'The tent of meeting taken to Shiloh and the apportioning of the land' is placed in the center. In 18:2-9 the rest of the land of Canaan is not only apportioned, but all the preceding divisions and regulations are authorized at Shiloh. This portion is introduced by 18:1. 'The whole assembly of the Israelites gathered at Shiloh and set up the Tent of Meeting there. The country was brought under their control'. Therefore the Tent of Meeting at Shiloh is situated in the center of the third main section and expresses the structural purpose of the whole book of Joshua. The erection of the Tent of Meeting at Shiloh is the fulfillment of an important promise in the Pentateuch. 'I will put my dwelling place among you, and I will not abhor you. I will walk among you and be your God, and you will be my people', Lev 26:11-12.[495]

Whether or not one fully agrees with Koorevaar's analysis of Joshua 14:6-19:51, one may nevertheless take note of Koorevaar's conclusion:

The editor [of the book of Joshua] knows nothing of the destruction and rejection of Shiloh. Quite contrary; Shiloh is the goal that must be accentuated. This is a deciding bit of evidence for dating the final theological structure of the book of Joshua. It must be placed

---

[493] Koorevaar 1990, p. 289.

[494] Ibid., pp. 289-290.

[495] Ibid., p. 290.

before the rejection and destruction of the sanctuary in Shiloh.[496]

According to Koorevaar,

> It is difficult to imagine that an editor would bring such a theological structure to the book [of Joshua] if Shiloh had already been rejected and laid waste and another city had come in her place: Zion-Jerusalem.[497]

Koorevaar also gives the following reasons why it is difficult to think that the glorification of Shiloh in Joshua is actually veiled argumentation for the importance of Jerusalem:

1. The author is in no way indicating that Shiloh has been rejected and superseded. Rather, "Shiloh is not rejected, but is even glorified in a structural-theological manner".[498]

2. From a rhetorical standpoint, "the editor would have a structural-theological message [for his contemporaries] that would not only have been superseded at the moment of writing, but it would also have been reprehensible".[499]

3. "The problem is wanting to see Jerusalem at all! For example, the Jerusalem of the time of the Judean king Josiah in 622 BC is the city that has been chosen by Jhwh for the promises of the royal house of David. In the view of the book of Joshua Jerusalem is the city of the Canaanite king Adoni-Zedek that had established a southern coalition with four other kings against Israel in Joshua 10. Although he is defeated there is no mention in that chapter concerning the possession of Jerusalem by Israel. On the contrary, one reads in 15:63, 'Judah could not dislodge the Jebusites, who were living in Jerusalem; to this day the Jebusites live there with the people of Judah'. Jerusalem is the city where Israel (Judah) had failed! But the city received no special meaning in this way. Previously just such a failure can be seen with the tribes east of the Jordan in 13:13 and thereafter one sees the same thing with Manasseh in 17:12-13. Jerusalem is a foreign place for Israel and Judah. There is absolutely no evidence that Jerusalem possessed a special theological position or that Israel had a special theological task in regard to Jerusalem. The editor has neither openly nor in

---

[496] Ibid., p. 292.
[497] Ibid.
[498] Ibid.
[499] Ibid.

veiled terms placed such a message in the book of Joshua. The Jerusalem of the time of Josiah with its theological purpose is actually a completely different Jerusalem and bears no resemblance to the Jerusalem of the book of Joshua."[500] Further, "How strange it is to want to see the Jerusalem of Josiah *behind* the Shiloh of Joshua, while there is the Jerusalem of Joshua *alongside* the Shiloh of Joshua!"[501]

There are also other reasons for a non-Judahite and non-Jerusalemite perspective and indications for an early rather than a late date for the book of Joshua. The first of these is the fact that the indisputable leader of Israel is Joshua *ben* Nun the Ephraimite (cf. Num 13:8). Thus, the facts that the tent of meeting was set at Shiloh and that Joshua *ben* Nun, the undisputable leader of the Israelites in the book of Joshua is an Ephraimite indicate that ultimately both political and religious leadership of the nation was in the North.[502] The situation in the book of Joshua is in fact essentially the same as in Genesis where Judah together with his brothers is subordinate to Joseph at the conclusion of the book (Gen 37-50; see esp. 37:5-11; 50:18 where Joseph's brothers bow down before him; cf. also 49:22-26), even though Judah and the South at least in places feature prominently in the Genesis narratives. Moreover, one has to note that if one excludes the cities of Judah in Josh 15,[503] all that really remains of the activities of the Judahites in the book of Joshua is the description of Caleb and his conquest of Hebron,[504] an account of his family describing allotment of land to Acsah and Othniel (vv. 13-19) and the mention about Jerusalem in v. 63.[505] In fact, that Judah fails to

---

[500] Ibid., pp. 292-293. Cf. Kaufmann 1985/1953, pp. 44-45.

[501] Koorevaar 1990, p. 293.

[502] That Joshua is an Ephraimite also casts doubt to the idea that he is construed as an ideal for Judahite kingship during the time of the monarchy (*contra* Ottosson 1991, pp. 23-24 and *passim*).

[503] See below for the city lists.

[504] Note that Hebron is portrayed as important also at around the time of the beginning of the Davidic monarchy (2 Sam 2:1; 5:1-5; cf. Noth 1930, p. 107).

[505] Note that Jerusalem was a significant city in the second millennium BC, attested by the fact that it is mentioned in the Egyptian Execration

conquer Jerusalem in Josh 15:63 and that the allotment of Judah is deemed too big for them (Josh 19:9)[506] imply that except for Caleb, the Judahites were not very proficient in settling their allotment.[507] Mention should also be made of the fact that according to Josh 7, Achan, the covenant-breaker is a Judahite (vv. 16-18).

Moreover, the Transjordanians are also strongly emphasized in the book of Joshua. As we have seen, the unity of the Transjordanians with Israel is emphasized in Josh 22:9-34. Also, as we have seen,[508] the Transjordanian issue is strongly emphasized in the overall conquest tradition of Numbers-Joshua. In the book of Joshua itself, the Transjordanians come first in the tribal allotments of Joshua 13-21, and this is consistent with Numbers 32-35 in which the Transjordanians already have received their share.[509] The emphasis on the Transjordanians is heightened by the statement that the Transjordanians cross over Jordan in front of the Israelites (לפני בני ישראל), armed and ready to take part in the conquest of Cisjordan (Josh 4:12; cf. Josh 1:14).

Furthermore, if one considers that neither the Transjordanians nor the Levites received an inheritance in the land of Canaan (i.e. west of Jordan), one may think that the Transjordanian allotments in Josh 13 and the Levitical cities in Josh 21 frame the allotments in the book of Joshua, and this may emphasize that provisions were made for those who were not part of the tribal inheritance of the land of Canaan.[510] If so, the arrangement of the Transjordanians and the Levites then emphasizes the unity of Israel, one of the great Deuteronomic themes of the book of Joshua. In any case, it is obvious that the

---

Texts from the 19th-18th centuries BC and in the Amarna letters (see e.g. P.J. King, *ABD* III, p. 751; cf. ibid., p. 753).

[506] Cf. Hawk 1991, p. 156n12.

[507] Cf. also our comments above, p. 148 regarding the archaeological evidence of the Israelite settlement.

[508] Cf. above, p. 210.

[509] In the book of Joshua itself, Josh 1:15 suggests that the Transjordanian conquest has been achieved, and Josh 1:12-18 as a whole naturally points back to the book of Numbers, esp. Num 32.

[510] As suggested by Koorevaar 1990, p. 289; cf. the emphasis in Polzin 1980 on the issue of "insiders" and "outsiders" in Israel in the book of Joshua as a whole.

depiction of the Transjordanians in the book of Joshua emphasizes the unity of Israel both in the conquest (Josh 1:12-18; 4:12; 22:1-6) and in the worship of Yahweh (Josh 22:9-34).

The strong emphasis on the Transjordanians in the book of Joshua fits best in the time before the eighth century when the Transjordanians and the people of the Northern kingdom were deported by the Assyrians (see 1 Chr 5:26). In fact, that Transjordan features prominently in the Judges narratives (e.g. Jdg 5:14-17; 8:4-17; 11:1-12:7), and is still relevant for the time of David according to the lists of the Chronicles (see esp. 1 Chr 12), but does not feature much afterwards (cf. 2 Ki 10:33), supports the idea that the book of Joshua is early rather than late. Specifically, it is hardly likely that the Transjordanian issue would have been current between the time of the Assyrian deportation and the exile.[511] Another factor which supports an early rather than a late date is that whereas the Transjordanian issue is strongly emphasized, there is little if any hint about the North-South divide in the book of Joshua.[512] In fact, the more one goes back in time, the easier it is to think how the emphasis on the Transjordanians would speak to the audience of the book of Joshua, including during the time of the United Monarchy and the premonarchic period.

Besides these considerations, there are other indications for the antiquity of the book of Joshua. First of all, one must remember that the book of Joshua presents itself as an ancient book. As Kaufmann points out, "A straightforward examination of Josh reveals that the latest event explicitly mentioned in it is the conquest of Leshem (Laish) by the Danites (Josh 19:47)."[513] A number of cities include their archaic names, such as Jebus/Jerusalem (Josh 15:63; 18:28), Kiriath-arbah/Hebron (15:54) and Kiriath Baal/Kiriath Jearim (Josh 15:60).[514] Both Jerusalem[515] and Gezer (Josh 16:10; cf. 1 Ki 9:16) are presented as not yet

---

[511] Recall also that based on various considerations in this chapter, it is difficult to think that Josh 22:9-34 was composed in the postexilic time.

[512] Cf. McConville 1993, pp. 100-101.

[513] Kaufmann 1985/1953, p. 21.

[514] Kaufmann 1985/1953, p. 44.

[515] Cf. above, p. 220.

conquered.[516] The Danites are assigned land from the south, not from the north where they are described as migrating later (Josh 19:40-48).[517] The Anakim, rather than the Philistines, are living in Gaza, Ashdod and Ashkelon (Josh 11:22).[518]

In addition to these, Hess lists the following features in the book of Joshua which are best explained by a second-millennium provenance. (1) The description of the borders of Canaan in Joshua 1:4 (and in the Pentateuch) "matches the Egyptian understanding of Canaan in the second-millennium BC sources, where the cities of Byblos, Tyre, Sidon, Acco and Hazor form part of the land".[519] In relation to this, "The northern boundary never was clear because the Egyptians, who saw Canaan as part of their empire, were in conflict with the Hittites on the northern border of the land. The Mediterranean sea formed the western border of Canaan and the Jordan River formed the eastern border (though north of the Sea of Galilee the region included areas farther east)."[520] (2) The plot of Joshua 2 accords with second-millennium ANE culture.[521] (3) The Hivites, Perizzites and the Girgashites (Josh 3:10) have a distinctive association with the second millennium BC.[522] (4) The act of God bringing down the walls of Jericho (Jos 6:20) has a parallel in a Hittite text.[523] (5) The list of items that Achan stole fits best in the latter half of the second millennium BC.[524] (6) The role of the Gibeonites in Josh 9 seems to fit well with the archaeology of their region.[525] (7) The names of a number of the original inhabitants of Canaan fit the context expressed by the fourteenth-century Amarna letters and second millennium Egyptian sources.[526] (8) The names of the three Anakites in Josh 15:14 indicate a mixed population in the region

---

[516] Kaufmann 1985/1953, pp. 44-45.
[517] Kaufmann 1985/1953, pp. 33-35.
[518] Kaufmann 1985/1953, p. 76.
[519] Hess 1996, p. 26.
[520] Ibid.
[521] See ibid., pp. 26-27.
[522] See ibid., pp. 27-28.
[523] See ibid., p. 28, including the Hittite text (in English translation).
[524] See ibid., pp. 28-29.
[525] See ibid., p. 29.
[526] See ibid., pp. 29-30.

around Hebron, which is compatible with what is known from extrabiblical evidence.[527] (9) The covenant in Josh 24:2-27 in its form and content most closely resembles the Hittite vassal-treaty structure which is unique to the second millennium BC.[528]

Hess also notes that, "There are difficulties with assumptions that Deuteronomistic theology must be confined to the period of Josiah and with the analysis of the Joshua narratives divorced from their Ancient Near Eastern context".[529] As Hess summarizes, "Block has argued that many of the theological ideas traditionally associated with Deuteronomistic themes are not distinctive to Israel or confined to the seventh century, but are common in countries throughout the ancient Near East."[530] Moreover, the attitude to the divine in the book of Joshua is compatible with what is known from Israel's surrounding cultures. As Hess summarizes, "Younger has demonstrated that the relationship of the central historical section of Joshua 9-12 is too close to that of contemporary (1300-600 BC) conquest accounts (which themselves are normally used as historical sources - though biased - by historians of the Ancient Near East) to allow certainty of identification of later insertions. Thus statements about the work and words of God are not later insertions into a battle chronicle, but are an essential feature of all Ancient Near Eastern battle accounts. The theology and the narrative should not be separated."[531]

In dating the book of Joshua, one also needs to take account of the currently prevailing philosophical presuppositions regarding Israelite historiography. As Van Seters points out, "The issues involved in the current discussion of history writing in ancient Israel arise primarily out of the views developed by H. Gunkel and H. Gressmann."[532] According to Gunkel and Gressmann, "history writing arises only under certain social and political conditions at

---

[527] See ibid., p. 30.

[528] See ibid., pp. 30-31.

[529] Ibid., p. 33.

[530] Ibid., p. 33, referring to Block 1988, which see for details.

[531] Hess 1996, p. 33, referring to Younger 1990, which see for details. Recall also above, Introduction, p. 23.

[532] Van Seters 1983, pp. 209-210.

the height of a culture".[533] In relation to this, according to Gunkel and Gressmann, Israelite historiography "evolved from early preliterate forms of the tradition to a sophisticated way of thinking and writing about the past, whether recent or more distant, by the time of the United Monarchy".[534] However, as Younger's comparative study of the ancient Near Eastern evidence indicates, this need not be the case. As Younger has shown, the genre of Josh 9-12 is perfectly compatible with other ancient Near Eastern conquest accounts, which demonstrably do not in any way result from a long oral tradition.[535] Moreover, many of these accounts date from the second millennium BC.[536] Thus, one may question the validity of a "traditio-historical" interpretation for the rest of the book of Joshua as well,[537] and consequently there exists no

---

[533] Van Seters 1983, p. 210.

[534] Van Seters 1983, p. 246.

[535] See Younger 1990, especially pp. 200-204 for his treatment of the account of the Gibeonites (Josh 9), which generally has been seen as a relatively late aetiology which explains the presence of the Gibeonites (see Younger 1990, p. 201). Younger gives examples from Assyrian, Hittite and Egyptian sources of attempts to gain favour without fight from conquerors. Especially, the account from the Ten Year Annals of Muršili indicates how Manapa-Datta, the ruler of Seha River land sent forth his mother, old men, and old women to meet Muršili in order to gain his favour. Muršili indicates that when the women bowed down at his feet, he treated them as they wished (ibid., p. 202; incidentally, cf. also Gen 32-33).

[536] See Younger 1990.

[537] Note also the following problems which are involved with the traditio-historical approach, as noted by Whybray (see Whybray 1987, pp. 133-219 for details):

1. According to the traditio-historical approach, writing was not used in the ancient Near East for producing such material as exists in the Pentateuch until a late period. (Whybray 1987, pp. 215-216)

2. "Attempts to establish the originally oral nature of the Pentateuchal material and its oral transmission over a long period of time on the basis of analogies drawn from the practice of oral tradition among other peoples and in different periods have, despite their acceptance by a large number of Old Testament scholars, been shown to lack cogency in several respects". (Whybray 1987, p. 216)

3. There is no evidence of a class of professional storytellers in ancient Israel. (Whybray 1987, p. 218)

prima facie reason to postulate a late dating for the Joshua narratives. Furthermore, as Westermann has pointed out, the period of the exile was hardly a moment of high culture in Israel, and yet scholarship generally thinks that the Deuteronomistic history was written during that time,[538] and thus it is not impossible to imagine that significant writing could have been done in Israel during the premonarchical period.[539] In this respect, one also needs to remember that the alphabet was known in Palestine at least from the middle of the second millennium BC,[540] and that we possess a reasonably extensive corpus of alphabetic texts from Ugarit from ca. 1400-1200 BC, including literary compositions.[541]

However, there are also features which may suggest a Judahite emphasis in the book of Joshua. First of all, even though Judah is listed after the Transjordanians in Josh 13-19, it nevertheless is listed first among the Cisjordanian tribes. Moreover, Judah clearly has the biggest number of cities which even have been divided into "districts" and its border is described most comprehensively. Another tribe whose allotment is described comprehensively is Benjamin,[542] whereas one sees less detail in the description of the allotments the further one goes from Judah and Benjamin.[543] Especially, there are practically no cities listed for Ephraim and Manasseh and their borders are described less carefully, even though there is every reason to think that they were the most

---

4. "It has been shown that no satisfactory techniques have yet been developed for detecting the origins of written narratives from evidence provided by the texts themselves." (Whybray 1987, p. 218)

[538] See Westermann 1994, p. 19.

[539] We must also note that scholars often have interpreted the view of the book of Judges about the premonarchical period quite uncritically and thus assumed that the period was in actuality so confused that nothing organized, including serious writing, could have been done during it and that no serious institutions could have existed (see also below, Chapter 4.6, including p. 251n642).

[540] For examples, see Albright 1966, esp. pp. 10-15, incl. figs 1-11. Cf. also Jdg 8:14.

[541] See e.g. *UT*; M. Yon, D. Pardee and P. Bordreuil, *ABD* VI, pp. 695-721, and the plethora of specialized works on Ugarit and Ugaritic.

[542] Benjamin has a detailed boundary description and a city list divided into two "districts".

[543] See Hawk 1991, pp. 111-113.

dominant political force in the period of the Judges.[544] Moreover, some tribes lack a boundary description (eg. Simeon and Dan), and the boundary and city lists are seemingly garbled for the Galilean tribes (Josh 19:10-39). Furthermore, the emphasis on Judean cities contrasts with the present state of archaeological knowledge from the hill country of Judea which suggests that there was much less settlement there than in the Northern hill country during Iron Age I, and that on the other hand, settlement in the South increased strongly from about the time of the beginning of kingship.[545] In fact, what makes the matter even more intriguing is that the large number of cities in Judah even contrasts with Josh 15 itself which only records Caleb's success at Hebron (Josh 15:13-15), the giving of land by Caleb to his daughter (Josh 15:16-19) and the failure of the Judahites to conquer Jerusalem (Josh 15:63).[546]

If one looks at the history of research, the major driving force behind the modern study of the boundary and city lists of Josh 13-19 was Alt,[547] whose views were accepted in principle by Noth who also connected Transjordan to the scheme suggested by Alt.[548] Alt distinguished a list of boundaries and two different lists of cities in Joshua 13-19, all of them official documents. The list of boundaries divides the whole western territory from the River of Egypt to the Ladder of Tyre between seven tribes: Judah, Benjamin, Ephraim, Manasseh, Zebulun, Asher, Naphtali, excluding Simeon, Dan and Issachar.[549] One of the city lists includes Judah (and Simeon), Benjamin and Dan, and the other includes the Galilean tribes as given in Josh 19:10-39.[550] According to Alt, the boundary list comes from the pre-monarchic period, independent of the twelve

---

[544] Cf. also above, Chapter 4.2, incl. p. 147.

[545] Cf. above, p. 148.

[546] Cf. above, p. 221. This also casts doubt on Hawk's (1991, pp. 109-110) suggestion that Caleb's priority in the narrative order and success in taking his allotment contrasts with the failure of the Josephites in Josh 17:14-18 in their progress and thus emphasizes the role of Judah.

[547] See esp. Alt 1953a/1925; Alt 1953b/1927; Alt 1927.

[548] See Noth 1935; Noth 1953.

[549] As summarized by Kaufmann 1985/1953, p. 23; see Alt 1953b/1927.

[550] See Alt 1953a/1925; Alt 1927.

tribe system,[551] and on the other hand, the city lists derive from the time of Josiah, reflecting the sociopolitical and geographical conditions of the kingdom of Josiah.[552]

The theories of Alt and Noth were criticised by Mowinckel, who rejected their documentary analysis of Josh 13-19.[553] According to Mowinckel, there existed no list of either Judean or Galilean cities.[554] Also, Mowinckel rejected the view that the boundary list originated in the period of the Judges.[555] Overall, Mowinckel suggested that the city and boundary lists of Joshua 13-19 are a postexilic creation by a Priestly writer, albeit drawing on older tradition stemming from different times between Solomon and the postexilic period.[556] One point where Mowinckel essentially agreed with Alt and Noth was that according to him, the list of the cities of Judah, Simeon, Benjamin and Dan is based upon tradition reflecting the conditions of Josiah's kingdom.[557]

Kaufmann has pointed out the basic problems involved with the reconstructions of Alt, Noth and Mowinckel.[558] Moreover, when one looks at research after Alt, Noth and Mowinckel, even though there have been many attempts at solution,[559] none are without problems, and none have been able to create a scholarly consensus. In fact, it may even be impossible to solve these problems in a definitive way. Thus, and as a detailed examination is beyond the scope of this study, we will limit ourselves to a limited number of observations.

---

[551] See Alt 1953b/1927, including pp. 197, 199.

[552] See Alt 1953a/1925, esp. pp. 279-284.

[553] See Mowinckel 1946; cf. Kaufmann 1985/1953, pp. 26-29.

[554] Mowinckel 1946, pp. 7-11.

[555] Ibid., pp. 11-20.

[556] See ibid., esp. pp. 7-11, 27-36.

[557] Ibid., p. 7.

[558] See Kaufmann 1985/1953, pp. 30-64.

[559] Suggested dates for the lists generally range from the time of the United Monarchy to the time of Josiah. For more details, see esp. Kallai 1986, Ottosson 1991, Svensson 1994, the appropriate sections of the commentaries of Boling-Wright 1982, Butler 1983, Fritz 1994 and Hess 1996, and the many monographs and articles mentioned in the bibliographies of these works.

Let us start by looking at Joshua 13-19 from the context of the order of the tribes in the genealogical/tribal lists in the Old Testament, as follows (Figure 11):[560]

Gn 29-30; 35:16-20:	R_{L1} S_{L2} L_{L3} JU_{L4} D_{B1} N_{B2} G_{Z1} A_{Z2} I_{L5} Z_{L6} J_{R1} B_{R2}
Gen 35:23-26:	R_{L1} S_{L2} L_{L3} JU_{L4} I_{L5} Z_{L6} J_{R1} B_{R2} D_{B1} N_{B2} G_{Z1} A_{Z2}
Gen 46:	R_{L1} S_{L2} L_{L3} JU_{L4} I_{L5} Z_{L6} G_{Z1} A_{Z2} J_{R1} B_{R2} D_{B1} N_{B2}
Gen 49:	R_{L1} S_{L2} L_{L3} JU_{L4} Z_{L6} I_{L5} D_{B1} G_{Z1} A_{Z2} N_{B2} J_{R1} B_{R2}
Ex 1:1-6:	R_{L1} S_{L2} L_{L3} JU_{L4} I_{L5} Z_{L6} B_{R2} D_{B1} N_{B2} G_{Z1} A_{Z2} J_{R1}

Num 1:5-16:	R_{L1} S_{L2} JU_{L4} I_{L5} Z_{L6} $J_{R1}(E_{R11}$ $M_{R12})$ B_{R2} D_{B1} A_{Z2} G_{Z1} N_{B2}
Num 1:17-54:	R_{L1} S_{L2} G_{Z1} JU_{L4} I_{L5} Z_{L6} $J_{R1}(E_{R11}$ $M_{R12})$ B_{R2} D_{B1} A_{Z2} N_{B2} L_{L3}
Num 2:1-31:	JU_{L4} I_{L5} Z_{L6} R_{L1} S_{L2} G_{Z1} L_{L3} E_{R11} M_{R12} B_{R2} D_{B1} A_{Z2} N_{B2}
Num 7:	JU_{L4} I_{L5} Z_{L6} R_{L1} S_{L2} G_{Z1} E_{R11} M_{R12} B_{R2} D_{B1} A_{Z2} N_{B2}
Num 10:	JU_{L4} I_{L5} Z_{L6} R_{L1} S_{L2} G_{Z1} E_{R11} M_{R12} B_{R2} D_{B1} A_{Z2} N_{B2}
Num 13:	R_{L1} S_{L2} JU_{L4} I_{L5} E_{R11} B_{R2} Z_{L6} M_{R12} D_{B1} A_{Z2} N_{B2} G_{Z1}
Num 26:	R_{L1} S_{L2} G_{Z1} JU_{L4} I_{L5} Z_{L6} $J_{R1}(M_{R12}$ $E_{R11})$ B_{R2} D_{B1} A_{Z2} N_{B2}

Num 34:	R_{L1} G_{Z1} M_{R12T} JU_{L4} S_{L2} B_{R2} D_{B1} $J_{R1}(M_{R12C}$ $E_{R11})$ Z_{L6} I_{L5} A_{Z2} N_{B2}[561]
Dt 4:43:	R_{L1} G_{Z1} M_{R12T}
Dt 27:12-13:	S_{L2} L_{L3} JU_{L4} I_{L5} J_{R1} B_{R2} (bless) R_{L1} G_{Z1} A_{Z2} Z_{L6} D_{B1} N_{B2} (curse)
Deut 33:	R_{L1} JU_{L4} L_{L3} B_{R2} $J_{R1}(E_{R11}$ $M_{R12})$ Z_{L6} I_{L5} G_{Z1} D_{B1} N_{B2} A_{Z2} -S_{L2}
Josh 13-19:	R_{L1} G_{Z1} M_{R12T} L_{L3} JU_{L4} $J_{R1}(E_{R11}$ $M_{R12C})$ B_{R2} S_{L2} Z_{L6} I_{L5} A_{Z2} N_{B2} D_{B1}
Josh 20:7-8:	N_{B2} E_{R11} JU_{L4} R_{L1} G_{Z1} M_{R12T}
Josh 21:4-7:	JU_{L4} S_{L2} B_{R2} E_{R11} D_{B1} M_{R12C} I_{L5} A_{Z2} N_{B2} M_{R12T} R_{L1} G_{Z1} Z_{L6}
Josh 21:9-40:	JU_{L4} S_{L2} B_{R2} E_{R11} D_{B1} M_{R12C} M_{R12T} I_{L5} A_{Z2} N_{B2} Z_{L6} R_{L1} G_{Z1}

Jdg 1:	JU_{L4} S_{L2} B_{R2} J_{R1} M_{R12C} E_{R11} Z_{L6} A_{Z2} N_{B2} D_{B1} -R_{L1} -G_{Z1} -M_{R12T} -I_{L5}
Judges deliverers:	JU_{L4} B_{R2} N_{B2} M_{R12} I_{L5} Gilead Gilead Z_{L6}?/JU_{L4}? Z_{L6} E_{R11} D_{B1}
Judges 5:	E_{R11} B_{R2} Machir Z_{L6} I_{L5} R_{L1} Gilead D_{B1} A_{Z2} Z_{L6} N_{B2} -JU_{L4} -S_{L2} -G_{Z1}
2 Sam 2:8-9:	Gilead A_{Z2} Jezreel E_{R11} B_{R2}

Ezek 48:1-28:	D_{B1} A_{Z2} N_{B2} M_{R12} E_{R11} R_{L1} JU_{L4} L_{L3} B_{R2} S_{L2} I_{L5} Z_{L6} G_{Z1}
Ezek 48:31-34:	R_{L1} JU_{L4} L_{L3} J_{R1} B_{R2} D_{B1} S_{L2} I_{L5} Z_{L6} G_{Z1} A_{Z2} N_{B2}
1 Chr 2:1-2:	R_{L1} S_{L2} L_{L3} JU_{L4} I_{L5} Z_{L6} D_{B1} J_{R1} B_{R2} N_{B2} G_{Z1} A_{Z2}
1 Chr 2-9:[562]	JU_{L4} S_{L2} R_{L1} G_{Z1} M_{R12T} L_{L3} I_{L5} B_{R2} N_{B2} M_{R12C} E_{R11} A_{Z2} -D_{B1} -Z_{L6}

---

[560] Cf. Noth 1930, pp. 7-28; Weippert 1973, pp. 76-78; Kallai 1997, esp. p. 90.

[561] Note that Joshua the Ephraimite and Eleazar the Priest are mentioned after Reuben, Gad and Transjordanian Manasseh. However, I have not mentioned them as they are spoken of as overseers of the land assignment. Reuben, Gad and Transjordanian Manasseh belong to the context, as they are mentioned first as tribes who already have received their share, even though they do not belong to the sublist which contains the men who would divide Cisjordan.

[562] Note that 1 Chr 8 picks Benjamin again and introduces the family of Saul, and Chapter 9 lists the inhabitants of Jerusalem, with Judah listed first, then Benjamin, Ephraim, Manasseh (v. 3), then Priests (vv. 10-13), then Levites (vv. 14-44).

1 Chr 6:39-48:	JU_{L4} B_{R2} E_{R11} D_{B1} M_{R12C} I_{L5} A_{Z2} N_{B2} M_{R12T} R_{L1} G_{Z1} Z_{L6} $-S_{L2}$
1 Chr 6:49-66:	JU_{L4} S_{L2} B_{R2} E_{R11} M_{R12C} M_{R12T} I_{L5} A_{Z2} N_{B2} Z_{L6} R_{L1} G_{Z1} $-D_{B1}$
1 Chr 12:24-38:	JU_{L4} S_{L2} L_{L3} B_{R2} E_{R11} M_{R12C} I_{L5} Z_{L6} N_{B2} D_{B1} A_{Z2} R_{L1} G_{Z1} M_{R12T}
1 Chr 27:16-22:	R_{L1} S_{L2} L_{L3} JU_{L4} Z_{L6} E_{R11} M_{R12C} M_{R12T} D_{B1} $-G_{Z1}$ $-A_{Z2}$ $-I_{L5}$ $-N_{B2}$ $-B_{R2}$
2 Chr 31:1:	JU_{L4} B_{R2} E_{R11} M_{R12}

Legend: * (in subscript:) L=Leah; R=Rachel; B=Bilhah; Z=Zilpah
                 * (in subscript:) L1= Leah's firstborn; L2=Leah's second, etc.
* R_{L1}=Reuben, S_{L2}=Simeon, L_{L3}=Levi; JU_{L4}=Judah; D_{B1}=Dan; N_{B2}=Naphtali; G_{Z1}=Gad;
A_{Z2}=Asher; I_{L5}=Issachar; Z_{L6}=Zebulun; J_{R1}=Joseph; E_{R11}=Ephraim; M_{R12}=Manasseh;
B_{R2}=Benjamin; M_{R12T}=Transjordanian Manasseh; M_{R12C}=Cisjordanian Manasseh
* non-mention of tribe is indicated by a minus sign (e.g. $-S_{L2}$ means that Simeon is not
mentioned), except in the case of Levi

Figure 11: Tribal lists in the Old Testament

Only in Josh 20:7-8, the list of the six cities of refuge, is
Ephraim mentioned before Judah. Ezekiel 48 is arranged
chiastically, with Judah and the sanctuary in the centre. Also, Judah
is not mentioned in Judges 5 (the Song of Deborah and Barak). 2
Sam 2:8-9 is a list of tribes which supported Ish-Bosheth, and
naturally Judah does not belong to the group. In all other places
Judah always comes before Ephraim. This is also consistent with
the presentations of the lists in Genesis-Exodus, where the Leah
tribes are always listed first and thus Judah always comes before
Ephraim.[563] The listing of the Leah tribes comes first also in
Numbers 1, 13, 26, and in the same order as in Genesis-Exodus,
with minor exceptions, and with Levi missing or last in the lists due
to the subject matter. The Leah tribes come first also in Numbers
2:1-31; 7 and 10, though in different order. Judah leads the way in
the wilderness (Num 10), and is also listed first in the camp order
in Num 2:1-31.[564] The dedicatory gifts of the princes in Num 7
follow the order of Num 2:1-31 and Num 10. Issachar and
Zebulun have been lifted together with Judah in these passages.
Leah tribes are also listed first in Dt 27:12-13, except that Reuben
heads the list of tribes who are to curse on Mt Ebal, and Zebulun is
quite far at the back. Dan, Asher and Naphtali, the sons of the
slave maids, always come last in Num 1-26 and in Deuteronomy 27
and 33. Gad, the remaining son of a slave maid sometimes comes

---

[563] Note also that even though the sons of the slave maids are
generally listed latest in Genesis-Exodus, sometimes Joseph and Benjamin
are also listed latest.
[564] Cf. Jobling 1980, p. 199.

somewhat early and sometimes together with the three other sons of slave maids. In Dt 33, Benjamin, Ephraim and Manasseh have moved toward the start of the list, yet Reuben, Judah and Levi head the list, with Simeon missing.

In the conquest and settlement tradition of Num 34 and Josh 13-19, the Transjordanian tribes stand at the head of the list. Judah comes next. After that, in Num 34, Simeon, Benjamin and Dan stand before Ephraim and Manasseh, whereas in Joshua 13-19 Ephraim and Manasseh come before Benjamin and Simeon. The Galilean tribes Zebulun, Issachar, Asher and Naphtali come last in both cases, except that Dan comes even after them in Josh 13-19.

Thus, one should not be too surprised that Judah is mentioned before Ephraim in Josh 15-17.[565] On the other hand, seen from the standpoint of comparison with the order of presentation of the tribes elsewhere in Genesis-Joshua, the fact that Ephraim stands closer to the head in Joshua 13-19 may be taken as an additional confirmation of a heightened importance for Ephraim in the conquest/settlement tradition of Joshua. One also has to remember that the inheritance of the Cisjordanian tribes is framed by the inheritance of Caleb (Josh 14) and the inheritance of Joshua (Josh 19:49-50), the faithful spies (Num 14),[566] and that this accords well with the fact that the share of Judah and Joseph are listed together separately from the rest of the tribes (Josh 15-17). In this respect, Caleb comes before Joshua in Num 13:2-16; 14:30;

---

[565] Note also that according to Noth "die Liste Num 26 einen vor David liegenden Stand der Dinge wiedergibt" (Noth 1930, p 129; similarly Milgrom 1989, p. 224). The main reason why Noth and Milgrom suggest such an early date for the list is that according to them, it lists localities in the hill country of Manasseh as belonging to Israel, but not in the plain, thus suggesting that it originates from a time when the hill country was already conquered/assimilated into Israel, but not yet the plain; see Noth 1930, pp. 122-132 and Milgrom 1989, p. 224 for details. Another reason for an early dating for Noth is the extraordinary fact that Gad comes between Simeon and Judah in the list, and that there is the order Manasseh-Ephraim instead of Ephraim-Manasseh, whereas later lists are more standardized (Noth 1930, p. 17). Then, if one accepts Noth's (and Milgrom's) view, it means that the original order of the list of Num 26 has not been changed, and thus Judah comes before Ephraim in a list which originates from before the time of David.

[566] Cf. above, p. 218 (incl. Figure 10).

32:12; Dt 1:36-38 (cf. Num 13:30-33 which only mentions Caleb as actively trying to pacify the people, and Num 14:24; Dt 1:36-38 which explicitly mention only Caleb's faithfulness), even though this is balanced by the fact that Joshua is mentioned before Caleb in Num 14:6, 38 and that Eleazar and Joshua lead the allotment process in Numbers and Joshua (Num 34:17; Josh 14:1; 19:51; 21:1; cf. also Josh 14:6, 13 where Judah and Caleb are explicitly subordinate to Joshua). Thus, both Judah and Ephraim are prominent in the conquest tradition, with Joshua the Ephraimite the overall leader (together with the Priest Eleazar), but Judah is listed first before Ephraim in accord with the general practice of tribal lists. Moreover, one must note that the order of the tribes in Josh 13-19 is compatible with the order of the all-Israelite conquest in the book of Joshua, that is, Transjordan - South - North (Josh 1:15; Josh 10-11).[567]

The situation is quite different in 1 Chronicles 2-9. Judah comes first,[568] including David and his descendants, then Simeon followed by the Transjordanians, but *Ephraim and Cisjordanian Manasseh stand almost at the end of the list.* Thus, if one compares 1 Chr 2-9 with Joshua 13-19, it seems that the influence of the Judean postexilic setting is clear: Judah is first and Ephraim and Cisjordanian Manasseh are not important. The situation is somewhat different with the other lists of the Chronicles, but 1 Chr 2:1-2 is based on the system attested in Genesis-Exodus, 1 Chr 12 and 27:16-22 are most naturally understood to derive from pre-exilic lists, and the lists of Levitical cities in 1 Chr 6 may be based on the book of Joshua,[569] whereas 1 Chr 2-9 is most naturally taken as a freer composition. A comparison with Chronicles thus implies that it is difficult to square Joshua 13-19 with postexilic conditions from a rhetorical standpoint.

As regards Judges 1, Judah and Simeon come first in the chapter, followed by Benjamin, Manasseh and Ephraim and three Galilean tribes, Zebulun, Asher and Naphtali. That the Transjordanian tribes have been omitted[570] and that Judah and Ephraim are not connected together as they are in Josh 13-19

---

[567] Cf. Ottosson 1991, p. 27; Kallai 1997.

[568] Cf. Jobling 1980, p. 199.

[569] See below, p. 235f. concerning Levitical cities.

[570] Issachar is also missing, but this may simply be due to oversight.

(Simeon and Benjamin are brought to the fore in Jdg 1) suggests a different rhetorical setting in Judges 1 from that in Joshua 13-19 and the conquest tradition. Moreover, a Judahite perspective is evident in Jdg 1 as Judah is listed first, and half of Jdg 1 (vv. 3-20 vs. 21-36) is devoted to the activities of Judah, even though on the other hand, the tribes are in an almost perfect South-North order. We may also add at this point that in the book of Judges as a whole, Judah is first in conquest (Jdg 1:2), has the first Judge (Jdg 3:7-11), and leads the way in an (according to the narrative itself) early intertribal conflict (Jdg 20:18).[571] Moreover, not only does Jdg 1 give for the description of Judah much more room than for the other tribes and record Judah's successes, but more or less criticises all other tribes which it lists.[572] On the other hand, for most of the Judges period, Ephraim and the northern and Transjordanian tribes feature most prominently.[573] However, this prominence, and a relative silence concerning Judah may also be partly due to the editorial strategy of the book of Judges which sees the period of judges as confused and apostate. Whereas the activities of Judah are emphasized during the early settlement when people still followed Yahweh (Jdg 1:1-2:5), the activities of the Northern tribes are emphasized during the time when the people were apostate.[574]

---

[571] Cf. O'Connell 1996, p. 270.

[572] See O'Connell 1996, pp. 58-72; Amit 1999, pp. 146-152. Jdg 1:19 records a failure by Judah, but nevertheless remains on the positive side in its estimation of Judah (cf. O'Connell 1996, p. 64; Amit 1999, p. 147).

[573] Cf. above, p. 147.

[574] Cf. Amit 1999, pp. 147-150; cf. also above, p. 148. One also should note that in any case, the area occupied by or assigned to Judah is quite large, and thus it would be surprising that Judah would not be considered of any importance during the settlement and Judges period, especially as Judah's territory also occupies almost all area southward from the entrance point of the tribes to Cisjordan (Gilgal and Jericho) according to the conquest tradition. Moreover, one should note that according to the biblical material, Judah stood separate from the rest of the tribes right before and after the monarchy of David and Solomon (2 Sam 2-3; 1 Ki 12; cf. also above, p. 137). The separation of Judah from the North is also attested geographically and climatically (See Finkelstein and Silberman 2001, pp. 131-132, 153-158; Finkelstein 1988, incl. p. 326). It is even possible that the terminology Judah vs Israel in reference to South vs

Then, the clear emphasis on Judah in the book of Judges as a whole contrasts with the concerns of the book of Joshua which is based on the overall leadership of Ephraim, the importance of the Transjordanians and the unity of Israel, even though Judah is listed first in the Cisjordanian allotments (Josh 13-19).

One should also point out that if it is possible to think in terms of a conquest of some kind, an area where population density is smaller might be easier to wage war against successfully than an area where population density is high. Similarly, one might expect more assimilation into indigenous population and consequently more religious syncretism in areas where the indigenous population is stronger.[575] Therefore, it would be easier to speak about conquest in the context of relatively more activity and accompanying success in the South than in the North.[576]

However, we still need to point out that if we look at the allotment of Levitical cities in Josh 21, they have been assigned in a South-North order, with Priestly cities having been assigned from the South (Judah, Simeon and Benjamin). Even though this would fit with the idea that priestly cities be assigned from an area which was easier to take control of, it is nevertheless rather intriguing especially as the tent of meeting itself was set at Shiloh according to the book of Joshua, and thus one would expect that it would rather be convenient to assign the Priestly cities around Shiloh in the North.

As far as scholarship is concerned, even though most scholars have dated the Levitical cities to the time of the monarchy or later,[577] Kaufmann interprets the list of Levitical cities as an "ancient utopia"[578] and dates it to the premonarchical period.[579] In

---

North may date from at least a relatively early period (cf. Josh 11:16, 21 vs. Ottosson 1991, p. 266; 2 Sam 2:4; 5:5; 24:1).

[575] Cf. also above, p. 232n565.

[576] See esp. Josh 10-12; cf. Ottosson 1991, pp. 100-104 for Southern prominence in the list of Josh 12:9-24.

[577] See e.g. Peterson 1980, pp. 1-18 for an overview of the history of scholarship on the Levitical cities.

[578] Kaufmann 1985/1953, pp. 65-71. Kaufmann suggests that the division of the country into two where one part is reserved for priests and the other for Levites only, and that the system was never implemented in practice reflect the utopian character of the list. In this respect, as Haran

any case, those who date the list late (the postexilic time, and conceivably at least for the time after the Assyrian deportation during the divided monarchy) must also take the list as programmatic.[580] Moreover, an early date is conceivable based on ancient Near Eastern parallels. As Hess has pointed out, the list has a parallel with land grants and the sale of properties found in texts from Alalakh.[581] Further, Milgrom points out that the word מטה in the list of Levitical cities is a term which is attested with the meaning 'tribe' in early, but not in late biblical documents.[582] As far as archaeology is concerned, only a half a dozen or so of the Levitical cities have been excavated to date,[583] and all of these attest occupation from Late Bronze Age or earlier.[584] Also, surveys have found pottery remains from almost all possible sites for Levitical

---

(1978, pp. 84-85, 128 incl. n27) points out, there hardly would have been enough Aaronides to populate thirteen cities right after the settlement, as Aaron's family could not have multiplied much in one or two generations from only Eleazar and Ithamar.

[579] According to Kaufmann (1985/1953, pp. 68-69), that the Levitical cities of Dan were assigned from the South, but not from the North whither the Danites later migrated attests the early date of the list of the Levitical cities.

[580] So Wellhausen 1905/1878, pp. 153-158; cf. e.g. Svensson 1994, p. 89.

[581] Hess 1996, p. 281; see Wiseman 1953, texts 1, 76-80, 86-88. Cf. Milgrom 1989, p. 504, who points out that the Akkadian word *tawwertum/tamertu* means extramural land (see also *AHw*, p. 1341, which lists also the second millennium as a period of use for the word).

[582] Milgrom 1983a, pp. 12-15 (cf. also above, p. 217n487). According to Milgrom, the word מטה is not attested after the ninth century in the meaning 'tribe', and that in this respect, the occurrence of the term in Chronicles (including the Levitical city list in Chronicles) always comes in material which the Chronicler took directly from early sources available to him.

[583] A. Mazar informally noted Beth Shemesh, Gibeon, Shechem, Gezer, Taanach and Heshbon in a personal communication, September 1999; cf. Peterson 1977. Peterson also notes minor excavations at Hebron (Peterson 1977, pp. 447-448) and excavations at Tell Jerishe, which is one of two places seen as candidates for Gath Rimmon (Peterson 1977, pp. 372-375).

[584] Cf. Peterson 1977 under cities listed above, n. 583.

cities at least from Iron Age I on,[585] and when one combines these finds with the problems of identification of the sites, which are at times considerable,[586] and the fact that no pottery sherds from earlier than 8th century have been found at suggested sites for Geba and Jattir,[587] even though Geba and Jattir are mentioned in the books of Samuel[588] which generally have been thought to give a reliable picture about the time they portray,[589] one may conclude that based on archaeological evidence, the Levitical cities could be dated to any period from the settlement on.[590]

Moreover, assigning the Priestly cities to the South is compatible with the Priestly tradition that Judah led in the wilderness (Num 2; Num 7), the South-North order of the Cisjordanian conquest,[591] and with Num 34 (assigned to P) which lists the representatives of the tribes who would allot Cisjordan. One might also even speculate that the assignment of the Priestly cities to the South would contrast with the setting of the tent of meeting at Shiloh and thus create a balance of religious power between North and South, serving to emphasize the all-Israelite character of the book of Joshua.[592] Yet, one must also remember

---

[585] See ibid. under each city and suggested site.

[586] See ibid. under each city and suggested site.

[587] See ibid., pp. 405-408, 496-499.

[588] 1 Sam 13-14; 2 Sam 5:25 (cf. Jdg 20:33); 1 Sam 30:27; see Peterson 1977, pp. 398-399, 491.

[589] See e.g. the comments in Hertzberg 1964, pp. 17-20. Note also that we have given added reasons above for thinking that the picture which the biblical sources present about the time which the books of Samuel portray is historically reliable (see above, Chapter 4.2, including p. 157, and also the treatment of the archaeology of Shiloh included in Chapter 4.1).

[590] One should also note that if the list is programmatic, a number of sites may have been selected even though Israelite occupation and/or settlement followed only later. In this respect, as Millard points out, even uninhabited places may have names (A.R. Millard, personal communication, May 2000).

[591] Cf. above, p. 233. As Transjordan was a somewhat "dubious" part of Israel, it would be listed last and one would not expect to settle priests there.

[592] Note also that, according to the current identification, the southern Levitical cities are concentrated around Hebron, the most important

that Josh 21 emphasizes that the Levitical cities were divided by lot (vv. 4-8, 10; cf. also Josh 14:1-2; 19:51; Num 26:55-56; 33:54).

Thus, we may suggest that the conquest tradition saw matters in a South-North order, but this is not necessarily an indication of an overall Judahite perspective. An earlier date than the monarchy is conceivable for the conquest and settlement tradition, and thus for the book of Joshua as well.

Finally, it is entirely possible that the city and boundary lists of Judah and Benjamin are extensive because their city lists were updated or expanded and the boundary lists sharpened during the period of the monarchy, including the divided monarchy. In fact, this is very logical, as it is clearly most natural to think that the text of Joshua was transmitted in the Southern Kingdom after the split with the North, and on the other hand, the knowledge of areas outside Judah and Benjamin would evidently have been more difficult to update after the split, and even more so after the Assyrian conquest. It is even possible that whereas the city and boundary lists of Judah and Benjamin were updated, expanded and sharpened, lists outside these suffered corruption. Especially, the fact that the boundary and city lists of the Galilean tribes (Josh 19:10-39) which are far from Judah and Benjamin are garbled suggests that the text has been corrupted. In this respect, it is also possible that an original list of cities of Ephraim and Manasseh was dropped out, as Kaufmann suggests.[593] Whether these updates, corruptions and possible excisions were intentional or not and if intentional, whatever their motive, the result would emphasize the role of Judah and Benjamin and naturally strengthen the impression of their relative importance in the final form of the book of Joshua.[594]

However, if there was updating or expansion in Judah during the monarchy,[595] it must nevertheless have been conservative overall, as the order of the tribes in Joshua 13-19 has not been

---

Judahite city during the premonarchical period according to the biblical documents (see Josh 15:13-14; 2 Sam 2: 1-4).

[593] Kaufmann 1985/1953, pp. 57-59. Kaufmann suggests that "scars" remain, especially in Josh 16:9 and 17:11. Kaufmann also suggests that portions of the Galilean lists were intentionally abridged (ibid., p. 59).

[594] Cf. Hawk 1991, pp. 111-113.

[595] Cf. also our comments above, Chapter 4.1, including p. 121n39.

changed to reflect the composition of the Southern Kingdom of Judah and Benjamin. Moreover, whereas Judah is lauded in various ways in Jdg 1 and spoken of much more than the other tribes, all that really is spoken of Judah in Josh 15 besides the city lists is the Caleb tradition in vv. 13-19 and the mention of Jerusalem in v. 63.[596] In this respect, that Josh 15:63 records the failure of Judah to conquer Jerusalem further suggests that there is no strong intentional pro-Judahite redaction in the book of Joshua, not even at the time of the monarchy if Josh 15:63 originates from that time. This becomes especially clear when one contrasts Josh 15:63 with the facts that according to the book of Joshua itself, Jerusalem is at the border of Judah and Benjamin but the city proper just belongs to Benjamin (Josh 15:8; 18:16, 28),[597] that according to Judges 1:21 it was *Benjamin* who failed to conquer Jerusalem, and that the book of Judges (Jdg 1:8) adds that *Judah* actually conquered Jerusalem during the early period of the conquest.[598]

---

[596] Cf. above, pp. 221, 228.

[597] Cf. Hawk 1991, pp. 104-105. However, as Kallai (1958, pp. 146-148; cf. Peterson 1977, pp. 294-295) points out, a city may occupy a territory, even a reasonably considerable one. Thus, even though the border strictly speaking leaves the city of Jerusalem itself to Benjamin, when one considers the possibility of territories outside the city proper, Jerusalem could be a true border city between Judah and Benjamin.

[598] It is possible that Josh 15:63 knew about the activity of Judah against Jerusalem and thus spoke about Judah rather than Benjamin in relation to Jerusalem (cf. also n. 597 above), knowing that Judah's activity, even though relatively successful, did not result in driving out the inhabitants of Jerusalem. Besides the issue of Jerusalem, Amit (1999, p. 146) adds further features in Jdg 1 which emphasize Judah as opposed to the presentation of the book of Joshua: "Judah conquered Hebron and smote the three giants, Sheshai, Ahiman and Talmai (v. 10), while Caleb drove the three giants out of Hebron. Similarly, Caleb was given Hebron by the tribe of Judah, who conquered the hill-country (v. 19), whereas the testimonies given in Joshua are quite different (cf. Josh 10:36-37; 12:10; 14:6-15; 15:13-14). Debir was conquered by Othniel son of Kenaz within a campaign by the tribe of Judah (vv. 11-13) rather than by one led by Joshua (cf. Josh 10:38-39; 12:13; 15:15-17)." In this respect, Judges 1 also includes Judahite successes and activity not recorded in the book of Joshua (besides Jdg 1:8 in this respect, see Amit 1999, pp. 145-146). It also has to be added here that even though a detailed examination of the matter is beyond the scope of this study, the differing attribution of

To conclude, one may consider the following comment by Hess concerning the boundary and city lists:

> The form of the boundary descriptions and town lists reflects both the ideal of the early settlement and their usage as legal and administrative documents in later periods. The early origin that the text assigns to these documents is supported by their topographical similarity with Late Bronze age city states of Palestine, by the need for some sort of boundaries - given the sociological dynamics present in the settlement of the land, and by archaeological evidence of settlement in the hill country of Palestine from 1200 BC.[599]

Thus, we may summarize that according to the book of Joshua, Deuteronomic conditions for bringing all sacrifices to the central sanctuary were attained during the last days of Joshua, and that Shiloh was the central sanctuary at the time. Josh 22:9-34 describes an incident where centralization was actually demanded from the Transjordanians. When we combine the results obtained in this section with the results of the previous section (Section 4.3 above), we may also point out that the picture of centralization of worship that the book of Joshua presents fits together with the picture of centralization in Pentateuchal legislation.

Moreover, the depiction of centralization in the book of Joshua need not be a late creation, but an early, even a premonarchical (before the disaster at Aphek) provenance of the book of Joshua at least in its basic form is a real possibility, including chapters 13-19 and 22:9-34. Such an early dating is in fact quite logical, as the emphasis on Shiloh in the book of Joshua does not fit with the conditions of the Judean-led monarchy for which Shiloh had been rejected and Jerusalem had taken its place. In this respect, the existence of Priestly material in the book of Joshua and on the other hand the existence of little Priestly material in Judges-Kings speaks for the same idea. An early dating for the book of Joshua also fits with the image of the book as an all-Israelite

---

conquests (esp. Judah vs Joshua) need not necessarily be a sign of contradiction, but only of differing emphasis (note also that [if referring to the same events] Josh 11:21-22 attributes victories at Hebron and Debir to Joshua, Josh 15:13-17 to Caleb and Othniel, and Jdg 1:10-11 to Judah and Othniel; cf. Younger 1994, p. 226).

[599] Hess 1996, p. 40.

document, contrasting with the later historical books Judges, Samuel, Kings and Chronicles which more or less attest Judean concerns. Moreover, the connections that the book of Joshua has with the conquest tradition in Numbers and the Priestly flavour of the conquest tradition in Numbers suggest that the conquest tradition of Numbers is early as well. Further, as the book of Joshua is heavily Deuteronomic overall, an early provenance of the book of Joshua would imply an early provenance for at least the core of the book of Deuteronomy as well. Naturally, such an early dating of the book of Joshua, the Priestly material, the conquest tradition of Numbers and the book of Deuteronomy would rather suggest that the picture that they present about the early history of Israel is more reliable than is often thought. And yet, especially keeping in mind the current state of archaeological research which relates to the Israelite settlement, it must also be said that an early date for these documents would not yet necessarily mean that the data contained in them is historically reliable in all of its parts. The material could still be a propagandistic and exaggerated portrayal of the time concerned, and we cannot be more precise in the context of this study. However, we must also emphasize that our basic results concerning the view of centralization that the book of Joshua presents are not dependent on the date of the book.

4.6.   Judges 17-21 and the Period of Judges

We have now covered the history of the central sanctuary and centralization for the period between the settlement and the building of Solomon's temple, except for the period portrayed by the book of Judges. In order to investigate the picture that the book of Judges presents about the central sanctuary and centralization, we will take Judges 17-21 as the basis for our discussion, simply for the reason that Jdg 17-21 contains references to Shiloh (Jdg 18:31), the ark (Jdg 20:27-28) and Phinehas the son of Eleazar son of Aaron (Jdg 20:28), and on the other hand, no such references exist outside these chapters in the book of Judges. We will start by discussing relevant aspects of the literary setting, structure and provenance of Jdg 17-21, also in relation to the book of Judges as a whole, and will then proceed to matters relating to what kind of picture Jdg 17-21 give regarding the central sanctuary and the centralization of worship, and how this picture relates to the rest of the book of Judges.

The overall structure of the book of Judges can naturally be divided into a prologue (1:1-3:6 which further divides logically into two parts, 1:1-2:5[600] and 2:6-3:6)[601], a main body consisting of the deliverer accounts of the book (3:7-16:31), and a conclusion (Chapters 17-21 which consists of two different accounts, chapters 17-18 and 19-21).[602] The main body which is at the heart of the book of Judges consists of a cyclical representation of Israel's history in the premonarchical era. The cycles, as is well known, consist of Israel's fall into idolatry, the resulting anger of Yahweh and subsequent enemy oppression, Israel's repentance and cry to Yahweh, Yahweh raising a deliverer who liberates Israel from enemy oppression, and resulting peace. On the other hand, neither the prologue nor the conclusion attest this cyclical pattern. The prologue consists of a limited conquest account (1:1-2:5) a lot of whose material can also be found in Joshua 13-21, and an introduction to the cyclical pattern of history in the period as depicted in the main body (2:6-3:6). The conclusion relates a pair of events (17-18 and 19-21) which according to the writer happened in the period of the Judges.

If one looks at the scholarship on the book of Judges,[603] one notices that, before Noth, most academic discussion treated Judges from a source-critical viewpoint.[604] On the other hand, since Noth, Judges generally has been seen as a part of the Deuteronomistic History.[605] However, as we have seen above,[606] there is good reason to think that such a history does not exist, and consequently, the book of Judges is not part of it either. This observation is confirmed by the fact that the presentation of history is very different in Judges from that in Joshua, in fact so much that the two books are in many ways complete opposites of each other.[607] Joshua is essentially optimistic, whereas Judges is essentially

---

[600] Even though 2:1-5 is rather slightly detached from both Ch. 1 and 2:6-3:6; cf. Amit 1999, pp. 152-153.

[601] See O'Connell 1996; Amit 1999; Weinfeld 1967 et al.

[602] Cf. O'Connell 1996, p. 2.

[603] See O'Connell 1996, pp. 345-368 for an excellent summary.

[604] See ibid., pp. 347-354.

[605] See ibid., pp. 355-368; cf. McConville 1997.

[606] See above, Chapter 4.5.

[607] Cf. Weinfeld 1967, pp. 105-113.

pessimistic. Joshua sees that the land has essentially been conquered during the last days of the life of the man Joshua and rather looks at the future finalization of this conquest, whereas Judges emphasizes the incompleteness of the conquest. Israel is dominant over its neighbours in the book of Joshua, whereas there are foreign oppressions in the book of Judges. There is peace at the end of the book of Joshua, whereas there rather is no peace in the book of Judges. In the book of Joshua, the people follow Yahweh, whereas in the book of Judges, the people are apostate and follow other gods. Finally, Joshua is written from an all-Israelite perspective, whereas Judges is written from a Judahite perspective.[608]

It is also recognized that the book of Judges has notably different concerns from the books of Kings. As von Rad stated it, "a new section begins for the Deuteronomist with Solomon".[609] According to O'Connell, von Rad has noted the following rhetorical incongruities between Judges and Kings: "cycles of apostasy and repentance versus an essentially downward trend of apostasy; idealization of the monarchy versus the idea that monarchy usually corrupts the nation; tacit assessment of the judges versus explicit judgment against the kings; YHWH's controlling of history through judges' charismata versus history as the fulfilment of YHWH's prophetic word; guilt of those opposed to judges (2:17) versus guilt of the moral disposition of kings".[610]

Naturally, if the book of Judges is at least basically an independent literary work, the considerations regarding the provenance of the book become very different from the case when the book is seen as a part of the Deuteronomistic History. In the latter case, all considerations naturally point to the exile as the basic time of composition of the book, whereas in the former case the dating of the book is much more open. Moreover, as O'Connell, who sees Judges as a product of the early monarchy, points out, the only textual evidence which could clearly imply a late date of composition is the mention עד־יום גלות הארץ in Judges 18:30, as

---

[608] Cf. above, Chapter 4.5.
[609] Von Rad 1953/1948, p. 75n2.
[610] O'Connell 1996, p. 360.

one could infer that this refers to the Assyrian deportation (734 or 722 BC).[611]

This then in fact has introduced us specifically to the question of the dating of Judges 17-21. Even though the note in 18:30 fits very well with the Assyrian deportation (see 2 Ki 15:29 where the land of Naphtali to which the city of Dan belonged, is taken into captivity), there are other possibilities as well. Some other earlier captivity, even one for which no historical information remains may be referred to.[612] Also, it has been suggested that there has been a textual error which has changed the word אֲרוֹן to אֶרֶץ, and that the reference was thus originally to the disaster of Aphek (1 Sam 4) where the ark was taken captive by the Philistines (recall גָּלָה כָבוֹד מִיִשְׂרָאֵל in 1 Sam 4:22).[613] Be that as it may, the dating of 18:30-31 may not be quite as important for our considerations as it might seem at first sight. This is because chapters 17-21 indicate that they portray an early period of Judges. According to 20:28, the events in chapters 19-21 happened within about a generation of the settlement, as they refer to Phinehas *ben* Eleazar *ben* Aaron, who also features in the Pentateuch and in Joshua (see Ex 6:25; Nu 25:7, 11; 31:6; Josh 22:13, 30, 31, 32; 24:33). Similarly, according to 18:30, Jonathan *ben* Gershom *ben* Moses[614] was the first priest of the Danites. Even though Jonathan might be a later descendant

---

[611] O'Connell 1996, p. 337. See e.g. Gray 1986, p. 347; Soggin 1981, p. 278; Boling 1975, p. 266 for interpreting the verse as referring to the Assyrian deportation.

[612] As noted by many conservative commentators time and again; cf. e.g. Cundall 1968, p. 192.

[613] See O'Connell 1996, pp. 481-483 for detailed argumentation in favour of this view. See also Schley 1989, p. 34 for the history of this line of interpretation. In fact, Keil (1983/1861-1865, *Judges*, p. 441), and Satterthwaite (1989, pp. 117-121) argue for a reference to the disaster at Aphek without suggesting textual emendation. Satterthwaite argues that verses 30 and 31 are parallel, and that both verses should thus refer to events of the same time. Moreover, Satterthwaite points out the fact that there is archaeological evidence for a destruction in Dan at the second half of the 11th century; for details of the archaeological evidence, see Biran 1994, pp. 125-146, 155, esp. pp. 135-138; cf. also Biran 1992, p. 14; Finkelstein 1988, pp. 102-103.

[614] See e.g. O'Connell 1996, p. 480n106 for textual issues concerning the name Moses in Jdg 18:30.

than grandson of Moses, as the usage of *ben* does not necessarily demand direct descent,[615] the fact that the Danite migration is mentioned in Joshua 19:47 suggests that at least a relatively early period of Judges is indicated. Then, even if Judges 17-21 was incorporated into the book of Judges as early as the time of David, if the accounts have any real historical basis, they must in any case have already been transmitted for up to 200-400 years before having been incorporated to the book of Judges, depending on whether one thinks of a 13th or 15th century settlement. Furthermore, it is clear that the 'no king' formulae in 17:6; 18:1; 19:1 and 20:25 date from a time after kingship has been established, and thus are additions which are later than the first composition (written or oral) of the chapters. Similarly, it is clear that 18:30 and 18:31 are later editorial comments as they look back to the events from a viewpoint which is detached from them.[616]

Nevertheless, there are a number of aspects worth clarifying as regards the provenance of Jdg 17-21, and these will also lead us to the interpretation of the chapters, and will naturally help us to interpret the rest of the book of the Judges as well. A tricky and important, even though less readily apparent, question in the interpretation of Jdg 17-21 is whether there is implied polemic in the chapters. In this respect, one may point out that the localities Bethel and Dan which are heavily involved in the narratives of both chapters 17-18 and 19-21 are the same localities where Jeroboam established royal sanctuaries in the Northern Kingdom (1 Ki 12:27-29). Especially, as Jdg 17-18, besides describing the Danite migration to the North and the conquest of the city of Laish, tell how a sanctuary originated at Dan, many scholars have seen the narrative connected with Jeroboam. In this respect, all scholars agree that the narrative views the Danite sanctuary negatively,[617] and most agree that the description contains plenty of

---

[615] See e.g. Keil 1983/1861-1865, *Judges*, p. 439.

[616] Cf. O'Connell 1996, pp. 421-424. Note however that Satterthwaite has made a good case for the overall unity of Judges 17-21 by means of literary criticism (Satterthwaite 1989). According to Satterthwaite, there is no need to consider even Judges 20:29-48 as composite, *contra* most commentators (Satterthwaite 1989, pp. 208-214).

[617] See e.g. Soggin 1981, p. 268; Gray 1986, p. 223; Noth 1968/1962, pp. 71-76; O'Connell 1996, pp. 231-241; Klein 1988, pp. 154-156;

irony.[618] Thus, a number of commentators think that the narrative
is polemic against the royal cult of Jeroboam I.[619] According to
Soggin, "in this polemic it is said that the premises of the sanctuary
in question had been false from the beginning: its cult was
syncretistic, the money which served to maintain it derived from a
theft, and its priesthood, though it boasted a most noble descent,
was not free, but subject to patronage".[620] However, this view has
its problems as the two sanctuaries are in many ways very different.
In Noth's words,

> Even if one supposes that the 'golden calf' of Jeroboam
> was erected at Dan on the very spot where formerly the
> silver image of Jdg 17-18 stood (which is nowhere
> stated and is by no means self-evident) and that
> therefore the 'calf' has superseded and replaced this
> cult image, nevertheless the cult objects are entirely
> different and accordingly different cultic practices are
> involved. One can hardly polemicize against the one
> when he has the other in mind. In almost all other
> respects as well, the two cultic establishments differ
> from one another. Whereas the earlier sanctuary was a
> recognized tribal sanctuary according to the explicit
> notation in Judges 18:19b, the one established by
> Jeroboam I at Dan was a royal sanctuary. Also, he
> fashioned in it a correspondingly new form by having a
> *bama*-house erected, and therefore he gave a new
> character to the whole thing, even though the spot was
> perhaps the same one where the tribal sanctuary had
> been located. The same applies to the priesthood.
> According to Jg. 17-18, the tribal sanctuary attached

Satterthwaite 1989, pp. 78, 123. There are however scholars, such as
Moore, Burney and Niemann who think that the original narrative was
either neutral or even pro-Danite, and that the polemic was introduced by
later editing (Satterthwaite 1989, p. 123). However, seeing an earlier pro-
Danite story is clearly a hypothesis which is impossible to verify.

[618] E.g. Soggin (1981, p. 268): "Now the attitude of the present text
towards the Danite sanctuary and what it contains is essentially negative,
with marked ironical thrusts, even if they are sometimes ambiguous."; cf.
Amit 1999, pp. 321-322, 328.

[619] Satterthwaite (1989, p. 124) lists Nötscher, Martin, Soggin in favour
of this view.

[620] Soggin 1981, p. 269.

great importance to having a 'Levitical' priesthood; but Jeroboam I, according to I Kg. 12:31b, installed non-Levites as priests in his state sanctuaries. Thus very little remains of concrete agreement between the two reports: only a general polemic against cultic establishments in the city of Dan and perhaps agreement that these establishments were located in the same place. For the rest we are dealing with phenomena of a quite different character and from different times.[621]

Noth himself thought that "the polemical narrative of Jg. 17-18 stems from the circle of the royal Israelite sanctuary of Dan which was established by Jeroboam I".[622] According to Noth, the 'no king' formula indicates that the cult was not performed correctly before king Jeroboam regulated it, as the story of Micah's sanctuary demonstrates.[623]

Noth himself did not think that the old tribal sanctuary existed alongside Jeroboam's sanctuary, but that it was discontinued.[624] On the other hand, Gray who also sees the narrative as pro-Jeroboam polemic thinks that the two sanctuaries existed contemporaneously and that the polemic stems from the "royal priests of Bethel or Dan as distinct from the oracle-priests of the tribal sanctuary at Dan who were descended from Micah's Levite".[625] According to Gray, "This is doubtless the source of the mild ridicule of the origin of the cult-symbols in money stolen and cursed, of the priesthood of a vagabond and disloyal Levite and of

---

[621] Noth 1968/1962, pp. 77-78. Noth points out in a footnote (no. 24 within quotation) that "Bethel, which is mentioned in connection with Dan in I Kg. 12:29, is expressly designated in Am 7:13 as a 'royal sanctuary' with a 'state temple'", and adds in a footnote (no. 26 within quotation) that it is reasonable to assume based on 1 Ki 12:31 that a *bama*-house was erected also at Bethel and Dan, even though this is not expressly stated.

[622] Noth 1968/1962, pp. 81-82.

[623] Ibid., pp. 82-83.

[624] Ibid., pp. 84-85. Note that archaeologically, evidence has been found of a sanctuary at the time of Jeroboam, but no evidence has been found of the tribal sanctuary at all (see Biran 1994, incl. p. 165; Biran 1992, pp. 14-15).

[625] Gray 1986, p. 223.

the high-handed appropriation of both by the Danites in their occupation of the defenceless settlement of Laish."[626] Also, according to Gray, the 'no king' formula in 17:6 and 18:1 refers to Jeroboam.[627]

In any case, all these explanations suffer from the problem that they do not account well for the fact that Judges 17-18 is connected with Judges 19-21.[628] If one sees polemical traits in Judges 17-18, one should equally see whether Judges 19-21 can be taken as polemical as well.[629] Now, the major thesis of O'Connell's book is that Judges is replete with anti-Saulide polemic and

---

[626] Ibid., pp. 223-224.

[627] Ibid., p. 224.

[628] According to Soggin (1981, p. 263), "Although these two episodes deal with different subjects, they have many things in common and therefore have been joined together on purpose" ... "they both deal with Levites residing in Ephraim who are not Ephraimites, who are wronged by the local population, and who somehow get involved with non-Israelite cities", referring to F. Crüsemann, *Der Widerstand Gegen das Königtum*, Neukirchen-Vluyn, 1978, pp. 156ff.). One may add that both narratives deal with a private incident escalating to public (tribal) level, and that in both narratives there is a false resolution (Micah's restoring the silver to his mother; reconciliation of the Levite with his concubine) which however is in each case overturned by subsequent events (Satterthwaite 1989, p. 287). Also, the 'no king' formula (17:6; 18:1; 19:1; 21:25) ties both narratives together. Amit's suggestion (see Amit 1999, pp. 337-341, 348-357) that Jdg 19-21 does not belong together with Jdg 17-18 is by no means certain. Above all, Amit's suggestion that Jdg 19-21 is too different from Jdg 17-18 and thus cannot describe roughly the same time or cannot have been written at roughly the same time is tenuous. For instance, *contra* Amit, it is not clear that Jdg 19-21 intends to praise the premonarchic system of the assembly of the tribes and its functioning (cf. e.g. the seizure of the maidens of Shiloh, if not directly at the instigation of the elders, at least in their full knowledge in 21:15-24). As another example for the tenuousness of Amit's argumentation, there may be many reasons why the Levite in Jdg 19-21 would resort to complaining/calling to the tribes after having been wronged, whereas Micah in Jdg 17-18 would not, and thus it is not clear that Jdg 19-21 differs from Jdg 17-18 in the way the tribal system works.

[629] Cf. Noth 1930, pp. 168-170, who does not detect any polemic in Jdg 19-21.

legitimization of the Davidic dynasty.[630] Surely Judges 19-21 can easily be read as anti-Saulide polemic. The culprits in the narrative are men of Gibeah, the future hometown of Saul (1 Sam 10:26; 15:34; 23:19; 26:1),[631] whose wickedness finds an analogy with Sodom, as commentators have noted.[632] Similarly, it is possible to argue that based on an analogy with Deut 13:13-19, the Israelites should have completely destroyed Benjamin,[633] and had they done so instead of reneging on covenant obligations (Jdg 21), there would have been no king Saul.[634]

Then, if one sees anti-Saulide polemic in Judges 19-21, it is easiest to conceive a *Sitz-im-Leben* for the polemic at the time of David, and the further one goes forward in time, the less relevant such polemic becomes.[635] In this respect, it is difficult to think that

---

[630] O'Connell 1996. Cf. also the portrayal of the conquest of Jerusalem in the book of Judges with that in the book of Joshua (see above, p. 239; cf. O'Connell 1996, p. 64).

[631] O'Connell 1996, p. 328.

[632] See O'Connell 1996, pp. 250-252 for a detailed comparison of Judges 19 with Genesis 19.

[633] So O'Connell 1996, p. 252

[634] Note also the similarity of custom between the slicing of the murdered concubine into twelve pieces and sending the pieces throughout Israel in Jdg 19:29 and Saul's similar act with an ox in 1 Sam 11:7 (as pointed out by Noth 1930, pp. 109-110), which also suggests a similar milieu for both Jdg 19-21 and 1 Sam 11.

[635] Amit (1999, pp. 349-350) suggests that Jdg 19-21 dates from the second temple period. According to Amit (ibid., p. 349n43), "It may be that the criticism against the Davidic dynasty following the destruction of the Temple and the disappearance of its representatives at the beginning of the Second Temple encouraged hopes for the renewal of the Benjaminite dynasty." In this respect, Amit implies that 1 Chr 10:13-14 was written due to such a situation of the postexilic community (ibid., p. 350). However, Amit herself suggests elsewhere that the view of kingship in the book of Judges differs from that of the postexilic Chronicles. According to Amit herself, Judges views kingship rather as a compromise than as an ideal, whereas Chronicles views it in a much more ideal light, where the Davidic king "is God's representative upon earth and the one who concretizes his rule (2 Chr 13:8)" (ibid., p. 115). Thus, even though Jdg 19-21, especially as a part of the book of Judges as a whole, fits with the idea gathered from Chronicles about possible renewed need of legitimation of the Davidic dynasty, it does not fit with the idea gathered

the Judahite author would have wanted to polemicize against Benjamin during the time of the divided monarchy when all other tribes had deserted Judah and only Benjamin was left. Moreover, as Judges 17-18 and 19-21 are connected together, one can only ask the question of why there is polemic against Dan in Judges 17-18, and yet on the other hand, one cannot see any polemic against Bethel in Judges 19-21,[636] even if one allows that the tradition in Jdg 20:26-28 which connects the "veritable" Phinehas (cf. Ex 6:25; Nu 25:7, 11; 31:6) with Bethel is a late, postexilic Priestly gloss;[637] on the contrary, in any case, the Israelites inquire from God at Bethel and finally succeed (Jdg 20:18ff.).[638] Furthermore, if Jdg 17-18 is anti-Jeroboam polemic, how could the 'no king' formula fit with polemic against Jeroboam, as Jeroboam himself was a king? And, if Jdg 17-18 is to be considered as pro-Jeroboam polemic, one may ask: How did the narrative come to be taken into the southern book of Judges?[639]

---

from Chronicles about the view of the Judean postexilic community of kingship. Cf. Noth 1968/1962, p. 80n29 regarding Jdg 17:6 and 18:1, "Only by doing violence to the sentences can we assign them to the post-exilic period 'which views the kingship in a glorious light'", and further (ibid., p. 80), "these sentences ... rather ... refer to a real, historical kingship which the author knows". These comments by Noth undoubtedly also fit to 19:1 and 21:25, especially as Jdg 19-21 in its present form is a part of the book of Judges as a whole (According to Amit herself, Jdg 19-21 has been edited in order to connect it to the exposition of the rest of the book, and as if to serve a compositional function of closing the circle of the entire book, even though in her opinion this connection can be seen to be artificial [see Amit 1999, pp. 353-357, esp. p. 357]).

[636] So O'Connell 1996, p. 298. See also ibid., p. 298n118 for a refutation of Amit 1990 who attempts to see hidden polemic against Bethel in Jdg 17-18.

[637] According to Gray (1986, p. 357), Phinehas the son of Eleazar, the Son of Aaron is "a post-Exilic redactional insertion". Similarly Soggin (1981, p. 293).

[638] Cf. below, p. 266, incl. n696.

[639] Moreover, as there are good reasons to think that the 'no king' formula (17:6; 18:1) is Deuteronomic (see below, p. 255), this makes it more unlikely that it has been used for pro-Jeroboam polemic.

To solve this dilemma, one can interpret Judges 17-18; 19-21 without seeing them as polemic connected with Jeroboam or as strongly anti-Saulide. If one looks at 1 Ki 12:29, Jeroboam established his chief sanctuaries at Bethel and Dan. Now, one notices that from the standpoint of the Northern Kingdom, Bethel and Dan were, roughly speaking, in the far south and far north, respectively. When one adds to this the fact that both were from early times known cult centres, it is quite natural that Jeroboam chose them as his major sanctuaries. Thus, it is not inconceivable that there was an illegitimate cult centre at Dan both in the period of the Judges and in the time of Jeroboam.[640] Furthermore, that there is a reference to the Danite migration elsewhere (Josh 19:47; cf. Jdg 1:34) suggests that at least the core of Judges 17-18 is based on early tradition.[641] Then, as the 'no king' formula (17:6; 21:25) indicates, both accounts were included in the book of Judges to illustrate the confused and apostate state of affairs during the period of Judges. In this respect, one could imagine that an account which involved Saul's hometown would have created interest in the reign of David. The selection of the narrative would also conveniently serve to emphasize the claims of David as against Saul, even if the narrative was not specifically created to polemicize against Saul.

Another matter which involves dating considerations in Jdg 17-21 is the already mentioned 'no-king' formula in 17:6; 18:1; 19:1; 21:25. That it is easy to read the 'no king' formula as optimism for kingship[642] contrasts with the presentation of the books of Kings

---

[640] Note also that Dan is a very fertile place due to powerful springs there.

[641] That Laish is called Leshem in Josh 19:47 also suggests that the Joshua and Judges traditions are independent, and thus rather confirm each other. It is also worth noting that O'Connell thinks that the variation of Laish and Leshem is dialectal (O'Connell 1996, p. 345n1).

[642] Cf. Weinfeld 1967, p. 111 "KAUFMANN is therefore correct in stating that the author of the general introduction 'has darkened the colors and depicted the period black on black ... in order to exalt the monarchy'. This dimming of colors also finds expression in the recurring refrain in chapters xvii-xxi: 'In those days there was no king in Israel; every man did what was right in his own eyes' (xvii 6; xviii 1; xix 1; xxi 25)". The suggestion of Boling (1975, p. 294) that, "in Micah's day Yahweh was not really being acknowledged as Israel's king (17:6)" is also

according to which kingship rather degenerated than improved with time.[643] Moreover, as it is clear that David is a good example of a king who was seen to be faithful to both covenant justice (as opposed to the events of Jdg 19-21) and to the cult (as opposed to the events of Jdg 17-18), the 'no king' formula could fit well to David's reign.[644] Moreover, according to O'Connell,

> In an Egyptian account of the chaos that preceded the accession of Setnakhte (ca. 1184-1182 BCE), Harris papyrus no. 1 states that "the land of Egypt had been overthrown with every man being his own standard of right (*s nb m ʿk3.f*) since they had no leader (*r ḥry*) for many years in the times of others". Not only does this furnish an ideological parallel to Judges' motif A1b[645]

---

a possible implied nuance in the 'no king' formula. However, one needs to also remember that, as e.g. Amit (1999, pp. 92-113) points out, the Abimelech and Gideon narratives are rather against kingship, with Jdg 8:22-27 specifically speaking for Yahweh's kingship instead of human kingship. According to Amit (1999, pp. 113-117), the closing section (Jdg 17-18 for Amit), taken together with the rest of the book, serves to suggest that for the author, kingship is ultimately a pragmatic compromise solution to a situation of anarchy which characterized the period of judges and the failure of the people to follow Yahweh (cf. also above, p. 249n635). Finally, one may say that for the book of Judges, it is also important that the king who would rule Israel is divinely appointed (O'Connell 1996, p. 271; cf. Amit 1999, p. 114).

[643] Cf. above, p. 243. One can of course argue that this degeneration of kingship was seen as such only by the exilic historian who wrote the book of Kings. However, for instance, if the tax burden on the people by Solomon as portrayed in 1 Ki 12:1-4 is accepted as historically reliable, there was disillusionment quite soon after the establishment of kingship. One should also note at least the political instability in the Northern Kingdom from Jeroboam on, even if one thought that the negative evaluation of the religious situation in the North stems from the exilic editor of the books of Kings.

[644] See O'Connell 1996, pp. 307-329. Regarding cult, one should especially emphasize that David brought the ark to Jerusalem (2 Sam 6; cf. 1 Chr 13:2-3) and prepared for the building of the temple (2 Sam 7 etc.; according to the Chronicles, David also prepared for temple worship [1 Chr 23-26]). The Bathsheba incident (2 Sam 11-12) is the only major ostensible tarnish in David's image.

[645] See O'Connell 1996 for the interpretation of this notation.

(איש הישר בעיניו יעשה) - indeed, Eg. ʾk3 'straightness, right' conveys a similar notion of conformity to norm as does BH ישר 'straightness, uprightness, right' - but it serves the interests of polemicizing the present order as a result of the previous period of history.[646]

O'Connell adds,

> Although no case should be made for direct dependence between Judges and this Egyptian parallel, two points may be made in regard to its similarity to Judg. 17:6b and 21:25b: (1) the characterization of the preceding period as one in which everyone followed his/her own standard of right is a negative characterization, and (2) it is claimed that the contemporary dynasty is the source of order that has brought an end to the anarchy of the preceding period.[647]

O'Connell concludes, "Other examples of negative characterization by Egyptian pharaohs against preceding periods, dynasties or pharaonic rules are extant."[648] Thus, it is entirely possible that the 'no king' formula implies an early date for Jdg 17-21.

The mention in Jdg 20:18 that Judah should go first against Benjamin echoes Jdg 1:2 and thus suggests that 1:1-2:5 and 17-21 belong together. Moreover, as Jdg 1:1-2:5 and 17-21 form a bracket around the main body of the book, this naturally suggests that the book as a whole is no later than this bracket. In this respect, if Jdg 1:1-2:5 is late, as is often thought,[649] this suggests that Jdg 17-21 must be late as well.[650] However, it is by no means certain that Jdg

---

[646] O'Connell 1996, p. 330. See also Greenspahn 1982. It has to be noted that apparently the anarchy of the preceding 19th dynasty has been exaggerated in order to extol the new ruler (A.R. Millard, personal communication, August 2000; cf. James 1979, p. 67).

[647] O'Connell 1996, p. 331.

[648] Ibid. Cf. also the Weidner Chronicle from Mesopotamia, apparently to be dated to the second millennium (text in *COS* 1, pp. 468-470, transl. & ed. by A.R. Millard; cf. Arnold 1994), and the Proclamation of Telipinu and the Apology of Hattušili II from Anatolia (both texts in *COS* 1, pp. 194-198, 199-204, transl. & ed. by T.P.J. van den Hout; cf. Chavalas 1994, pp. 123-125).

[649] See Noth 1991/1943, pp. 23-24; Amit 1999, p. 120n1.

[650] Cf. Satterthwaite 1989, p. 302.

1:1-2:5 is late, especially if the book of Joshua is early, as Jdg 1:1-2:5 in itself can be read quite naturally based on the book of Joshua.[651] Moreover, as the ravished concubine was from the tribe of Judah (Jdg 19:1), it would be natural that Judah should take the lead in avenging the matter (cf. Dt 13:10; 17:7).[652] Finally, as we have seen above, Judah's relative prominence is attested consistently throughout Genesis-Joshua, and both Joshua and Judges suggest that Judah was active, and even relatively prominent during the early settlement.[653] Thus, the "bracket" may be early and may also be based on early tradition.[654]

The large numbers of troops and intertribal unity as portrayed in Judges 19-21 have been taken as a sign of lateness. But, as Satterthwaite points out, "If we allow that the idea of the tribes acting in this way [as a unity] in the judges period is a mistaken retrojection, it still does not follow that Ju 20-21 have to be dated much later than the period of the judges. Such a narrative could easily stem from the time of the early monarchy."..."Someone writing at this time could well have thought it realistic that Israel in the period before the monarchy had functioned as the twelve-tribe unit with which he was familiar in his own day."[655] Regarding large numbers, Satterthwaite points out the following examples elsewhere: "1 Sam 4.2, 10 (34.000 Israelites killed in the course of two battles with the Philistines; 1 Sam 11.8 (30.000 mustered from Judah, 300.000 from the rest of Israel); 1 Sam 13.5 (30.000 Philistine chariots, 6.000 horsemen, and innumerable foot soldiers); 1 Sam 15.4 (10.000 from Judah, 200.000 from the rest of Judah [*sic*; should be from the rest of Israel]); 1 Ki 20.29 (the Israelites kill 100.000 foot soldiers on one day); Ju 16.27-30 (a temple collapses

---

[651] Cf. O'Connell 1996, pp. 58-80, 268-342 for seeing Jdg 1:1-2:5 as an integral part of the book of Judges and dating it early based on rhetorical analysis.

[652] O'Connell 1996, p. 262.

[653] Cf. also above, p. 231, Figure 11, and the accompanying analysis.

[654] Recall also that the relative silence about Judah in the "body" of the book of Judges may be partly intentional in order to heighten the failures of the other tribes (cf. Amit 1999, pp. 147-150; cf. our comments above, p. 147), and thus may not necessarily be used to argue that nothing much happened in Judah during the time.

[655] Satterthwaite 1989, pp. 299-300.

killing 3.000 Philistines); 1 Ki 20.30 (a wall collapses killing 27.000 Syrians)".[656] Thus, large numbers are nothing peculiar to Judges 19-21, and consequently not necessarily a sign of lateness.

A very important question in regard to the provenance and the interpretation of Jdg 17-21 is its relation to the book of Deuteronomy. Whereas it is clear that the main body of the book is Deuteronomic,[657] any connections between chapters 17-21 and Deuteronomy are not apparent at first sight. Noth saw no Deuteronomistic features in Jdg 19-21,[658] and explicitly denied any Deuteronomistic conceptions in Judges 17-18.[659] Thus, Noth did not consider the chapters as part of the original Deuteronomistic History, but as a later addition.[660] Similarly, Gray states that, "Containing no saving act or any saviour-figure and without the introductory framework of lapse, oppression, penitence and grace, neither this passage (Judges 17-18) nor Appendix B (Judges 19-21) was part of the pre-Deuteronomistic compilation of the traditions of the great judges. The absence of positive censure on cultic unorthodoxy and the significant fact that it stands outside the chronological scheme of the Deuteronomistic History indicate that those appendices were not part of the Deuteronomistic History."[661]

However, especially Veijola and Jüngling have argued for Deuteronomistic editing in Judges 17-21,[662] and the following four Deuteronomic features proposed by them are the most conspicuous ones in Jdg 17-21.[663] (1) The phrase איש הישר בעיניו יעשה in the 'no king' formula is similar to Deut

---

[656] Ibid., p. 299n45. Cf. lines 85-101; 175-193 of KRT A (see *COS* 1, pp. 334, 336; translated by D. Pardee), the Ugaritic Legend of King Krt, which poetically speaks about large numbers of troops (as pointed out by Milgrom 1989, pp. 337-338).

[657] For the issues involved with 1:1-2:5, see e.g. Weinfeld 1967.

[658] See Noth 1930, pp. 162-170.

[659] Noth 1968/1962, p. 82n35.

[660] Noth 1991/1943, p. 77n2; cf. Noth 1930, p. 168.

[661] Gray 1986, p. 224. Cf. Veijola 1977, pp. 15-16 (incl. p. 16n4) for a summary of the approach of seeing Jdg 17-21 as a post-Deuteronomistic appendix to the book of Judges; cf. ibid., p. 27 (incl. n86).

[662] Satterthwaite 1989, p. 308, referring to Veijola 1977 and Jüngling 1981.

[663] Cf. Satterthwaite 1989.

12:8, and similar phrases recur frequently in Deuteronomy and Kings (esp. Dt 12:25; 13:19; 21:9; 1 Ki 11:33, 38; 2 Ki 10:30; 12:3).[664] (2) The position of Levites in 17:7 and 19:1 is similar to that found in Deut 18:1-8 which indicates that Levites are permanent aliens.[665] (3) The בית־אלהים in 17:5 contrasts with the בית־האלהים at Shiloh in 18:31 (note also the use of the article ה), indicating that Micah's shrine is illegal as opposed to the legitimate 'house of God' at Shiloh.[666] (4) In 20:1-17, the process of inquiry is similar to Deut 13:13-19 and 17:2-7; the expression of burning out (בער) evil from Israel in v. 13 occurs also in Deuteronomy (e.g. Dt 17:7, 12; 21:21); and the expression in 20:10 of the נבלה in Israel occurs also in Deuteronomy (Dt 22:21).[667]

Due to these features, it is difficult to at least conclusively deny that the writer/incorporator of Jdg 17-21 was aware of Deuteronomy,[668] and that the chapters are part of the design of the book of Judges as a whole. Moreover, features (1) and (3) suggest that cult centralization may be involved. In this respect, as O'Connell suggests, Judges 17-18

> attests a clear rhetorical focus upon concern about cultic disloyalty. The plot-structure of Judges 17:1-18:31 begins with an account of Micah's family cult (an aberration from the ideal of one intertribal cult enjoined by Deut. 12), becomes complicated by the Levite's quest for a Priestly position apart from Yahweh's cult, becomes further complicated by the Danites' departure from their tribal territory and culminates in the promotion of Micah's family-cult

---

[664] Veijola 1977, pp. 15-17.

[665] Veijola 1977, pp. 17-19, 20-21. For details of the various hypotheses of what can be inferred about Levites based on Jdg 17:7, cf. the discussion in Satterthwaite 1989, pp. 89-90.

[666] See Veijola 1977, pp. 26-27.

[667] Jüngling 1981, pp. 264-269.

[668] Satterthwaite who argues against Deuteronomic editing admits, "at least parts of Ju 17-21 would have been congenial to one who agreed with ideology found in Deuteronomy" (Satterthwaite 1989, p. 315), and further, "Though I do not believe that the chapters necessarily have been shaped by a Deuteronomistic editor, it is a possibility which must be considered" (ibid.).

apostasy to the level of tribal-cult apostasy by the Danites (Jdg. 18:30a, 31).[669]

O'Connell has also carefully analyzed possible connections between Judges 17-18 and Deut 12:1-13:1, as follows.[670]

	Deut 12:1-13:1	*Jdg 17-18*
Cult sites on hills	to be destroyed (12:2)	constructed (17:1-5)
Idols	to be cut down (12:3)	manufactured (17:3, 4)
Ideal of central shrine	repeatedly endorsed (12:4-7, 11, 13-14, 17-18, 26-27)	repeatedly and ironically ignored (17:2-5, 13; 18:31)
What is right in... own eyes	prohibited (12:8)	practised (17:6)
Popular support of Levites	at central shrine (12:12, 18-19)	at private shrine (17:7-13; 18:19-20, 30)
Inheritance not yet settled	Israel excused (12:9-10)	Micah (settled)/ Danites (un-settled) unexcused (17:1; 18:1 [cf. 1:34-36])
YHWH to let live in safety	Future Israel (12:10)	not Dan but Laish (18:7, 10, 28)[671]

Figure 12: Judges 17-18 vs. Deuteronomy 12:1-13:1 (O'Connell)

Even if one does not accept all of O'Connell's allusions, one nevertheless has to admit that they may be allusions. Thus, the comparison of Jdg 17-18 with Dt 12 suggests that the centralization of the cult was a concern of the writer/incorporator of Judges 17-18. Then, as was suggested already by Veijola,[672] Jdg 18:31 indicates that Micah's shrine is illegal as opposed to the legitimate 'house of

---

[669] O'Connell 1996, p. 232.

[670] Cf. also the table of comparison of Judg 19:29-21:24 and Deut 13:13-19 in O'Connell 1996, pp. 256-257.

[671] Adapted from O'Connell 1996, pp. 239-240.

[672] Veijola 1977, p. 26; cf. above, p. 256.

God' at Shiloh.[673] However, we may go further. As the writer of
Jdg 17-18 alludes to Deuteronomy 12, he was aware of the
centralization requirement of Deuteronomy. Then, as the writer
suggests that the 'house of God' was at Shiloh during the days of
the judges, he implies that Shiloh was the central sanctuary in the
sense of Dt 12 during that period.[674] In other words, Jdg 17-18
implies that Yahweh's name dwelt in Shiloh during the days of the
judges.[675] In any case, Jdg 17-18 is *fully compatible* with the idea that
Yahweh's name dwelt in Shiloh in the Deuteronomic sense during
the days of the judges.

On the other hand, as the 'no king' formula states specifically
in the context of Jdg 17-18 and the cultic aberrations it portrays
that everyone 'did what was right in his eyes'
(איש הישר בעיניו יעשה; Jdg 17:6), and the same phrase occurs in Dt
12:8, it is very conceivable that the writer suggests that cultic
centralization was not observed in the days of the Judges. In any
case, the 'no king' formula is fully compatible with such a concept.
This then provides us with a decisive bit of information for the
interpretation of centralization in the book of Judges: Everyone did
what he himself wanted, and thus did not follow the injunction to
centralize the cult at Shiloh.

Moreover, external conditions were hardly conducive to cultic
centralization during the period of the judges. As we have
discussed above, the books of Joshua and Judges contrast with
each other.[676] According to the book of Joshua, people essentially
followed Yahweh during Joshua's time, whereas according to the

---

[673] Cf. also the comments above, p. 140 regarding the meaning of
'house' in this verse.

[674] Cf. Veijola 1977, p. 26 concerning Jdg 18:31b: "... wollte er [DtrG]
sagen, dass die Daniten schon damals einen illegitimen Kult besassen, als
sich das Zentralheiligtum mit der Lade in Silo befand - eine frühe
Entsprechung für den späteren unheilvollen Gegensatz: *bāmōt* auf dem
Lande, das Zentralheiligtum in Jerusalem."

[675] Note that whether or not the sanctuary at Dan continued after the
rejection of Shiloh does not change our considerations, even thought if
the reading ארון were followed in Jdg 18:30, or the verse anyway referred
to the disaster at Aphek, verses 30 and 31 would parallel each other better
(cf. also above, p. 243, esp. n613).

[676] See above, p. 242.

book of Judges, the people turned to apostasy after Joshua's time. Moreover, this apostasy resulted in Yahweh's anger (Jdg 2:1-3). Then, because of the apostasy, Yahweh gave the Israelites to foreign powers which oppressed them (Jdg 2:11-15). The Israelites would then cry to Yahweh (Jdg 2:18) who would raise a deliverer (Jdg 2:16) who then would judge Israel (see e.g. 12:7-15). Yet, the people would not even listen to the judges, but would still follow other gods (Jdg 2:17). Especially, after the judge would die, the Israelites would do wrong, even more than before (Jdg 2:19). Thus, the judges period is overall a downward spiral,[677] and from a theological viewpoint, the logical conclusion to this downward spiral is the rejection of Shiloh and the transition from the political system of judgeship to kingship and the election of Jerusalem. The old order is rejected because of its wickedness, and the new order of kingship brings hope with it (Ps 78:68-72; Jdg 17:6; 21:25). The writer of Judges speaks from the viewpoint of the hope which Judean kingship has brought with it.[678]

Thus, according to the book of Judges, the period of judges is a period of wickedness, unrest, and foreign oppression. Even though the deliverances of individual judges bring times of intermittent peace (see e.g. Jdg 3:11; 3:30; 8:28), such peace is not at least directly related to a Deuteronomic concept of peace by the author of Judges.[679] Also, even if one is to understand these periods of intermittent peace as related to the concept of peace in Deuteronomy, the author nevertheless overall indicates that the people do not follow Yahweh even during these periods (Jdg 2:17). Thus, we may conclude that during the times of foreign oppression, the Deuteronomic conditions which were required for implementing the centralization of worship in practice did not exist, and moreover, the book of Judges indicates that even if the land had rest, people did not honour Yahweh (note esp. Jdg 2:17 and Jdg 17:6), and this naturally includes that they did not honour the centralization requirement. In this respect, if one compares the book of Judges with the book of Joshua, whereas worship is

---

[677] Cf. e.g. Cundall 1968, p. 28.

[678] Cf. Cundall 1968, p. 28.

[679] Cf. above, Chapter 3.3 for our discussion of the concept of peace in Deuteronomy, and cf. above, Chapter 4.5 for our discussion of the last days of Joshua and their comparison with the time of Solomon.

centralized at the end of the book of Joshua (Josh 21:43-45; 22:9-34), in the book of Judges there are many places of worship, and the state of the centralization of worship thus presents an added contrast among the many perceived contrasts between the book of Joshua and the book of Judges.

When one then looks at the sacrifices of Gideon and Manoah, both occur during the time of foreign oppression, setting forward a chain of events which leads to deliverance. In Gideon's case, there is a Midianite oppression (Jdg 6:1-6, 13), and in the case of Manoah, there is a Philistine oppression (Jdg 13:1). Thus, in either case, the conditions would hardly have allowed the Israelites to go to the central sanctuary either from a theoretical or from a practical viewpoint, even if they wanted to do so.[680] Moreover, had they gone up, there would have been nothing to rejoice about (cf. Dt 12; Dt 16). Thus, in the conditions attested at the times of Gideon and Manoah, building an altar to Yahweh locally would be the only possible way to worship Yahweh in practice. Especially, during the time of Gideon, Baal worship was common (Jdg 6:25-32). Thus, for Gideon, to build an altar to Yahweh was not just to worship Yahweh, but to profess that Yahweh is god and that he should be worshipped.[681] Then, one may think that if worship of Yahweh could be established, the Deuteronomic promises of peace and security could also eventually be attained, and this would then ideally open the way for centralizing all worship to the central sanctuary.[682]

---

[680] Jdg 6:2 even indicates that during the Midianite oppression the Israelites had to recede to mountain clefts and to caves and strongholds for safety, instead of living a normal life in their towns and villages (so also Cundall 1968, p. 103).

[681] See Bluedorn 1999, pp. 61-62, 67-68; similarly, according to Levine (1974, p. 24), Gideon initiated the legitimate cult of Yahweh as against Baal worship.

[682] See above, Chapter 3.3. Without trying to go too much into details, as the matter is basically beyond the scope of this study, the conditions during the time of Elijah are reasonably comparable to those at the time of Gideon. Jeroboam had established the golden calf worship in Bethel and Dan in order to prevent people from going to Jerusalem to sacrifice, in fear that religious allegiance to Jerusalem will bring about political allegiance to the South and a loss of his kingship (1 Ki 12:25-33). Even if the text does not indicate so, it would be logical to think that Jeroboam

Thus, it is logical to think that as the author of the book of Judges is resigned to the fact that the Israelites do not follow Yahweh and the conditions generally do not allow centralization, he does not advocate the concept of centralization strongly. Moreover, as the author of the book of Judges sees matters from the standpoint of Judean kingship and the rejection of Shiloh, it is

---

might even have actively discouraged or even persecuted those who still wished to go to Jerusalem after the establishing of the golden calf worship. Moreover, according to the books of Kings, subsequent kings followed the sins of Jeroboam (Nadab: 1 Ki 15:25-26; Baasha: 15:33-34; Omri: 16:25-26). In this respect, according to the books of Kings, Ahab, the king during Elijah's time, did even more evil than Jeroboam. He married a Sidonian woman and started to serve Baal, setting up an altar to Baal in Samaria and an Asherah (1 Ki 16:29-33). Moreover, just before the time of Ahab and Elijah there is recorded a war with the Arameans (1 Ki 15:20; 20:34), a war with the Southern Kingdom (1 Ki 15:32), and a civil war (1 Ki 16:15-23) and overall, the threat of war must have been looming all the time (1 Ki 20; 22:1). Under these circumstances, it would have been very difficult for the people of the Northern Kingdom to travel to Jerusalem in order to sacrifice (cf. 2 Chr 15:3-6). A local altar of Yahweh would in practice have been the only way an Israelite could worship Yahweh. However, matters had gone so far that even Yahweh's altars, if they existed, had been torn down (1 Ki 18:30; 19:10, 14), and there was prosecution against the prophets who would advocate the worship of Yahweh (1 Ki 18:4; 19:10, 14). In this respect, that Elijah was not aware of Yahweh worshippers indicates that Yahweh worshippers had to keep a low profile (1 Ki 19:10, 14, 18). Thus, Elijah could say that not only had the Israelites forsaken the covenant of Yahweh, including all that pertains therein (also going up to Jerusalem to sacrifice among other things), but they also had actively torn down Yahweh's altars, the only possible way to worship Yahweh under the present circumstances, and more than the material damage, also killed by the sword the spokesmen of Yahweh, the prophets (1 Ki 19:10, 14). Then, from the standpoint of Yahwism and the narrative of 1 Ki 18, Elijah's task was to call Israel back from the bottom of a dark pit back to the worship of Yahweh, and this was to be done by building an altar to Yahweh and showing that Yahweh is God through the spectacular show of fire from heaven which consumed the burnt offering (1 Ki 18:30-39). Only after the king and the people would follow Yahweh, could there be hope of even thinking of conditions (including future peace and security from enemies) which would allow one to go to Jerusalem to sacrifice.

quite logical to think that the author does not wish to promote Shiloh strongly any more, but only hints at the role of Shiloh in Jdg 17-18, including Jdg 18:31.[683] Furthermore, if Judges was written during the time of David, it is logical to infer that the writer may have been influenced by the state of affairs that it was not yet necessary to centralize worship to Jerusalem.

After these considerations, we may nevertheless still ask how the role of Shiloh and the central sanctuary is to be understood in Jdg 19-21, especially when Jdg 20:26-28 locates the ark (ארון ברית האלהים) and Phinehas *ben* Eleazar *ben* Aaron, and thus seemingly the high priest, at Bethel.[684] In this respect, as the

---

[683] Cf. above, Chapters 4.1 and 4.2.

[684] As noted above (p. 250, incl. n. 637), the mention of Phinehas is often seen as a late addition. However, we may first point out that the mention of Phinehas is not the only Priestly expression in Judges 19-21. As Schley (1989, p. 132) points out, the expression זקני העדה (Jdg 21:16) occurs otherwise only in Lev 4:15, "while the term עדה is itself nearly always Priestly". Furthermore, as Schley points out, המחנה שלה ('the camp at Shiloh', Jdg 21:12) occurs only one other time in the Hebrew Bible, in Josh 18:9 (Schley 1989, p. 132; cf. above, p. 208). Similarly, the expression שלה אשר בארץ כנען ('Shiloh, which is in the land of Canaan', Jdg 21:12) is found only in Josh 22:9, and in the related expression שלה בארץ כנען ('Shiloh in the land of Canaan') in Josh 21:2 (Schley 1989, p. 132; cf. above, p. 208). Also, of these expressions in Jdg 19-21, at least זקני העדה (Jdg 21:16) is an integral part of the narrative. Moreover, without taking recourse to our earlier results of the earliness of the Priestly material (for these, cf. above, Chapter 1, and Chapter 4.5), we may also point out that if a late, perhaps postexilic Priestly editor added Phinehas to the text, one would have to ask the question of why he would have placed the revered Phinehas at Bethel, especially if Shiloh was the place where the tent of meeting stood and/or the only legitimate place of sacrifice for him, and moreover, the time was deemed a time of apostasy by Jdg 19-21. In other words, the mention of Phinehas does not fit with the Wellhausenian thinking on the Priestly material, and therefore we may also doubt the idea that the mention of Phinehas is a postexilic Priestly gloss. (Note also that if we write out the mention of the ark and Phinehas in Jdg 20:27-28 as follows,

ושם ארון ברית האלהים בימים ההם
‎,ופינחס בן־אלעזר בן־אהרן עמד לפניו בימים ההם

expression בימים ההם is vague,[685] it is not clear whether the ark was merely brought to Bethel for the war so that the Israelites could inquire from Yahweh,[686] or whether it should be understood that the ark was in Bethel for a longer time.[687] One might even conceive that the tent of meeting had been brought to Bethel as

---

we can see that there is good reason to think that the mention of Phinehas has been integrated well into the text [note especially that the expression בימים ההם terminates both clauses, and that לפניו refers back to ארון ברית האלהים].) Finally, we may add that the fact that the explanatory comment in Judges 20:27-28 mentions the ark and Phinehas, but not the tent of meeting also fits well with a monarchic appropriation. First of all, since there are more Priestly words and expressions than Phinehas in Jdg 19-21, the mention of Phinehas is connected to the Priestly tradition, and from this it follows that we may think that the editor who mentioned Phinehas also knew about the tent of meeting. If we then remember that the book of Judges is a document written from the standpoint of the Judean monarchy and the rejection of the old order of Shiloh, we may think that the reason for the overall scantiness of Priestly material in Judges 19-21 and the rest of the book does not need to be that the Priestly material did not exist at the time of the writer, but rather that to use Priestly material was not in accord with the concerns of the writer, since for him Shiloh and the institutions relating to it, including the tent of meeting, had been rejected and a new order based on Judah and Jerusalem had taken their place (cf. above, esp. Chapter 4.2; note however that the mention of the bringing of the tent of meeting to the temple in 1 Ki 8:4 fits well with the concerns of the Judahite monarchy [cf. above, p. 153, incl. n. 200]). On the other hand, as the ark, as before, was the symbol and locus of Yahweh's presence (cf. above, Chapters 2.2.1, 4.2), it would naturally be in the interest of the writer and his audience to mention it. Moreover, that at least later Jerusalemite tradition connects Phinehas with Zadok (1 Chr 6; 24:2-3) suggests that Phinehas was a revered figure for the Jerusalemite priesthood, and thus it would be relevant for the book's intended audience to mention about Phinehas.

[685] As pointed out by Wenham 1971a, p. 107.

[686] So Wenham 1971a, p. 107.

[687] Even the extracanonical Greek text of Josh 24:33, Ἐν ἐκείνη τῇ ἐμέρᾳ λαβόντες οἱ υἱοὶ Ἰσραὴλ τὴν κιβωτὸν τοῦ Θεοῦ, περιεφέροσαν ἐν ἑαυτοῖς "On that day, the Israelites took the ark of God and carried it around among them" is not clear of whether the ark was carried around only at the time of the death of Eleazar, or whether the practice continued for a longer time.

well, especially if one can think that the ark was in Bethel for a longer time. Also, it is not clear what was the exact role of the festival mentioned in Jdg 21:19, and whether the festival should be considered as orthodox or not.[688] One might also ask whether the festival was the only festival which took place at Shiloh,[689] and even question how often it took place,[690] even though we may also add that it is not necessary to think that the exact details of the festival had to be a particular concern of the writer.[691] Finally, it is not clear

---

[688] Cf. Schley 1989, pp. 135-137; Gray 1986, p. 363 for thoughts on possible Canaanite influence on the cult of Shiloh. Cf. on the other hand also Keil (1983/1861-1875, *Judges*, pp. 461-462), according to whom the festival was "one of the three great annual festivals, probably one which lasted seven days, either the passover or the feast of tabernacles, most likely the former, as the dances of the daughters of Shiloh were apparently an imitation of the dances of the Israelitish women at the Sea of Reeds under the superintendence of Miriam (Ex 15:20)".

[689] So also Haran 1978, p. 299.

[690] The expression מימים ימימה is usually taken to mean 'yearly' (see esp. Haran 1969b; Haran 1978, pp. 304-309, 312-313; Levine 1974, pp. 132-135). Literally, the expression means 'from days to days'. Greek reads αφ'/ἐξ ἡμερῶν εἰς ἡμέρας in every case for מימים ימימה. A related expression זבח הימים is attested in 1 Sam 1:21; 2:19; 20:6, for which Greek reads θυσία(ν) τῶν ἡμερῶν, implying the possibility of translating it as a 'sacrifice of a fixed, appointed time'. In this respect, the expression מועד הימים occurs in 1 Sam 13:11, meaning, "a fixed, appointed time". Coming back to the expression מימים ימימה, it occurs in the Old Testament in Ex 13:10; Jdg 11:40; 21:19; 1 Sam 1:3; 2:19 (EVEN-SHOSHAN, p. 457). In each case, it is possible to retain the meaning "regularly", and see the meaning "yearly" only by implication from the context (esp. Ex 13:10 [למועדה מימים ימימה]; Jdg 11:40 [ארבעת ימים בשנה ... מימים ימימה]). Moreover, if one translates 1 Sam 1:7,

וכן יעשה שנה בשנה מדי עלתה בבית יהוה כן תכעסנה ותבכה ולא תאכל as, "And thus she (Peninnah) did every year whenever she went to the house of Yahweh. Thus she (Peninnah) teased her and she (Hannah) cried and did not eat", 1 Sam 1:7 may be understood to indicate that more than one yearly trip could have been made to the sanctuary, and the expression שנה בשנה in the verse to mean that the event happened continuously as the years passed by.

[691] Cf. Satterthwaite 1989, pp. 325-326, "All the writer appears to be interested in is the fact that the festival provides an opportunity for the

whether the instructions concerning the location of Shiloh in Jdg 21:19 are intended as part of the speech of the elders,[692] or whether they are an editorial comment.[693] In the former case, the text would suggest that at least the Benjaminite men who escaped the slaughter to the rock of Rimmon (Jdg 20:44-48) did not even know where Shiloh was,[694] whereas in the latter case the text would suggest that the readers of the book of Judges did not know well where Shiloh was located.

However, we may note that whichever way these matters may be, what is important for our purposes is that the time of judges, and specifically the time portrayed by Jdg 19-21 in this context was a confused time during which 'every man did what was right in his own eyes' (Jdg 21:25; cf. Jdg 19:1). Therefore, it is not inconceivable that the narrative implies that even Phinehas, the devout servant of Yahweh according to the Priestly tradition (Num 25), might have been in Bethel together with the ark, even though he and the ark strictly speaking should be in Shiloh.[695] Also, it is

---

seizure of the Shilonite virgins. He does not identify the festival in question with one of the three national festivals listed at Ex 34.18f (cf. 1Sam 1.3f); he does not say whether or not the dancing procession is the main element in the festival or merely a 'side-show'; nor does he say anything about the origins of the festival; or whether he considers it 'heterodox' or 'orthodox'. None of these matters appears to have been relevant to him." Note also that according to O'Connell, the main thrust of the narrative of Judges 19-21 is the Benjaminite war and cultic matters are subservient to this theme (see O'Connell 1996, pp. 231-264). In this respect, whereas O'Connell compares Judges 17-18 with Dt 12 which speaks of cultic centralization, he compares Judges 19-21 with Dt 13:13-19 which speaks of covenant justice.

[692] So Boling (1975, p. 293); Satterthwaite (1989, p. 248).

[693] So Gray (1986, p. 363); Soggin (1981, p. 299); Moore (1895, p. 451).

[694] In this respect, one may imagine that only the swiftest, that is, the youngest could escape, and their ignorance even about the location of Shiloh could then actually be compatible with the idea that the generation(s) following Joshua generally did not follow Yahweh.

[695] One might even conjecture that for some reason, during the early days of the judges, the ark was taken from Shiloh, perhaps forcibly, by the Israelites and subsequently taken to different places (especially, Josh 24:33 LXX [quoted above, p. 263n687] may imply this), and Phinehas may have

not inconceivable that under these circumstances, Yahweh finally heard the Israelites when they fasted before him and sacrificed before him (Jdg 20:26-28), even though this did not take place at Shiloh.[696] The time was not a time when it was possible to demand perfection in cultic matters, including centralizing all sacrifices at Shiloh.

On the other hand, the narrator does not necessarily approve the building of the altar by the Israelites in Jdg 21:2-4.[697] According to Satterthwaite, "the building of a special altar, and the offering of two sorts of sacrifices, suggests a determined effort to seek Yahweh's favour. However, these sacrifices are not said to have had any immediate effect: Yahweh does nothing in response of them, and plays no further part in the planning and actions narrated in the rest of the chapter. The sacrifices appear to be offered more to induce Yahweh not to bring further evil upon them than out of a desire that their actions should be subject to his guidance. What follows, therefore, is presented as solely the initiative of the tribes. Throughout this chapter Yahweh remains a distant figure: it is almost as though Israel's actions in the aftermath of the war against Benjamin are a mess with which he will have nothing to do."[698] According to O'Connell, instead of meting out covenant retribution by destroying Benjamin utterly (cf. Dt 13:13-19), the Israelites instead kill the inhabitants of Jabesh-Gilead, and cause the rape of the Shilonite maidens (Jdg 21:19-23), reminiscent of the way the Gibeonites had treated the Levite's concubine earlier

---

wanted to go with the ark rather than to stay at Shiloh, or may even have been forced to go with the ark.

[696] Note also how Polzin (1980, pp. 202-203) recognizes the following changes in the narrator, the Israelites, and Yahweh during the course of the inquiries: (1) God changes to Yahweh in the narrator's parlance (2) Benjamin changes to Benjamin my brother in Israelite parlance, (3) simple inquiry changes to sacrifices, (4) premeditated certainty of action before inquiry changes to hesitancy, (5) people who are said to come to inquire change from Israelites to *all* Israelites, (6) Little detail of response by Yahweh changes to more detail of response and finally to a success promise.

[697] That the narrative states that the Israelites built the altar at that point naturally indicates that it was a different altar from that in Jdg 20:26-28.

[698] Satterthwaite 1989, pp. 235-236.

(Jdg 19:22-28).[699] No wonder that Yahweh does not agree to these plans and keeps quiet. Thus, Jdg 21 shows that not all attestations of building altars and offering sacrifices to Yahweh are viewed positively in the book of Judges.[700]

In association with our considerations of the time of the judges, we may also ask whether there was a sanctuary in Bethel where the ark had been brought, and if there was, of what kind. Similarly, we might ask whether there was a sanctuary in Mizpah, especially as the expression לפני יהוה is used in Jdg 11:11 and 20:1.[701] In response, we have seen that during the time of Joshua, there was a sanctuary at least in Shechem (Josh 24),[702] and consequently, there may similarly have been sanctuaries in Bethel and Mizpah. If so, as we have seen above, leaving the ark out of consideration, from the standpoint of orthodox/canonical Yahwism, these sanctuaries should not have included any cult objects as seats of Yahweh's presence,[703] and moreover, in a centralized situation, no sacrifices should have been offered in them.[704] However, it is an entirely different matter what the actual practice was in these sanctuaries, especially as the book of Judges indicates that the practices of the time were in general less than ideal, and on the other hand, the texts do not give information of the exact details of these sanctuaries. Yet, we may think that even if aspects were involved which were not legitimate from the standpoint of orthodox/canonical Yahwism, as the people were gathering in the context of Yahweh worship and Yahwism in the narratives of Jdg 11; 20, it is possible to conceive that the expression לפני יהוה could be used.[705]

---

[699] O'Connell 1996, pp. 262-263.

[700] It is difficult to ascertain what the narrator thinks about the sacrifices at Bochim (Jdg 2:1-5).

[701] Note also that the Mizpah in Jdg 11:11 may be located in Gilead and thus may be a different Mizpah than that of Jdg 20:1.

[702] See above, p. 199f.

[703] Cf. above, Chapter 2.2.2.

[704] Cf. also above, Chapter 4.5, incl. p. 199f.

[705] Also, as the ark, the seat of Yahweh's presence was at Bethel, this would give an added reason to use the expression *lipne YHWH* in Jdg 20:26.

Finally, one may ask the question of what happened to the priesthood during the time of the judges. Specifically, if Phinehas the son of Eleazar was the high priest during the early period of the judges, how could it be that in the beginning of the books of Samuel we find Eli as the high priest, when according to the biblical testimony in the books of Chronicles Eli was not a descendant of Eleazar, but of Ithamar, Eleazar's brother, and moreover, the line switches back to Eleazar with Zadok (1 Chr 6; 24:2-3)?

There have been various attempts at a solution.[706] However, it has to be emphasized that the data is scanty, and thus all proposed solutions must essentially remain hypothetical. Also, one should point out that according to the tradition in the books of Samuel (see 1 Sam 2:27-30), and even according to the Priestly tradition (1 Chr 24:3; cf. 1 Sam 22:20; 23:6; 2 Sam 8:17), the priesthood of Eli was legitimate, and Eli's naming his son Phinehas (1 Sam 1:3) suggests that the Elide line held Phinehas in high esteem. Moreover, there are no indications in the Pentateuch that there was anything wrong with Ithamar himself (cf. e.g. 1 Chr 24:3-5; note also Ithamar's work in association with the tent of meeting in Num 4:29-33). Further, the Priestly tradition does not necessarily indicate a hereditary succession of priesthood, or that the high priest can come only from the line of Eleazar. As Milgrom states, Num 25:12-13 "explicitly mentions 'a pact of priesthood for all time' – 'priesthood', not 'High Priesthood'".[707] Even though Eleazar was appointed as the successor of Aaron in the Pentateuch (Num

---

[706] See Schley 1989, *passim*, and Cody 1969, esp. pp. 88-93 for a review of scholarship of the priesthood of Zadok and Abiathar. Zadok has often been seen as a Jebusite priest taken over by David and connected later to the line of Aaron through Eleazar (see Cody 1969, pp. 88-93, including other, less popular theories for the origin of Zadok). According to Wellhausen (1905/1878, pp. 136), the Elides (and other priests as well) originally considered Moses as their ancestor. One could also mention that Schley (1989, pp. 142-151) suggests that the Elide line originally descended from Aaron through Eleazar, but was assigned to Ithamar during the monarchy and the postexilic time, whereas the Jebusite Zadok was connected to Eleazar. It has to be noted that one of the reasons for these varying theories is the perceived difficulty with the ancestry of Abiathar to Eli (see above, p. 151n186).

[707] Milgrom 1989, p. 479.

20:25-29; 27:21), and seemingly Phinehas succeeded Eleazar (cf. also Josh 24:33 LXX), this does not necessarily mean that a hereditary succession must be assumed to be a rule.[708] Thus, if one takes the biblical tradition seriously, one may state that for some reason the priesthood changed from Phinehas and his sons to the Elides during the time of the Judges,[709] and this is as far as one can go based on the evidence.

Thus, the book of Judges gives a confused picture of an apostate Israel. As regards the central sanctuary and centralization, the book suggests that, theoretically, worship should have been centralized to Shiloh. However, centralization was not possible in practice due to the external conditions of the nation. Also, even if times of relative peace existed, centralization was evidently not implemented. Jdg 19-21 even describes a situation where the ark was for some reason displaced from Shiloh where it naturally belonged. In these less than ideal conditions, Yahweh worked through local sacrificial places of worship as well, and this is compatible with the view of Deuteronomy, according to which local altars are acceptable in less than ideal conditions.[710]

---

[708] Cf. Amit 1999, pp. 72-73 who points out that Joshua did not appoint a successor.

[709] One might perhaps even conjecture that if Phinehas and the ark stayed at Bethel (Jdg 20:26-28) for a longer time and the tent of meeting stayed at Shiloh, someone else, most conceivably an ancestor of the Elides, took the reins at Shiloh during that time. Then, one might imagine that the ark returned to Shiloh later, and was accommodated within the new leadership of the line descending to the Elides.

[710] Cf. above, Chapter 3.3.

5. SUMMARY AND CONCLUSIONS

We have seen above how the central sanctuary is a place where Yahweh dwells among his people Israel. Yahweh's presence is manifested at the ark which is normally housed in the tent of meeting or in the temple. This Israelite conception of divine presence is analogous with ancient Near Eastern concepts and practices. The ark is functionally equivalent to an ancient Near Eastern god image, and the tent of meeting and temple to an ancient Near Eastern temple.

However, whereas in the ancient Near East gods took their residence in the image and the image came to be more or less equated with the god, Yahweh is basically invisibly present at the ark, but is not to be equated with the ark, and it is not clear exactly how he is spatially present at the ark. That there is only one ark, and only one tent of meeting or temple, implies that there can be only one "house" of Yahweh. This is corroborated by the fact that all references to Yahweh's dwelling or Yahweh's house in the Old Testament after the Sinai revelation occur in relation to the central sanctuary. The dwelling of Yahweh in his sanctuary in the midst of the people is an important concept in the Old Testament, especially in the Priestly material. However, Deuteronomy is compatible with the concept of Yahweh's presence at the central sanctuary and in fact emphasizes that people come to Yahweh's presence at the central sanctuary.

Local altars are not places of Yahweh's dwelling, and are thus conceptually subordinate to the central sanctuary. However, Yahweh promises to "come" to worshippers at local altars which have been built at an appropriate place. The simple form of local altars, including lack of regulations concerning cultic personnel and the way sacrifices are made, also emphasizes the subordination of the local altars to the central sanctuary. Moreover, knowing that a god-image is a place or a token of a god's dwelling and presence in the ancient Near East, the Exodus altar law implies that no image is needed as a token of the presence of Yahweh, but a local altar by itself is sufficient for meeting Yahweh in worship and to be blessed by him. Similarly, a *massebah* is not needed as a seat of Yahweh either.

The Priestly material demands centralization in the wilderness, but does not demand centralization after the wilderness period. However, the fact that the Priestly material requires centralization in the wilderness serves as rhetoric for the importance of the central sanctuary. The motive for the importance of the central sanctuary in the Priestly material is the unity of Israel, avoidance of idolatry, and provision for priests. The altar laws of the Priestly material and the Covenant Code are complementary since the focus of the Covenant Code is local altars, whereas the focus of the Priestly material is the central sanctuary and the Priestly material argues for the importance of the central sanctuary after the settlement without demanding centralization. The narrative setting of the Covenant Code and the Priestly material in the Pentateuch implies that the author carefully crafted the two together, which also suggests that they are to be seen as complementary with each other rather than contradictory.

Deuteronomy sees centralization as an ideal, to be attained after settlement is complete and conditions are ideal, with Israel dwelling in peace. The ideals which go together with centralization in Deuteronomy are the unity of Israel, avoidance of idolatry, and provision for the Levites. The ideal conditions envisaged by Deuteronomy are to be obtained by following Yahweh wholeheartedly. On the other hand, Deuteronomy also provides for conditions before complete settlement, or if conditions are not ideal for other reasons. Before complete settlement, or in less than ideal conditions, local altars are allowed. However, the rhetoric of Deuteronomy serves to encourage the people to follow Yahweh so that ideal conditions can be attained. Deuteronomy is dependent both on the Covenant Code (verbally dependent) and the Priestly material (even though not verbally dependent) and develops their viewpoints. This also fits well with the narrative arrangement of the Pentateuch where Deuteronomy follows the Covenant Code and Priestly material in narrative sequence. The order of the laws and their narrative setting in the Pentateuch strongly suggests that they were deliberately and carefully placed in their present contexts and were meant to be seen together as complementary entities.

Jeremiah 7:12-15; 26:4-6, 9 explicitly state that Shiloh was formerly the place where Yahweh's name dwelt. Also, based on the prominence of Shiloh in the premonarchical period attestable both textually and archaeologically, and on an analogy of the way literary material, including stock phrasing, was transmitted in the ancient Near East, it is possible that this tradition in Jeremiah is itself based on ancient tradition. Moreover, as the fate of Shiloh is a paradigm of the fate of Jerusalem for Jeremiah, this suggests that Shiloh may have been destroyed, and archaeological evidence suggests that there was a destruction in Shiloh in the 11th century BC. In any case, Jer 7:12-15; 26:4-6, 9 suggest that Yahweh had previously rejected Shiloh.

Psalm 78 implies that Shiloh was the chosen place before Jerusalem, and 1 Sam 1-3 confirms that Shiloh was at least a prominent sanctuary in Israel in the late period of the Judges. However, after the disaster at Aphek (1 Sam 4), Shiloh was rejected and there was no central sanctuary where offerings should have been sacrificed exclusively. That the ark was carried into captivity was a sign that Yahweh had rejected Shiloh. That the ark and the tent of meeting stayed separated reinforced the resulting uncertainty of how and where worship should be conducted in the future. In the days of David and Solomon, Jerusalem was designated as the new chosen place, and officially became the chosen place by the building and dedication of the temple. The rejection of Shiloh and the choice of Jerusalem also involved the change of priesthood from the Elides to the Zadokites. That the tent of meeting is not mentioned directly in the books of Samuel, whereas the ark is rather emphasized, fits well with the fact that the old order of worship including the tent of meeting was seen as basically having been abandoned after the rejection of Shiloh, but the ark continued to be prominent as the seat of Yahweh, being later brought into the temple of Solomon.

Deuteronomy 27 which commands the building of the altar on Mount Ebal by Joshua is a well integrated part of the book of Deuteronomy. Similarly, its counterpart in Joshua 8:30-35 which records the fulfilment of the command fits conceptually very well to the beginning of the book of Joshua, even if the passage sits somewhat loosely in its place in the book from a literary standpoint. The occasion of the building of the altar on Mt Ebal is the time of the early settlement / early days of Joshua when the chosen place has not yet been set and when centralization of sacrifices is not yet required. The finds by Zertal on Mount Ebal may be connected with Joshua's altar, even though this is by no means certain.

Josh 22:9-34 is an integral part of the book of Joshua, and not a later isolated addition as is often thought. Josh 22:9-34 incorporates Priestly material for Deuteronomic purposes and also has strong connections with the Priestly conquest tradition of the book of Numbers. This suggests that Priestly material precedes Deuteronomic material in the book of Joshua, which is in line with our examination of the Pentateuchal altar laws. Moreover, this implies that Joshua is not part of a Deuteronomistic History as proposed by Noth. In regard to centralization, Josh 22:9-34 portrays events during the last days of Joshua when according to the book of Joshua the Deuteronomic conditions for setting the chosen place have been fulfilled, and the book of Joshua implies that Shiloh was the chosen place during the last days of Joshua. That the monarchic period saw Shiloh and the tent of meeting as the house of Yahweh as rejected after the disaster at Aphek is in direct contrast with the positive emphasis on Shiloh and the tent of meeting and the existence of Priestly material in the book of Joshua, suggesting that the book has been composed in the premonarchical period before the disaster at Aphek. Also, the fact that Joshua has an all-Israelite character, whereas later historical books have been written from a Judahite perspective would fit with the idea of a premonarchic provenance of the book of Joshua. Moreover, the emphasis on the Transjordanians makes it difficult to think of a late date, and a number of other features in the book suggest an early provenance. The boundary and city lists may originally date from the premonarchical period, but seemingly have gone through editing during the period of the monarchy.

During the judges period the Israelites do not follow Yahweh but serve other gods. For this reason, Yahweh causes foreign oppression and other difficulties. Thus, the Deuteronomic conditions of peace often do not apply. Moreover, even if there are periods of peace after a deliverance by a judge, nevertheless "everyone does what is right in his own eyes". Thus, the conditions required for centralization often do not apply, and even if they apply, centralization is not implemented in practice. In these less than ideal circumstances, when centralization is not possible in practice, Yahweh works also through local altars (e.g. Gideon, Manoah). An early, Davidic date is possible for the book of Judges, even though the interpretation of centralization does not hinge strongly on the date of the book. In any case, the book attests the concerns of the Judean-led monarchy, which include a lack of emphasis on Shiloh and the tent of meeting, in agreement with the view that they have been rejected and Jerusalem and the temple have taken their place.

Thus, we may conclude that according to the available sources, Shiloh and Jerusalem were the places where Yahweh's name dwelt during the period spanning the settlement to the building of Solomon's temple. In chronological sequence, in the beginning of the settlement there was no place where Yahweh's name dwelt. Shiloh became the place where Yahweh's name dwelt in the last days of Joshua. Shiloh was rejected during the early days of Samuel, and there was no place where Yahweh's name dwelt until the building of Solomon's temple when Jerusalem became the chosen place. According to the biblical material, the last days of Joshua were the only time when centralization was achieved in practice. During the period of the judges, centralization was either not feasible or it was simply not followed. Solomon did not centralize even though he should have, and is explicitly criticized in this respect.

Finally, we may conclude that the history and theology of the centralization of worship are compatible with each other, at least for the time period between the settlement and the building of Solomon's temple,[1] and this conclusion does not depend on the date and provenance of the biblical materials discussed. Therefore, this study leads to the conclusion that it is not necessary to date Deuteronomy to the seventh century BC, and similarly, there is no

---

[1] Cf. also the brief considerations above, p. 260n682 as regards the time of Elijah which belongs to the period between the building of Solomon's temple and the Exile. On the other hand, even though we suspect that our results regarding the compatibility of Deuteronomic legislation and actual practice might well be valid for this period as well, a detailed study would be needed for the period, and similarly for the exilic and the postexilic periods (cf. also our remarks regarding the exilic and the postexilic periods above, p. 155n202, and aspects of our discussion of Josh 24 above, Chapter 4.5, p. 199f., incl. the comment in p. 203n431).

requirement to date any other material which advocates centralization to the seventh century or later. On the other hand, if one compares the rhetorical concerns of the book of Joshua with those of the books of Judges, Samuel and Kings and takes into account the religious and political relationship between North and South and Shiloh and Jerusalem in the history of Israel as expressed in the extant literary material, there are reasons for supposing that the book of Joshua was written in its essential form before the disaster of Aphek described in 1 Sam 4. For similar reasons, one may think that the Priestly material of the Pentateuch in general fits best in the time before the disaster of Aphek and the rejection of Shiloh. An early dating for the book of Joshua also fits with the image of the book as an all-Israelite document, contrasting with the later historical books Judges, Samuel, Kings and Chronicles which more or less attest Judahite concerns. Moreover, the connections that the book of Joshua has with the conquest tradition in Numbers and the Priestly flavour of the conquest tradition in Numbers suggest that the conquest tradition of Numbers is early as well. Finally, as the book of Joshua is heavily Deuteronomic, this naturally suggests that at least the core of the book of Deuteronomy was also written before the loss of the ark from Shiloh to the Philistines at the disaster of Aphek at around 1050 BC. If these conclusions are valid, they suggest a number of important implications for Old Testament scholarship in general. Above all, if the date of Deuteronomy to the seventh century can no more be taken as axiomatic as has generally been done since the time of de Wette and Wellhausen, Old Testament scholarship becomes much more open to various possibilities of interpretation than before.

APPENDIX: AN EXAMINATION OF THE PROPERTIES OF HISTORICAL RECONSTRUCTIONS

In the following, I will construct a model of historical reconstructions. Then, based on this model, I will determine a number of general properties of historical reconstructions and apply them to Old Testament studies.

A.1. Modelling the Flow of History

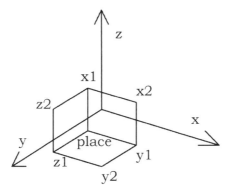

Figure A 1: An example of a place

Let us start from the premise that the past can be divided into time and space. Let us call a specific space at a specific time a *place*. Let us also define that it is required of a place that it is an enclosed volume. To illustrate the concept, let us consider the special case that our enclosed volume is a cube. Then, if we would use x, y, and z coordinates, one possible place would be a set of points x, y, and z, where $x1 <= x <= x2$, $y1 <= y <= y2$, and $z1 <= z <= z2$ (Figure A 1). However, we could also for example consider the volume occupied by any object as a place, such as a book or a house. We could also subdivide the house into smaller units. Or, we could take the volume occupied by a human as a place. Then, we could have the colour of the house or the weight and name of a human as properties. In this way, by dividing places into smaller units and by adding further information to each place, we could add detail into our model.

Now, a specific space at a specific time, that is, a place is often not empty, but contains something, such as people, objects or the like. If so, we may think that some kind of information is also associated with such a place. Let us call this information *properties* of a place.

Let us next define a concept called a *state of reality*. We will say that a state of reality is a place at a specific time, including the properties of the place. We could think that a state of reality amounts to "freezing" the reality within a specific location at a specific time. It would be like taking a three-dimensional picture of reality.

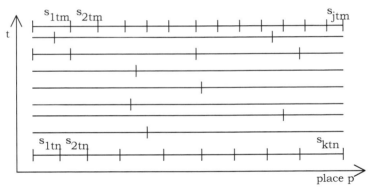

Figure A 2: Reality consisting of states of reality

Now, let us see how reality could be modeled with these states of realities. Let us first think of a specific time, and call it t_m. If we divide reality into a set of contiguous and mutually distinct places (let us call those places as p_{itm}) at that time t_m, our places will cover the whole of reality at t_m. If we then add all possible properties to each p_{itm}, we can describe the whole of reality at t_m. Then, if we do the same for all times t, we can describe the whole of reality throughout history. Figure A 2 illustrates the idea (a sample of times and corresponding states of reality drawn). Note that it depends on us and our interests how we divide the reality into places at each time t_m. Each line segment, such as s_{1tn}, s_{2tn}, s_{ktn}, s_{1tm}, s_{2tm}, and s_{jtm} in the picture represents a state of reality. Each line segment is a two-dimensional rendering of a three-dimensional place and the properties of that place.

However, in practice we would not be interested in the whole of universe and the whole of history. Also, we usually would not be interested in all possible properties at a given place. We would want to be selective. For example, the following picture (Figure A 3) illustrates a selective set of states of reality, also assuming that the properties of each place include only selected information.

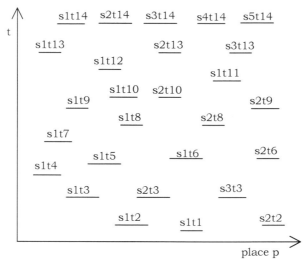

Figure A 3: A selected set of states of reality

Next, let us assume that we have selected a set of states of reality, such as in Figure A 3. Each state of reality can model reality in a particular place at a particular time. Then, if a state of reality s_{xty} is somehow the result of another state s_{atb}, where $ty>tb$, we say that s_{xty} is *dependent* on s_{atb}. For example, s_{xty} could be an author and s_{xty} could be a book written by the author. We also define that a state can be dependent on more than one state, and more than one state can be dependent on a state. For example, a book can have more than one author and an author can write more books than one.

Then, let us define that a process which changes a state s_{atb} into another state s_{xty}, where $ty>tb$, is called an *event*. Moreover, we will denote such an event as e, and the resulting relationship as $s_{xty}=e(s_{atb})$. It is clear that e is a function. For example, a process which changes a state s_{atb}, where s_{atb} is an author, to a state s_{xty}, where s_{xty} is a book written by him, and $ty>tb$, can be an example of an event.

We further define that there can be more than one event associated with any state, in accord with defining that a state can be dependent on more than one state, and more than one state can be dependent on a state. For example, a book can have more than one author and an author can write more books than one. Then, let us assume that we have a set of states of realities, such as in Figure A 3. If we define events between selected states and draw them as arrows, we can arrive at the following picture (Figure A 4).

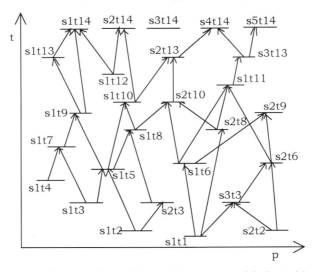

Figure A 4: States of realities with events added (a historical reconstruction)

We note that events in our model, which can only happen forward in time, are approximations of the process of infinitely small changes that change states of realities into other states of realities, where states of realities are a sample of reality at a particular place at a particular time. Consequently, it is clear that the more states and events we draw, the more extensive our model will be. Also, conceptually, as events can happen only forward in time, there can be no arrows pointing downward or sideways in Figure A 4.

Now, by selecting a set of states of realities and events suitably, in the similar way as in Figure A 4, we will be able to represent any historical reconstruction. This becomes apparent if we think that what we are interested in history is selected information. The more we would add states and events, the more closely we could model reality. If our number of states of realities approached infinity, events would become virtually unnecessary, since adjacent states of realities would get to be very close to each other. Looking at such closely connected states of reality would be like looking at a film, with a very big number of frames per second. As a comparison, if a film shows enough frames per second, it seems to the human eye as if he would be looking continuous, real events, even though the film in fact is showing only selected information. Thus, events in our model approximate the total result of the infinitely small changes that change states of realities into other states of realities.

Let us next look at Figure A 4 in more detail. We notice that a number of states in have no arrows (events) starting from them. Also, a number of states have no arrows coming in to them. We will call such states which have no arrows leaving them as *terminal states*. Also, we will call those states which have no arrows coming in to them as *initial states*. We also note that terminal states are not necessarily last in time in the reconstruction (e.g. s_{2t9}), and that initial states are not necessarily first in time in the reconstruction (e.g. s_{1t12})

Moreover, let us think of the information that we, who are living in the present, have available from the past. Obviously, such information must coincide with the terminal states of the reconstruction model, since terminal states are the results of the historical processes that the model portrays. Let us look at Figure A 4. Then, states s_1t_{14}, s_2t_{14}, s_3t_{14}, s_4t_{14}, and s_5t_{14} could correspond to our historical record. Now, in order to be able to think of certain states as a historical record, let us define a concept called *frame of reference*. We define the frame of reference of a reconstruction as the time of the latest state in the reconstruction, and call it T_F. If we look at the reconstruction of Figure A 4, t_{14} is its frame of reference, since the states s_1t_{14}, s_2t_{14}, s_3t_{14}, s_4t_{14}, and s_5t_{14} are latest in the reconstruction. Next, we define that all states whose time is T_F, are called *record states*. We further call a collection of all record states as *present record*. Consequently, in Figure A 4, the states s_1t_{14}, s_2t_{14}, s_3t_{14}, s_4t_{14}, and s_5t_{14} are record states, together forming a present record. It is clear that all record states are also terminal states, since there are no states in the reconstruction later than record states, and there can thus be no events away from record states. On the other hand, all terminal states are not necessarily record states. For instance, in Figure A 4, s_2t_9, even though it is a terminal state, is not a record state.

A.2.　Properties of Historical Reconstructions

Above, we have outlined a model of historical reconstruction. However, we might ask, how would we build a historical reconstruction? Also, what should be required of a reconstruction so that it can be deemed to be acceptable in practice?

First of all, we note that we will have to start our examination based on the historical record that we have from the past, as that is the only information which we can observe by empirical means. All the rest of the information in a historical reconstruction has to be deduced based on studying the record states. We would deduce the states of realities and individual events that pertain to the reconstruction based on the historical record. In order to see how such a process of deduction can be done practice, let us make a comparison with physical sciences. For physical sciences, the process of finding natural laws would typically go as follows (Figure A 1).

Step 1:　Start with an initial set of data X and dependent data Y, obtained by measuring nature.
Step 2:　Find an F which satisfies Y=F(X) for the given X and Y, or at least an F which satisfies Y=F(X) best (initial hypothesis).
Step 3:　Make more measurements of X and Y.
Step 4:　Modify F to fit the new measurements as well as possible and go to Step 3, or discard F and go to Step 2.

Figure A 5: Finding natural laws for physical sciences

On the other hand, for historical reconstructions, first, in Step 1, instead of data X and dependent data Y, we would most conveniently start with a subset S_R of the historical record. In Step 2, we should find a reconstruction which explains the subset of the historical record, or at least explains it as well as possible. For Step

3, including more of the historical record S into S_R would most naturally correspond to making more measurements of X and Y. Naturally, the historical record is in practice often limited, say for example, by available manuscripts. Step 4 would be the same as for physical sciences. Let us now write this process of constructing a historical reconstruction out as a diagram (Figure A 6).

Step 1:   Start with an initial subset S_R of the available historical record.
Step 2:   Find a reconstruction which explains S_R, or at least explains S_R as well as possible (initial hypothesis).
Step 3:   Include more of historical record to S_R.
Step 4:   Modify the reconstruction to fit the new data as well as possible and go to Step 3, or discard the reconstruction and go to Step 2 for a different hypothesis.

Figure A 6: Constructing a historical reconstruction

The process could also terminate in Step 4 if all of available historical data S were covered by the model. Also, the process could be resumed later if more historical data were discovered.

Now, if we look at Figure A 6, Steps 2 and 4 are about determining whether a specific reconstruction can explain the available historical record. In other words, the theory is *tested* in Steps 2 and 4.

Then, what kind of tests should be made for historical reconstructions? We can readily see two tests from Figure A 6. The first test is whether a reconstruction can explain all of the available data, or whether there is some data which it cannot explain. The second test, a little less readily apparent, is whether the reconstructed states and events are acceptable, plausible and related to each other in a logical manner. We call this second criteria as the requirement of *logical consistency*. The two criteria can also be interrelated. For example, there might be a theory which explains all of the data, but does not do so in a logically consistent manner. On the other hand, a theory could explain only a subset of the historical record in a logically consistent manner.

Let us next examine the properties of historical reconstructions further, keeping the above test criteria in mind. We will first define the concept of causality. We call a historical reconstruction *causal* if none of its initial states is a record state and if non of its non-record states is a terminal state. It is obvious that a reconstruction needs to be causal in order to account for all available historical record. On the other hand, it is generally not acceptable if a terminal state of a reconstruction is not a record state, as it corresponds to a historical state and corresponding event which are not in any way reflected in the historical record. In practice, we can make a reconstruction causal by leaving out those initial states that are record states and those states (and events) from which there is no path of events to record states. As an example, let us make the reconstruction of Figure A 4 causal. In Figure A 4, state s_{3t14} is an initial state but not a record state. Also, there is no path to a record state from state s_{2t9}. Removing s_{3t14}, s_{2t9} and arrows leading to s_{2t9} results in the following picture (Figure A 7).

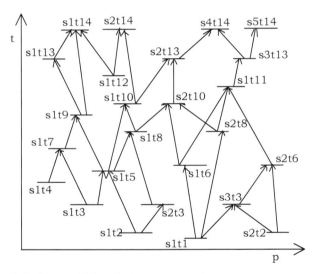

Figure A 7: A causal historical reconstruction

Let us continue by examining causal reconstructions further. If we have a causal reconstruction R with present record $S_R = s_{p1t1}$, $s_{p2t2}, \dots, s_{pntn}$ and initial states $S_I = s_{putv}, s_{pu+1tv+1}, \dots, s_{pu+k\ tv+k}$ (s_{pxty} are states of realities), it is demonstrable that,

$S_R = E(S_I)$, where E is a function made up combining all events of R as follows:

For each s_{piti} in S_R, $s_{pitj} = e_{pitj,patb,pa+1ta+1, \dots pa+ztb+z}(s_{patb}, s_{pa+1tb+1}, \dots, s_{pa+ztb+z})$, where $s_{patb}, s_{pa+1tb+1}, \dots, s_{pa+ztb+z}$ which we will denote as $S_I(s_{pitj})$ is a nonempty subset of S_I, and $S_I(s_{pitj})$ and $e_{pitj,patb,pa+1ta+1, \dots pa+ztb+z}$ can be found as follows (Note: this is equivalent to finding and/or going from each s_{pitj} in reverse direction down the reconstruction tree through all possible arrows and states; cf. Figure A 7 above): For each s_{pitj}, start with two sets S_s and E_s, where S_s is empty, and E_s consists of all events $e_{pitj,pxty}$ that influence s_{pitj} (i.e. arrows which lead to s_{pitj} starting point of each arrow $e_{pitj,pxty}$ would be s_{pxty}; there would be no $e_{pitj,pxty}$, or s_{pxty} of course, if s_{pitj} belonged to S_I). For each $e_{pitj,pxty}$, call recursive subroutine S1 (S1: Add $e_{pitj,pxty}$ to E_s. If s_{pxty} is not in S_s, add s_{pxty} to S_s, find all $e_{pxty,pmtn}$ which influence s_{pxty}, and call S1 for each $e_{pxty,pmtn}$). When finished, $E_s = e_{piti,patb,pa+1ta+1, \dots pa+ztb+z}$, S_s = states that influence s_{piti}, and $S_I(s_{piti})$ = those s_{pgth} in S_s that belong to S_I.

Now, for example, for the causal reconstruction in Figure A 7, $S_R = (s_{1t14}, s_{2t14}, s_{4t14}, s_{5t14})$ and $S_I = (s_{1t1}, s_{1t2}, s_{2t2}, s_{1t3}, s_{1t4}, s_{1t12})$, and thus $(s_{1t14}, s_{2t14}, s_{4t14}, s_{5t14}) = E(s_{1t1}, s_{1t2}, s_{2t2}, s_{1t3}, s_{1t4}, s_{1t12})$. We call the equation $S_R = E(S_I)$ as *reconstruction equation*.

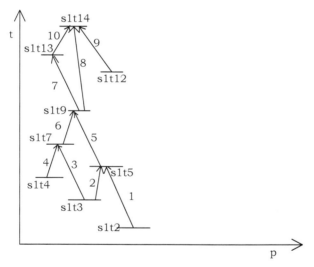

Figure A 8: Formation of a single record state

We note that in order to determine a causal reconstruction, it is only necessary to know the record states S_R, the initial states S_I and E. The remaining states can be deduced from them. Thus, S_R, S_I and E determine a causal reconstruction.

We also note that any causal reconstruction can be represented as a combination of reconstructions for each individual record state. For example, the reconstruction of Figure A 7 can be split into four reconstructions, one for each of the states s_{1t14}, s_{2t14}, s_{4t14}, s_{5t14}, in the manner drawn out for s_{1t14} in Figure A 8.[1]

The fact that two of the entities in the reconstruction equation are unknown makes it clear that we can expect that there may be many possible solutions to historical reconstruction problems. In fact, if we compare the reconstruction equation $S_R=E(S_I)$ for causal reconstructions to the equation $Y=F(X)$ of physical sciences, we notice that whereas whereas in physical sciences for the equation $Y=F(X)$, X and Y are known and only F is unknown, for historical reconstructions, only S_R is known and both E and S_I are unknown. That two of the entities in the reconstruction equation are unknown makes it clear that we can expect that there may be many more possible solutions to historical reconstruction problems than to the problems of physical sciences. We can also illustrate the matter as follows. We could at first choose E in a number of ways and then find a suitable S_I so that S_I and E satisfy the reconstruction equation. Or, we could first choose S_I in a number of ways and then find a suitable E so that S_I and E satisfy the reconstruction equation. Or, in Figure A 7 (p. 284 above), we could change the places of the states of reality and corresponding arrows at will, add new states of reality and corresponding events, or delete old ones. Even if the states and arrows were fixed, the contents of the states of reality and corresponding events could be selected at least in a number of different ways so that they would produce the historical record s_{1t14}, s_{2t14}, s_{4t14}, s_{5t14}. In terms of application to reality, it is obvious that many of the possible reconstructions could

---

[1] In real life, we would often have two separate reconstructions which we would like to fit together. For example, we might have one reconstruction based on the textual material of the Old Testament and one based on Syro-Palestinian archaeological data. If so, theoretically, we could first split both reconstructions into combinations of reconstructions for each individual record state. Then, we could try to combine all resulting reconstructions for each individual record state into a single reconstruction. Ideally, we would want the resulting reconstruction to be causal. However, this might not be the case. If so, the most natural way to correct the problem would be to modify either one or both of the individual reconstructions so that when combined, the reconstructions would fit together.

give a substantially different, even mutually conflicting idea about history.[2]

Since we know (or at least believe) that there was only one past, it should be clear that not all historical reconstructions which can be devised based on a historical record approximate historical reality correctly. Epecially, if there are vastly differing historical reconstructions, it may be that only one of them (if any) approximates historical reality correctly. The rest may approximate historical reality either partially, or totally incorrectly. To illustrate this concept, let us look at Figure A 9 below. For the reconstruction R1, all of the events and states of reality really took place in history, even though R1 cannot reconstruct everything that belongs to history. For the reconstruction R2, some of the events and states of reality really took place in history, and some did not. On the other hand, none of the events and states of reality as portrayed by reconstruction R3 correspond to historical reality. We also note that some of the information contained in R1 coincides with information in R2, and on the other hand some of the information in R2 coincides with R3.

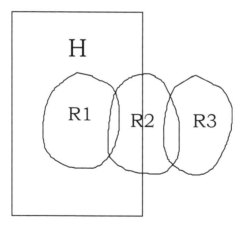

Figure A 9: The relation of historical reconstructions to historical reality

---

[2] If causality were not required, a yet larger number of additional reconstructions could be devised.

We define that a reconstruction which approximates history correctly (such as R1 above) is called a *corresponding reconstruction*. Also, we define that a solution which reconstructs history totally incorrectly (such as R3 above) is called a *non-corresponding reconstruction*. Finally, we define that a solution which reconstructs history totally partially correctly (such as R2 above) is called a *partially corresponding reconstruction*. It should be obvious that in real life, most reconstructions would be partially corresponding reconstructions.

However, how can we choose among a possibly large number of historical reconstructions which can be devised based on a given historical record? Even a causal reconstruction might be a non-corresponding reconstruction, or only a partially corresponding reconstruction. This is above all due to the fact that multiple, substantially differing reconstructions might be possible. Therefore, even if our our academic process of constructing a historical reconstruction (Figure A 6 above) found a causal reconstruction, we could not be sure at face value that it is a corresponding reconstruction.

As Thomas S. Kuhn has demonstrated[3], scientific communities are usually committed to one single paradigm. But, how can one be certain that a paradigm which an academic community holds for constructing historical reconstructions can converge to a corresponding solution, as there might be a number of considerably different causal reconstructions which can be devised based on the historical record and a paradigm can converge to only one of them?

Fortunately, with most historical reconstructions, there are certain events and states of reality in the reconstruction which are virtually certain and can serve as a starting point in building a reconstruction. For example, in the field of Old Testament studies, everyone agrees that there was an exile to Babylonia at the beginning of the sixth century BC. Or, it is agreed that Sennacherib attacked Judah at the end of the seventh century BC. And yet, even though this is a good way to limit possible solutions, these virtually certain historical 'facts' are nevertheless part of the reconstruction and not directly verifiable empirically.

---

[3] Kuhn 1962.

Also, if we start from those 'facts', or associated states of realities and events which are certain, and add more detail, we will sooner or later come to details which are more or less debatable. For example, in relation to Old Testament studies, how many Judahites were deported in Sennacherib's campaigns? Or, can one believe in a long process of oral tradition in forming the biblical traditions, and if so, how did this tradition form? Or, on a yet more intriguing level, if the biblical record is not confirmed by contemporary archaeological evidence, can it be used for reconstructing events that it refers to, and if it can, in which way? Naturally, answering these questions differently will lead to differing historical reconstructions. Consequently, methodological decisions are of prime importance. And yet, as it is evident that methodological judgments are often very subjective, one needs to exercise caution before claiming that a reconstruction which has been obtained using particular methodology corresponds to historical reality.

Thus, above, we have established a number of properties for historical reconstructions. We have noted the importance of causality and logical consistency, and have pointed out the possibility of multiple corresponding reconstructions. Keeping in mind these properties of historical reconstructions, I have striven to build a reconstruction which accounts for all biblical, archaeological and ancient Near Eastern data relevant to centralization of worship in ancient Israel in the period considered. In this, I have not considered it of prime importance to follow the current scholarly paradigm, but have defined my own methodology and have tried to apply it as consistently as possible.[4] Whether and how much the historical reconstruction I have produced might be causal, logically consistent and corresponding, and whether it could ultimately accommodate data which falls outside the scope of this study is left for the reader to decide.

---

[4] Cf. above, Introduction.

BIBLIOGRAPHY

Ahlström, G.W.
1993   *The History of Ancient Palestine.* Minneapolis: Fortress Press.

Albright, W.F.
1927   'The Danish Excavations at Seilun - A Correction'.
        PEFQS 59: 157-158.
1966   *The Proto-Sinaitic Inscriptions and Their Decipherment.* Harvard
        Theological Studies XXII, Cambridge: Harvard University
        Press and London: Oxford University Press.

Allen, L.C.
1997   'The Intertexture of Divine Presence and Absence in the
        Book of Ezekiel', for *SBL conference 1997: Theological
        Perspectives in the book of Ezekiel.* http://
        shemesh.scholar.emory.edu/ scripts/ SBL/ ezekiel/
        allen.html, pp. 1-17.

Alt, A.
1927   'Eine galiläische Ortsliste in Jos. 19'. *ZAW* 45: 59-81.
1953a   'Judas Gaue unter Josia'. *KS II*, München: C.H. Beck, pp.
        276-288. Original in *PJB* 21 (1925): 100-117.
1953b   'Das System der Stammesgrenzen im Buche Josua'. *KS I*,
        München: C.H. Beck, pp. 193-202. Original in Sellin-
        Festschrift 1927, pp. 13-24.
1953c   'Israels Gaue unter Salomo'. *KS II*, München: C.H. Beck,
        pp. 76-89, original in *Alttestamentliche Studien R. Kittel zum
        60. Geburtstag dargebracht*, 1913, pp. 1-19.
1953d   'Josua', in *KS I*, München: C.H. Beck 1953, pp. 176-192;
        original in *BZAW* 66 (1936): 13-29.
1966a   'The Settlement of the Israelites in Palestine', in *Essays on
        Old Testament History and Religion*, Oxford: Basil Blackwell,
        pp. 133-169. German original: *Die Landnahme der Israeliten in*

Palästina, Reformationsprogramm der Universität Leipzig, 1925.

1966b   'The God of the Fathers', in *Essays on Old Testament History and Religion*, Oxford: Basil Blackwell, pp. 1-77. German original: *Der Gott Der Väter*, BWANT III. Folge Heft 12, 1929.

1966c   'The Origins of Israelite Law', in *Essays on Old Testament History and Religion*, Oxford: Basil Blackwell, pp. 79-132. German original: *Die Ursprünge des Israelitischen Rechts*, Berichte über die Verhandlungen der Sächsischen Akademie die Wissenschaften zu Leipzig, Philologisch-historische Klasse, 86. Band, 1. Heft, 1934.

1966d   'The Formation of the Israelite State in Palestine', in *Essays on Old Testament History and Religion*, Oxford: Basil Blackwell, pp. 171-237. German original: *Die Staatenbildung der Israeliten in Palästina*, Reformationsprogramm der Universität Leipzig, 1930.

Amit, Y.

1990   'Hidden Polemic in the Conquest of Dan: Judges XVII-XVIII'. *VT* 40, 1: 4-20.

1999   *The Book of Judges: The Art of Editing*. Biblical Interpretation Series 38, Leiden: E.J. Brill.

Anbar, M.

1985   'The Story about the Building of an Altar on Mount Ebal', in N. Lohfink, ed., *Das Deuteronomium: Entstehung, Gestalt und Botschaft* (BETL LXVIII), Leuven: University Press, pp. 304-309.

Anderson, A.A.

1989   *2 Samuel*, in WBC. Waco, Texas: Word Books.

Archer, G.L.

1994   *A Survey of Old Testament Introduction*, Revised and Expanded Edition. Chicago: Moody Press.

Arnold, B.T.

1994   'The Weidner Chronicle and the Idea of History in Israel and Mesopotamia', in *Faith, Tradition and History: Old Testament Historiography in Its Near Eastern Context*, Winona Lake, Indiana: Eisenbrauns, 1994, pp. 129-148.

Ashley, T.R.
1993   *Numbers*. NICOT, Grand Rapids, Michigan: Eerdmans.

Assmann, J.
1984   *Ägypten - Theologie und frömmigkeit einer frühen Hochkultur.*
        Stuttgart: W. Kohlhammer.

Auld, A.G.
1980   *Joshua, Moses & the Land: Tetrateuch-Pentateuch-Hexateuch in a*
        Generation since 1938. Edinburgh.

Avner, U.
1993   *Mazzebot* Sites in the Negev and Sinai and their
        Significance', in *Biblical Archaeology Today, 1990: Proceedings of*
        the Second International Congress on Biblical Archaeology.
        Jerusalem: Israel Exploration Society / Keterpress, pp.
        166-181.

Bakon, S.
1988   'Centralization of Worship'. *JBQ* 26,1: 26-33.

Bamberger, B.J.
1979   *Leviticus.* The Torah: A Modern Commentary, New York:
        The Union of American Hebrew Congregations.

Barker, P.A.
1998   *The Theology of Deuteronomy 27. TB* 49.2: 277-303.

Barnett, R.D.
1981   'Bringing the God into the Temple', in A. Biran, ed.,
        Temples and High Places in Biblical Times: Proceedings of the
        Colloquium in Honor of the Centennial of Hebrew Union College -
        Jewish Institute of Religion, Jerusalem: Hebrew Union College,
        pp. 10-20.

Bimson, J.J.
1981   *Redating Exodus and the Conquest.* JSOTSS 5, Sheffield: The
        Almond Press.

Biran, A.
1981   "To the God who is in Dan", in A. Biran, ed., *Temples and*
        High Places in Biblical Times: Proceedings of the Colloquium in
        Honor of the Centennial of Hebrew Union College - Jewish Institute
        of Religion, Jerusalem: Hebrew Union College, pp. 142-151.
1992   'Dan (Place)'. *ABD* II: 12-17.

1994 *Biblical Dan.* Jerusalem: Israel Exploration Society.

Bittel, K.
1981 'Hittite Temples and High Places in Anatolia and North Syria', in A. Biran, ed., *Temples and High Places in Biblical Times: Proceedings of the Colloquium in Honor of the Centennial of Hebrew Union College - Jewish Institute of Religion*, Jerusalem: Hebrew Union College, pp. 63-73.

Bleeker, C.J.
1967 *Egyptian Festivals: Enactments of Religious Renewal.* Studies in the History of Religions 13, Leiden: E.J. Brill.

Block, D.
1988 *The Gods of the Nations: Studies in Ancient Near Eastern National Theology.* Evangelical Theological Society Monograph Series 2, Jackson: Evangelical Theological Society.
1997 'The Portrayal of God's Absence in the Book of Ezekiel', for *SBL conference 1997: Theological Perspectives in the book of Ezekiel.* http://shemesh.scholar.emory.edu/scripts/SBL/ezekiel/block.html, pp. 1-17.
1997b *The Book of Ezekiel, Chapters 1-24.* NICOT, Grand Rapids, Michigan / Cambridge, U.K.: Eerdmans.
1998 *The Book of Ezekiel, Chapters 25-48.* NICOT, Grand Rapids, Michigan / Cambridge, U.K.: Eerdmans.

Bluedorn, W.
1999 *Yahweh versus Baalism: A Theological Reading of the Gideon-Abimelech Narrative.* PhD Thesis; Cheltenham & Gloucester College of Higher Education, Cheltenham, U.K.

Boling, R.G.
1975 *Judges: Introduction, Translation and Commentary.* AB, Garden City, New York: Doubleday.

Boling, R.G. and Wright, G.E.
1982 *Joshua: A New Translation with Introduction and Commentary.* AB, Garden City, New York: Doubleday.

Brandl, B.
1986-1987 'Two Scarabs and a Trapezoidal Seal from Mount Ebal'. *TA* 13-14: 166-172.

Braun, R.
1986   *1 Chronicles*. WBC, Waco, Texas: Word Books.

Brichto, H.C.
1976   'On Slaughter and Sacrifice, Blood and Atonement'.
        HUCA 47: 19-55.

Briggs, C.A. and Briggs, E.G.
1907   *A Critical and Exegetical Commentary on the book of Psalms*.
        ICC, Edinburgh: T&T Clark.

Bright, J.
1965   *Jeremiah*. The Anchor Bible, New York: Doubleday.

Budd, P.J.
1984   *Numbers*. WBC, Waco, Texas: Word Books.Budge, E.A.W.,
        ed.

1914   *Assyrian Sculptures in the British Museum, Reign of Ashur Nasir-
        Pal, 885-860 B.C.* London.

Bunimovitz, S.
1993   'Area C: The Iron Age I Pillared Buildings and Other
        Remains', in I. Finkelstein, ed., *Shiloh: The Archaeology of a
        Biblical Site*, Tel Aviv: The Institute of Archaeology of Tel
        Aviv University, pp. 15-34 (Chapter 2).

Bunimovitz, S., and Finkelstein, I.
1993   'Pottery', in I. Finkelstein, ed., *Shiloh: The Archaeology of a
        Biblical Site*, Tel Aviv: The Institute of Archaeology of Tel
        Aviv University, pp. 81-196 (Chapter 6).Burney, C.F.

1903   *Notes on the Hebrew Text of the Books of Kings, with an
        Introduction and Appendix*. Oxford: Clarendon Press.

Butler, T.C.
1983   *Joshua*. WBC, Waco, Texas: Word Books.

Campbell, A.F.
1975   *The Ark Narrative (1 Sam 4-6; 2 Sam 6): A Form-Critical and
        Traditio-Historical Study*. Dissertation Series 16, Missoula,
        Montana: SBL and Scholars Press.
1979   'Psalm 78: A Contribution to the Theology of Tenth
        Century Israel'. *CBQ* 41: 51-79.

Carroll, R.P.
1971   'Psalm LXXVIII: Vestiges of a Tribal Polemic'. *VT* 21, 2: 133-150.
1986   *Jeremiah*. Old Testament Library, London: SCM Press.

Cassuto, U.
1961   *The Documentary Hypothesis and the Composition of the Pentateuch: Eight Lectures.* Jerusalem: Magnes Press.
1983   *A Commentary on the Book of Exodus.* Jerusalem: The Magness Press, the Hebrew University. First published in Hebrew 1951, first English edition 1967.

Chavalas, M.
1994   'Genealogical History as "Charter": A Study of Old Babylonian Period Historiography and the Old Testament', in *Faith, Tradition and History: Old Testament Historiography in Its Near Eastern Context*, Winona Lake, Indiana: Eisenbrauns, 1994, pp. 103-128.

Childs, B.S.
1963   'A Study of the Formula "Until This Day"', *JBL* 82:279-292.
1974   *Exodus*. OTL, London: SCM Press.

Christensen, D.L.
1991   *Deuteronomy 1-11*. WBC, Dallas, Texas: Word Publishers.

Clements, R.E.
1965   *God and Temple*. Oxford: Basil Blackwell.
1976   *One Hundred Years of Old Testament Interpretation.* Philadelphia: Westminster Press.
1989   *Deuteronomy*. OTG, Sheffield: Sheffield Academic Press.
1998   *The Book of Deuteronomy: Introduction, Commentary, and Reflections.* NIB II: 271-538. Nashville, Tennessee: Abingdon Press.

Clifford, R.J.
1971   'The Tent of El and The Israelite Tent of Meeting'. *CBQ* 33: 221-227.
1972   *The Cosmic Mountain in Canaan and the Old Testament.* Cambridge, Massachusetts: Harvard University Press.
1981   'In Zion and David a New Beginning: An Interpretation of Psalm 78', in *Traditions in Transformation: Turning Points in*

Biblical Faith, ed. B. Halpern and J.D. Levenson. Winona Lake: Eisenbrauns.

Cody, A.
1969   *A History of the Old Testament Priesthood.* AnBib 35, Rome: Pontifical Biblical Institute.

Cogan, M.
1974   *Imperialism and Religion: Assyria, Judah and Israel in the Eighth and Seventh Centuries B.C.E.* SBL Monograph Series 19, Missoula: Scholars Press.

Collon, D.
1987   *First Impressions: Cylinder Seals in the Ancient Near East.* London: British Museum Publications.

Cooper, J.S.
1983   *The Curse of Agade.* Baltimore and London: Johns Hopkins Press.

Coote, R.B. and Whitelam, K.W.
1987   *The Emergence of Early Israel in Historical Perspective.* Sheffield: Almond Press.

Cortese, E.
1990   *Josua 13-21: Ein priesterschriftlicher Abschnitt im deuteronomistischen Geschichtswerk.* Göttingen: Vandenhoeck & Ruprecht.

Cowley, A.
1967   *Aramaic Papyri of the Fifth Century B.C.* Osnabrück: Otto Zeller (Reprint of 1923 edition).

Craigie, P.C.
1976   *The Book of Deuteronomy.* NICOT, Grand Rapids, Michigan: Eerdmans.
1991   'Jeremiah 1:1-8:3', in P.C. Craigie, P.H. Kelley and J.F. Drinkard Jr., *Jeremiah 1-25.* WBC, Dallas: Word Books.

Cross, F.M.
1947   'The Priestly Tabernacle'. *BA* 10: 45-68.
1981   'The Priestly Tabernacle in the Light of Recent Research', in A. Biran, ed., *Temples and High Places in Biblical Times: Proceedings of the Colloquium in Honor of the Centennial of Hebrew*

Union College - Jewish Institute of Religion, Jerusalem: Hebrew Union College, pp. 169-180.

Cundall, A.E.
1968   'Judges', in A.E. Cundall and L. Morris, *Judges and Ruth: An Introduction and Commentary.* TOTC, Downers Grove, Illinois: Inter-Varsity Press, pp. 7-215.

Curtis, A.H.W.
1994   *Joshua.* OTG, Sheffield: Sheffield Academic Press.

Dahood, M.
1965   *Psalms 1-50.* AB, New York etc.: Doubleday.
1968   *Psalms 51-100.* AB, New York etc.: Doubleday.
1970   *Psalms 101-150.* AB, New York etc.: Doubleday.

Dalley, S.
1984   *Mari and Karana: Two Old Babylonian Cities.* London and New York: Longman.
1989   *Myths from Mesopotamia: Creation, the Flood, Gilgamesh, and Others.* Oxford: Oxford University Press.

Davies, G.H.
1963   'The Ark in the Psalms', in *Promise and Fulfilment: Essays Presented to Professor S.H. Hooke,* ed. F.F. Bruce. Edinburgh: T.&T. Clark, pp. 51-61.

Davies, P.R.
1992   *In Search of 'Ancient Israel'.* JSOTSS 148, Sheffield: JSOT Press.

Day, J.
1979   'The Destruction of the Shiloh Sanctuary and Jeremiah vii 12, 14'. VTSup 30: 87-94.
1986   'Pre-Deuteronomic Allusions to the Covenant in Hosea and Psalm LXXVIII'. *VT* 36, 1: 1-12.

Dever, W.G.
2001   *What Did the Biblical Writers Know and When Did They Know It? What Archaeology Can Tell Us about the Reality of Ancient Israel.* Grand Rapids, Michigan / Cambridge, U.K.: Eerdmans.

DeVries, S.J.
1985   *1 Kings.* WBC, Waco, Texas: Word Books.

Dillard, R.B.
1987   *2 Chronicles*. WBC, Waco, Texas: Word Books.

Dossin, G.
1938   'Les archives épistolaires du palais de Mari'. *Syria* 19: 105-126.

Dothan, T.
1981   'Sanctuaries along the Coast of Canaan in the MB period: Nahariyah', in A. Biran, ed., *Temples and High Places in Biblical Times: Proceedings of the Colloquium in Honor of the Centennial of Hebrew Union College - Jewish Institute of Religion*, Jerusalem: Hebrew Union College, pp. 74-81.

Driver, S.R.
1901   *A Critical and Exegetical Commentary on Deuteronomy*, 3rd ed. ICC, Edinburgh: T.&T. Clark. First edition 1895.

Duhm, B.
1899   *Die Psalmen erklärt*. KHAT, Freiburg, Leipzig und Tübingen: J.C.B. Mohr (Paul Siebeck).

Dunand, M.
1958   *Fouilles de Byblos*, Tome II. Paris.

Durand, J.-M.
1985   'Le culte des bétyles en Syrie', in J.-M. Durand and J.-R. Kupper, eds., *Miscellanea Babylonica: Mélanges offerts a Maurice Birot*. Paris: Éditions Recherche sur les Civilisations, pp. 79-84.
1986   'Fragments rejoints pour une histoire Elamite', in L. de Meyer, H. Gasche and F. Vallat, eds., *Fragmenta historia Elamicae: Mélanges offerts a M.J. Steve*. Paris: Éditions Recherche sur les Civilisations, pp. 111-128.

Durham, J.I.
1987   *Exodus*. WBC, Waco, Texas: Word Books.

Dus, J.
1964   'Die Lösung des Rätsels von Jos 22'. *AO* 32: 529-546.

Edel, E.
1994   *Die ägyptisch-hethitische Korrespondenz aus Boghazköi in babzlonischer und hethitischer Sprache* (Band 1: Umschriften

und Übersetzung; Band 2: Kommentar). Oplag: Westdeutscher Verlag.

Eichrodt, W.
1950   'The Right Interpretation of the Old Testament: A Study of Jeremiah 7:1-15'. *TToday*: 15-25.

Eissfeldt, O.
1956   'Silo und Jerusalem', in *Congress Volume, Strasbourg 1956*, ed. J.A. Emerton et al. VTSup 4, Leiden: E.J. Brill, pp. 138-148.

1958   'Das Lehrgedicht Asaphs Psalm 78', in *Berichte über die Verhandlungen der Sachsichsen Akademie der Wissenschaften zu Leipzig*, Phil.-hist. Klasse 104, 5. Berlin: Akademia. pp. 26-43.

1962-1979a 'Kultzelt und Tempel'. *KS* 6, Tübingen: J.C.B. Mohr, pp. 1-7. Original in *Wort und Geschichte. FS Karl Elliger*, Neukirchen-Vluyn 1973, pp. 51-55.

1962-1979b 'Monopol-Ansprüche des Heiligtums von Silo'. *KS* 6, Tübingen: J.C.B. Mohr, pp. 8-14. Original in *OLZ* 68 (1973): 327-333.

1962-1979c 'Jahwe Zebaoth'. *KS* 3, Tübingen: J.C.B. Mohr, pp. 103-123. Original in *Miscellanea Academica Berolinensia*, Berlin 1950, vol II, 2, pp. 128-150.

1970   'Gilgal or Shechem?', in *Proclamation and Presence: Old Testament Essays in Honour of Gwynne Henton Davies*, ed. J.I. Durham and J.R. Porter. London: SCM Press, pp. 90-101.

Elliger, K.
1966   *Leviticus*. HAT 4, Tübingen: J.C.B. Mohr (Paul Siebeck).

Fabry, H.-J.
1978   הדֹם *hadhom*'. *TDOT* 3: 325-334.

Finet, A.
1993   'Le sacrifice de l'âne en Mésopotamie', in J. Quaegebeur, ed., *Ritual and Sacrifice in the Ancient Near East: Proceedings of the International Conference organized by the Katholieke Universiteit Leuven from the 17th to the 20th of April 1991*. Orientalia Lovaniensia Analecta 55, Leuven: Uitgeverij Peeters en Departement Oriëntalistiek, pp. 135-142.

Finkelstein, I.
1986   'Shiloh Yields Some, But Not All, of Its Secrets'. *BAR* 12,
         1: 22-41.
1988   *The Archaeology of the Israelite Settlement.* Jerusalem: Israel
         Exploration Society.
1993a   'Introduction', in I. Finkelstein, ed., *Shiloh: The Archaeology
         of a Biblical Site*, Tel Aviv: Institute of Archaeology of Tel
         Aviv University, pp. 1-12 (Chapter 1).
1993b   'Excavations Results in Areas E, G, J, K, L and M', in I.
         Finkelstein, ed., *Shiloh: The Archaeology of a Biblical Site*, Tel
         Aviv: Institute of Archaeology of Tel Aviv University, pp.
         65-78 (Chapter 5).

Finkelstein, I. and Silberman, N.A.
2001   *The Bible Unearthed: Archaeology's New Vision of Ancient Israel
         and the Origin of Its Sacred Texts.* New York: Simon &
         Schuster.

Fowler, M.D.
1987   'The Meaning of *lipne* YHWH in the Old Testament'.
         ZAW 99:384-390.

Frankfort, H.
1996   *The Art and Architecture of the Ancient Orient.* Fifth edition,
         New Haven and London: Yale University Press. First
         published 1954 by Penguin Books Ltd.

Freedman, D.N.
1981   'Temple Without Hands', in A. Biran, ed., *Temples and High
         Places in Biblical Times: Proceedings of the Colloquium in Honor of
         the Centennial of Hebrew Union College - Jewish Institute of
         Religion*, Jerusalem: Hebrew Union College, pp. 21-30.

Freedman, R.E.
1992   'Tabernacle'. *ABD* VI: 292-300.

Fretheim, T.E.
1968   'The Ark in Deuteronomy'. *CBQ* 30: 1-14.

Fritz, V.
1977   *Tempel und Zelt: Studien zum Tempelbau in Israel und zu dem
         Zeltheiligtum der Priesterschrift.* Neukirchen: Neukirchener
         Verlag.

1993   'Open Cult Places in Israel in the Light of Parallels from Prehistoric Europe and Pre-Classical Greece', in *Biblical Archaeology Today, 1990: Proceedings of the Second International Congress on Biblical Archaeology*. Jerusalem: Israel Exploration Society / Keterpress, pp. 182-187.

1994   *Das Buch Josua*. HAT I/7, Tübingen: J.C.B. Mohr.

George, A.R.
1993   *House Most High: Temples of Ancient Mesopotamia*. Mesopotamian Civilizations 5, Eisenbrauns: Winona Lake, Indiana.Gilmour, G.H.

1995   *The Archaeology of Cult in the Southern Levant in the Early Iron Age: An Analytical and Comparative Approach*. PhD Thesis, Oxford: St Cross College / Trinity.

Gleis, M.
1997   *Die Bamah*. BZAW 251, Berlin/New York: Walter de Gruyter.

Gordon, C.H.
1935   אלהים in its Reputed Meaning of 'Rulers, Judges'". *JBL* 54: 139-144.

Görg, M.
1977   'Eine neue Deutung für *kapporet*'. *ZAW* 89: 115-118.

Gray, G.B.
1903   *A Critical and Exegetical Commentary on Numbers*. ICC, Edinburgh: T.&T. Clark.

1912   *A Critical and Exegetical Commentary on the Book of Isaiah*. ICC, Edinburgh: T.&T. Clark.

Gray, J.
1964   *I & II Kings: A Commentary*. OTL, London: SCM Press.

1986   *Joshua, Judges, Ruth*. NCBC, Grand Rapids: Eerdmans and Basingstoke: Marshall, Morgan & Scott.

Green, A.
1996   'Ancient Mesopotamian Religious Iconography', in J.M. Sasson, ed. in chief, *Civilizations of the Ancient Near East*. New York: Simon & Schuster Macmillan, vol III, pp. 1837-1855.

Greenspahn, F.E.
1982   'An Egyptian Parallel to Judg 17:6 and 21:25'. *JBL* 101/1: 129-135.

Greenstein, E.L.
1990   'Mixing Memory and Design: Reading Psalm 78'. *Prooftexts* 10: 197-218.

Gregory, R.
1990   'Irony and the Unmasking of Elijah', in A.J. Houser (ed.) and R. Gregory, *From Carmel to Horeb: Elijah in Crisis.* JSOTSS 85 (Bible and Literature Series 19), Sheffield: Almond Press.

Grimal, N.
1992   *A History of Ancient Egypt.* Oxford: Basil Blackwell. French original 1988.

Grünwaldt, K.
1999   *Das Heiligkeitsgesetz Leviticus 17-26: Ursprüngliche Gestalt, Tradition und Theologie.* Berlin: Walter de Gruyter.

Gunkel, H.
1925-1926 *Die Psalmen übersetzt und erklärt.* GHAT, II Abteilung, 2. Bänd, 4. Auflage, Göttingen: Vandenhoeck & Ruprecht.

Gurney, O.R.
1977   *Some Aspects of Hittite Religion.* The Schweich Lectures of the British Academy 1976, Oxford: Oxford University Press.

Haag, E.
1990   'Zion und Schilo: Traditionsgeschichtliche Parallelen in Jeremia 7 und Psalm 78', in Josef Zmijevski, ed., *Die Alttestamentliche Botschaft als Wegweisung: Festschrift für Heinz Reinelt.* Stuttgart: Verlag Katholisches Bibelwerk GmbH, pp. 307-328.

Hägg, R.
1993   'Open Cult Places in the Bronze Age Aegean', in *Biblical Archaeology Today, 1990: Proceedings of the Second International Congress on Biblical Archaeology.* Jerusalem: Israel Exploration Society / Keterpress, pp. 188-195.

Hallo, W.W.
1996a *Origins: The Ancient Near Eastern Background of Some Modern Western Institutions.* Leiden, New York, Köln: E.J. Brill.
1996b 'Lamentations and Prayers in Sumer and Akkad', in J.M. Sasson, ed. in chief, *Civilizations of the Ancient Near East.* New York: Simon & Schuster Macmillan, vol III, pp. 1871-1881.

Halpern, B.
1981 'The Centralization Formula in Deuteronomy'. *VT* 31, 1: 20-38.

Haran, M.
1960 'The OHEL MOED in Pentateuchal Sources'. *JSS* 5: 50-65.
1962 'Shiloh and Jerusalem: The Origin of the Priestly Tradition in the Pentateuch'. *JBL* 81: 14-24.
1965 'The Priestly Image of the Tabernacle'. *HUCA* 36: 191-226.
1969a 'The Divine Presence in the Israelite Cult and the Cultic Institutions'. *Biblica* 50: 251-67.
1969b 'Zebah Hayyamim'. *VT* 19.1: 11-22.
1978 *Temples and Temple Service in Ancient Israel: An Inquiry into the Character of Cult Phenomena and the Historical Setting of the Priestly School.* Oxford: Clarendon Press.
1981 'Temples and Cultic Open Areas as Reflected in the Bible', in A. Biran, ed., *Temples and High Places in Biblical Times: Proceedings of the Colloquium in Honor of the Centennial of Hebrew Union College - Jewish Institute of Religion,* Jerusalem: Hebrew Union College, pp. 31-37.

Hartley, J.E.
1992 *Leviticus.* WBC, Dallas, Texas: Word Books.

Hawk, D.L.
1991 *Every Promise Fulfilled: Contesting Plots in Joshua.* Louisville: Westminster / John Knox.
1997 'The Problem with Pagans', in *Reading Bibles, Writing Bodies: Identity and the Book,* ed. by T.K. Beal and D.M. Gunn. London and New York: Routledge.

Heger, P.

1999   *The Three Biblical Altar Laws: Developments in the Sacrificial Cult in Practice and Theology - Political and Economic Background.* BZAW 279, Berlin: Walter de Gruyter.

Heinrich, E.

1982   *Die Tempel und Heiligtümer in Alten Mesopotamien: Typologie, Morphologie, Geschichte.* 2 vols, Berlin: Walter de Gruyter.

Hertzberg, H.W.

1964   *I & II Samuel.* OTL, London: SCM Press. German original: *Die Samuelbücher*, ATD 10, second revised edition, Göttingen: Vandenhoeck & Ruprecht, 1960.

Herzog, Z.

1981   'Israelite Sanctuaries at Arad and Beer-Sheba', in A. Biran, ed., *Temples and High Places in Biblical Times: Proceedings of the Colloquium in Honor of the Centennial of Hebrew Union College - Jewish Institute of Religion*, Jerusalem: Hebrew Union College, pp. 120-122.

Hess, R.S.

1993   'Early Israel in Canaan: A Survey of Recent Evidence and Interpretations'. *PEQ* 125: 125-142.

1994   'Asking Historical Questions of Joshua 13-19: Recent Discussion Concerning the Date of the Boundary Lists', in *Faith, Tradition and History: Old Testament Historiography in Its Near Eastern Context*, Winona Lake, Indiana: Eisenbrauns, 1994, pp. 191-205.

1996   *Joshua*, in TOTC. Leicester: Inter-Varsity Press.

Hill, A.E.

1988   'The Ebal Ceremony as Hebrew Land Grant?'. *JETS* 31: 399-406.

Hobbs, T.R.

1985   *2 Kings.* WBC, Waco, Texas: Word Books.

Hoffmann, H.D.

1980   *Reform und Reformen: Untersuchung zu einen Grundthema der Deuteronomistischen Geschichtsschreibung.* AThANT 66, Zürich: Theologischer Verlag.

Hoffmeier, J.K.
1997   *Israel in Egypt: The Evidence for the Authenticity of the Exodus Tradition*. Oxford: Oxford University Press.

Hoffner, H.A.
1969   'Some Contributions of Hittitology to Old Testament Study'. *TB* 20: 27-55.

Holladay, J.S., Jr.
1987   'Religion in Israel and Judah Under the Monarchy: An Explicitly Archaeological Approach', in *Ancient Israelite Religion: Essays in Honor of Frank Moore Cross*, ed. by P.D. Miller, Jr., P.D. Hanson, S.D. McBride. Philadelphia: Fortress Press, pp. 249-299.

Holladay, W.L.
1974   *Jeremiah: A Spokesman out of Time*. Philadelphia: United Church Press.
1986   *Jeremiah 1: A Commentary on the Book of the Prophet Jeremiah Chapters 1-25*. HERMENEIA, Philadelphia: Fortress Press.
1989   *Jeremiah 2: A Commentary on the Book of the Prophet Jeremiah Chapters 26-52*. HERMENEIA, Philadelphia: Fortress Press.

Holt, E.K.
1986   'Jeremiah's Temple Sermon and the Deuteronomists: an Investigation of the Redactional Relationship between Jeremiah 7 and 26'. *JSOT* 36: 73-87.

Hornung, E.
1983   *Conceptions of God in Ancient Egypt: The One and the Many*. London: Routledge & Kegan Paul. German original: *Der Eine und die Vielen*, Darmstadt: Wissenschaftliche Buchgesellschaft, 1971.
1996   'Ancient Egyptian Religious Iconography', in J.M. Sasson, ed. in chief, *Civilizations of the Ancient Near East*. New York: Simon & Schuster Macmillan, vol III, pp. 1711-1730.
1999   *Akhenaten and the Religion of Light*. Ithaca and London: Cornell University Press. Original German edition: *Echnaton: Die Religion des Lichtes*, Düsseldorf and Zürich: Artemis & Winkler Verlag, 1995.

Horwitz, L.K.
1986-1987 'Faunal Remains from the Early Iron Age Site on Mount Ebal'. *TA* 13-14: 173-189.

House, P.R.
1995 *1, 2 Kings*. NAC, Broadman & Holman Publishers.

Hout, T.P.J. van den
1995 *Der Ulmitešub-Vertrag: Eine prosopographische Untersuchung.* StBoT 38, Wiesbaden: Otto Harrassowitz Verlag.

Humphreys, C.J.
1998 'The Number of People in the Exodus from Egypt: Decoding Mathematically the Very Large Numbers in Numbers I and XXVI'. *VT* 48, 2: 196-213.

Hurowitz, V.A.
1992 *I Have Built You an Exalted House: Temple Building in the Bible in Light of Mesopotamian and Northwest Semitic Writings.* JSOTSS 115, Sheffield: Sheffield Academic Press.

Hurvitz, A.
1982 *A Linguistic Study of the Relationship Between the Priestly Source and the Book of Ezekiel: A New Approach to an Old Problem.* Cahiers de la Revue Biblique 20, Paris: J. Gabalda.

Hutter, M.
1993 'Kultstelen und Baityloi: Die Ausstrahlung eines syrischen religiösen Phänomens nach Kleinasien und Israel', in B. Janowski, K. Koch and G. Wilhelm, eds., *Religionsgeschichtliche Beziehungen zwischen Kleinasien, Nordsyrien und dem Alten Testament.* OBO 129, Freiburg, Schweiz: Universitätsverlag and Göttingen: Vandenhoeck & Ruprecht, pp. 87-108.
1996 *Religionen in der Umwelt des Alten Testaments I: Babyloner, Syrer, Perser.* Stuttgart: W. Kohlhammer GmbH.

Jacobsen, T.
1987 'The Graven Image', in *Ancient Israelite Religion: Essays in Honor of Frank Moore Cross*, ed. by P.D. Miller, Jr., P.D. Hanson, S.D. McBride. Philadelphia: Fortress Press, pp. 15-32.

James, T.G.H.
1979   *An Introduction to Ancient Egypt*. London.

Jobling, D.
1980   "'The Jordan a Boundary'": A Reading of Numbers 32 and Joshua 22'. *SBL Seminar Reports* 19: 183-207.
1984   'Levi-Strauss and the Structural Analysis of the Hebrew Bible', in *Anthropology and the Study of Religion*, ed. R. Moore and F. Reynolds. Chicago: Center for the Scientific Study of Religion, pp. 192-211.

Jones, G.H.
1984   *1 and 2 Kings*, vol 1. NCBC, London: Grand Rapids, Michigan: Eerdmans and London: Marshall, Morgan & Scott.

Joosten, J.
1996   *People and Land in the Holiness Code: An Exegetical Study of the Ideational Framework of the Law in Leviticus 17-26*. Leiden: E.J. Brill.

Jüngling, H.W.
1981   *Richter 19.1-30a; 21:25: Ein Plädoyer für das Königtum*. Analecta Biblica 84, Rome: Pontifical Biblical Institute.

Junker, H.
1953   'Die Entstehungszeit des Ps. 78 und des Deuteronomiums'. *Biblica* 34: 487-500.

Kaiser, O.
1974   *Isaiah 13-39: A Commentary*. OTL, London: SCM Press. German original: *Der Prophet Jesaja, Kap 13-39*, ATD 18, Göttingen: Vandenhoeck & Ruprecht, 1973.

Kaiser, W.C., Jr.
1990   *Exodus*. EBC 2: 285-497, Grand Rapids, Michigan: Zondervan.

Kallai, Z.
1958   'The Town Lists of Judah, Simeon, Benjamin and Dan'. *VT* 8: 134-160.
1986   *Historical Geography of the Bible: The Tribal Territories of Israel*. Jerusalem: Magnes Press / Leiden: E.J. Brill.
1991   'The Twelve-Tribe Systems of Israel'. *VT* 47, 1:53-90.

Kapelrud, A.S.
1965   *The Ras Shamra Discoveries and the Old Testament*. Oxford: Basil Blackwell. Translated by G.W. Anderson.

Kaufmann, Y.
1985   *The Biblical Account of the Conquest of Canaan*. 2nd ed, Jerusalem: Magnes Press. Original in Hebrew 1955.

Keil, C.F., and Delitzsch, F.
1983   *Commentary on the Old Testament*. Grand Rapids: Eerdmans. Original in German 1861-1875.

Kempinski, A.
1986   'Joshua's Altar - An Iron Age Watchtower'. *BAR* 12,1: 42, 44-49.

Kidner, D.
1973   *Psalms 1-72*. TOTC 10, London: Inter-Varsity Press.
1975   *Psalms 73-150*. TOTC 11, London: Inter-Varsity Press.

King, L.W.
1912   *Babylonian Boundary-Stones and Memorial Tablets in the British Museum*. London.

Klein, L.R.
1988   *The Triumph of Irony in the Book of Judges*. JSOTSS 68, Sheffield: Almond Press.

Klein, R.W.
1983   *1 Samuel*. WBC, Waco, Texas: Word Books.

Kloppenborg, J.S.
1981   'Joshua 22: The Priestly Editing of an Ancient Tradition'. *Biblica* 62, 3: 347-371.

Knohl, I.
1995   *The Sanctuary of Silence: The Priestly Torah and the Holiness School*. Minneapolis: Fortress Press.
1997   'Two Aspects of the "Tent of Meeting"', in M. Cogan, B.L. Eichler, J.H. Tigay eds., *Tehillah le-Moshe: Biblical and Judaic Studies in Honor of Moshe Greenberg*. Winona Lake, Indiana: Eisenbrauns, pp. 73-79.

Koopmans, W.T.
1990   *Joshua 24 as Poetic Narrative*. JSOTSS 93, Sheffield: Sheffield
        Academic Press.

Koorevaar, H.J.
1990   *De Opbouw van het Boek Jozua*. Heverlee: Centrum voor
        Bijbelse Vorming Belgie v.z.w. (In Dutch, with an English
        summary).

Kramer, S.N.
1940   *Lamentation over the Destruction of Ur*. Assyriological Studies
        12, Chicago, Illinois: The University of Chicago Press.
1963   *The Sumerians: Their History, Culture, and Character*.
        Chicago/London: The University of Chicago Press.

Kraus, F.R.
1984   *Königliche Verfügungen in Altbabylonischer Zeit*. Studia et
        Documenta ad iura orientis antiqui pertinentia, vol XI,
        Leiden: E.J.Brill.

Kraus, H.J.
1966   *Worship in Israel: A Cultic History of the Old Testament*.
        Oxford: Basil Blackwell. German original 1962.
1989   *Psalms 60-150*. Minneapolis: Augsburg Fortress. German
        original: Psalmen, 2. Teilband, *Psalmen 60-150*, in Biblischer
        Kommentar, copyright 1961/1978 Neukirchener Verlag
        des Erziehungsvereins GmbH, Neukirchen-Vluyn.

Kübel, P.
1971   'Epiphanie und Altarbau'. *ZAW* 83:225-231.

Kuhn, T.S.
1962   *The Structure of Scientific Revolutions*. Chicago: The University
        of Chicago Press.

Kuhrt, A.
1995   *The Ancient Near East: c. 3000-330*. 2 vols, London and
        New York: Routledge.

Kuschke, A.
1951   'Die Lagervorstellung der priesterschriftlichen Erzählung'.
        ZAW 63: 74-105.

Kutscher, R.
1975   *Oh Angry Sea (a-ab-ba hu-luh-ha): The History of a Sumerian Congregational Lament,* New Haven and London: Yale University Press, 1975.

Lambert, W.G.
1957-1958 'Three Unpublished Fragments of the Tukulti-Ninurta Epic'. *AfO* 18: 38-51.
1967   'Enmeduranki and Related Matters'. *JCS* 21: 126-138.

Langdon, S.
1919   'Two Sumerian Liturgical Tezts'. *RA* 16: 207-209.

Lebrun, R.
1980   *Hymnes et Prières Hittites.* Louvain-la-Neuve: Centre D'Histoire des Religions.

Lee, A.C.C.
1990   'The Context and Function of the Plagues Tradition in Psalm 78'. *JSOT* 48: 83-89.

Lemche, N.P.
1998   *The Israelites in History and Tradition.* London: SPCK / Louisville, Kentucky: Westminster John Knox Press.

Levenson, J.D.
1981   'From Temple to Synagogue: 1 Kings 8', in *Traditions in Transformation: Turning Points in Biblical Faith,* ed. B. Halpern and J.D. Levenson. Winona Lake: Eisenbrauns.

Levine, B.A.
1974   *In the Presence of the Lord: A Study of Cult and Some Cultic Terms in Ancient Israel.* Leiden: E.J. Brill.
1989   *Leviticus.* JPS Torah Commentary, Philadelphia / New York / Jerusalem: The Jewish Publication Society.
1993   '*Lpny YHWH* - Phenomenology of the Open-Air-Altar in Biblical Israel', in *Biblical Archaeology Today, 1990: Proceedings of the Second International Congress on Biblical Archaeology.* Jerusalem: Israel Exploration Society / Keterpress, pp. 196-205.

Levinson, B.M.
1997   *Deuteronomy and the Hermeneutics of Legal Innovation.* Oxford: Oxford University Press.

Levinson, B.M., ed.
1994   *Theory and Method in Biblical and Cuneiform Law: Revision, Interpolation and Development.* JSOTSS 181, Sheffield: Sheffield Academic Press.

Lindblom, J.
1961   'Theophanies in Holy Places in Hebrew Religion'. *HUCA* 32: 91-106.

Liphschitz, N.
1986-1987 'Paleobotanical Remains from Mount Ebal'. *TA* 13-14: 190-191.

Lloyd, S.
1984   *The Archaeology of Mesopotamia: From the Old Stone Age to the Persian Conquest*, revised edition. London: Thames and Hudson.

Lohfink, N.
1991   'Zur deuteronomischen Zentralisationsformel', in N. Lohfink, *Studien zum Deuteronomium und zur deuteronomistischen Literatur II*, Stuttgart: Verlag Katholisches Bibelwerk, pp. 147-177.
1992   'Opfer und Säkularisierung im Deuteronomium', in A. Schenker, ed., *Studien zu Opfer und Kult im Alten Testament, mit einer Bibliographie 1969-1991 zum Opfer in der Bibel*, Tübingen: J.C.B. Mohr (Paul Siebeck), pp. 15-43.
1995   'Opferzentralisation, Säkularisierungsthese und mimetische Theorie', in N. Lohfink, *Studien zum Deuteronomium und zur deuteronomistischen Literatur III*, Stuttgart: Verlag Katholisches Bibelwerk, pp. 219-260.
1996   'Fortschreibung?: zur Technik von Rechtsrevisionen im deuteronomischen Bereich, erörtet an Deuteronomium 12, Ex 21,2-11 und Dtn 15,12-18', in T. Veijola, ed., *Das Deuteronomium und seine Querbeziehungen*, Schriften der Finnischen Exegetischen Gesellschaft 62, Helsinki: Finnische Exegetische Gesellschaft / Göttingen: Vandenhoeck & Ruprecht, pp. 127-171.

Long, V.P.
1994   *The Art of Biblical History*. Foundations of Contemporary Interpretation 5, Leicester: Apollos.

Lorton, D.
1999   'The Theology of Cult Statues in Ancient Egypt', in *Born in Heaven, Made on Earth: The Making of the Cult Image in the Ancient Near East*. Winona Lake, Indiana: Eisenbrauns, pp. 123-210.

Machinist, P.
1976   'Literature as Politics: The Tukulti-Ninurta Epic and the Bible'. *CBQ* 38: 455-482.

Macqueen, J.G.
1996   *The Hittites*. London: Thames and Hudson.

Manley, G.T.
1957   *The Book of the Law: Studies in the Date of Deuteronomy*. London: Tyndale Press.

Margueron, J.
1975   'Quatre campagnes de fouilles a Emar (1972-1974): Un bilan provisoire'. *Syria* 52: 53-85.
1982   'Architecture et Urbanisme', in D. Beyer, ed., *Meskéné-Emar: Dix ans de travaux 1972-1982*. Paris: Editions Recherche sur les Civilisations, pp. 23-39.

Mayer, W.
1983   'Sargons Feldzug gegen Urartu - 714 v. Chr. Text und Übersetzung'. *MDOG* 115: 65-132.

Mayes, A.D.H.
1974   *Israel in the Period of the Judges*. London: SCM Press.
1979   *Deuteronomy*. NCBC, Grand Rapids, Michigan: Eerdmans / London: Marshall, Morgan & Scott.
1985   *Judges*. OTG, Sheffield: JSOT Press.

Mazar, A.
1990a   *Archaeology and the Land of the Bible 10000-586 BCE*. The Anchor Bible Library, New York: Doubleday.
1990b   'Iron Age I and II Towers at Giloh and the Israelite Settlement'. *IEJ* 40, 2-3: 77-101.
1997   'Iron Age Chronology: A Reply to I. Finkelstein'. *Levant* XXIX: 157-167.

McCann, J.C., Jr.
1996   *The Book of Psalms: Introduction, Commentary, and Reflections.* NIB IV: 641-1280. Nashville, Tennessee: Abingdon Press.

McCarter, P.K.
1980   *I Samuel: A New Translation with Introduction, Notes & Commentary.* AB, Garden City, New York: Doubleday.

McConville, J.G.
1984   *Law and Theology in Deuteronomy.* JSOTSS 33, Sheffield: JSOT Press.
1993a   *Grace in the End - A Study in Deuteronomic Theology.* Grand Rapids, Michigan: Zondervan Publishing House / Carlisle, UK: Paternoster Press.
1993b   *Judgment and Promise: An Interpretation of the Book of Jeremiah.* Leicester: Apollos / Winona Lake: Eisenbrauns.
1997   'The Old Testament Historical Books in Modern Scholarship'. *Themelios* 22, 3: 3-13.

McConville, J.G and Millar, J.G.
1994   *Time and Place in Deuteronomy.* JSOTSS 179, Sheffield: Sheffield Academic Press.

McCown, C.C.
1950   'Hebrew High Places and Cult Remains'. *JBL* 69: 205-219.

McMahon, G.
1996   'Theology, Priests, and Worship in Hittite Anatolia', in J.M. Sasson, ed. in chief, *Civilizations of the Ancient Near East,* New York: Simon & Schuster Macmillan, vol III, pp. 1981-1995.

Mendenhall, G.E.
1954   'Ancient Orient and Biblical Law'. *BA* 17: 26-46.

Merrill, E.H.
1994   *Deuteronomy.* NAC, Broadman & Holman Publishers.

Meshel, Z.
1981   'A Religious Center at Kuntillet-Ajrud, Sinai', in A. Biran, ed., *Temples and High Places in Biblical Times: Proceedings of the Colloquium in Honor of the Centennial of Hebrew Union College - Jewish Institute of Religion,* Jerusalem: Hebrew Union College, p. 161.

Mettinger, T.N.D.
1982   *The Dethronement of Sabaoth: Studies in the Shem and Kabod Theologies.* CBOTS 18, Lund: CWK Gleerup.
1995   *No Graven Image? Israelite Aniconism in its Ancient Near Eastern Context.* CBOTS 42, Stockholm: Almqvist & Wiksell.

Meyers, E.M.
1992   'Synagogue'. *ABD* VI: 251-260.

Michalowski, P.
1989   *The Lamentation over the Destruction of Sumer and Ur.* Mesopotamian Civilizations 1, Eisenbrauns: Winona Lake.

Milgrom, J.
1971   'A Prolegomenon to Leviticus 17:11'. *JBL* 90: 149-156.
1976   'Profane Slaughter and a Formulaic Key to the Composition of Deuteronomy'. *HUCA* 47: 1-17.
1983a   'Priestly Terminology and the Political and Social Structure of Pre-Monarchic Israel', in J. Milgrom, *Studies in Cultic Theology and Terminology*, Leiden: E.J. Brill, pp. 1-17.
1983b   'The Term עבדה', in J. Milgrom, *Studies in Cultic Theology and Terminology*, Leiden: E.J. Brill, pp. 19-46. Original in J. Milgrom, *Studies in Levitical Terminology*, Berkeley: University of California, 1970, pp. 60-87.
1989   *Numbers.* JPS Torah Commentary, Philadelphia and New York: Jewish Publication Society.
1991   *Leviticus 1-16.* AB, New York: Doubleday.

Millar, J.G.
1998   *Now Choose Life: Theology and Ethics in Deuteronomy.* New Studies in Biblical Theology 6, Leicester: Apollos.

Millard, A.R.
1985   *Treasures from Bible Times.* Tring, Herts, England: Lion Publishing.
1988   'King Og's Bed and Other Ancient Ironmongery', in *Ascribe to the Lord: Biblical & Other Studies in Memory of Peter C. Craigie*, JSOTSS 67, Sheffield: Sheffield Academic Press, pp. 481-492.
1994   'Abraham, Akhenaten, Moses and Monotheism', in *He Swore an Oath: Biblical Themes in Genesis 12-50*, Grand Rapids, Michigan: Baker Book House, pp. 119-129.

1995   'The Knowledge of Writing in Iron Age Palestine'. *TB* 46.2: 207-217.

Miller, J.M. and Hayes, J.H.
1986   *A History of Ancient Israel and Judah*. London: SCM Press.

Miller, P.D.
1990   *Deuteronomy*. INTERPRETATION, Louisville: John Knox Press.

Miller, P.D., Jr. and Roberts, J.J.M.
1977   *The Hand of the Lord: A Reasssesment of the "Ark Narrative" of 1 Samuel*. Baltimore and London: Johns Hopkins University Press.

Moberly, R.W.L.
1992   *The Old Testament of the Old Testament: Patriarchal Narratives and Mosaic Yahwism*. Minneapolis: Fortress Press.

Montgomery, J.A.
1951   *A Critical and Exegetical Commentary on the Books of Kings*, ed. by H.S. Gehman. ICC, Edinburgh: T.&T. Clark.

Moore, G.F.
1895   *A Critical and Exegetical Commentary on Judges*. ICC, Edinburgh: T.&T. Clark.

Moorey, P.R.S.
1991   *A Century of Biblical Archaeology*. Cambridge: Lutterworth Press.

Morenz, S.
1973   *Egyptian Religion*. London: Methuen & Co. German original 1960.

Mowinckel, S.
1946   'Zur Frage nach dokumentarischen Quellen in Josua 13-19', in *Avhandlingar utgitt av Det Norske Videnskaps-Akademi i Oslo II. Hist-Filos. Klasse 1946*, No. I. Oslo: A.W. Broggers Boktryggeri A/S.
1964   *Tetrateuch-Pentateuch-Hexateuch*. BZAW 90, Berlin: Alfred Töpelmann.

Munn-Rankin, J.M.
1956   'Diplomacy in Western Asia in the Early Second Millennium BC'. *Iraq* 18: 68-110.

Murphy, R.E.
1992   'Wisdom in the OT'. *ABD* 6:920-931.

Nelson, R.D.
1981   'Josiah in the Book of Joshua'. *JBL* 100,4: 531-540.

Nicholson, E.W.
1963   'The Centralization of the Cult in Deuteronomy'. *VT* 13: 380-389.
1982   'The Covenant Ritual in Exodus XXIV 3-8'. *VT* 32,1: 74-86.

Niehaus, J.J.
1985   *The Deuteronomic Style: An Examination of the Deuteronomic Style in the Light of Ancient Near Eastern Literature.* PhD Thesis, University of Liverpool, Liverpool, U.K.
1992   'The Central Sanctuary: Where and When?'. *TB* 43.1: 3-30.
1994   'The Warrior and His God: The Covenant Foundation of History and Historiography', in *Faith, Tradition and History: Old Testament Historiography in Its Near Eastern Context,* Winona Lake, Indiana: Eisenbrauns, 1994, pp. 299-312.
1995   *God at Sinai: Covenant and Theophany in the Bible and Ancient Near East.* Carlisle, UK: Paternoster Press.

Nielsen, K.
1986   *Incense in Ancient Israel.* VTSup 38, Leiden: E.J. Brill.

Noort, E.
1998   *Das Buch Josua: Forschungsgeschichte und Problemfelder.* Darmstadt: Wissenschaftliche Buchgesellschaft.

Noth, M.
1930   *Das System der zwölf Stämme Israels.* Stuttgart: W. Kohlhammer Verlag.
1935   'Studien zu den historisch-geographischen Dokumenten des Josuabuches'. *ZDPV* 58, pp. 185-255.
1953   *Das Buch Josua,* zweite, verbesserte auflage. HAT 7, Tübingen: J.C.B. Mohr (Paul Siebeck).
1960   *The History of Israel,* reissue of the second edition in revised and corrected translation. London: SCM Press.

1962   *Exodus: A Commentary.* OTL, London: SCM Press. German original: *Das zweite Buch Mose, Exodus*, ATD 5, Göttingen: Vandenhoeck & Ruprecht, 1959.

1963   'Samuel und Silo'. *VT* 13: 390-400.

1965   *Leviticus: A Commentary.* OTL, London: SCM Press.

1968   'The Background of Judges 17-18', in B.W. Anderson and W. Harrelson, eds., *Israel's Prophetic Heritage: Essays in Honor of J. Muilenberg.* New York: Doubleday, pp. 68-85. German original 1962: 'Der Hintergrund von Richter 17-18', reprinted in *Archäologische, exegetische und topographische Untersuchungen zur Geschichte Israels,* in *Aufsätze zur Biblischen Landes- und Altertumskunde,* 2 vols., H.W. Wolff, ed., Neukirchen-Vluyn, 1971, vol 1, pp. 133-147.

1972   *A History of Pentateuchal Traditions.* Englewood Cliffs, N.J.: Prentice Hall. German original: *Überlieferungsgeschichte des Pentateuchs,* Stuttgart: W. Kohlhammer, 1948.

1987   *The Chronicler's History.* JSOTSS 50, Sheffield: Sheffield Academic Press. German original: *Überlieferungsgeschichtliche Studien II,* Halle: M. Niemeyer, 1943.

1991   *The Deuteronomistic History.* 2nd ed, JSOTSS 15, Sheffield: Sheffield Academic Press. German original: *Überlieferungsgeschichtliche Studien I,* Halle: M. Niemeyer, 1943.

O'Connell, R.H.

1996   *The Rhetoric of the Book of Judges.* Leiden: E.J. Brill.

Oppenheim, A.L.

1964   *Ancient Mesopotamia: Portrait of a Dead Civilization.* Chicago: The University of Chicago Press.

Orlinsky, H.

1962   'The Tribal System of Israel and Related Groups in the Period of the Judges', in *Studies and Essays in Honor of A.A. Neuman,* ed. M. Ben-Horin et al. Leiden and Philadelphia, pp. 375-387.

Otto, E.

1976   'Silo und Jerusalem'. *TZ* 32: 65-77.

1994   'Aspects of Legal Reforms and Reformulations in Ancient Cuneiform and Israelite Law', in B.M. Levinson ed., *Theory and Method in Biblical and Cuneiform Law.* JSOTSS 181, Sheffield: Sheffield Academic Press, pp. 160-196.

Ottosson, M.
1980   *Temples and Cult Places in Palestine.* Acta Universitatis
         Uppsaliensis / Boreas 12, Motala: Borgströms Tryckeri.
1991   *Josuaboken: en programskrift för davidisk restauration.* Acta
         Universitatis Uppsaliensis, Studia Biblica Uppsaliensia 1,
         Stockholm: Almqvist & Wiksell.

Pagolu, A.
1995   *Patriarchal Religion as Portrayed in Genesis 12-50: Comparison
         with Ancient Near Eastern and Later Israelite Religions.* PhD
         Thesis; Open University/Oxford Centre for Mission
         Studies. Published as *The Religion of the Patriarchs,* JSOTSS
         277, Sheffield: Academic Press, 1998.

Parpola, S.
1987   *The Correspondence of Sargon II, Part I: Letters from Assyria and
         the West.* SAA I, Helsinki, Finland: Helsinki University
         Press.

Parpola, S., and Watanabe, K.
1988   *Neo-Assyrian Treaties and Loyalty Oaths.* SAA II, Helsinki,
         Finland: Helsinki University Press.

Patterson, R.D. and Austel, H.J.
1988   *1, 2 Kings.* EBC, Grand Rapids, Michigan: Zondervan
         Publishing House, Volume 4, pp. 1-300.

Pearce, R.A.
1973   'Shiloh and Jer 7:12, 14 & 15'. *VT* 23:105-108.

Peterson, J.L.
1977   *A Topographical Surface Survey of the Levitical "Cities" of Joshua
         21 and I Chronicles 6: Studies on the Levites in Israelite Life and
         Religion.* ThD Thesis, Chicago Institute of Advanced
         Theological Studies and Seabury-Western Theological
         Seminary, Evanston, Illinois.

Polzin, R.
1980   *Moses and the Deuteronomist: A Literary Study of the
         Deuteronomic History, Part One: Deuteronomy, Joshua, Judges.*
         New York: Seabury Press.
1989   *Samuel and the Deuteronomist: A Literary Study of the
         Deuteronomic History, Part Two: 1 Samuel.* Bloomington and
         Indianapolis: Indiana University Press.

Pongratz-Leisten, B., Deller, K., and Bleibtreu, E.
1992   'Götterstreitwagen und Götterstandarten: Götter auf dem Feldzug und ihr Kult im Feldlager'. *BM* 23: 291-356.

Postgate, J.N.
1992   *Early Mesopotamia: Society and Economy at the Dawn of History.* London and New York: Routledge.

Provan, I.W.
1995   *1 and 2 Kings.* NIBC, Peabody, Massachusetts: Hendrickson Publishers.

Quirke, S.
1992   *Ancient Egyptian Religion.* London: British Museum Press.

Rad, G. von
1953   *Studies in Deuteronomy.* Studies in Biblical Theology 9, Chicago: Henry Regnery Company. German original: *Deuteronomium-Studien*, Göttingen: Vandenhoeck & Ruprecht, 1948.
1965a   'The Tent and the Ark', in *idem, The Problem of the Hexateuch and other Essays*, Edinburgh and London: Oliver Boyd, pp. 103-124. German original: Zelt und Lade, *KZ* 42 (1931): 476-498.
1965b   'There Remains Still a Rest for the People of God: An Investigation of a Biblical Conception', in *idem, The Problem of the Hexateuch and other Essays*, Edinburgh and London: Oliver Boyd, pp. 94-102. German original in *Zwischen den Zeiten*, 11th year, Munich 1933, pp. 104-11.
1965c   'The Form-Critical Problem of the Hexateuch', in *idem, The Problem of the Hexateuch and other Essays*, Edinburgh and London: Oliver Boyd, pp. 1-78. German original in BWANT 4th series, vol XXVI, 1938.
1965d   'The Beginnings of Historical Writing in Ancient Israel', in *idem, The Problem of the Hexateuch and other Essays*, Edinburgh and London: Oliver Boyd, pp. 166-204. German original in *Archiv für Kulturgeschichte*, vol XXXII, Weimar 1944, pp. 1-42.
1966   *Deuteronomy.* OTL, London: SCM Press. German original: *Das fünfte Buch Mose: Deuteronomium*, ATD 8, Göttingen: Vandenhoeck & Ruprecht, 1964.

Rendtorff, R.

1990   *The Problem of the Process of Transmission in the Pentateuch.*
        JSOTSS 89, Sheffield: JSOT Press. German original: *Das
        überlieferungsgeschichtliche Problem des Pentateuch.* BZAW 147,
        Berlin: Walter de Gruyter, 1977.

1995   'Another Prolegomenon to Leviticus 17:11', in D.P.
        Wright, D.N. Freedman, and A. Hurvitz, ed., *Pomegranates
        and Golden Bells: Studies in Biblical, Jewish, and Near Eastern
        Ritual, Law, and Literature in Honor of Jacob Milgrom,* Winona
        Lake, In: Eisenbrauns, pp. 23-28.

Reuter, E.

1993   *Kultzentralisation: Entstehung und Theologie von Dtn 12.* BBB
        87, Frankfurt am Main: Verlag Anton Hain.

Reventlow, H.G.

1969   'Gattung und Überlieferung in der Tempelrede Jeremias,
        Jer 7 und 26'. *ZAW* 81, 3: 315-352.

Richardson, A.T.

1927   'The Site of Shiloh'. *PEFQS* 59: 85-88.

Riley, W.

1993   *King and Cultus in Chronicles: Worship and the Reinterpretation of
        History.* JSOTSS 160, Sheffield: JSOT Press.

Ringgren, H.

1973   *Religions of the Ancient Near East.* London: SPCK.

Robertson, E.

1948   'The Altar of Earth (Exodus XX, 24-26)'. *JJS* 1: 12-21.

Roos, J. de

1996   'Hittite Prayers', in J.M. Sasson, ed. in chief, *Civilizations of
        the Ancient Near East,* New York: Simon & Schuster
        Macmillan, vol III, pp. 1997-2005.

Rost, L.

1982   *The Succession to the Throne of David.* Historic Texts and
        Interpreters in Biblical Scholarship I, Sheffield: Almond
        Press. German original: *Die Überlieferung von der
        Thronnachfolge Davids,* Stuttgart: Kohlhammer, 1926.

Rothenberg, B.
1972 *Timna: Valley of the Biblical Copper Mines.* London: Thames and Hudson.

Rowley, H.H.
1967 *Worship in Ancient Israel.* London: SPCK.

Saggs, H.W.F.
1984 *The Might That Was Assyria.* London: Sidgwick & Jackson.

Satterthwaite, P.E.
1989 *Narrative Artistry and the Composition of Judges 17-21.* PhD Thesis, University of Manchester, Manchester, U.K.

Scalise, P.
1995 'Jeremiah 26-34', in G.L. Keown, P.J. Scalise and T.G. Smothers, *Jeremiah 26-52.* WBC, Dallas, Texas: Word Books.

Schicklberger, F.
1973 *Die Ladeerzählungen des ersten Samuel-Buches: Eine literaturwissenschaftlicher und theologiegeschichtliche Untersuchung.* Forschung zur Bibel 7, Würzburg: Echter Verlag.

Schley, D. G.
1989 *Shiloh: A Biblical City in Tradition and History.* JSOTSS 63, Sheffield: Sheffield Academic Press.

Schmitt, R.
1972 *Zelt und Lade als Thema alttestamentlicher Wissenschaft. Eine kritische forschungsgeschichtliche Darstellung.* Gütersloh: Gütersloher Verlagshaus Gerd Mohn.

Schreiner, J.
1990 'Geschichte als Wegweisung: Psalm 78', in Josef Zmijevski, ed., *Die Alttestamentliche Botschaft als Wegweisung: Festschrift für Heinz Reinelt.* Stuttgart: Verlag Katholisches Bibelwerk GmbH, pp. 307-328.

Schwartz, B.J.
1991 'The Prohibitions Concerning the 'Eating' of Blood in Leviticus 17', in *Priesthood and Cult in Ancient Israel*, ed. G.A. Anderson and S.M. Olyan. JSOTSS 125, Sheffield: JSOT Press, pp. 34-66.

1996   '"Profane" Slaughter and the Integrity of the Priestly Code'. *HUCA* 67: 15-42.

Schwienhorst-Schönberger, L.
1990   *Das Bundesbuch (Ex 20,22-23,33): Studien zu seiner Entstehung und Theologie.* BZAW 188, Berlin and New York: Walter de Gruyter.

Selman, M.J.
1994   *1 Chronicles.* TOTC, Leicester, England / Downers Grove, Illinois: Inter-Varsity Press.
1994b   *2 Chronicles.* TOTC, Leicester, England / Downers Grove, Illinois: Inter-Varsity Press.

Seow, C.L.
1992   'Ark of the Covenant'. *ABD* 1: 386-393.

Sheriffs, D.C.T.
1979   'The Phrases *ina IGI DN* and *lipeney Yhwh* in Treaty and Covenant Contexts'. *JNSL* 7: 55-68.

Singer, I.
1983   *The Hittite KI.LAM Festival,* Part One. StBoT 27, Wiesbaden: Harrassowitz.
1984   *The Hittite KI.LAM Festival,* Part Two. StBoT 28, Wiesbaden: Harrassowitz.

Smith, H.P.
1912   *A Critical and Exegetical Commentary on the books of Samuel.* ICC, Edinburgh: T.&T. Clark.

Snaith, N.H.
1978   'The Altar at Gilgal: Joshua XXII 23-29'. *VT* 28: 330-335.

Soden, W. von
1994   *The Ancient Orient: An Introduction to the Study of the Ancient Near East.* Translated by D.G. Schley. Grand Rapids, Michigan: Eerdmans.

Soggin, J.A.
1972   *Joshua.* OTL, London: SCM Press. Original in French 1970.
1981   *Judges.* OTL, Philadelphia: Westminster Press.

Spaey, J.
1993   'Emblems in Rituals in the Old Babylonian Period', in *J. Quaegebeur, ed., Ritual and Sacrifice in the Ancient Near East: Proceedings of the International Conference organized by the Katholieke Universiteit Leuven from the 17th to the 20th of April 1991*. Orientalia Lovaniensia Analecta 55, Leuven: Uitgeverij Peeters en Departement Oriëntalistiek, pp. 411-420.

Sprinkle, J.M.
1994   *The Book of the Covenant: A Literary Approach*. JSOTSS 174, Sheffield: Sheffield Academic Press.

Stern, E.
1981   'Late Bronze Age Sanctuary at Tel Mevorakh', in A. Biran, ed., *Temples and High Places in Biblical Times: Proceedings of the Colloquium in Honor of the Centennial of Hebrew Union College - Jewish Institute of Religion*, Jerusalem: Hebrew Union College, p. 160.

Stoebe, H.J.
1973   *Das erste Buch Samuelis*. KAT VIII, Gütersloh: Gütersloher Verlagshaus Gerd Mohn.

Strong, J.T.
1997   'God's Kabod: The Presence of Yahweh in the Book of Ezekiel', for *SBL conference 1997: Theological Perspectives in the book of Ezekiel*. http:// shemesh.scholar.emory.edu/ scripts/ SBL/ ezekiel/ strong.html, pp. 1-25.

Svensson, J.
1994   *Towns and Toponyms in the Old Testament with Special Emphasis on Joshua 14-21*. CBOTS 38, Stockholm: Almqvist & Wiksell.

Tarragon, J.-M. de
1980   *Le Culte à Ugarit: D' apres les textes de la pratique en cuneiformes alphabetiques*. Paris: J. Gabalda et Cie.

Tate, M.E.
1990   *Psalms 51-100*. WBC, Dallas, Texas: Word Books.

Thompson, J.A.
1963   *The Ancient Near Eastern Treaties and the Old Testament.*
        London: The Tyndale Press.
1974   *Deuteronomy: An Introduction and Commentary.* TOTC,
        Leicester, England / Downers Grove, Illinois: Inter-
        Varsity Press.
1980   *The Book of Jeremiah.* NICOT, Grand Rapids, Michigan:
        Eerdmans.

Thompson, T.L.
1992   *Early History of the Israelite People: From the Written &*
        Archaeological Sources. Leiden: E.J. Brill.
2000   *The Bible in History: How Writers Create a Past.* London.

Thureau-Dangin, F.
1975   *Rituels Accadiens.* Osnabrück: Otto Zeller Verlag
        (reimpression of 1921 edition).

Tigay, J.H.
1996   *Deuteronomy.* JPS Torah Commentary, Philadelphia and
        Jerusalem: The Jewish Publication Society.

Toorn, Karel van der
1996   *Family Religion in Babylonia, Syria and Israel: Continuity and*
        Change in the Forms of Religious Life. Leiden, New York,
        Köln: E.J. Brill.

Tuell, S.S.
1997   'Deus Absconditus in Ezekiel's Prophecy', for *SBL*
        conference 1997: Theological Perspectives in the book of Ezekiel.
        http:// shemesh.scholar.emory.edu/ scripts/ SBL/
        ezekiel/ tuell.html, pp. 1-13.

VanGemeren, W.A.
1991   *Psalms.* EBC 5:1-880. Grand Rapids, Michigan: Zondervan
        Publishing House.

Van Seters, J.
1983   *In Search of History.* New Haven: Yale University Press.
1996   'Cultic Laws in the Covenant Code and their Relationship
        to Deuteronomy and the Holiness Code', in *Studies in the*
        Book of Exodus: Redaction-Reception-Interpretation, pp. 319-345.
        Leuven: Leuven University Press.

Vaughan, P.H.
1974   *The Meaning of "bama" in the Old Testament*, SOTSMS 3, Cambridge: Cambridge University Press.

Vaux, R. de
1961   *Ancient Israel: Its Life and Institutions*. London: Lutterworth Press. French original: *Les Institutions de l'Ancien Testament*, Paris: Les Editions du Cerf, 2 vols, 1958-1960.

1972   'Ark of the Covenant and Tent of Reunion', in *The Bible and the Ancient Near East*. London: Darton, Longman & Todd, pp. 136-151. French original: *Bible et Orient*, Paris: Les Éditions du Cerf, 1967.

1978   *The Early History of Israel*. London: Darton Longman & Todd. French original: *Histoire Ancienne d'Israel*, Paris: J. Gabalda et Cie, 1971.

Veijola, T.
1977   *Das Königtum in der Beurteilung der deuteronomistischen Historiographie: Eine redaktionsgeschichtliche Untersuchung*. AASF Series B, vol 198, Helsinki: Suomalainen Tiedeakatemia.

Velde, H. te
1996   'Theology, Priests, and Worship in Ancient Egypt', in J.M. Sasson, ed. in chief, *Civilizations of the Ancient Near East*, New York: Simon & Schuster Macmillan, vol III, pp. 1731-1749.

Walker, C., and Dick, M.B.
1999   'The Induction of the Cult Image in Ancient Mesopotamia: The Mesopotamian *mīs pî* Ritual', in *Born in Heaven, Made on Earth: The Making of the Cult Image in the Ancient Near East*. Winona Lake, Indiana: Eisenbrauns, pp. 55-121.

Walsh, J.T.
1996   *1 Kings*. Berit Olam: Studies in Hebrew Narrative and Poetry, Collegeville, Minnesota: The Liturgical Press.

Walton, J.H.
1989   *Ancient Israelite Literature in Its Cultural Context: A Survey of Parallels Between Biblical and Ancient Near Eastern Texts*. Grand Rapids, Michigan: Regency Library of Biblical Interpretation, Zondervan Publishing House.

Watts, J.D.W.
1985   *Isaiah 1-33*. WBC, Waco, Texas: Word Books.

Weinfeld, M.
1964   'Cult Centralization in Israel in the Light of a Neo-Babylonian Analogy'. *JNES* 23: 202-212.
1967   'The Period of the Conquest and of the Judges as Seen by the Earlier and the Later Sources'. *VT* 17: 93-113.
1972   *Deuteronomy and the Deuteronomic School.* Oxford: Clarendon Press. Reprint Winona Lake, In: Eisenbrauns 1992.
1991   *Deuteronomy 1-11.* AB, New York: Doubleday.

Weippert, H.
1973   'Das geographische System der Stämme Israels'. *VT* 23: 76-89.
1980   'Der Ort, den Jahwe erwählen wird, um dort seinen Namen wohnen zu lassen: Die Geschichte einer alttestamentlichen Formel'. *BZ* 24, 1: 76-94.

Weiser, A.
1962   *The Psalms.* OTL, London: SCM Press. German original: *Die Psalmen,* ATD 14/15, Göttingen: Vandenhoeck & Ruprecht, 1959.

Wellhausen, J.
1905   *Prolegomena zur Geschichte Israel,* sechste Ausgabe. Berlin: Druck und Verlag Georg Reimer. First published 1878.
1963   *Die Composition des Hexateuchs und der historischen Bücher des alten Testaments,* vierte unveränderte Auflage. Berlin: Walter de Gruyter. First published 1876.

Wenham, G.J.
1971a   'Deuteronomy and the Central Sanctuary'. *TB* 22: 103-118.
1971b   'The Deuteronomic Theology of the Book of Joshua'. *JBL* 90, pp. 140-148.
1975   'Were David's Sons Priests?'. *ZAW* 87, 1: 79-82.
1979   *The Book of Leviticus.* NICOT, Grand Rapids, Michigan: W.B. Eerdmans.
1981   *Numbers: An Introduction and Commentary.* TOTC, Leicester: Inter-Varsity Press.
1987   *Genesis 1-15.* WBC, Waco, Texas: Word Books.
1993   'Deuteronomy and the Central Sanctuary', in D.L. Christensen, ed., *A Song of Power and the Power of Song: Essays*

on the Book of Deuteronomy, Winona Lake, Indiana: Eisenbrauns, pp. 94-108.

1994   *Genesis 16-50.* WBC, Dallas, Texas: Word Books.

1997a   'The Gap Between Law and Ethics in the Bible'. *JJS* XLVII, 1: 17-29.

1997b   *Numbers.* OTG, Sheffield: Sheffield Academic Press.

1999a   'Pondering the Pentateuch: The Search for a New Paradigm', in D.W. Baker and B.T. Arnold, ed., *The Face of Old Testament Studies: A Survey of Contemporary Approaches.* Grand Rapids, Michigan: Baker Books, pp. 116-144.

1999b   'The Priority of P'. *VT* XLIX, 2: 240-258.

Westbrook, R.

1994   'What is the Covenant Code?', in B.M. Levinson ed., *Theory and Method in Biblical and Cuneiform Law.* JSOTSS 181, Sheffield: Sheffield Academic Press, pp. 15-36.

Westermann, C.

1981a   *Praise and Lament in the Psalms.* Atlanta: John Knox Press. Translated from German original: *Lob und Klagen in den Psalmen*, 1961-1977.

1981b   *Genesis 12-36.* BKAT I/2, Neukirchen-Vluyn: Neukirchener Verlag.

1994   *Die Geschichtsbücher des Alten Testaments: Gab es ein deuteronomistisches Geschichtswerk?* Gütersloh: Chr. Kaiser/ Gütersloher Verlagshaus.

Wette, W.M.L. de

1830   'Dissertatio critica qua a prioribus Deuteronomium Pentateuchi libris diversum, alius cuiusdam recentioris auctoris opus esse monstratur', pro venia legendi publice defensa Ienae a. 1805, in W.M.L. de Wette, *Opuscula Theologica*, Berlin: G. Reimerum, pp. 149-168.

Whitelam, K.W.

1994   'The Identity of Early Israel: The Realignment and Transformation of Late Bronze-Iron Age Palestine'. *JSOT* 63: 57-87.

Whybray, R.N.

1987   *The Making of the Pentateuch: A Methodological Study.* JSOTSS 53, Sheffield: JSOT Press.

Wiggermann, F.A.M.
1996   'Theologies, Priests, and Worship in Ancient Mesopotamia', in J.M. Sasson, ed. in chief, *Civilizations of the Ancient Near East*. New York: Simon & Schuster Macmillan, vol III, pp. 1857-1870.

Wildberger, H.
1997   *Isaiah 13-27*. Continental Commentary, Minneapolis: Fortress Press. German original: *Jesaja, Kapitel 13-27*, BKAT Band X/2, Neukirchen-Vluyn: Neukirchener Verlag, 1978.

Wilson, I.
1995   *Out of the Midst of the Fire: Divine Presence in Deuteronomy*. SBL Dissertation Series, Atlanta: Scholars Press.

Wiseman, D.J.
1953   *The Alalakh Tablets*. Occasional Publications of the British Institute of Archaeology at Ankara 2, London: British Institute of Archaeology at Ankara.

Woudstra, M.H.
1961   *The Ark of the Covenant from Conquest to Kingship*. PhD Thesis, Philadelphia, Pennsylvania: Westminster Theological Seminary.
1981   *The Book of Joshua*. NICOT, Grand Rapids: Eerdmans.

Wright, C.J.H.
1996   *Deuteronomy*. NIBC, Peabody, Massachusetts: Hendrickson Publishers.

Wright, H.C.
1982   *Ancient Burials of Metallic Foundation Documents in Stone Boxes*. University of Illinois, Graduate School of Library and Information Science Occasional Papers 157. Champaign, Illinois: University of Illinois at Urbana-Champaign.

Youngblood, R.F.
1992   *1, 2 Samuel*. EBC 3: 551-1104. Grand Rapids, Michigan: Zondervan Publishing House.

Younger, K.L.

1990 *Ancient Conquest Accounts: A Study in Ancient Near Eastern and Biblical History writing*. JSOTSS 98, Sheffield: Sheffield Academic Press.

1994 'Judges 1 in its Near Eastern Literary Context', in *Faith, Tradition and History: Old Testament Historiography in Its Near Eastern Context*, Winona Lake, Indiana: Eisenbrauns, 1994, pp. 207-227.

1999 'Early Israel in Recent Biblical Scholarship', in D.W. Baker and B.T. Arnold, ed., *The Face of Old Testament Studies: A Survey of Contemporary Approaches*. Grand Rapids, Michigan: Baker Books, pp. 176-206.

Zertal, A.

1986 'How Can Kempinski Be So Wrong!'. *BAR* 12,1: 43, 49-53.

1986-1987 'Mount Ebal: Excavation Seasons 1982-1987, Preliminary Report'. *TA* 13-14: 105-165.

Zobel, H.-J.

1977 אֲרוֹן *aron*. *TDOT* 1: 363-374.

INDEX OF SCRIPTURE AND OTHER ANCIENT SOURCES

Index of Passages Quoted in Hebrew and Other Ancient Languages

INDEX OF STANDALONE WORDS AND EXPRESSIONS IN HEBREW AND OTHER ANCIENT LANGUAGES

INDEX OF AUTHORS

GENERAL INDEX

INDEX OF TERMS USED IN THE APPENDIX